Standard Chemistry

MALCOLM DICKSON
and
BOB WILSON

UNWIN HYMAN

Published by
UNWIN HYMAN LIMITED
15/17 Broadwick Street
London W1V 1FP

© Malcolm Dickson and Bob Wilson

First published 1990

All rights reserved. No part of this publication may be reproduced, stored in a retrieval system, or transmitted in any form or by any means, electronic, mechanical, photocopying or otherwise, without the prior permission of Unwin Hyman Limited

British Library Cataloguing in Publication Data
Wilson, Bob
 Standard chemistry.
 1. Chemistry
 I. Title   II. Dickson, Malcolm
 540

ISBN 0-04-448165-6

Designed by Geoff Wadsley
Artwork by Panda Art and RDL Artset Ltd
Typeset by MS Filmsetting Ltd, Frome, Somerset
Printed and bound in Great Britain by
Butler and Tanner Ltd, Frome, Somerset

Acknowledgements

We would like to thank Joe Boyd for his astute editing in the early stages of this book, and David Wright of Exxon Chemicals, at Mossmorran in Fife, for his help with the Spotlight on Industry section in chapter two.

May we also thank the following for supplying information of a general nature: ICI, The Fertilisers Manufacturers Association, Steetley's (UK) at Hartlepool, and BP at Grangemouth.

The authors and publisher would like to thank the following for permission to reproduce photographs:

Heather Angel 5, 171 (top); Anglesey Aluminium Metal Ltd/J C Davies 155; The Associated Press Ltd 181; Barnaby's Picture Library 1 (centre, left), 11, 39 (bottom, right), 122 (left), 201; BBC Hulton 122 (right); Bibby Sterilin Ltd 112; British Alcan Aluminium Plc/Don Williams 154 (top); British Alcan Aluminium 156; British Leyland 163 (bottom); British Steel Plc 140 (bottom), 142 (top); CEGB 39 (top, left), 45 (centre), 52, 71; Centre for Alternative Technology 171 (bottom); Norman Childs Photography 140 (top), 154 (bottom); Ciba-Geigy Plastics 1 (top, right); © Crown Copyright 196; M Dickson 159 (right), 164; Exxon Chemicals 67; Barry Finch Photography 198 (bottom); Friends of the Earth Trust (London) 125; Geoscience 110 (top); Hutchison Picture Library 45 (left); Michael Holford 143 (right), 146 (top); ICI 1 (centre, right), 39 (bottom, left), 127, 129 (right), 177, 190, 193 (left; right); Holford 143 (right), 146 (top); ICI 1 (centre, right), 39 (bottom, left), 127, 129 (right), 177, 190, 193 (left, right); Intermedics Inc 92; C James Webb 6, 14, 81, 93 (top; bottom), 195 (centre), 211; Lever Brothers Ltd 19; The Malaysian Rubber Producers Research Association 198 (top); The Mary Rose Trust 146 (left); Metropolitan Police 225; MK Electric Ltd 194 (left); NASA 2; National Coal Board 39 (centre, left), 42; NHPA/G I Bernard 119 (top); Nadia Nightingale 169 (bottom); Nimbus Records/Jim Lowe 166; Nuclear Electric 142 (bottom); Ogilvy and Mather 217; Oxford Scientific Films/Michael Fugden 128; Oxford Scientific Films/Ronald Toms 124 (left); Pacemaker Press International 147; Pains Wessex Schermully 18 (bottom); Panos Pictures/Jeremy Hartley 169 (top); Pasminco Europe (Impalloy Division) 163 (top); Prestige Group (UK) Plc 20 (bottom); Pyranha Mouldings Ltd 194 (bottom); RAF Museum 39 (top, right); Rotherham Engineering Steels 144; RSPB 44; The Royal Mint 143 (left); Safeway Plc 12, 91, 200; Salt Museum/ICI 129 (left); Science Photo Library/Peter Menzel 94; The Scotch Whisky Association 227; Scottish and Newcastle Brewery 230; Scottish Agricultural Industries 120 (bottom); Shell Photo Service 45 (right), 51, 60 (bottom), 62 (top; bottom), 63; Sodatream Ltd 110 (bottom, left); The Soil Association 172; Statoil 96; Steetley's (UK) Ltd 132; Syndication International 1 (top, left), 159 (left); Topham Picture Library 120 (top); Tunewell Transformers Ltd 20 (top); Sandra Wegerif 60 (top), 108 (top; centre; bottom), 110 (bottom, right), 119 (bottom); Wildlife Matters 180, 195 (top); ZEFA Picture Library (UK) Ltd 150.

The author and publisher would also like to thank the following for permission to reproduce diagrams and text:

Friends of the Earth (Scotland) 214; ICI 175, 198; Longman Group Ltd 187; Thomas Nelson and Sons Ltd 22; The Scotsman 96; Shell (UK) Ltd 208–209

Special thanks are given to the Scottish Examination Board for permission to reproduce questions from the Standard Grade specimen question papers, in the Study Question sections of this book.

Contents

Acknowledgements — ii
To The Teacher — iv
To The Student — iv

Reactions and the Atom — 1
1 Reactions All Around
2 Substances and Their States
3 Speed of Reactions
4 The Periodic Table
5 What's In An Atom?
6 Molecules
7 Chemical Formulae
8 The Mole
9 Chemical Equations
Study Questions

Fuels and Hydrocarbons — 39
1 Energy from Fuels
2 Formation of Fossil Fuels
3 Using Oil
4 Polluting the Air
5 The Alkanes
6 The Alkenes
7 Cracking Hydrocarbons
8 Homologous Series and Isomerism
9 Spotlight on Industry
Study Questions

Electricity in Chemistry — 71
1 Conductors and Insulators
2 Formation of Bonds
3 Ionic Formulae and Equations
4 Electricity from Chemicals
5 The Chemistry of the Cell
6 Electrochemical Cells
7 Spotlight on Industry
Study Questions

Acids and Alkalis — 108
1 Acids and Alkalis all Around
2 Reactions of Acids
3 Neutralisers in Action
4 Acid Rain
5 Making Salts
6 Spotlight on Industry
7 Concentration
Study Questions

Metals and Corrosion — 140
1 All About Metals
2 Chemical Properties of Metals
3 Extracting the Metal from its Ore
4 Extracting Ores by Electrolysis
5 Corrosion
6 Protecting Metals from Corrosion
Study Questions

Fertilisers — 169
1 Our Hungry World
2 Synthetic Fertilisers
3 Making Ammonia
4 Making Nitric Acid
5 Spotlight on Industry
Study Questions

Plastics — 193
1 The Plastic Age
2 Making Plastic (Polymers)
3 Spotlight on Industry
Study Questions

Carbohydrates — 211
1 The Energy Foods
2 A Closer Look at Carbohydrates
3 Making and Breaking Carbohydrates
4 Alcohol
5 Spotlight on Industry
Study Questions

Index/Glossary — 234

To The Teacher

Standard Chemistry has been written for all students preparing for the Scottish Standard Grade Chemistry examination (or similar examinations) and covers all the learning outcomes, as outlined in the Scottish Examination Board (SEB) Arrangements Document (1988). The book was written in such a way as to be both accessible and enjoyable to a wide range of students. Particular attention has been paid to how language is used and throughout we have tried to keep the text as simple as the subject matter would allow.

Each section is laid out so that *General* and *Credit* material are kept separate and thereby aid a differentiated learning approach. This ease of identification of *Credit* material will also be useful for pupils revising or "topping up" pre-requisite credit knowledge for the SEB Revised Higher Chemistry course.

Throughout the book, there is an emphasis on "everyday" chemistry, the socio-economic importance of the chemical industry and the effect of chemistry on the environment – all to reinforce the importance of chemistry in our lives. This also provides useful background information for a variety of problem solving activities.

Information is presented in a variety of forms including photos, diagrams, graphs and flowcharts to aid students in the development of selecting information skills.

Each section of a chapter begins with a **Key Ideas** box, which summarises the main features within the section. Chapter 1 covers topics 1–4 of the Standard Grade syllabus and in addition introduces writing formulae, equations and calculations, which are reinforced throughout all chapters. In *General* text, equations are written in both the unbalanced and balanced forms. Again, this is to help students in a differentiated learning approach.

All the topics of the Standard Grade syllabus are included, and the order in which the topics and learning outcomes are covered are summarised below:

Chapter	Standard Grade Topic
1	1–4
2	5, 6
3	7, 10
4	8, 9
5	11–13
6	15
7	14
8	16

At the end of each section within a chapter, there are a variety of graded **Activities** to aid revision, covering Knowledge and Understanding, and Problem Solving. There are also graded **Study Questions**, taken from SEB past examination papers at the end of each chapter.

Most chapters include a **Spotlight on Industry** section which reinforces the importance of the chemical industry in our everyday lives. There is a comprehensive index/glossary at the end of the book and throughout the text, important terms appear in bold print.

To The Student

How to use this book:

1. If you want to find out about a topic, look it up in the **Contents** page at the front of the book.

2. If you cannot find the topic in the **Contents** page, you should look it up in the alphabetical **Index/Glossary** at the back of the book. This also gives you the meanings of some chemical words.

3. The **Key Ideas** box introduces each section and summarises the main points which you will be able to read about.

4. If a word is printed in **bold** it means that it is especially important.

5. The main text covers *General* level material and the *Credit* text is marked with arrows (see the key).

6. The **Activities** at the end of each section and the **Study Questions** at the end of each chapter allow you to check that you have remembered and understood what you have read. Some of the activities give you practice at solving problems.

Key to Symbols

▼▬▬▬▬ Start of *Credit* material

▬▬▬▬▲ End of *Credit* material

○ *General* level question

◐ *General/Credit* level question

● *Credit* level question, or balanced equation

KU Covers Knowledge and Understanding

PS Covers Problem Solving

1 Reactions All Around

When bread is baked it changes the way it looks

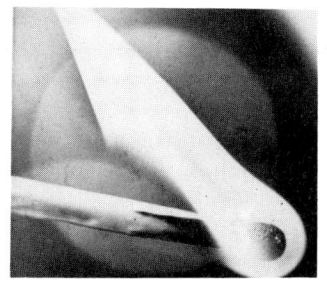

Striking a match produces heat

Key Ideas

Chemical reactions are happening around us all the time. Some reactions happen *naturally*. *We* cause others to happen. When a reaction occurs, one or more *new substances* are formed. We can tell if a reaction takes place, because *changes* occur: a substance can change the *way it looks* and *energy* may be given out or taken in.

Elements and *compounds* are involved in reactions. Elements can be given *symbols* instead of names. The *name* of a compound often tells us what's in it.

Liquid epoxy glues soon solidify when mixed with hardener, and often give out heat

New substances, like plastics, are made in the chemical industry

Everyday Reactions

All the activities shown in the photographs have something in common – **chemical reactions** are taking place. When a chemical reaction takes place, one or more **new substances** are formed. We can tell if a chemical reaction has taken place in two ways:

1 A substance usually changes **the way it looks**;
2 **Energy** is normally either **given out** or **taken in**.

All the reactions in the photographs are caused by **us**. However, natural reactions are happening around us all the time.

All the time plants are growing many chemical reactions are taking place. Some need light or heat energy to make the chemicals inside them react to form new substances. Many plants are eaten by humans and other animals. They then undergo chemical reactions in our digestive system.

Chemical reactions occur in plants and animals

When a car body rusts the shiny metal slowly turns brown, and loses its strength. The metal has reacted with water and oxygen in the air to form new substances which are completely different from the original metal.

Reactions and the Atom

2 REACTIONS AND THE ATOM

Reactions in the Laboratory

Chemical reactions can be carried out in the laboratory. In each example below, some kind of **change** takes place, showing a reaction has occurred.

Magnesium and Oxygen

When magnesium (a grey metal) burns in air it gives out bright light and a lot of heat. A white powder called magnesium oxide is produced.

We can write a **word equation** for this reaction:

magnesium + oxygen → Magnesium oxide

| grey metal | means "reacts with" | from the air | means "produces" | white powder |

In this reaction, magnesium and oxygen are reacting together and so are called the **reactants**. Magnesium oxide is produced and so it is called the **product**.

Magnesium burning in air

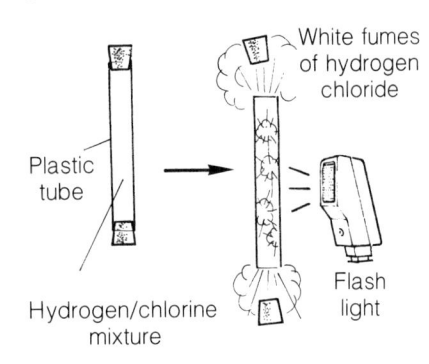

Exploding hydrogen and chlorine

Hydrogen and Chlorine

When the gases hydrogen and chlorine are mixed and a bright light is shone on the mixture, an explosion occurs and white fumes of hydrogen chloride are produced.

Word equation: hydrogen + chlorine → hydrogen chloride

      colourless   green   white fumes
         gas   gas

REACTANTS → **PRODUCT**

Hydrogen and Oxygen

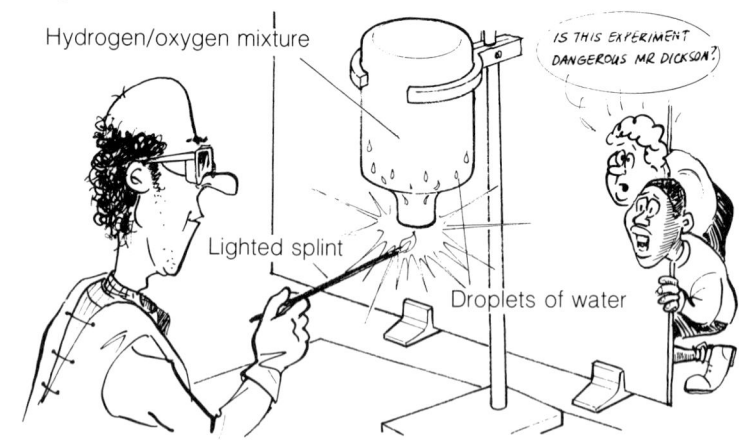

When a flame is held near a mixture of hydrogen and oxygen, it explodes and colourless droplets of hydrogen oxide form. Hydrogen oxide is commonly known as **water**.

Word equation: hydrogen + oxygen → water

      colourless   colourless   colourless
         gas   gas   liquid

REACTANTS → **PRODUCT**

In all three of these chemical reactions, **energy** has been given out and **new substances** have been produced. These new substances are called **compounds**. In each case they have been formed from **elements** joining together in some way.

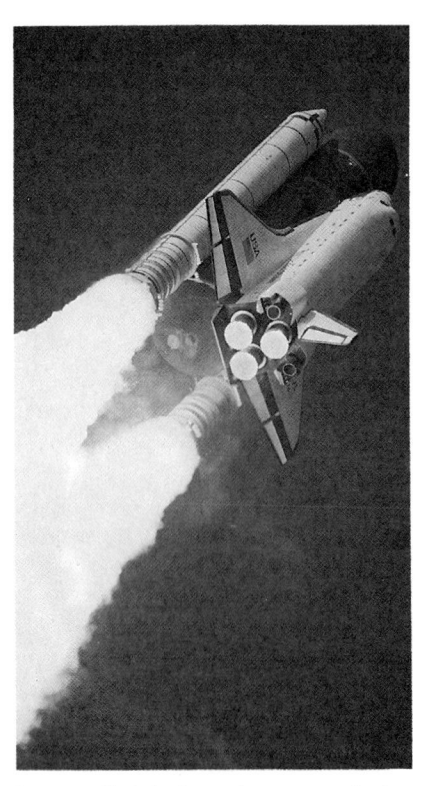

A controlled hydrogen/oxygen explosion powers the launch rocket on the space shuttle

REACTIONS AND THE ATOM 3

Elements

It was Robert Boyle in the seventeenth century who gave the name "element" to any substance which could not be changed into anything simpler. Today, there are **over 100** known elements. They are listed in a chart called the **Periodic Table**. Each element has a name and a code for this name called its **symbol**. You will see a periodic table on page 16. Find the symbols for the **reactants** in the three reactions described on page 2.

A symbol can be either:
  a capital letter only, e.g., hydrogen is **H**, oxygen is **O**;
  or a capital letter with a small letter, e.g., chlorine is **Cl**, magnesium is **Mg**.

These symbols are from the English names. Other symbols come from different languages. For example, the symbol for lead is **Pb**. This is from its Latin name "plumbum". Why do you think the person who comes to fix your water pipes is called a plumber?

If the name of a substance is not in the periodic table, then the substance is not an element. The name water is **not** in the periodic table, so water is not an element.

Compounds

Compounds are made when elements react. New compounds can also be made when compounds react with elements or other compounds.

Chalk and Acid

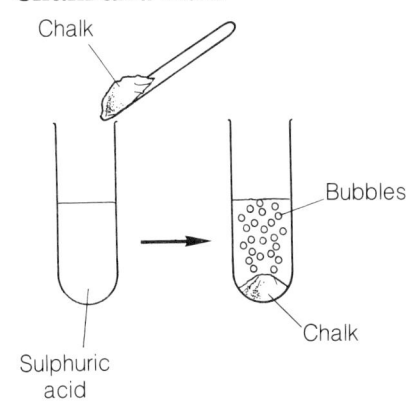

The **bubbles of gas** show a reaction is taking place.

Hydrochloric Acid and Sodium Hydroxide

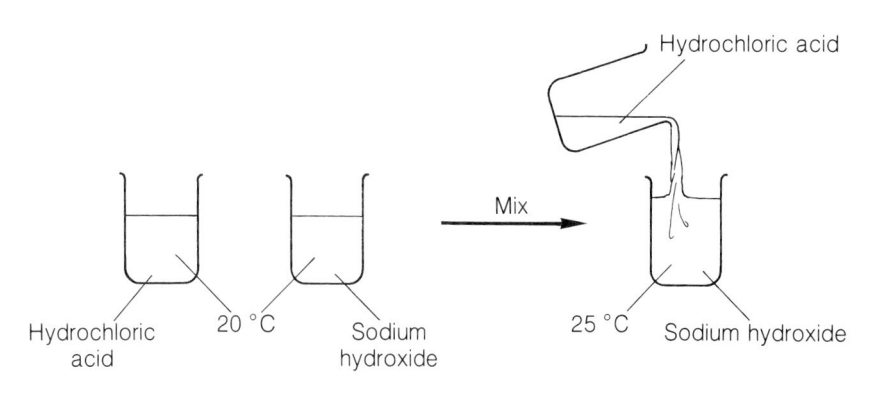

No change in appearance occurs. However, the **rise in temperature** shows a reaction is taking place.

Magnesium and Copper Sulphate

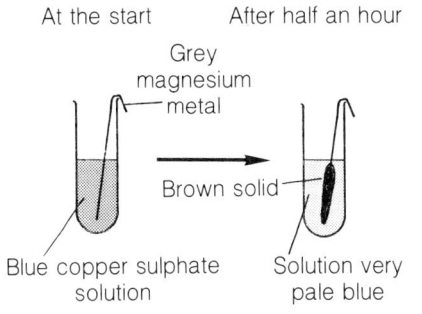

The appearance of brown copper solid, and the fading blue of the copper sulphate solution indicates a reaction is occurring.

What's in a Name?

Names of **compounds** can tell us which elements are in them. There are some general rules:

1 Compounds with names ending in **-ide**, usually contain **two** elements. Table 1.1 gives some examples.

Table 1.1

Compound	Elements
hydrogen chloride	hydrogen (H) and chlorine (Cl)
calcium oxide	calcium (Ca) and oxygen (O)
iron sulphide	iron (Fe) and sulphur (S)
sodium fluoride	sodium (Na) and fluorine (F)

4 REACTIONS AND THE ATOM

There are a few exceptions to this rule:
Names ending in **hydroxide** – compound includes hydrogen, oxygen and some other element(s).
Names ending in **cyanide** – compound includes carbon, nitrogen and some other element(s).
Table 1.2 gives some examples.

Table 1.2

Compound	Elements
magnesium hydroxide	magnesium (Mg), oxygen (O) and hydrogen (H)
potassium cyanide	potassium (K), carbon (C) and nitrogen (N)

2 Compounds with names ending in **-ate** or **-ite** tell us that **oxygen** is present, as well as other elements.

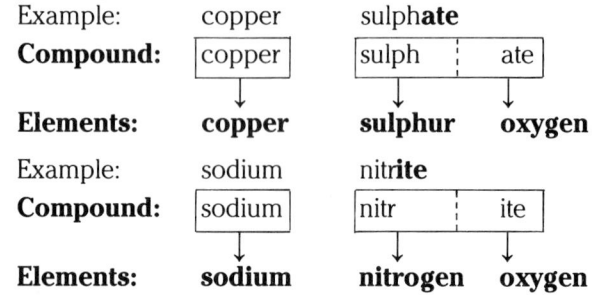

Example: copper sulph**ate**

Compound: copper | sulph : ate
↓ ↓ ↓
Elements: **copper** **sulphur** **oxygen**

Example: sodium nit**rite**

Compound: sodium | nitr : ite
↓ ↓ ↓
Elements: **sodium** **nitrogen** **oxygen**

Activities

1. Two solutions were mixed in a beaker and no change was **seen** to have taken place. However, a pupil said a reaction had occured.
   (a) What change could have taken place to make the pupil realise a reaction had occurred?
   (b) How could she prove that this change had taken place?

2. When zinc is added to a solution of blue copper sulphate, zinc sulphate and copper are formed.
   (a) Zinc sulphate is colourless. How does this help us tell that a chemical reaction has taken place?
   (b) Write a word equation for this reaction.
   (c) In the reaction, which substances are elements and which are compounds?
   (d) Explain your answers to (c).
   (e) Name the elements present in copper sulphate.

3. Choose your answers to (a), (b) and (c) below, from the grid

sodium chloride	potassium sulphate	oxygen
calcium nitrate	magnesium	helium

   (a) Write down the name of each element and beside each, its symbol.
   (b) Write down the names of the compounds containing oxygen.
   (c) Write down the name of each compound in the grid and the names of the elements in each, with their symbols.

4. Write down four chemical reactions that you saw happening (or even did) yesterday.

2 Substances and Their States

Which State?

Substances exist as solids, liquids or gases. Sometimes they are **mixtures**. Many fruit juices are mixtures of different liquids. They can also be in solution. The copper sulphate used in the reaction with magnesium earlier was in a water **solution**. To make the solution, **solid** copper sulphate was **dissolved** in water. In this example, the solid copper sulphate is a **solute** – it is the substance being dissolved. Water is the **solvent**. It is the liquid in which the solute is being dissolved.

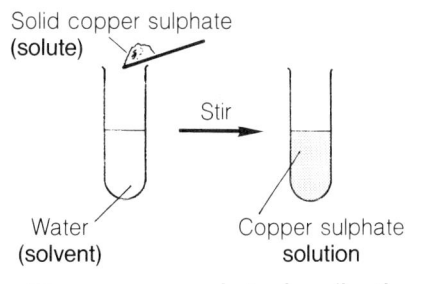

Solid copper sulphate (solute)

Stir

Water (solvent)   Copper sulphate solution

We can use a code to describe the **state** of a substance. The code uses **symbols** instead of words to describe state. The symbols are:

- **(s)** for solid
- **(l)** for liquid
- **(g)** for gas
- **(aq)** for solutions in water

(aq) comes from the Latin "**aq**ua", meaning water. An **aqua**rium is a container in which fish and other **water** animals can be kept.

We can use state symbols to describe how to make copper sulphate solution.

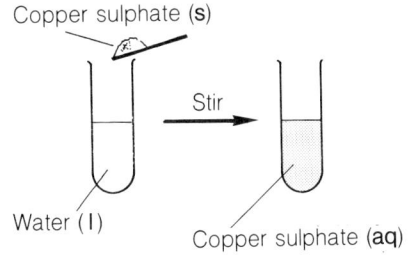

Copper sulphate (s)

Stir

Water (l)   Copper sulphate (aq)

If too much solute is added so that no more can dissolve, the solution formed is said to be **saturated** – it is "full of solute". Table 1.3 shows the solubility of some substances in water at 20 °C. It is important to state the temperature. The solubility of most substances changes as the temperature of the solvent changes.

Table 1.3

Substance	Mass dissolving in 100 g of water at 20°C (in grams)
Salt (sodium chloride)	36
Sugar (sucrose)	204
Copper sulphate	20
Oxygen	0.004

Solutions All Around

Solutions are not just made in the laboratory – they are all around us. When you make a cup of instant coffee, you are making a solution. Dissolve the coffee (solute) in hot water (solvent) and a solution is made. If you add sugar, it too dissolves to form a solution.

Sea water tastes salty. This is because the water contains substances dissolved in it. The sea is a giant solution! If sea water is heated until all the water evaporates, a mixture of solid substances is left behind. These are called **salts**.

The Dead Sea, in Israel, has six times the amount of salts dissolved in it than other sea water. The water evaporates naturally in shallow pools and the mixture of salts left behind is collected and separated. The salts can then be changed into other, more useful, substances like sodium hydroxide and bromine. These are needed in the chemical industry.

Water is not the only useful solvent. White spirit and turpentine are used to clean paint brushes. The paint dissolves in the solvent, forming a solution. Nail varnish remover contains propanone which dissolves the nail varnish. Many common substances such as glues, gloss paint and varnish are in solvents other than water.

Key Ideas

Chemical reactions can happen whether the reacting substances are solid, liquid or gas. They also occur in *solution*. A solution is formed when a *solute* dissolves in a *solvent*. State symbols can be used to show which state a substance is in. *Mixtures* of substances in the same, or different, states can be separated. *Filtering*, *chromatography* and *distillation* are common ways of separating substances.

Crude salt crystallising in shallow waters

6 REACTIONS AND THE ATOM

Mixtures

As you saw in the previous section, a **mixture** of hydrogen and oxygen can be made to react and form a **compound**. Once the compound is formed (in this case water) it is very difficult to separate the elements from each other. This is because during a reaction elements **join together**. This doesn't happen with mixtures. Mixtures can be separated more easily.

A mixture of sweets can easily be separated by picking out the ones that look the same. Other mixtures, like custard powder and drinking chocolate, are harder to separate, because the substances are powdered and more thoroughly mixed together.

In the laboratory, the elements in a mixture of iron and sulphur can easily be separated by passing a magnet over it – only the iron sticks to the magnet. If the mixture is heated, however, a chemical reaction takes place and a compound, iron sulphide, is formed. The iron and sulphur cannot then be separated with a magnet.

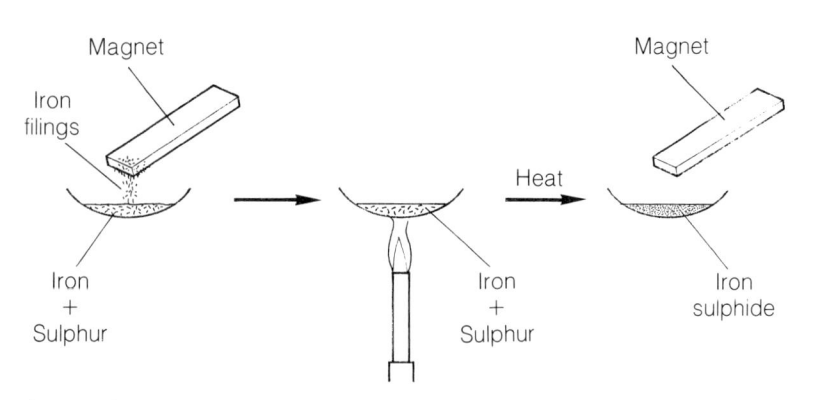

Iron can be separated from the mixture but not the compound

Rock salt is a naturally occurring mixture of salt and sand, which is more difficult to separate. Think about how you might do it in the laboratory. Check your ideas with the method given in the section on **filtering**.

Separating Mixtures

There are many ways of separating mixtures, depending on what they are. Three common methods are **filtering**, **distillation** and **chromatography**.

Filtering

Filtering is a way of separating a mixture of a solid and a liquid or a solid and a solution.

Making filter coffee

In the home: ground (filter) coffee is a mixture of soluble and insoluble substances. Hot water dissolves the soluble coffee, forming a coffee solution. This drips through the filter paper, leaving the insoluble part of the coffee behind.

In the laboratory: a mixture of chalk and water can be filtered, just like the coffee. The water drips through the filter paper, leaving the insoluble chalk in the paper. The solid left in the filter paper is called the **residue**. The liquid or solution which goes through the paper is called the **filtrate**.

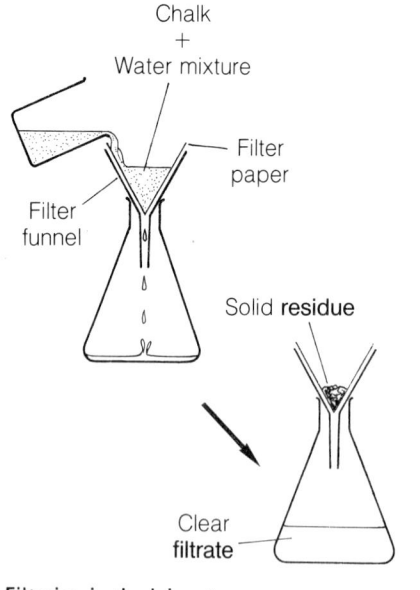

Filtering in the laboratory

Our drinking water is filtered after it leaves the reservoir. It is passed through layers of clean sand and gravel to remove small particles of mud and other solids.

Separating "Rock Salt"

The salt and sand in "rock salt" can be separated by first mixing it with water. The salt dissolves to give a salt solution/sand mixture which is then filtered. The salt solution passes through the filter paper, leaving the sand behind. The salt water can be heated to evaporate the water, and leave just the dry salt.

Distillation

Mixtures of liquids or solutions can be separated by distillation. In a distillery, the whisky is separated from a mixture of whisky, water, and other materials. The whisky (alcohol) has a lower boiling point than the water. When the mixture is heated, the whisky **evaporates** before the water. The vapour is cooled in a **condenser**, and the liquid is collected. A similar process can be carried out in the laboratory using a mixture of alcohol and water. Separating liquids in this way is called **fractional distillation**.

In some parts of the world there is a shortage of drinking water. In parts of the Middle East, where fuel is cheap, pure water can be obtained from sea water by **simple distillation**. When heated, the pure water is evaporated (and later condensed) leaving the salts behind. It is a very expensive process. We don't have to do it in this country because we have plenty of fresh rainwater to drink. We shouldn't take this for granted though. Water can easily be polluted by industrial waste, acid rain (see Acids and Alkalis) or nitrate fertilisers washed from the soil (see Fertilisers).

Chromatography

Mixtures in solution can be separated by a method called **paper chromatography**. The word "chromatography" comes from the Greek word "khroma", meaning colour. The ink in some felt tip pens, and food colourings are mixtures of coloured dyes. Mixtures like these can be separated by paper chromatography.

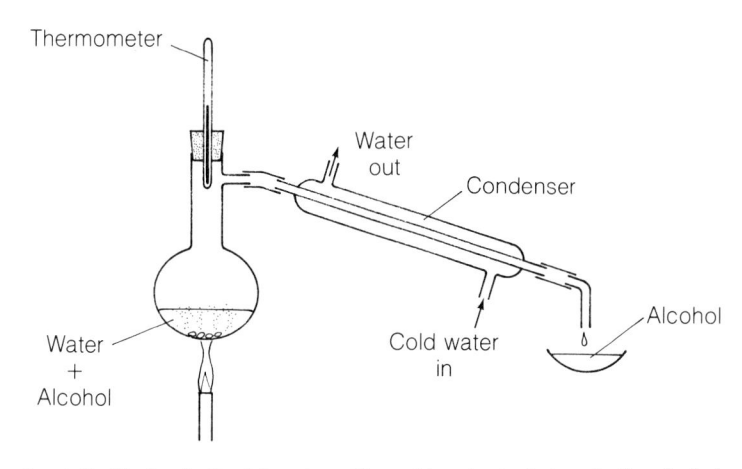

REACTIONS AND THE ATOM 7

Fractional distillation in the laboratory. The cold water jacket cools the alcohol vapour.

How to Set Up a Chromatogram

1. A small spot of ink is put at the centre of a piece of filter paper.
2. The paper is dipped into a **solvent** – in this case a mixture of alcohol and water.

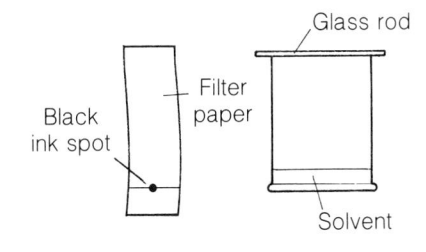

How Does it Work?

The solvent slowly moves up the filter paper. When it reaches the ink, the dyes start to spread out with the solvent, at different speeds.

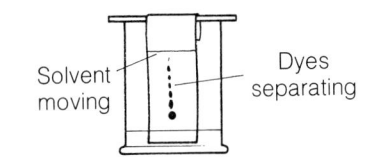

Testing for Pure Substances

Paper chromatography can be used to test if a substance is pure. With pure substances only one colour is seen. The method can also be used to separate **colourless** mixtures. Once the chromatogram is run, it is sprayed with a chemical which reacts with any substances on the paper to form coloured compounds. If more than one spot is seen the substance being tested is a mixture.

Using Chromatography

Chemists use chromatography in many useful ways:
- In the **food industry**, synthetic (man-made) dyes, used to colour foods, can be separated out to check that they are harmless.
- In **hospitals**, chemicals found in blood and urine can be separated out to see if they contain drugs or other impurities.
- A **forensic scientist** can identify ink used by a forger to change a bank cheque!

In Carbohydrates you can see how paper chromatography can be used to separate mixtures of carbohydrates.

REACTIONS AND THE ATOM

Activities

1. Think about making yourself a cup of hot chocolate.
   (a) Name the solute and solvent you would use.
   (b) Describe how you might separate the mixture you have made.

2. When a solution of sodium hydroxide is made, pellets of the compound are dissolved in water. When hydrogen chloride gas is dissolved in water hydrochloric acid is formed. If the two solutions are mixed, they react to form sodium chloride and water.
   Write down:
   (a) the substances mentioned in the passage above, together with their state symbols;
   (b) a word equation for the reaction between the two solutions. Include state symbols.

3. You are given a mixture of salt and sand, and any laboratory equipment you need. Describe what you would do to separate the mixture into sand and salt crystals. Diagrams would be helpful in your description.

4. Some ethanol (boiling point 79 °C) and butanol (boiling point 117 °C) are accidentally mixed.
   (a) Draw the apparatus you would use to separate the two liquids and label it clearly.
   (b) Describe what you would do.
   (c) Which liquid would separate first?
   (d) Explain your answer to (c).
   (e) Both liquids burn. What safety precaution would you have to take when separating them?

5. A sample of urine taken from a patient in hospital is known to contain a mixture of chemicals. Describe how you would test the urine to find out how many substances it contained.

6. The table below shows the solubility of potassium sulphate over a range of temperatures.

Temperature (°C)	Solubility (g per 100 g of water)
0	7
20	10
40	12
60	16
80	20

   (a) Draw a line graph of solubility against temperature, on graph paper.
   (b) From your graph, predict what the solubility might be at 100 °C.

7. The graph below shows the solubility of certain compounds at different temperatures.

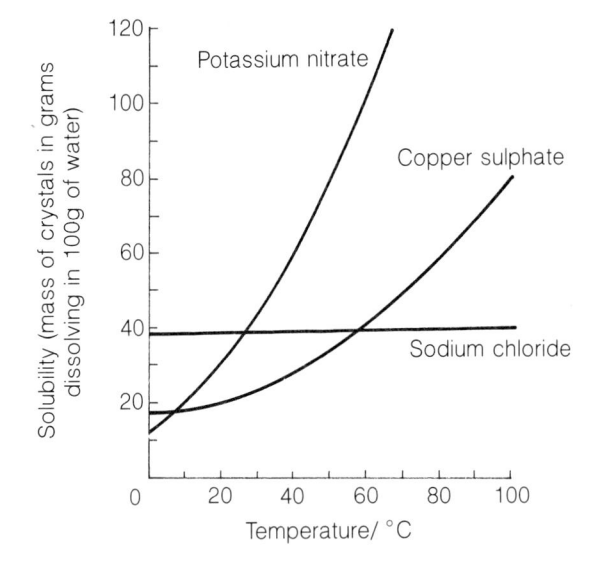

   (a) How much solvent is each solute dissolved in?
   (b) Which compound is most soluble at 60 °C?
   (c) Which compound's solubility is least affected by an increase in temperature?
   (d) If a saturated solution of copper sulphate was cooled from 60 °C to 20 °C, what mass of crystals would form?

3 Speed of Reactions

How Fast?

In Reactions All Around you saw that chemical reactions are happening around us all the time. These reactions are all happening at different **speeds**, or **rates**. The speed of a reaction is a measure of **how fast** it happens. It indicates **how much** of the product is formed in a particular time.

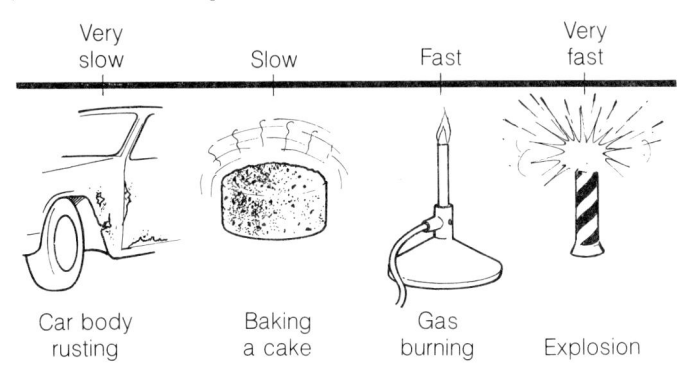

Very slow — Car body rusting
Slow — Baking a cake
Fast — Gas burning
Very fast — Explosion

Chemical reactions happen at different rates

Key Ideas

Chemical reactions occur at different *speeds* or *rates*. The speed of a reaction is a measure of *how fast* it happens. The *particle size, concentration* and *temperature* of reactants all play a part in how fast a reaction occurs. *Catalysts* can be added to speed up reactions. Many important reactions in our body and chemical reactions in industry rely on catalysts to make them happen at a particular rate.

How the Speed of a Reaction Changes

We can find out how the speed of a reaction changes, as the reaction progresses. To do this we need to carry out a reaction and measure the amount of product formed over a period of time. A suitable reaction is chalk or marble (both calcium carbonate) with hydrochloric acid. During this reaction carbon dioxide gas is produced. The gas can be collected and its **volume** measured at regular time intervals. Alternatively, we can measure the **loss in mass** of flask and reactants as carbon dioxide is given off, at regular intervals. The results from both methods can be shown on a graph.

Measuring Gas Volume

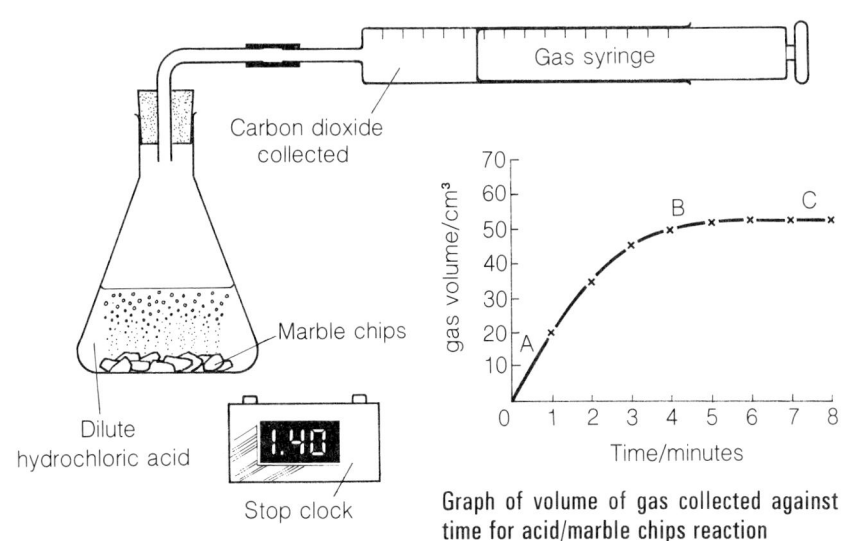

Table 1.4 – Results

Time (min)	Gas Volume (cm³)
0	0
1	20
2	35
3	45
4	50
5	52
6	53
7	53
8	53

Graph of volume of gas collected against time for acid/marble chips reaction

Look at the graph of volume of gas against time.

At **A**, the graph is a straight line with a fairly steep slope. The gas is being produced quickly. The reaction is **fast**.

At **B**, the graph starts to level off. The gas is no longer being produced quickly. The reaction is **slower**.

At **C**, the graph has completely levelled off. No more gas is being produced. The reaction has **stopped**.

10 REACTIONS AND THE ATOM

Measuring Loss in Mass

In this experiment a **computer** is used to take readings every 60 seconds and plot a graph of loss in mass against time.

Table 1.5 – Results

Time (min)	Loss in Mass (g)
0	0.000
1	0.037
2	0.064
3	0.082
4	0.092
5	0.095
6	0.097
7	0.097
8	0.097

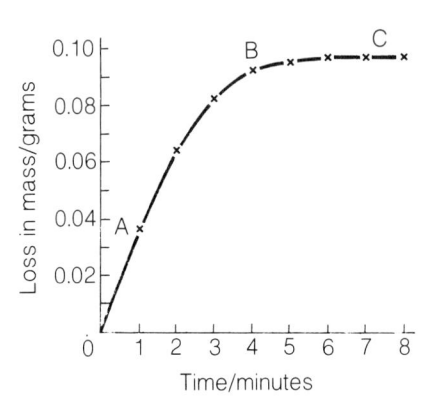

Graph of loss in mass against time for acid/marble chips reaction

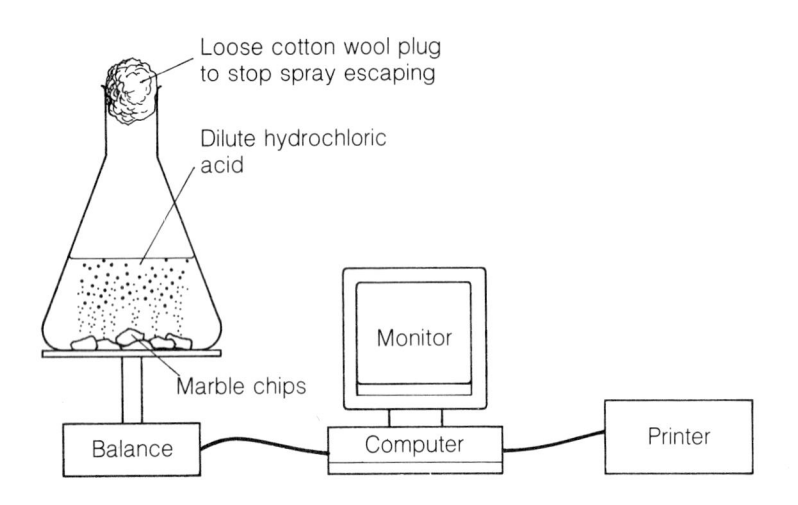

As you might expect, the graph is similar to the one for volume of gas against time in the last experiment. The shape of the graph can be explained in a similar way:

At **A**, the graph is a straight line with a fairly steep slope. The gas is being produced quickly, so the loss in mass is large. The reaction is **fast**.

At **B**, the graph starts to level off. The gas is no longer being produced quickly, and the loss in mass is not as large. The reaction is **slower**.

At **C**, the graph has completely levelled off. No more gas is being produced, and there is no further loss in mass. The reaction has **stopped**.

Why Does the Speed Change?

At the beginning of the reaction there are a lot of acid and marble particles. Therefore they are more likely to **collide** with one another and react. As the acid and marble are used up, there are less particles around, and so less chance of collision and reaction. The reaction slows down. Eventually all the acid or marble (or both) is used up and the reaction stops.

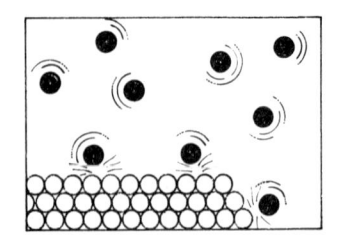

Near the start of the reaction: lots of acid and marble particles

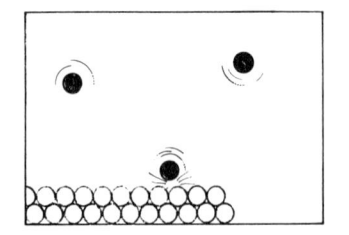

Near the end of the reaction: fewer acid and marble particles

● acid   ○ marble

Changing the Speed of a Reaction

1 Particle Size

The **size of the reacting particles** has an effect on the speed of the reaction. We can show this by repeating the marble and acid experiment, using different sizes of particles (see page 11).

What do you notice about the temperature of the acid and the amount of acid and marble in each experiment? Do you think it would be a fair comparison if the amounts of acid and marble were different?

The amount of acid and marble, the temperature of the acid and the size of the particles can all be changed. They are known as **variables**. It is important when investigating the effect of changing one variable, that all the other variables remain the same. Otherwise, you could not be sure that any change in rate observed was due only to the variable you deliberately changed.

In this experiment, only the sizes of the marble particles are different. This is because we are trying to find the effect of particle size on the speed of reaction.

The results from both experiments are shown on the same graph. This makes it easier to compare changes in reaction rate.

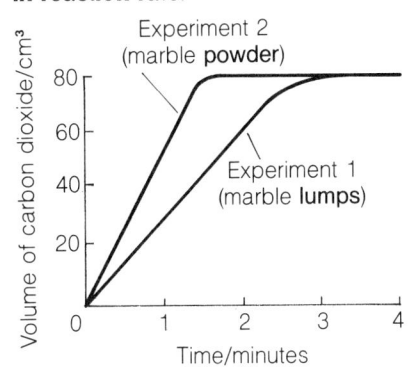

Graph to show the effect of particle size on rate of reaction

Notice that initially (at the beginning of the reaction) the slope of the powdered marble graph is **steeper** than the slope of the marble lumps graph. This shows that the powdered marble produces carbon dioxide **quicker** – in other words the **speed** of reaction is **faster** with **smaller particles**. This is true for most chemical reactions.

Notice also that the total volume of gas collected is the same in each experiment. This is because the same amounts of acid and marble were used each time.

It's not just in laboratory experiments that particle size can be shown to be important:

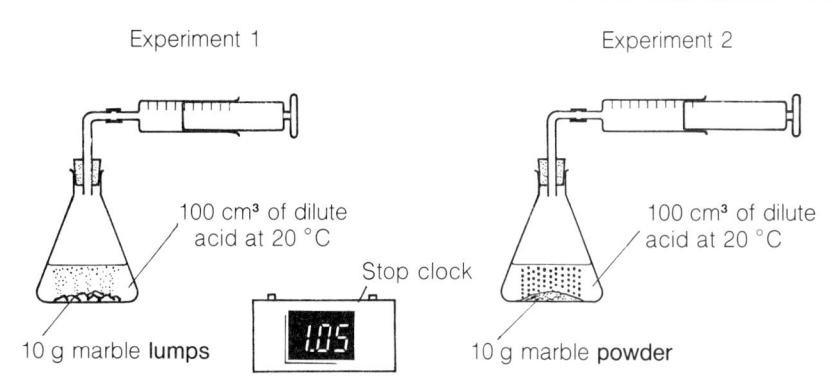

Experiment 1: 100 cm³ of dilute acid at 20 °C, 10 g marble **lumps**
Experiment 2: 100 cm³ of dilute acid at 20 °C, 10 g marble **powder**
Stop clock

- Potatoes will cook quicker if they are cut into small pieces.
- In flour mills, fans continuously extract fine particles of flour from the air. This is to stop the small particles reacting with the oxygen in the air and causing an explosion – a **very** fast kind of reaction.
- In coal mines there is a similar problem with coal dust. The air is kept damp to reduce the risk of explosion.
- In coal-fired power stations the coal is deliberately crushed into small pieces so that it will burn quicker.
- Fireworks often contain metals which burn quickly, with bright coloured flames. Do you think the metals would be powdered or in lumps?

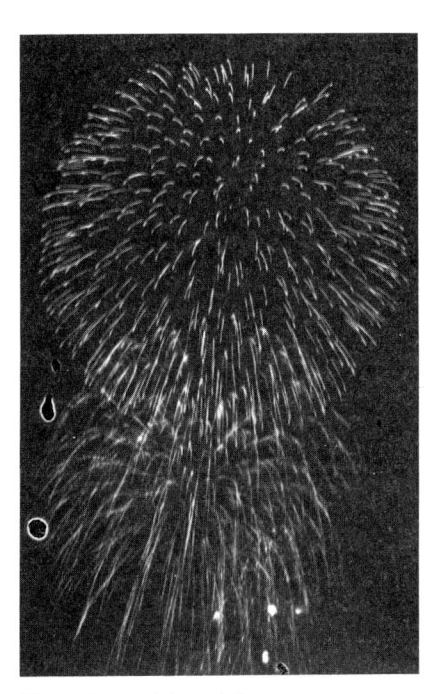

Fireworks contain metals

Why do Small Particles React Faster?

For two or more substances to react their particles have to collide. Smaller particles have a larger overall **surface area**, so there is more chance of other particles colliding and reacting.

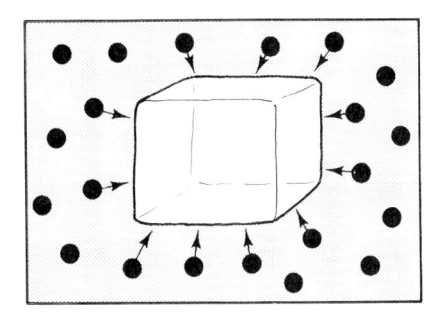

A large lump of solid has quite a small surface area. The reaction can only happen at the outside surface.

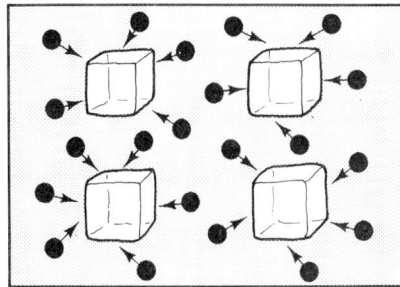

Smaller lumps of solid have a larger surface area at which the reaction can happen. The reaction rate is much faster.

12 REACTIONS AND THE ATOM

2 Temperature

The **temperature** at which a reaction is carried out also affects the speed of reaction. This can be shown in a similar experiment.

We can use the reaction between marble and acid again. The experimental details are the same, except this time the particle size, and the amount of marble and acid used are not altered. Only the **temperature** of the acid is changed.

The results of both experiments are shown in the graph below.

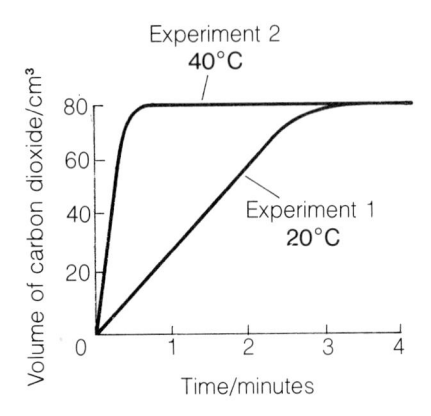

Graph to show the effect of temperature on reaction rate

The initial slope of the graph for the experiment at the higher temperature is **steeper**, and shows that the reaction speed is **faster**. This is true for most chemical reactions. Notice again that the total volume of gas collected is the same in each experiment.

Temperature affects chemical reactions that occur in our everyday life:
- Car exhausts get very hot because gases leaving the engine are hot. The heat causes the exhaust to rust more quickly than the rest of the car.
- Many foods are kept in fridges or freezers to make them last longer. The **reduced** temperature **slows down** any chemical reactions which make the food "go off".
- Many industrial chemical processes need high temperatures. The manufacture of ammonia requires a temperature of around 450°C to produce the chemical at an economical speed.

Why are reactions faster at higher temperatures?

Temperature can be used as a measure of how much energy particles have. The higher the temperature, the more energy they have and the faster they move around. This causes more collisions, but more importantly, the particles have **a lot of energy** and are more likely to react with each other.

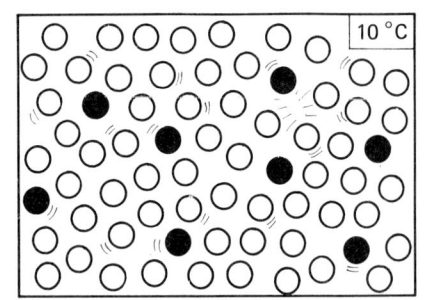

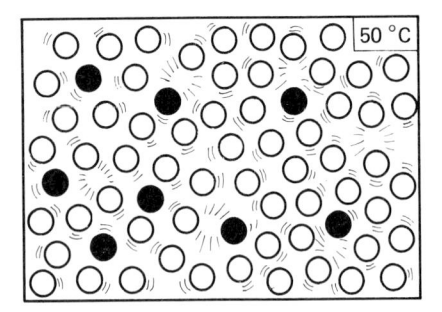

3 Concentration

The concentration of reactants affects the speed of a reaction too. This can again be shown in an experiment.

Let us use the reaction between marble and acid once more. The experimental details are again the same except this time particle size, amount of marble, and temperature are not altered. Although the volume of acid is the same, the **concentration** is different – there is, however, enough acid in each experiment to react completely with the marble.

The results of both experiments are shown in the graph below.

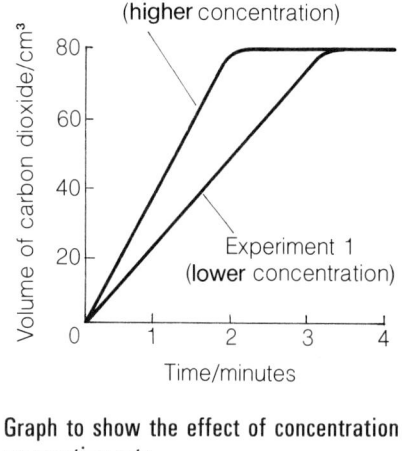

Graph to show the effect of concentration on reaction rate

The steeper initial slope of the graph at the **higher** concentration, shows that the reaction is faster. This is true for most chemical reactions. Again the total volume of gas collected is the same in each case because the same amount of marble has reacted.

Concentration affects chemical reactions that occur in our everyday lives, and in industry too:
- Charcoal in a barbecue burns much faster when you fan it. This is because a higher concentration of oxygen (in the air) is then reacting with the charcoal.

Low temperatures slow chemical reactions down

REACTIONS AND THE ATOM   13

- Concentration of reactants in industrial processes is often critical. If concentrations are wrong then reactions can happen too slowly to be economically practical.
  For some reactions involving **gases**, increasing **pressure** can have a similar effect to increasing concentration. The higher the pressure, the faster the reaction.
- Cooking food in a pressure cooker cuts down the cooking time needed. Inside the pot, water changes to steam, and because it can't escape the pressure builds up.
- Many industrial processes involving gases are speeded up by increasing pressure, e.g., when making ammonia, pressures of around 200 times atmospheric pressure are used (see Fertilisers).

Why do more concentrated mixtures react faster?

Concentration is a measure of the number of particles in a certain amount of substance. The more particles, the higher the concentration. When two reactants are mixed and the concentration of one (or both) is high, then there is a greater chance of collision taking place.

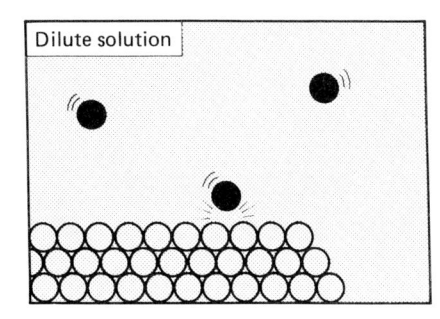

Dilute solution
Particles are far apart and are less likely to meet and react.

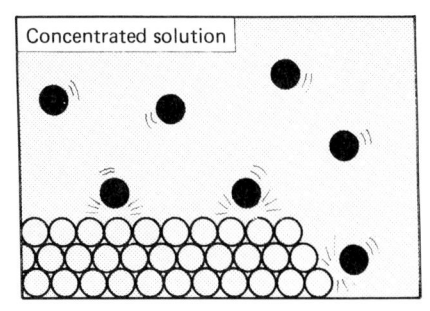

Concentrated solution
More particles are present in the same volume, so they are closer together. They are more likely to meet and react.

4 Catalysts

A catalyst is a substance, which, when added to a reaction mixture, speeds up the reaction. However, catalysts themselves are not used up during reaction.

In the Laboratory

Hydrogen peroxide solution **slowly** breaks up (decomposes) to form water and oxygen. However, when a **small** amount of a black solid compound called manganese dioxide is added, the reaction suddenly speeds up. The manganese dioxide is acting as a **catalyst**.

When the reaction is over, the manganese dioxide looks just the same as it did at the start. It has not undergone any chemical change

Manganese dioxide catalyst speeds up the decomposition of hydrogen peroxide

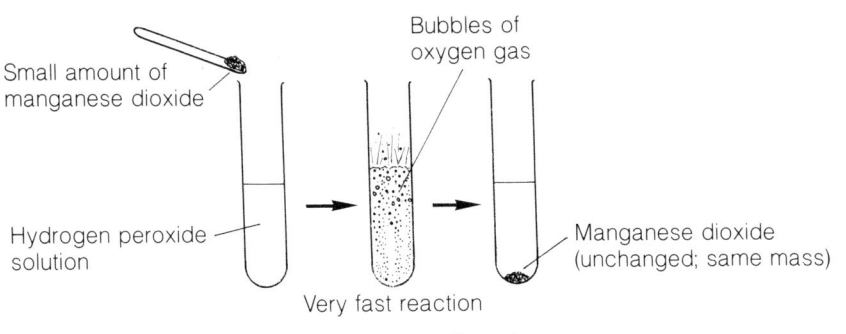

Table 1.6

Catalyst	Reaction
Vanadium oxide	The Contact Process for making sulphuric acid (see Fuels and Hydrocarbons)
Iron	The Haber Process for making ammonia (see Fertilisers)
Nickel	Hydrogenation – converting vegetable oils into margarine (see Fuels and Hydrocarbons)
Platinum/Rhodium	The Ostwald Process for making nitric acid (see Fertilisers)

and none of it has been used up. The manganese dioxide can be weighed before the reaction, then filtered off, dried and reweighed afterwards. No change in mass will be found. This is the same for all catalysts – only **small amounts** are needed and they are **not used up** or **chemically changed**.

In Industry

Catalysts are very important for speeding up some chemical reactions on a large scale. Table 1.6 lists some important industrial catalysts.

Car exhausts are now being fitted with catalytic converters. They contain transition metals, like platinum and rhodium, which convert polluting gases in the exhaust fumes (nitrogen oxide and carbon monoxide) into less harmful gases (see Fuels and Hydrocarbons).

In Nature

Plants and animals contain natural catalysts called **enzymes** to control reactions inside them. Potatoes and blood contain an enzyme called **catalase**, which breaks up hydrogen peroxide. **Amylase**, an enzyme in

14 REACTIONS AND THE ATOM

the saliva in our mouth, speeds up the first stage in the breakdown of starch in foods like bread and potatoes.

Some industrial processes use enzymes extracted from living things. The manufacture of beer, yoghurt, some medicines and cheese all involve enzymes. Biological washing powders even contain enzymes.

All these products involve enzymes

Activities

1. What **four** things could an industrial chemist do to try and increase the speed at which a chemical is made from its reactants?

2. (a) Give **one** example of an everyday reaction, the speed of which is affected by a change in temperature.
   (b) Give examples of **two** other reactions, one in which the speed is affected by concentration and one in which the speed is affected by particle size.

3. Catalysts can be added to reactions to speed them up.
   (a) What **two** things might you notice about a catalyst if you compared it before and after a chemical reaction?
   (b) Give an example of a catalyst used in:
      (i) an important industrial process (name the process);
      (ii) car exhausts.
   (c) Explain what an enzyme is and give an example of how one might be used in industry.

4. The table below shows the volume of hydrogen produced when acid reacts with magnesium metal.

Time (min)	
0	0
1	15
2	25
3	31
4	34
5	36
6	37
7	38
8	38

   (a) Plot the results in the table on a graph of volume of gas collected against time. Use graph paper.
   (b) From the graph, at what time is the reaction faster, 1 minute or 4 minutes?
   (c) Explain how you worked out your answer to (b).

5. Graphs 1 and 2 below are for acids of **different** concentrations reacting with zinc metal to form hydrogen gas.

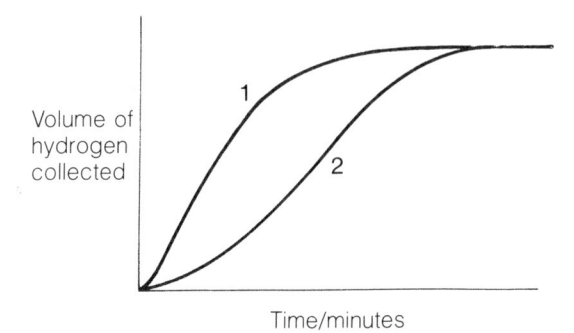

   (a) Which graph would be obtained using the more concentrated acid?
   (b) Explain your answer to (a).
   (c) If the particles of zinc are made bigger:
      (i) what would happen to the initial speed of both reactions?
      (ii) how would the final volumes of gas compare to those shown in the graph?
   (d) What would happen to the speed of both reactions if the temperature of the acid was increased?

6. Manganese dioxide and lead dioxide both catalyse the decomposition of hydrogen peroxide into water and oxygen gas.
   (i) Describe how you could compare the two catalysts, to see which was the best at decomposing hydrogen peroxide.
   (ii) Draw a diagram of the arrangement you would use in your experiment.

4 The Periodic Table

Key Ideas

There are over 100 known elements. Most occur *naturally* but some have been *made* by scientists. The elements are arranged in the *periodic table* so that those with similar chemical properties are *grouped* together.

Grouping the Elements

An element is a substance which cannot be broken down into any simpler substance. Some of the 105 elements were already known about thousands of years ago. **Gold** and **silver** jewellery and ornaments have been found, which are over 5000 years old. **Iron** weapons and tools over 2000 years old have also been found. In the Middle Ages, alchemists tried to change **lead** into gold!

Today the elements are arranged in the **periodic table**. The one we use is not a lot different from the one proposed by a Russian chemist called Dmitri Mendeleev in 1869; even though few elements had been discovered at that time. He showed that the elements grouped themselves into families with **similar chemical properties** when they were arranged in order of their increasing atomic mass. These families appeared "periodically" (at regular intervals) – hence the name periodic table.

Mendeleev was prepared to leave gaps in the table and predict that elements would be discovered to fill the gaps – and they were! He was even able to predict the chemical properties of some of these elements by looking at other elements in the "family".

In today's periodic table, elements are listed in order of increasing **atomic number**. In schools, we tend to use a shortened version of the periodic table, like the one shown on page 16.

Sorting Out the Elements

A close look at the periodic table shows that all the elements are either **metals** or **non-metals** (most are metals). Metals and non-metals have different **physical properties**. Physical properties can be measured or observed, such as conductivity, state (solid, liquid or gas), colour and boiling point. Table 1.7 compares some of the physical properties at room temperature of metals and non-metals.

Table 1.7

Metals	Non-metals
All but one are solid e.g., Gold (Au), Iron (Fe), Aluminium (Al) } solid Mercury (Hg) is the only liquid	Can be solid, liquid or gas e.g., Sulphur (S) – solid Bromine (Br) – liquid (the only one) Helium (He) – gas
Good conductors of electricity e.g., copper wires	Only carbon in the form of graphite is a good conductor of electricity
Good conductors of heat e.g., aluminium pots	Most are poor conductors of heat
Shiny when polished	Mostly dull
Many are strong and can be bent or beaten into shape e.g., car bodies made of iron (steel)	Solids tend to be hard and break easily (brittle)

Most elements occur naturally in the Earth, a few as free elements (such as gold), and the rest combined with other elements in the form of compounds. For example, iron is found as **iron oxide** (iron ore), and aluminium as **aluminium oxide** (bauxite).

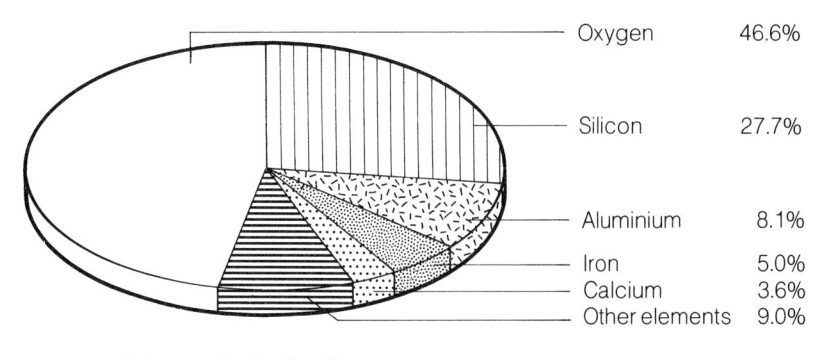

Oxygen	46.6%
Silicon	27.7%
Aluminium	8.1%
Iron	5.0%
Calcium	3.6%
Other elements	9.0%

Percentage of elements in the Earth's crust

Some elements, like **uranium**, give out tiny particles and rays of energy. These are **radioactive** elements. Scientists have been able to make some new elements in the laboratory. Other elements have been detected after nuclear explosions. Elements are often named after places, countries or

16 REACTIONS AND THE ATOM

The Periodic Table of Elements

Groups	1 alkali metals	2 alkaline earth metals						transition metals						3	4	5	6	7 halogens	0 noble gases
Periods																			
1							1766 **H** hydrogen 1 (date of discovery, symbol, name, atomic number)												1868 **He** helium 2
2	1817 **Li** lithium 3	1798 **Be** beryllium 4												1808 **B** boron 5	B.C. **C** carbon 6	1772 **N** nitrogen 7	1774 **O** oxygen 8	1771 **F** fluorine 9	1898 **Ne** neon 10
3	1807 **Na** sodium 11	1775 **Mg** magnesium 12												1827 **Al** aluminium 13	1823 **Si** silicon 14	1669 **P** phosphorus 15	B.C. **S** sulphur 16	1774 **Cl** chlorine 17	1894 **Ar** argon 18
4	1807 **K** potassium 19	1808 **Ca** calcium 20	1879 **Sc** scandium 21	1791 **Ti** titanium 22	1830 **V** vanadium 23	1797 **Cr** chromium 24	1774 **Mn** manganese 25	B.C. **Fe** iron 26	1735 **Co** cobalt 27	1751 **Ni** nickel 28	B.C. **Cu** copper 29	~1500 **Zn** zinc 30	1875 **Ga** gallium 31	1886 **Ge** germanium 32	1250 **As** arsenic 33	1817 **Se** selenium 34	1826 **Br** bromine 35	1898 **Kr** krypton 36
5	1861 **Rb** rubidium 37	1790 **Sr** strontium 38	1794 **Y** yttrium 39	1789 **Zr** zirconium 40	1801 **Nb** niobium 41	1778 **Mo** molybdenum 42	1937 **Tc** technetium 43	1844 **Ru** ruthenium 44	1803 **Rh** rhodium 45	1804 **Pd** palladium 46	B.C. **Ag** silver 47	1817 **Cd** cadmium 48	1863 **In** indium 49	B.C. **Sn** tin 50	~1450 **Sb** antimony 51	1782 **Te** tellurium 52	1811 **I** iodine 53	1898 **Xe** xenon 54
6	1860 **Cs** caesium 55	1808 **Ba** barium 56	1839 **La** lanthanum 57	1923 **Hf** hafnium 72	1802 **Ta** tantalum 73	1783 **W** tungsten 74	1925 **Re** rhenium 75	1804 **Os** osmium 76	1804 **Ir** iridium 77	1500's **Pt** platinum 78	B.C. **Au** gold 79	B.C. **Hg** mercury 80	1861 **Tl** thallium 81	B.C. **Pb** lead 82	1450 **Bi** bismuth 83	1898 **Po** polonium 84	1940 **At** astatine 85	1900 **Rn** radon 86
7	1939 **Fr** francium 87	1898 **Ra** radium 88	1899 **Ac** actinium 89	1969 **Unq** unnilquadium 104	1970 **Unp** unnilpentium 105													

metals ↔ non-metals

1803 **Ce** cerium 58	1885 **Pr** praseodymium 59	1885 **Nd** neodymium 60	1947 **Pm** promethium 61	1879 **Sm** samarium 62	1896 **Eu** europium 63	1880 **Gd** gadolinium 64	1843 **Tb** terbium 65	1886 **Dy** dysprosium 66	1879 **Ho** holmium 67	1843 **Er** erbium 68	1879 **Tm** thulium 69	1879 **Yb** ytterbium 70	1907 **Lu** lutetium 71
1828 **Th** thorium 90	1917 **Pa** protactinium 91	1789 **U** uranium 92	1940 **Np** neptunium 93	1940 **Pu** plutonium 94	1944 **Am** americium 95	1944 **Cm** curium 96	1949 **Bk** berkelium 97	1950 **Cf** californium 98	1952 **Es** einsteinium 99	1953 **Fm** fermium 100	1955 **Md** mendelevium 101	1957 **No** nobelium 102	1961 **Lr** lawrencium 103

Elements of atomic number 85, 87 and 93 – 105 are not found naturally, but manufactured by scientists

solid | liquid | gas

REACTIONS AND THE ATOM 17

famous scientists. Look at the periodic table. You will probably recognise some elements named this way. Table 1.8 gives some examples.

Table 1.8

Element	Named after
Strontium, Sr	the town in Scotland, Strontian, near where it was discovered.
Einsteinium, Es	the famous scientist, Albert Einstein.
Berkelium, Bk	Berkeley University in America, where it was made.
Francium, Fr	the country, France.
Neptunium, Np	the Roman God of the Sea (the first element to be made in the laboratory).

Using Elements

The elements themselves are very useful – ten of them go into making a computer.

Circuit Board
Joined to each other. Socket of one board made from **Cu** and **Be** mixture (alloy). It is springy, makes good contact and is covered in **Au**.

Au is a good conductor.

Connector of other board is **Ni** (strong). Also covered in **Au**.

Package
This must be air tight as it becomes defected if small atoms leak in or out. It is tested in a container of helium.

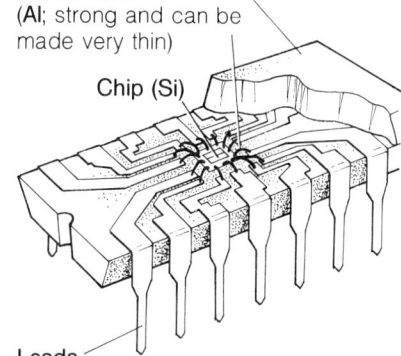

Connectors
(**Al**; strong and can be made very thin)

Chip (Si)

Leads
(an alloy of **Fe** and **Ni**, covered by **Au** or **Sn**). These are attached to tracks on circuit board with **solder** (an alloy of **Sn** and **Pb**, which has a sharp, low melting point).

Elements are most useful for making compounds. Although there are just over 100 elements, there are more than six million compounds – and more are being made all the time.

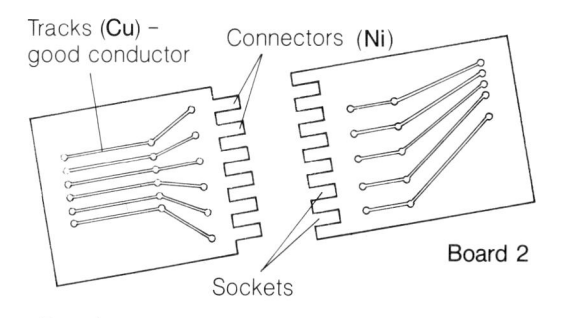

Tracks (**Cu**) – good conductor
Connectors (**Ni**)
Sockets
Board 1
Board 2

The human body contains only eleven elements (apart from trace elements) but thousands of different compounds

Families of Elements

The elements in the periodic table are arranged in **groups**. The groups are in vertical **columns**. Elements in the **same** group show similar **chemical properties**. This means they react with other substances in a similar way. Groups next to each other also show similarities.

Group 1: The Alkali Metals

The group 1 metals are **very reactive** (the most reactive in the periodic table) and do not occur naturally as elements. They are found in the Earth as compounds, like sodium chloride and potassium bromide. To obtain the metal, the compounds are melted and then electricity is passed through them. Electricity is expensive, so it costs a lot of money to extract group 1 metals.

How Reactive Are They?
Rubidium and **caesium** are so reactive that they have to be kept in a vacuum. Caesium is in fact the most reactive of all metals. Francium has never been seen and has only ever been detected in very small amounts by a machine.

Lithium, **sodium**, and **potassium** are so reactive that they have to be stored under **oil**, to keep them from combining with gases in the **air**, including water vapour.

Reaction With Air
The alkali metals are very soft. They can be cut with a knife and they look like a typical metal when freshly cut. However, they lose their shine within seconds as they react with the oxygen in the air. A coating of metal oxide is formed. Potassium forms potassium oxide:

potassium + oxygen → potassium oxide

Alkali metals burn in air, giving very colourful flames. Sodium has a **yellow** flame and potassium **lilac**. Their compounds give similarly coloured flames. Flame colours can be used to tell which group 1 elements are in a compound.

18 REACTIONS AND THE ATOM

Sodium vapour street lamp

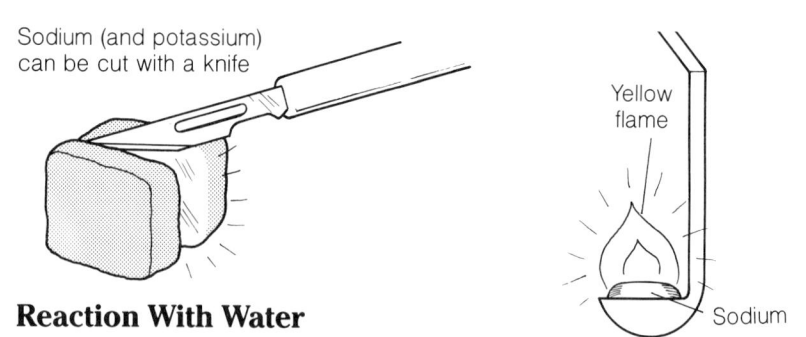

Reaction With Water

The group 1 metals react violently with water. The metal hydroxide and hydrogen gas are formed:

e.g., potassium + water → potassium hydroxide + hydrogen

The hydroxides formed are soluble in water and form **alkaline** solutions. This is why they are called alkali metals.

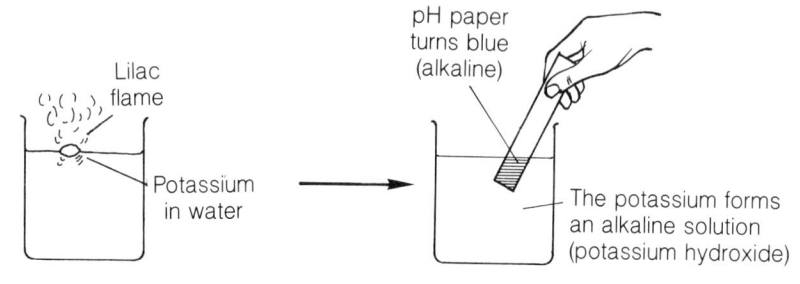

Using the Alkali Metals

Sodium vapour gives street lamps their yellow colour and liquid **sodium** is used as the coolant in some nuclear reactors. **Lithium** batteries power heart pacemakers and **potassium** is an important element in fertilisers. Sodium chloride is common table salt and a variety of compounds can be made from it, like sodium hydroxide and sodium carbonate.

Group 2: The Alkaline Earth Metals

The group 2 metals show many similarities within the group, and also to the group 1 metals. They exist as compounds. Sea water contains a lot of **magnesium chloride**. The metal is extracted by passing electricity through the molten chloride.

How Reactive Are They?

They are not as reactive as the group 1 metals and do not have to be stored under oil. They undergo similar reactions, but more slowly.

Reaction With Air

The metal oxide is formed when group 2 metals burn in air:

e.g., magnesium + oxygen → magnesium oxide

Like the group 1 metals, the alkaline earth metals and their compounds give colourful flames. Strontium has a **red** flame and barium **green**.

Reaction With Water

Magnesium reacts very slowly with cold water, but calcium reacts quite vigorously to form calcium hydroxide and hydrogen gas:

calcium + water → calcium hydroxide + hydrogen

Like the group 1 metals, group 2 metals become more reactive as we go down the group.

A magnesium distress flare

REACTIONS AND THE ATOM 19

Using Group 2 Metals

Magnesium burns with a very bright light and it is used in distress flares, fired by ships in trouble at sea. **Magnesium hydroxide** relieves indigestion. **Strontium** compounds are used in fireworks, because of their brilliant red colour.

Barium sulphate shows up on an X-ray. It is used in hospitals as a "barium meal". The patient swallows it mixed with water and its progress through the body is followed to detect digestive and other medical problems.

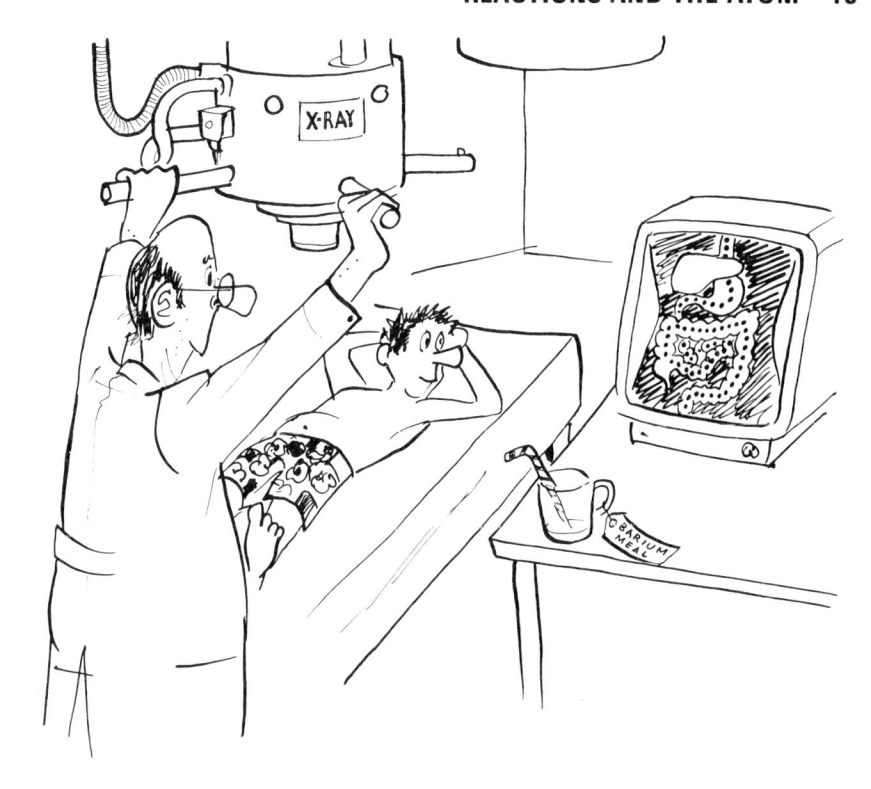

Group 7: The Halogens

These are the most reactive of the non-metals. Their name comes from Greek meaning "salt makers". The halogens form **salts** with metals. Many of these salts are found in the sea. Each kilogram of sea water contains about 30 g of **sodium chloride**.

Reaction With Metals

sodium + chlorine → sodium chloride ⎫
magnesium + bromine → magnesium bromide ⎬ salts

Reactions With Non-metals

hydrogen + chlorine → hydrogen chloride ⎫ form acids when
hydrogen + bromine → hydrogen bromide ⎬ dissolved in water

The halogens are less reactive down the group.

Using Halogens

Chlorine is in bleach, which is used to remove coloured stains and also kill germs. You can smell chlorine in swimming pools. **Silver bromide** is sensitive to light turning from white to black. It is coated onto photographic film. **Fluoride** compounds are added to water and toothpaste, to help protect teeth from decay.

Chlorofluorocarbons (CFC's) are halogen compounds used as the coolant in fridges. They are also used in aerosols. Manufacturers are cutting back on the use of CFC's, because they destroy the ozone layer in the atmosphere. The **ozone layer** protects the Earth from harmful ultraviolet rays from the sun. If too many ultra-violet rays reach the earth, they can lead to harmful effects such as skin cancer.

Chlorine is used in bleach

Group 0: The Noble Gases

The noble gases are **very unreactive** and many of their uses are based on this property. At one time they were known as the "inert" gases, because they were thought not to react at all. However, in the 1960's, xenon and krypton compounds of fluorine were made. All the noble gases are found in air. They are separated by cooling air to liquify it, and then warming to boil each gas off in turn.

Using Noble Gases

Helium is less dense than air and doesn't burn. It is used in weather balloons and airships. Deep sea divers breathe a mixture of helium and oxygen instead of air because the nitrogen in air forms tiny bubbles in the blood. This causes the "bends" when divers come to the surface too quickly.

Argon is used in light bulbs as it will not react with the hot filament. **Neon** is used in some advertising signs since it glows brightly when electricity is passed through it. **Krypton** is used in certain types of lasers.

advertising sign

The Transition Metals

The transition metals form a large grouping in the middle of the periodic table. Many of the names are probably familiar to you. Although the grouping is different from the other groups, they still show many similarities.

Reactions

They are generally unreactive. Those that do react form very colourful compounds. Emeralds and sapphires are jewels containing transition metal compounds. Precious metals like gold and silver are unreactive.

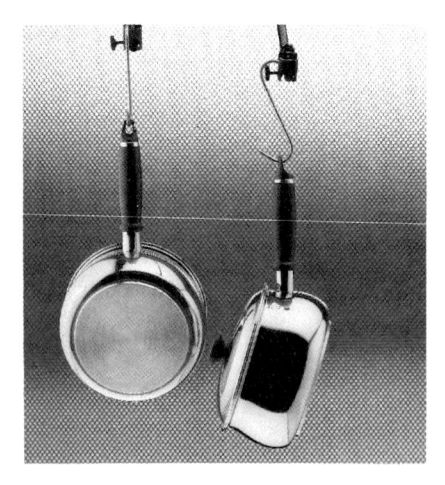

Copper pots are good heat conductors

Using Transition Metals

Many are **catalysts** – platinum, iron and nickel are widely used in industry. Some of them are very strong. Iron can be converted into steel for building ships and bridges. Over 700 million tonnes of iron are produced every year, throughout the world. It is the most widely used metal.

Some metals can be bent and shaped, or made into wires. Copper is one of these. It is used to make electrical wires and also hot water tanks. It is a good conductor of electricity and heat.

Activities

1. (a) to (g) below give descriptions of some of the elements in the periodic table. Use the information in this section and the periodic table to find an element which fits each description. When you have identified each element, write down its **name** and **symbol** and state which **group** and **period** it belongs to.
   (a) A metal which is liquid at room temperature.
   (b) A gas which dissolves in water to form a solution which can be used as a bleach.
   (c) A metal which can be cut with a knife and burns with a yellow flame.
   (d) A gas which is very unreactive and is used in weather balloons.
   (e) An element named after a famous scientist.
   (f) An element named after a country.
   (g) An element with a symbol taken from a foreign language.

2. Find **rubidium** in the periodic table. From its position, predict the following:
   (a) How reactive it will be with water.
   (b) What the products of a reaction with water would be. Write a word equation for the reaction.
   (c) What you would see if it was exposed to the air. Write a word equation for any reaction you think would take place.
   (d) How it would have to be stored.

3. Metals can be joined together by welding, which involves heating the metals to a very high temperature. Some welding processes use argon to stop air getting near the metal.
   (a) Why do you think air has to be kept away from the metals?
   (b) What property of argon makes it useful in this kind of welding?
   (c) Which group of elements does argon belong to?
   (d) Argon occupies about 0.93 per cent of the air. If air is cooled down to around $-200°C$, it turns into a liquid.

   The table below shows the boiling points of the main gases in air.

Element	Boiling Point (°C)
Nitrogen	−196
Oxygen	−182
Argon	−186

   Using this information, describe how pure argon could be obtained from air.

5 What's In An Atom?

Atoms

Every element is made up of very small particles called **atoms**. The atoms themselves are made up of even smaller particles.

At one time the atom was thought to be the smallest particle possible. However, scientists carried out a variety of experiments around the turn of this century and proved that this wasn't the case. It was found that atoms contained **charged particles**. The charges were **positive** (+) and **negative** (−). The positively charged particles were called **protons**, and the negative particles **electrons**. We still use these names today.

How Are These Particles Arranged?

In 1898, Sir J J Thomson looked at all the evidence. He suggested that an atom was shaped like a sphere (like a ball but much smaller), with the charged particles spread through it. Other people described it as a "plum pudding" picture.

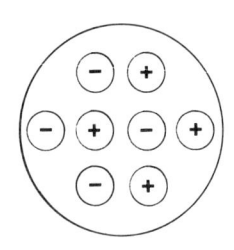

The "plum pudding" model of the atom

In 1909, Geiger and Marsden set up an experiment to test this idea.

They fired newly discovered alpha particles at a thin gold leaf screen. Most of the particles went straight through the gold leaf, but occasionally one would be deflected, and some even came back again.

Thomson's model could not explain these results. Ernest Rutherford concluded that the results made sense only if the positive particles were arranged together in the **middle** of the atom. He called this collection of particles the **nucleus**. He also suggested that the electrons were very light and moved around the outside of the nucleus. His ideas are still used today.

Key Ideas

Elements are made up of *atoms*. Atoms themselves consist of *electrons, protons* and *neutrons*. The numbers of these particles varies from element to element. The electrons in an atom are arranged in *energy levels*. Each atom has an *atomic number* and a *mass number*. The atomic number identifies the element. Not all atoms in an element have exactly the same mass – they are *isotopes*.

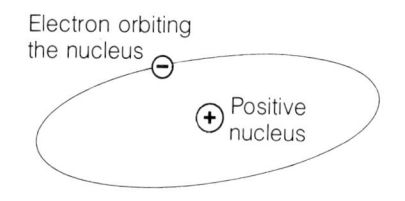

Rutherford's model of the atom

Neutral Atoms

Elements and compounds have a neutral charge overall. They are neither positive nor negative. This must mean that the total positive charge of the nucleus is the **same as** the total negative charge of the electrons – they cancel out each others' charge.

Most alpha particles pass straight through; only some are deflected.

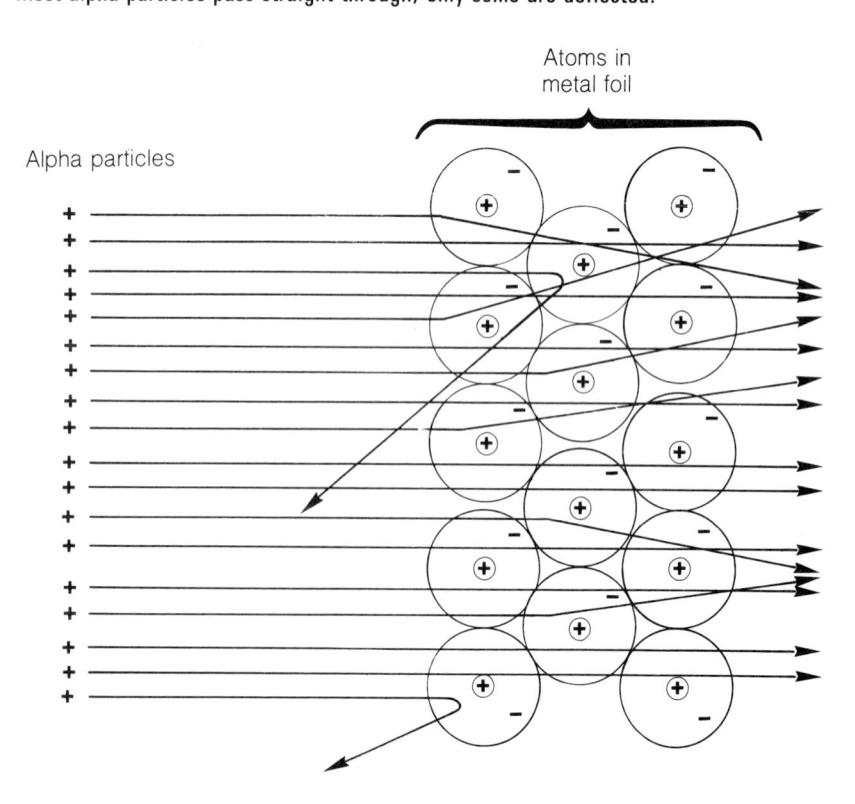

REACTIONS AND THE ATOM

A Closer Look at the Atom

Despite the success of Rutherford and others in explaining the arrangement of protons and electrons in the atom, one problem still remained unsolved. The **mass** of most atoms was greater than the mass of protons in the nucleus. Rutherford predicted the presence of another particle to account for the extra mass. It wasn't until 1932 that a member of the Rutherford team, J Chadwick, was able to show the existence of another particle within the nucleus. This particle had **no charge** and almost the same mass as a proton. He called it a **neutron**. Table 1.9 summarises the charges and masses of particles in an atom.

Table 1.9

Particle	Mass (amu)	Charge	Where found
Proton (p)	1	1+	nucleus
Neutron (n)	1	0	nucleus
Electron (e)	$\frac{1}{1840}$	1−	outside nucleus

(Mass and charge values as compared to each other.)

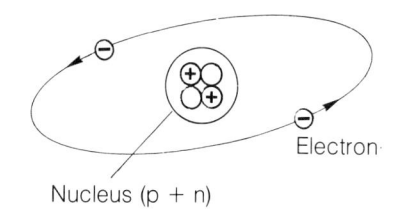

The arrangement of protons, neutrons and electrons in an atom of helium

Mass is measured in atomic mass units (amu). From the table, we see that the proton and the electron have opposite charges of one unit each. Atoms are **neutral**, so the number of protons and electrons must be the **same** in an atom. In this way, the total positive charge cancels the total negative charge.

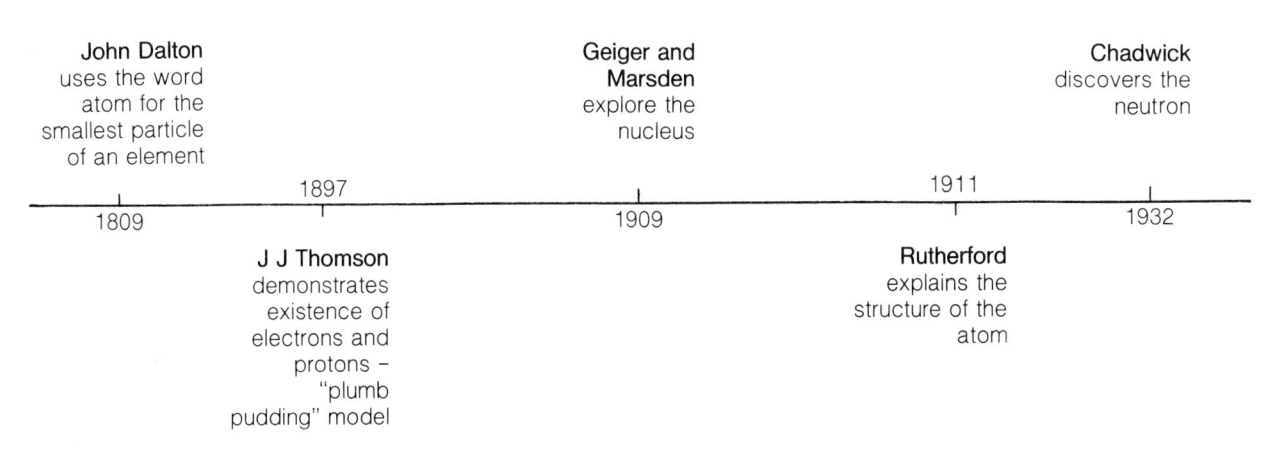

John Dalton uses the word atom for the smallest particle of an element — 1809

J J Thomson demonstrates existence of electrons and protons – "plumb pudding" model — 1897

Geiger and Marsden explore the nucleus — 1909

Rutherford explains the structure of the atom — 1911

Chadwick discovers the neutron — 1932

The search for the structure of the atom

Ions

During chemical reactions, it is possible for the atoms of elements to **lose** or **gain** electrons. When the atoms lose or gain electrons they are no longer neutral. They become **charged**. A charged atom is called an **ion**. If an atom **loses** an electron (or electrons) it loses some negative charge and so becomes **positively** charged. A positive ion is formed, because the atom now has more protons than electrons.

Metals tend to form positive ions when they react. We can represent the ion charge by adding it to the chemical symbol.

Using **sodium** as an example:
Na is the symbol for a **sodium atom**
Na$^+$ is the symbol for a **sodium ion**
The **one positive** charge (+) shows the sodium atom has lost **one electron.**

If an atom **gains** an electron (or electrons), it becomes a **negative** ion. This is because there are now more electrons than protons. **Non-metal** elements tend to form **negative ions** when they react. Using **chlorine** as an example:
Cl is the symbol for a **chlorine atom**
Cl$^-$ is the symbol for a **chloride ion**
The one negative charge (−) shows the chlorine atom has gained one electron.

Scientists are still finding out more about the atom. Particles which are parts of protons and neutrons have now been discovered. They have been given unusual sounding names like "quark" and "lepton". Although their discovery is important, the existence of protons, neutrons and electrons is enough for us to explain the chemistry of elements and compounds.

24 REACTIONS AND THE ATOM

The Atomic Number

We have seen that all atoms contain positive and negative particles. The atoms of **different** elements have **different** numbers of these particles. This is what makes them different from each other. The elements are arranged in the periodic table according to their **atomic number**. The number tells us how many protons each atom of an element has.

Look at the periodic table on page 16. You will see that each element has a different atomic number. The higher the atomic number, the **bigger** and **heavier** the atoms of that element are. This is because the number of particles is increasing so the **mass** and **size** of the atom also increases.

The Significance of the Atomic Number

The atomic number describes the atom as belonging to a particular element. The number of protons and electrons in an atom are the same and so the atomic number also tells us how many electrons are in a particular (neutral) atom. Table 1.10 gives some examples.

Table 1.10

Element	Atomic number	Protons	Electrons	Overall charge on atom
Hydrogen (H)	1	1	1	0
Carbon (C)	6	6	6	0
Sodium (Na)	11	11	11	0
Aluminium (Al)	13	13	13	0

Notice how the atomic number tells us nothing about the number of neutrons in an atom.

The Mass Number

The **mass number** is the number of protons added to the number of neutrons:

mass number = protons + neutrons

The number of neutrons can be calculated by subtracting the atomic number (protons) from the mass number (protons + neutrons).

number of neutrons = mass number − atomic number

How are the Electrons Arranged?

The electrons in an atom are arranged in an organised way. Having, say, 100 electrons, moving about a nucleus in any direction and in any area of space, would be like having 100 pupils running around a classroom in any direction! It would be impossible for them to avoid hitting each other.

The electrons move about in layers of space, sometimes called shells, like the layers of an onion. Each shell can hold only so many electrons. Table 1.11 shows (for the first 20 elements) the maximum number of electrons "allowed" in each shell.

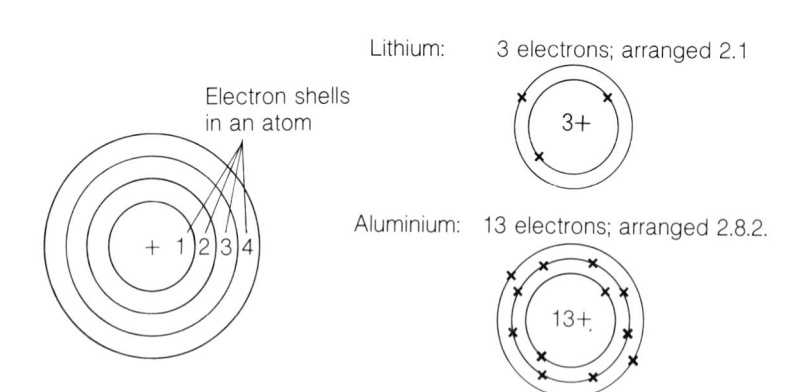

Table 1.11

Shell number	Maximum number of electrons
1	2
2	8
3	8
4	2

Lithium: 3 electrons; arranged 2.1

Aluminium: 13 electrons; arranged 2.8.2

Calcium: 20 electrons; arranged 2.8.8.2

Arrangement of electrons in "shells". Note that the shells are filled from Shell 1, and each shell is full before another is started.

Look at the electron arrangements of the elements in groups 1 to 0, in the periodic table below. Compare the group number to the number of electrons in the outer shell of each element in that group. You should notice that they are the same (apart from group 0). In some periodic tables group 0 is referred to as a group 8. Can you think why? The chemical similarities between elements in the same group are largely due to them having the same number of electrons in their outer shell.

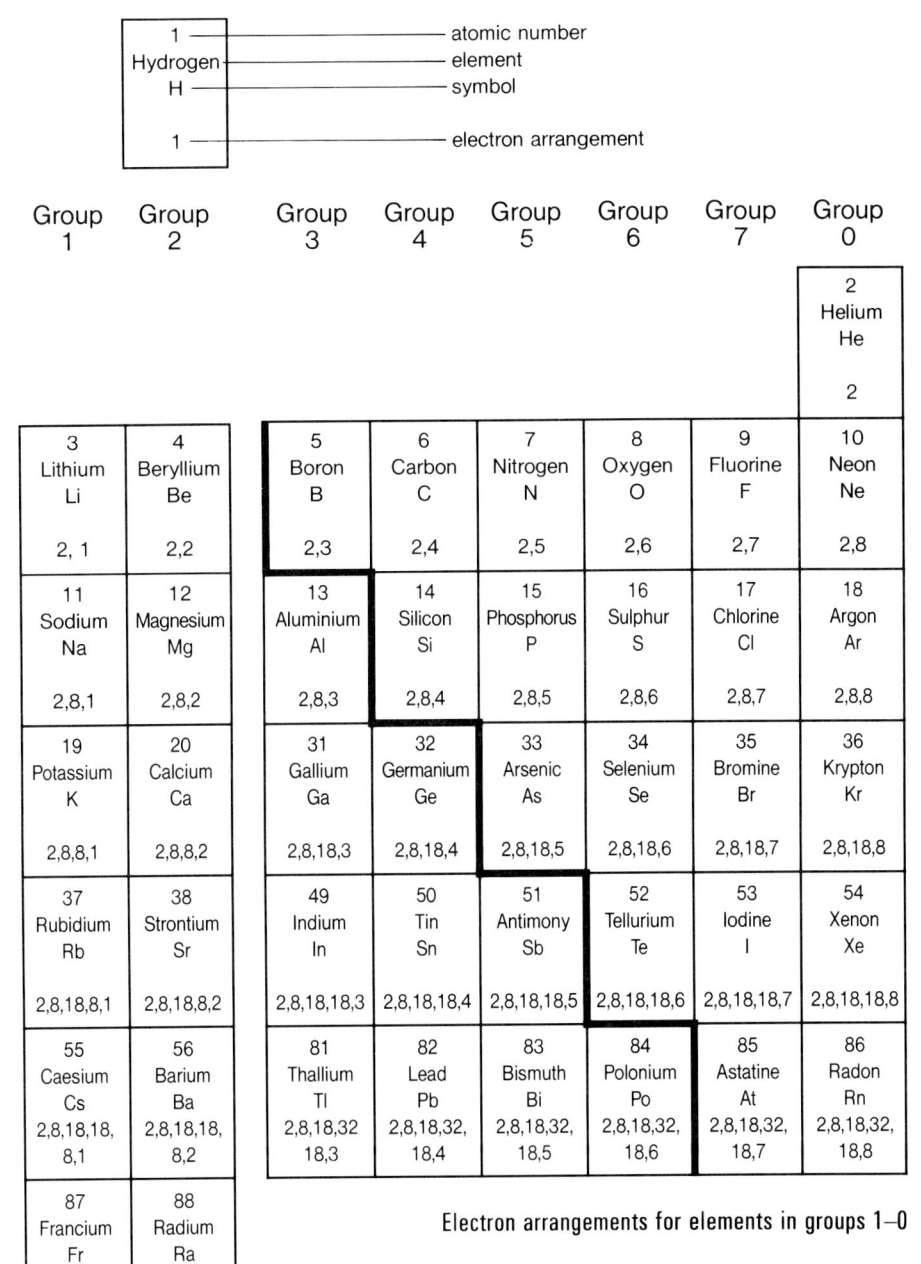

1			atomic number
Hydrogen			element
H			symbol
1			electron arrangement

Group 1	Group 2	Group 3	Group 4	Group 5	Group 6	Group 7	Group 0
							2 Helium He 2
3 Lithium Li 2,1	4 Beryllium Be 2,2	5 Boron B 2,3	6 Carbon C 2,4	7 Nitrogen N 2,5	8 Oxygen O 2,6	9 Fluorine F 2,7	10 Neon Ne 2,8
11 Sodium Na 2,8,1	12 Magnesium Mg 2,8,2	13 Aluminium Al 2,8,3	14 Silicon Si 2,8,4	15 Phosphorus P 2,8,5	16 Sulphur S 2,8,6	17 Chlorine Cl 2,8,7	18 Argon Ar 2,8,8
19 Potassium K 2,8,8,1	20 Calcium Ca 2,8,8,2	31 Gallium Ga 2,8,18,3	32 Germanium Ge 2,8,18,4	33 Arsenic As 2,8,18,5	34 Selenium Se 2,8,18,6	35 Bromine Br 2,8,18,7	36 Krypton Kr 2,8,18,8
37 Rubidium Rb 2,8,18,8,1	38 Strontium Sr 2,8,18,8,2	49 Indium In 2,8,18,18,3	50 Tin Sn 2,8,18,18,4	51 Antimony Sb 2,8,18,18,5	52 Tellurium Te 2,8,18,18,6	53 Iodine I 2,8,18,18,7	54 Xenon Xe 2,8,18,18,8
55 Caesium Cs 2,8,18,18, 8,1	56 Barium Ba 2,8,18,18, 8,2	81 Thallium Tl 2,8,18,32 18,3	82 Lead Pb 2,8,18,32, 18,4	83 Bismuth Bi 2,8,18,32, 18,5	84 Polonium Po 2,8,18,32, 18,6	85 Astatine At 2,8,18,32, 18,7	86 Radon Rn 2,8,18,32, 18,8
87 Francium Fr 2,8,18,32, 18,8,1	88 Radium Ra 2,8,18,32, 18,8,2						

Electron arrangements for elements in groups 1–0

The Energy of Electrons

The orbiting electrons in different shells have different amounts of **energy**. Those nearest the nucleus have the **lowest** energy. They are in the lowest **energy level**. As the energy level (shell number) increases, so the energy of the electrons occupying those energy levels increases. Electrons in the outer energy level of an atom have the highest energy. It is the outer electrons which are involved in chemical reactions.

26 REACTIONS AND THE ATOM

Chemical Shorthand

Chemists use a shorthand method of presenting information about an atom. They use a combination of symbols and numbers. Information about an atom of chlorine, for example, may be given like this:

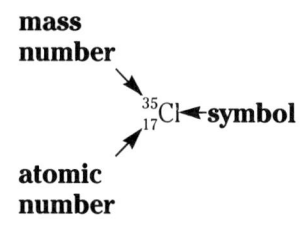

mass number ↘
$^{35}_{17}Cl$ ← **symbol**
↗ **atomic number**

Decoding the chemical shorthand used for chlorine, tells us:

atomic number = 17, so **no. of protons** = 17
no. of electrons = 17 (atoms are neutral)
mass number = 35, so **no. of neutrons** = 35 − 17 = 18

This sort of notation can be used for atoms of any element. It can also be used for ions. The number of electrons is the only thing which changes when an atom forms an ion. This means the atomic number (number of protons) and the mass number (number of protons + neutrons) doesn't change. The shorthand for an atom and ion of both sodium and chlorine is shown below:

$^{23}_{11}Na$ { 23−11 = 12 neutrons / 11 protons / 11 electrons }
a sodium **atom**

$^{23}_{11}Na^+$ { 23−11 = 12 neutrons / 11 protons / **10 electrons** }
a sodium **ion**

$^{35}_{17}Cl$ { 35−17 = 18 neutrons / 17 protons / 17 electrons }
an **atom** of chlorine

$^{35}_{17}Cl^-$ { 35−17 = 18 neutrons / 17 protons / **18 electrons** }
an **ion** of chlorine

Isotopes

For most elements, not all the atoms in that element are **identical**. For such an element, the **number of neutrons** can vary. When atoms of the same element have different numbers of neutrons, they are known as **isotopes**. Chlorine has two isotopes:

$^{35}_{17}Cl$ and $^{37}_{17}Cl$

The atomic numbers are the same – they must be, otherwise they would be atoms of different elements. The mass numbers are different, because the number of neutrons is different. Table 1.12 shows the number of each particle in isotopes of chlorine and hydrogen.

Many elements have naturally occurring isotopes. Other isotopes are man-made. Some isotopes are **radioactive** – they give off **radiation**. Radiation can be both useful and harmful. For example, doctors can use it to kill cancerous cells in the body, but too much of it can damage healthy cells too.

Table 1.12

Element	Istotopes	Protons	Electrons	Neutrons
Chlorine	$^{37}_{17}Cl$	17	17	20
	$^{35}_{17}Cl$	17	17	18
Hydrogen	$^{1}_{1}H$	1	1	0
	$^{2}_{1}H$	1	1	1
	$^{3}_{1}H$	1	1	2

Relative Atomic Mass (A_r)

The total mass of an atom comes from the mass of its neutrons and protons. The electrons are so light that they don't add significantly to the overall mass. Most elements, however, have isotopes. Therefore, an average is taken of the mass of all the isotopes and this average mass is called the **relative atomic mass** (A_r) (see page 234).

"Relative" to What?

Any measurement that is made, whether length or temperature, etc, must be measured compared to a **standard** of some kind. The standard that all atomic masses are compared to is the mass of the isotope of carbon, $^{12}_{6}C$. Its mass is taken as exactly 12 amu. The average masses of the atoms of all other elements are measured **relative** (compared with) the mass of the $^{12}_{6}C$ atom.

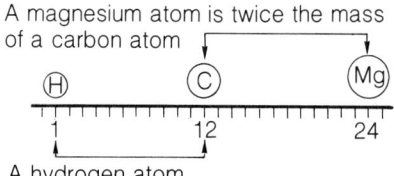

A magnesium atom is twice the mass of a carbon atom

H — 1
C — 12
Mg — 24

A hydrogen atom is 1/12 of the mass of a carbon atom

The masses of atoms of all elements are compared with the mass of the carbon – 12 atom ($^{12}_{6}C$)

Counting and Weighing Isotopes

The relative atomic mass of chlorine is 35.5. The two isotopes of chlorine are ^{35}Cl and ^{37}Cl. If the average mass is 35.5, there must be more isotopes with mass number 35 than 37. We get this information from a machine called the **mass spectrometer**. It tells us:

1 how many isotopes there are
2 the mass of each isotope
3 the percentage of each isotope.

The information is often given in a graph, like the one shown for chlorine. We can use it to calculate the relative atomic mass.

REACTIONS AND THE ATOM

Mass spectrum of chlorine

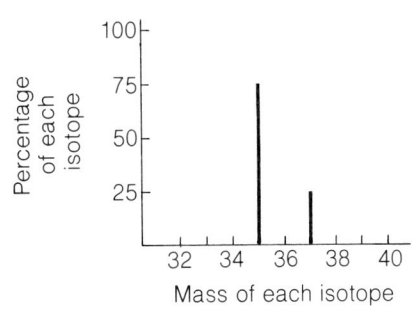

From the graph we see:
1 chlorine has two isotopes (two peaks)
2 the isotopes have atoms of mass 35 and 37
3 75 per cent of atoms have mass 35 ⎫
  25 per cent of atoms have mass 37 ⎬ average 35.5

There are usually more atoms of one isotope than another and so relative atomic masses are seldom whole numbers. However, they are often rounded up (or down) to make calculations easier.

Activities

1. An atom contains positively and negatively charged particles.
   (a) What are the negative and positive particles called?
   (b) Sketch the structure of an atom to show where the positive and negative particles are found.
   (c) What is the overall charge on an atom?
   (d) Explain your answer to (c).

2. Find the elements lithium and potassium in the periodic table on page 25.
   Construct a table to present the following information about each element:
   symbol; atomic number; electron arrangement.

3. In 1932 a third particle was discovered in the atom.
   (a) Name this third particle.
   (b) What is its charge?
   (c) Where in the atom is it found?
   (d) Sketch a diagram to show the structure of the atom. Include all three different kinds of particle found.
   (e) Draw out a table showing the mass and charge of the particles in an atom.

4. The table below shows the relative atomic masses of some group one elements, and their melting points.

Element	Relative Atomic Mass (RAM)	Melting Point (°C)
Li	6.9	180
Na	23.0	98
K	39.1	64
Rb	85.5	39

   (a) Draw a line graph, showing melting point against relative atomic mass.
   (b) From the graph, predict the approximate melting point of caesium (RAM 132.9).
   (c) By what other name is this group of elements known?

5. An atom of the element aluminium can be represented as $^{27}_{13}$Al.
   (a) What do the numbers 27 and 13 represent?
   (b) How many protons, neutrons and electrons does this atom have?
   (c) Draw a diagram to show the arrangement of the electrons in the atom.
   (d) Aluminium atoms tend to lose three electrons when they form ions. Write down the shorthand notation for this ion to show how it compares with the atom ($^{27}_{13}$Al).

6. A **mass spectrometer** separates the **isotopes** of an element according to their **mass number**. The information can be used to calculate the **relative atomic mass** of an element. The graph obtained for the element magnesium, is shown below.

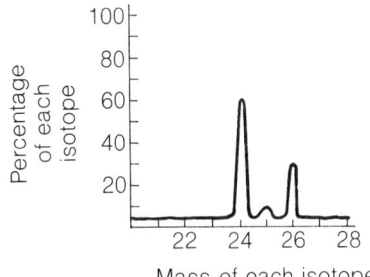

   (a) Explain the meaning of the terms shown in bold type.
   (b) Use the graph to answer the following questions.
      (i) How many isotopes does magnesium have?
      (ii) Which isotope is there most of?
      (iii) Explain why the relative atomic mass of magnesium is 24.3.

28 REACTIONS AND THE ATOM

6 Molecules

What is a Molecule?

The **noble gases** are the only elements which exist as individual atoms. All other elements, and compounds, exist as structures in which atoms are joined together in some way. The **non-metal elements** (except the noble gases) exist as different sized groups of atoms. The smaller groups of atoms are called **molecules**. The smallest molecules have just **two** atoms joined together. They are called diatomic molecules. Table 1.13 shows some diatomic elements.

Table 1.13

Diatomic Molecule	State
hydrogen	(g)
nitrogen	(g)
oxygen	(g)
fluorine ⎫	(g)
chlorine ⎬ halogens	(g)
bromine ⎭	(l)
iodine	(s)

A chlorine molecule

Other non-metal elements form larger molecules. **Phosphorus** (solid), for example, has **4 atoms** in each molecule and **sulphur** (solid) has **8 atoms** in each molecule.

A phosphorous molecule

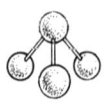

A sulphur molecule

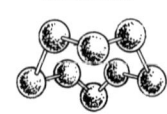

Compounds formed when atoms of non-metal elements react together range from diatomic to giant molecules. **Hydrogen chloride** (gas) is a diatomic molecule. **Starch** (solid) is a giant molecule containing thousands of carbon, hydrogen and oxygen atoms, joined together.

Key Ideas

Atoms often join together to form *molecules*. Molecules are groups of atoms held together by *covalent bonds*. Molecules are usually formed from atoms of *non-metals*. Some *elements* and *compounds* exist as covalent molecules. The smallest molecules are made up of *two atoms*. Larger molecules may contain thousands of atoms. Molecules have a variety of *shapes*.

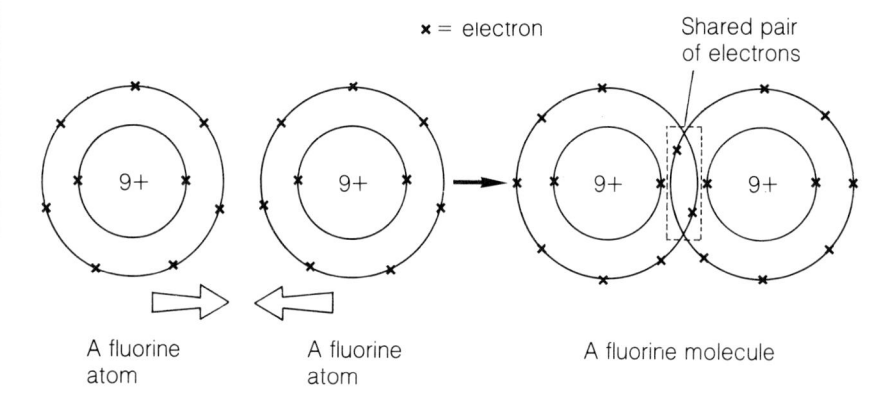

Covalent bonding in a fluorine molecule

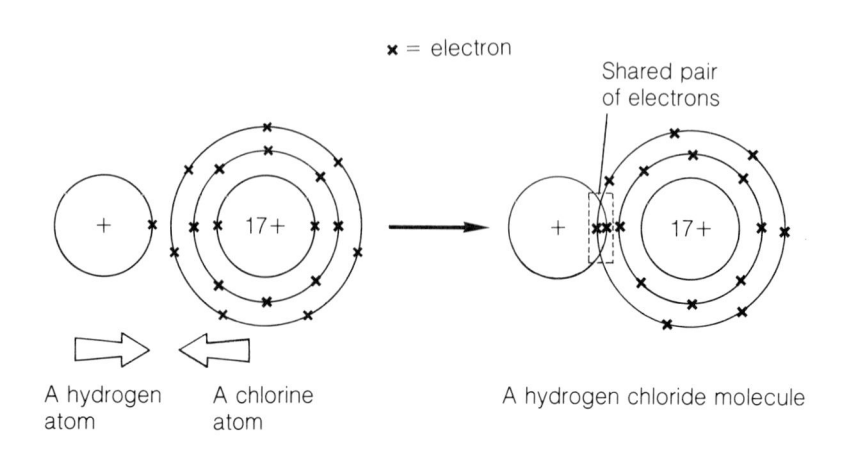

Covalent bonding in a hydrogen chloride molecule

What Holds Molecules Together?

Atoms of all elements (except noble gases) and compounds are held together by forces of attraction called **bonds**. In molecules formed between atoms of non-metal elements, the bonds are called **covalent bonds**. In a covalent bond two atoms **share a pair of electrons** between them.

A covalent bond is often shown by a line between the symbols of the elements in the molecule. The fluorine molecule may be written as **F—F**. The hydrogen chloride molecule may be written as **H—Cl**.

Why Do Atoms Bond?

The noble gases are very **stable** elements. They are very **unreactive**. The noble gases are so stable that they exist as single, unbonded atoms – they are **monatomic**. Table 1.14 shows the electron arrangements for some noble gases. In each case the outer energy level is **full**. This is what makes them stable.

Atoms of elements in other groups do not have a full outer energy level. These atoms are unstable. Atoms of non-metal elements achieve a stable electron arrangement by sharing electrons and forming a covalent bond. Have a close look at the diagrams which show the covalent bonding in fluorine and hydrogen chloride (page 28). Count the total number of electrons that each atom has in its outer energy level, both before and after the covalent bond is formed. You should find that only after bonding does each atom have a full outer energy level.

A Closer Look at Covalent Bonding

All atoms have a nucleus which is **positively** charged. The negatively charged electrons orbit around the nucleus. It is the **attraction** between positive and negative charges which hold the electrons in the atom. When two (or more) atoms bond, the shared pair of electrons is attracted to the nucleus of **both** atoms. It is this **shared** attraction which holds the atoms together in the molecule.

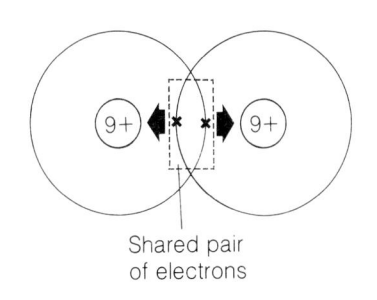

Both nuclei in a fluorine molecule attract the shared pair of electrons

Table 1.14

Element	Electron Arrangement		
He	2		first energy level full
Ne	2.8		second energy level full
Ar	2.8.8		third energy level full

Shapes of Molecules

The electrons in the outer energy levels of atoms are moving in space around the nucleus of an atom. They are arranged in such a way that when they bond (to make molecules), certain shapes are formed, depending on the atoms involved. Table 1.15 shows the shapes of some common covalent molecules. Note that all the atoms in the molecules have full outer energy levels.

Table 1.15

Molecule	Arrangement of atoms	Shape	Diagram of model
Hydrogen chloride	H—Cl	linear	
Hydrogen oxide (water)	H—O—H (bent)	planar (flat)	
Nitrogen hydride (ammonia)	N with three H	pyramidal	
Carbon hydride (methane)	C with four H	tetrahedral	

It is difficult to draw molecules in three dimensions so they are often drawn flat. However, as the diagrams of the models show, they are **not** all flat.

REACTIONS AND THE ATOM

Multiple Bonds

In some molecules the atoms are held together by **double** or **triple** covalent bonds. A double bond is formed when **two pairs** of electrons are shared. A triple bond is formed when **three pairs** of electrons are shared. The atoms in **oxygen** and **nitrogen** molecules are held together by multiple bonds.

Nitrogen molecules are very difficult to break because the triple bond is very strong.

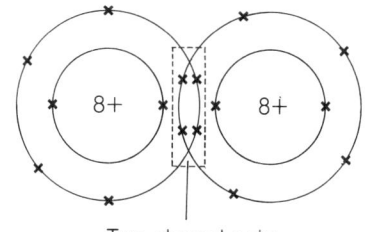

Two shared pairs of electrons

O=O double covalent bond

Bonding in an oxygen molecule

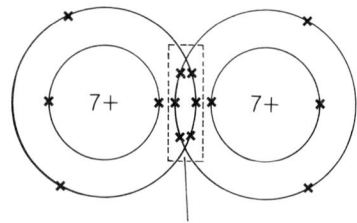

Three shared pairs of electrons

N≡N triple covalent bond

Bonding in a nitrogen molecule

Activities

● 1 The element bromine exists as **diatomic molecules**.
   (a) Explain what is meant by "**diatomic molecules**".
   (b) What is it that holds the bromine molecule together?
   (c) Draw diagrams to show how bromine atoms form a bromine molecule.
   (d) From the following list, select the pairs of elements which would form covalent bonds if they were reacted together:
   sodium and fluorine; oxygen and phosphorus; hydrogen and sulphur; magnesium and iodine.

● 2 (a) Explain why an atom reacts and forms a covalent bond with another atom.
   (b) Explain why the atoms involved in a covalent bond stay together.

● 3 Silicon is in the same group of the periodic table as carbon. Silicon reacts with hydrogen to form a compound called silane. Draw a molecule of silane and describe its likely shape.

7 Chemical Formulae

Key Ideas

A *chemical formula* is a shorthand way of telling us which *elements* are in a molecule. It also tells us *how many atoms* of each element there are. There are *valency* rules which can be used to work out the formulae of most molecules. Many elements and compounds are not made up of individual molecules. We can still use chemical formulae to tell us what is in them.

Formulae from Molecular Models

From the diagrams of covalent molecules it is possible to work out **which elements** are present in a molecule and **how many atoms** of each element there are. This information can be presented in a shorthand way called the **chemical formula**. For example:

Hydrogen chloride   H—Cl

The drawing shows that a hydrogen chloride molecule contains **one hydrogen** atom and **one chlorine** atom. This can be written as:

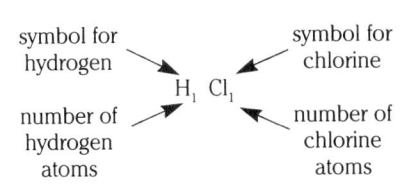

symbol for hydrogen → H_1 ← symbol for chlorine
number of hydrogen atoms → Cl_1 ← number of chlorine atoms

The number "1" is usually not shown, because writing down a symbol must mean that there is at least one of these atoms present. The **chemical formula** for hydrogen chloride is therefore written **HCl**. Table 1.16 shows the chemical formulae for water, ammonia and methane.

Table 1.16

Name	Shape of Molecule	Chemical Formula
Water	H—O—H (bent)	H_2O
Ammonia	H—N(—H)—H	NH_3
Methane	H—C(—H)(—H)—H	CH_4

Valency

Chemical formulae can be worked out by experiment. Using the results of earlier experiments, chemists have devised a way of working out chemical formulae without having to do further experiments. Each element now has a **valency** number, depending on which group in the periodic table it is found. Valency is another word for **combining power**. The valency allows us to work out how many **other** atoms a particular atom can combine with. Table 1.17 shows the valencies of elements in groups 1 to 7.

Table 1.17

Group	Valency	Example
1–4	same as group number	Na: group 1 **valency = 1** C: group 4 **valency = 4**
5–7	8 – group number	O: group 6 **valency 8 – 6 = 2** N: group 5 **valency 8 – 5 = 3**

The **noble gases** (group 0) have a valency of **zero**. This means they have no combining power. Although this is not strictly true, it is extremely difficult to get noble gases to react, and so they exist as individual atoms (monatomic). **Hydrogen** has a valency of **1**.

32 REACTIONS AND THE ATOM

Using Valency

Valency tells us how many atoms of the **other** element in a **compound** a particular atom will react with. This is easily shown in an example:

Water (hydrogen oxide)
Elements   H   O
Valency   1 $8-6=2$

Number of atoms   2   1
Formula   **H₂O**

The arrows show the valencies being swapped over. Table 1.18 shows how valency can be used to work out further formulae.

Valencies must always be reduced to the smallest number possible.

Example: **carbon dioxide**
Elements   C   O
Valency $8-4=4$ $8-6=2$

Reduce to smallest ratio   2   1
No. of atoms   1   2
Formula   **CO₂**

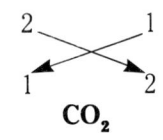

Exceptions to the Rule

The formulae of some compounds cannot be worked out using the valency method. Often, however, the **name** tells us how many atoms are in the molecules:

Example 1
carbon **mon**oxide
one oxygen } formula **CO**

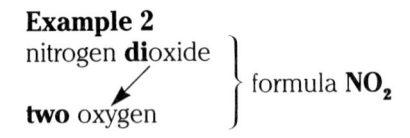

Example 2
nitrogen **di**oxide
two oxygen } formula **NO₂**

Example 3
sulphur **tri**oxide
three oxygen } formula **SO₃**

Other prefixes include tetra- (four), pent- (five) and hex- (six).

Table 1.18

	Hydrogen chloride	Ammonia (nitrogen hydride)	Methane (carbon hydride)
Elements Valency	H Cl 1 $8-7=1$	N H $8-5=3$ 1	C H $8-4=4$ 1
No. of atoms Formula	1 1 HCl	1 3 NH₃	1 4 CH₄

Giant Structures

The examples so far have all been covalent molecules. The numbers in the formulae tell us exactly how many atoms of each element are in a molecule. Valency can also be used to work out the formulae of compounds which exist as **giant structures** of some kind. Some non-metal elements combine to form **giant covalent networks** (see also Electricity in Chemistry).

Silicon dioxide is an example. It occurs naturally in the form of quartz and sand.

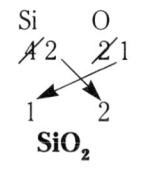

Formula: Si   O
           2   1
           1   2
       SiO₂

The formula suggests that silicon dioxide is made up of small molecules. However, it is really a giant covalent network with millions of atoms joined to each other. What the formula does tell us is that oxygen and silicon are present in a 2:1 ratio (for every **one** silicon atom there are **two** oxygen atoms – see page 78).

This is one of the limitations of a chemical formula – it doesn't tell us whether the compounds exist as small molecules or giant networks.

Formulae of Elements

The formula of most elements is just the **symbol**. Some elements exist as **diatomic molecules** and their formulae are written to show this. Table 1.19 gives some examples of the formulae of elements.

Table 1.19

Element (Diatomic)	Formula	Element	Formula
hydrogen	H₂	helium	He
nitrogen	N₂	carbon	C
oxygen	O₂	sodium	Na
fluorine	F₂	sulphur	S
chlorine } Group 7	Cl₂	argon	Ar
bromine } (halogens)	Br₂	silver	Ag
iodine	I₂		

Activities

○ 1 (a) Use the periodic table on page 16 to help you work out the valencies of the following elements:
boron, hydrogen, silicon, phosphorus, bromine, selenium.
(b) Use the valencies found in (a) to work out the formulae for compounds which might be formed between the following pairs of elements:
boron and hydrogen; silicon and bromine; silicon and phosphorus; selenium and carbon.
(c) Write down the **names** of the compounds formed in (b).

○ 2 Use the names of the following compounds to work out their formulae:
sulphur dioxide; phosphorous trichloride; phosphorous pentachloride (think how many sides a "pentagon" has).

○ 3 Use the periodic table on page 16 to help you write down the formulae for:
(a) one noble gas
(b) one halogen
(c) an alkali metal
(d) a gas in group 5
(e) a liquid metal
(f) hydrogen.

● 4 (a) Work out the formulae for carbon dioxide and silicon dioxide.
(b) Describe the state of these compounds at room temperature.
(c) Explain your answers to (b), by referring to the structures of the compounds.

8 The Mole

Key Ideas

Single atoms are small and impossible to weigh. Chemists use a quantity called the *mole*. One mole of an *element* is its *relative atomic mass* (A_r) measured in *grams*. One mole of a *covalent compound* is its *relative molecular mass* (M_r) measured in *grams*. The mole is used to work out masses of reactants and products in chemical reactions.

Masses of Substances

Atoms are so small that we cannot possibly weigh them out individually. However, by doing experiments, chemists have found out that if we weigh out the **relative atomic mass** (A_r) in grams of several **elements**, each will have exactly the **same number of atoms**.

The relative atomic mass of any element measured in **grams** is called **one mole**. The symbol for the mole is **mol**. Table 1.20 shows the masses of 1 mole of three elements.

Table 1.20

Element	Symbol	Relative Atomic Mass (A_r)	Mass of 1 Mole
Carbon	C	12	12 g
Aluminium	Al	27	27 g
Potassium	K	39	39 g

These all contain the same number of atoms

For a covalent **compound**, 1 mole is the **relative molecular mass (M_r)** measured in **grams**. The relative molecular mass of a compound is simply the relative atomic mass of each element in the formula, added together. This is best shown in an example:

Water (formula H_2O)

$M_r = (1 \times 2) + (16 \times 1) = 18$

- A_r of hydrogen
- No. of hydrogen atoms in formula
- A_r of oxygen
- No. of oxygen atoms in formula

1 mol H_2O = 18 g

Table 1.19 on page 32 lists the **elements** which exist as **diatomic molecules**. The mass of 1 mole of a diatomic element is its relative molecular mass measured in grams. For example:

Oxygen (formula O_2)

$M_r = 16 \times 2 = 32$

1 mole O_2 = 32 g

Moles and Mass

You have seen how we can work out the mass of 1 mole of a substance. Often multiples (and fractions) of 1 mole are required. It is possible to convert moles into masses (and masses into moles) by using a simple equation:

$$\textbf{Moles} = \frac{\text{mass (g)}}{\text{mass of 1 mole (g)}}$$

from this $\boxed{\textbf{mass (g)} = \text{moles} \times \text{mass of 1 mole (g)}}$

This triangle can be a useful memory aid:

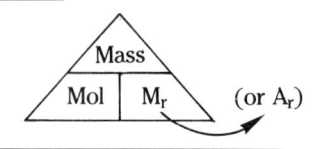

Mass / Mol / M_r (or A_r)

For **elements**: $\text{moles} = \dfrac{\text{mass}}{A_r}$

and $\boxed{\text{mass} = \text{moles} \times A_r}$

For **compounds**: $\text{moles} = \dfrac{\text{mass}}{M_r}$

and $\boxed{\text{mass} = \text{moles} \times M_r}$

REACTIONS AND THE ATOM

Table 1.21 gives some examples of moles/mass calculations.

Table 1.21

How Many Moles?	*What Mass?*
Elements 1 How many moles are in 20 g of calcium? $$\text{moles} = \frac{\text{mass}}{A_r}$$ $$= \frac{20}{40}$$ $$= \mathbf{0.5 \ mol}$$ 2 How many moles are in 42 g of silicon? $$\text{moles} = \frac{\text{mass}}{A_r}$$ $$= \frac{42}{28}$$ $$= \mathbf{1.5 \ mol}$$ **Compounds** 1 How many moles are in 33 g of carbon dioxide? Formula: CO_2 $$M_r = 12 + (16 \times 2) = 44$$ $$\text{moles} = \frac{\text{mass}}{M_r} = \frac{33}{44} = \mathbf{0.75 \ mol}$$ 2 How many moles are in 42.5 g of hydrogen sulphide? Formula: H_2S $$M_r = (1 \times 2) + 32 = 34$$ $$\text{moles} = \frac{\text{mass}}{M_r} = \frac{42.5}{34} = \mathbf{1.25 \ mol}$$	**Elements** 1 How many grams are in 0.2 moles of magnesium? $$\text{mass} = \text{moles} \times A_r$$ $$= 0.2 \times 24$$ $$= \mathbf{4.8 \ g}$$ 2 How many grams are in 1.75 moles of sulphur? $$\text{mass} = \text{moles} \times A_r$$ $$= 1.75 \times 32$$ $$= \mathbf{56 \ g}$$ **Compounds** 1 How many grams are in 0.25 moles of methane? Formula: CH_4 $$M_r = 12 + (1 \times 4) = 16$$ $$\text{mass} = \text{moles} \times M_r$$ $$= 0.25 \times 16 = \mathbf{4 \ g}$$ 2 How many grams are in 2.2 moles of ammonia? Formula: NH_3 $$M_r = 14 + (1 \times 3) = 17$$ $$\text{mass} = \text{moles} \times M_r$$ $$= 2.2 \times 17 = \mathbf{37.4 \ g}$$

Activities

(A_r can be found on page 234)

○ 1 Calculate the mass of 1 mole of the following: (a) helium atoms; (b) hydrogen molecules; (c) carbon dioxide molecules; (d) magnesium atoms; (e) fluorine molecules; (f) sulphur dioxide molecules.

● 2 Find the mass of each of the following: (a) 4 moles of aluminium atoms; (b) 1.5 moles of chlorine molecules; (c) 0.02 moles of carbon atoms; (d) 0.05 moles of sodium atoms; (e) 2.5 moles of hydrogen fluoride; (f) 3.3 moles of ammonia; (g) 0.3 moles water; (h) 0.04 moles hydrogen chloride.

● 3 How many moles are in each of the following? (a) 24 g of carbon; (b) 112 g of iron; (c) 3.5 g of lithium; (d) 1.6 g of copper; (e) 1.62 g of hydrogen bromide; (f) 46 g of nitrogen dioxide (NO_2); (g) 18.25 g of hydrogen chloride; (h) 24 g of sulphuric acid (H_2SO_4).

9 Chemical Equations

In Reactions All Around you saw how a word equation could be used to show what is happening in a chemical reaction. However, the words can be replaced by **formulae**. The rules from Chemical Formulae must be used (look back to refresh your memory). Chemical equations were first worked out by doing experiments. Equations sum up the results of these experiments. The following examples are both from Reactions All Around.

Example 1
Word equation: hydrogen + chlorine → hydrogen chloride
Formulae equation: $H_2 + Cl_2 \rightarrow HCl$
Example 2
Word equation: hydrogen + oxygen → water
Formulae equation: $H_2 + O_2 \rightarrow H_2O$

State symbols can also be used in equations. If they are added to the previous examples, we have:
Example 1 $H_2(g) + Cl_2(g) \rightarrow HCl(g)$
Example 2 $H_2(g) + O_2(g) \rightarrow H_2O(l)$

> **Key Ideas**
>
> A **chemical equation** is a shorthand way of showing reactants and products in a reaction. *Formulae* are used for elements and compounds instead of words. A *balanced* equation shows the *ratios* of reactants and products in the reaction.

Balanced Equations

If you look closely at the equations in examples 1 and 2 above, you will see that the number of reactant atoms and product atoms are different.

In example 1:

$$H_2 + Cl_2 \rightarrow HCl$$
2 hydrogen atoms   2 chlorine atoms   1 hydrogen atom, 1 chlorine atom

These equations are said to be **unbalanced**. Unbalanced equations are adequate for showing what is reacting and what is produced, but they don't give a true picture of the **quantities** involved. The number of reactant and product atoms must be the same – they need to be **balanced**. The way to balance an equation is shown below. We will use examples 1 and 2 again.

Example 1 Unbalanced equation:
$$H_2(g) + Cl_2(g) \rightarrow HCl(g)$$

There are more hydrogen and chlorine atoms on the left-hand side of the equation, than on the right-hand side. The atoms can't just "disappear" – they have to be accounted for. The "missing" hydrogen and chlorine atoms must have combined to form **another** hydrogen chloride molecule (as this is the only product):

H₂ molecule   Cl₂ molecule →   2 HCl molecules
(2 H atoms)   (2 Cl atoms)   (2 H atoms + 2 Cl atoms)

There are now the same number of hydrogen and chlorine atoms on each side of the equation. The equation is **balanced**. It can be written without the pictures of the atoms and molecules:

$$H_2(g) + Cl_2(g) \rightarrow 2\,HCl(g)$$

Number of reactant atoms = Number of product atoms

Notice that the formulae of the reactants and products are the same as they were in the unbalanced equation. **Formulae never change**. To balance an equation numbers may only be put **in front** of formulae.

Example 2 Unbalanced equation:
$$H_2(g) + O_2(g) \rightarrow H_2O(l)$$

The molecule pictures again show the equation is unbalanced. There is one more oxygen atom on the left-hand side of the equation than on the right-hand side. It must have formed a second water molecule by reacting with another hydrogen molecule:

2 H₂ molecules   1 O₂ molecule →   2 H₂O molecules
(4 H atoms)   (2 O atoms)   (4 H atoms + 2 O atoms)

Number of reactant atoms = Number of product atoms

Without the atom pictures we have:
$$2H_2(g) + O_2(g) \rightarrow 2H_2O(l)$$

Although in each separate equation the number of reactant and product atoms are the same, it must be remembered that they have changed the way they are arranged. Bonds between reactant molecules have been **broken** and **new bonds** have been made. In other words, **new substances** have been formed. This happens in all chemical reactions.

Calculations from Equations

When we write a balanced equation, the numbers we put in front of formulae can also represent the number of **moles** of substance, either reacting or being produced. This allows us to **calculate** masses from balanced equations.

For example:

	hydrogen	+	chlorine	→	hydrogen chloride
Balanced equation:	H_2	+	Cl_2	→	$2HCl$
No. of moles reacting and being produced:	1 mol		1 mol		2 mol
	(1×2)	+	(1×71)	→	$2(1 + 35.5)$
No. of grams:	2 g	+	71 g	→	73 g

This tells us that 2 g of hydrogen reacts with 71 g of chlorine to produce 73 g of hydrogen chloride. Notice that the total mass of reactants equals the total mass of products. This is not surprising as all the atoms have to be accounted for. During a reaction the atoms rearrange themselves – they don't just disappear! The balanced equation gives the proportions of reactants and products.

In the above example:

	H_2	+	Cl_2	→	$2HCl$
	1 mol		1 mol		2 mol
By simple proportion	10 mol		10 mol		20 mol
or	0.1 mol		0.1 mol		0.2 mol

In other words, if we know how much reactant or product we have, we can work out other quantities by simple proportion.

Example 1 How many grams of hydrogen chloride would be produced when 0.5 mol of hydrogen reacted with excess chlorine? ("Excess" means there is more than enough for complete reaction.)

Answer

Balanced Equation:	H_2	+	Cl_2	→	$2HCl$
No. of moles:	1 mol		1 mol		2 mol
By simple proportion	0.5 mol		0.5 mol		1 mol
	↑				
	(from question)				
In grams	1 g	+	35.5 g	→	36.5 g

So, **36.5 g** of hydrogen chloride would be produced.

Example 2 How much hydrogen would have to be burned (reacted with oxygen) to produce 72 g of water?

Answer

Balanced Equation:	$2H_2$	+	O_2	→	$2H_2O$
No. of moles:	2 mol		1 mol		2 mol
In grams	4 g	+	32 g	→	36 g
By simple proportion	8 g	+	64 g	→	72 g

So, **8 g** of hydrogen would be required to produce 72 g of water.

Activities

(Make sure each question is correct before going on to the next)

○ 1 Write formulae equations for the following reactions:
  (a) carbon + oxygen → carbon dioxide
  (b) nitrogen + hydrogen → ammonia (nitrogen hydride)
  (c) hydrogen + sulphur → hydrogen sulphide
  (d) hydrogen + bromine → hydrogen bromide

● 2 Balance all the equations in question one above.

● 3 Use the balanced equations in question two to work out the following:
  (a) How much carbon dioxide would be produced if 4 g of carbon is burned?
  (b) How much hydrogen would be needed to produce 34 g of ammonia?

● 4 Water produced when fuels like methane are burned, can cause condensation in homes. The balanced equation for the burning of methane in oxygen is:
$$CH_4(g) + 2O_2(g) \rightarrow CO_2(g) + 2H_2O(g)$$
Calculate the amount of water produced when 8 kg of methane is burned.

Reactions and the Atom – Study Questions

1 On Andy's first day in chemistry, his teacher demonstrated an experiment to the class. Here is the report that Andy wrote in his note book.

> Mr Murphy took this really thin kind of copper and put it in a jar of gas. The gas was chlorine. We had to keep clear of the chlorine he said. When the copper went in the gas it shrivelled up. Then it went on fire. When it stopped there was green stuff in the jar. This is a CHEMICAL REACTION
>
> — copper
> — chlorine

(a) From Andy's report, give **two** pieces of evidence which suggest that a chemical reaction had taken place. **PS**
(b) Write a **word** equation for this reaction. **KU**

2 Each box in the grid refers to an element.

A Element with electron arrangement 2.8.3	B Element of atomic number 19	C Ar
D Sodium	E A brown liquid at room temperature	F Element which has 6 electrons in each atom

Which box (or boxes) refers to:
(a) a metal which does **not** react violently with water?
(b) a very unreactive element?
(c) elements in the same group of the periodic table?
(d) an element which is a gas at room temperature? **KU**

3

A Gas burning at a cooker ring	B Boiling water in an electric kettle	C Dissolving sugar in a cup of tea
D Bubbles in a cake as it rises	E An epoxy resin glue setting	F Nail varnish drying on nails

Which box (or boxes) shows a chemical change? **KU**

4 Each box in the grid gives information about the numbers of particles in atoms.

A Mass number	B Number of electrons in outer energy level	C Atomic number
D Number of electons	E Number of protons	F Number of neutrons

Which box (or boxes) refers to:
(a) a number which is the same as the number in box E?
(b) a number which is the sum of the numbers in boxes E and F?
(c) a number which is different for different isotopes of the one element? **KU**

5 Read the statements below.
(a) In elements with small atomic numbers, the atomic nucleus contains equal, or nearly equal, numbers of protons and neutrons.
(b) Where the atomic number is large, there are more neutrons than protons. The larger the atomic number, the larger is the percentage of neutrons in the nucleus.

Information can be presented in a variety of ways: tables, diagrams, flowcharts, keys, piecharts, bar graphs, line graphs, etc.
Consider the following four atomic symbols:

$${}^{28}_{14}Si \quad {}^{40}_{20}Ca \quad {}^{120}_{50}Sn \quad {}^{200}_{80}Hg$$

Choose a suitable way and present this information to support **both** statements (a) and (b). The information should be taken **only** from the four atomic symbols above. **PS**

6 Heavy water is used in some nuclear reactors.
It is like ordinary water except that the normal hydrogen atoms, ${}^{1}_{1}H$, known as protium atoms, are replaced by deuterium atoms, ${}^{2}_{1}H$.
(a) Calculate the mass of two moles of heavy water. **PS**
(b) Tritium, ${}^{3}_{1}H$, is another type of hydrogen atom. Make a table to show the number of protons, neutrons and electrons in a tritium atom. **KU**
(c) What term is used to describe atoms like protium, deuterium and tritium? **KU**

7 Some elements exist as diatomic molecules.
Two such elements, formulae X_2 and Y_2, react together to form a compound.
Experiment shows that 1 mole of element X reacts exactly with 2 moles of element Y to give 2 moles of the compound.
Use this information to derive the formula for the compound formed between X and Y. **PS**

1 Energy from Fuels

Key Ideas

Energy is needed to power cars and trains, to make electricity in power stations and to keep our homes and schools warm. Most of our energy comes from *coal, oil* and *natural gas.* These are our *fossil fuels.*

Burning in Air

Fuels are made from **chemicals**. To get the energy out of the fuels, we have to **burn** them. Burning is a chemical reaction where the fuel reacts with **oxygen** from the air. Burning is also known as **combustion**. The energy is given out as **heat**.

This experiment can be used as a special test for oxygen.

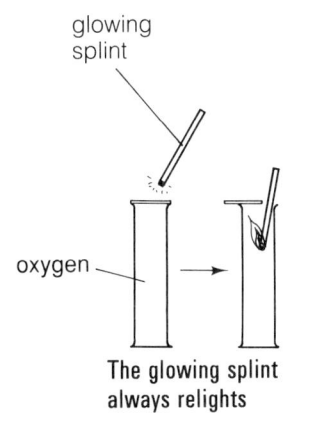

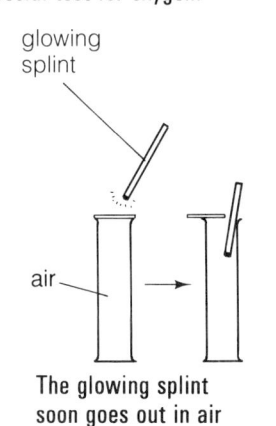

glowing splint

oxygen

The glowing splint always relights

glowing splint

air

The glowing splint soon goes out in air

Why does the splint go out? Air contains other gases as well as oxygen; it's a **mixture** of gases, as shown in the pie chart. The small amount of oxygen (21%) is soon used up. When a substance burns in pure oxygen energy is released much more efficiently than when it is burned in air.

Noble gases (1%): helium, neon argon, krypton, and xenon

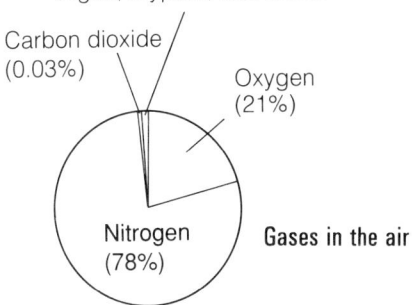

Carbon dioxide (0.03%)

Oxygen (21%)

Nitrogen (78%)

Gases in the air

Fuels and Hydrocarbons

40 FUELS AND HYDROCARBONS

Energy and waste products from fuels

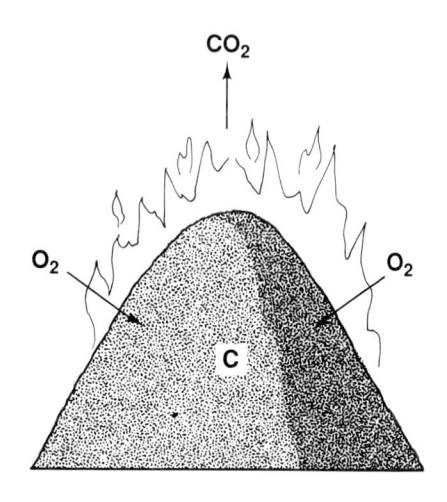

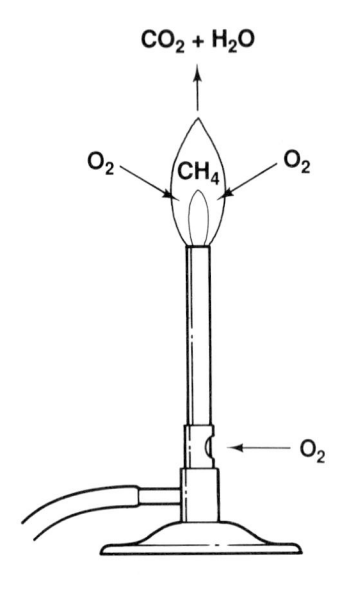

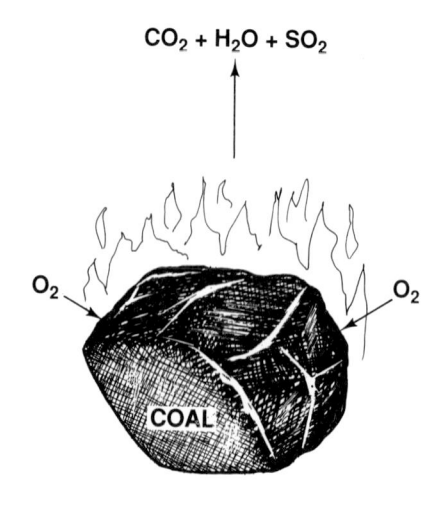

Carbon is an element found in all fossil fuels. Carbon burns to give carbon dioxide.

Carbon + oxygen → carbon dioxide

$C(s) + O_2(g) \rightarrow CO_2(g)$

Carbon dioxide is a **waste** product which can be released into the atmosphere without causing harm.

Natural gas is mainly **methane**. This gas contains carbon bonded to hydrogen to form CH_4 molecules. Methane burns to give carbon dioxide and water. Water, like carbon dioxide, is also a harmless waste product.

methane + oxygen → carbon dioxide + water

$CH_4(g) + O_2(g) \rightarrow CO_2(g) + H_2O(l)$

● $CH_4(g) + 2O_2(l) \rightarrow CO_2(g) + 2H_2O(l)$

When **coal** burns, carbon dioxide and water are produced again. However, coal also contains sulphur, which forms a waste gas called **sulphur dioxide**. This harms our atmosphere. Harmful gases, like sulphur dioxide, are known as **pollutants** and you will see later how scientists prevent these pollutants from getting into the air.

Combustion is an example of an **exothermic** reaction. Any chemical reaction which gives out energy is exothermic.

Exothermic reaction in the laboratory

Acid + Alkali

Exothermic reaction in the body

FUELS AND HYDROCARBONS

Where Does the Heat Come From?

If we examine the way the atoms in elements and compounds are **bonded**, we can see where the energy comes from during combustion. In all chemical reactions, bonds between the atoms of each reactant have to be **broken**. This requires energy to be put in. However, when the new compound is formed, new bonds are **made** and this results in energy being released.

When the bond-making energy is greater than the bond-breaking energy, then, overall, energy is given out; we say the reaction is **exothermic**. This explains why you need a flame or spark to light a gas fire: to get the reaction going you need to put in energy, but once the reaction starts, the flame can be taken away because overall the reaction is exothermic.

The table shows how we can use bond energies from the data books to calculate how much energy we can obtain from a **set amount** of methane.

Energy from methane gas

$$CH_4 + 2O_2 \rightarrow CO_2 + 2H_2O$$

Bonds broken:

$4 \times C-H + 2 \times O=O$

Bond breaking energy:

$(4 \times 414) + (2 \times 497)$
$1656 + 994$
2650 kJ mol^{-1}

Bonds made:

$2 \times C=O + 4 \times O-H$

Bond making energy:

$(2 \times 724) + (4 \times 458)$
$1448 + 1832$
3280 kJ mol^{-1}

Overall energy = Bond breaking energy − Bond making energy
= 2650 − 3280
= **−630 kJ mol⁻¹**

The minus sign indicates energy is given out, i.e. the reaction is **exothermic**.
(The unit of energy is kilojoules per mole of substance reacted, i.e. kJ mol⁻¹)

Activities

○ 1 Explain what a fuel is.
○ 2 What does "combustion" mean?
○ 3 You are given three test tubes containing different gases. Describe how you could show which one was oxygen.
○ 4 The table on the right shows the composition of the gases in air. Copy the table and fill in the blanks.
○ 5 Explain what is meant by an "exothermic" reaction and give two examples.

Gas	%
oxygen	
	almost 80
	very little

● 6 Hydrogen reacts with oxygen to produce water.

$$2H_2(g) + O_2(g) \rightarrow 2H_2O(l)$$

Use the bond energies in the data book to work out if the reaction is exothermic or not. Also, show which bonds are being broken and which are being made.

● 7 (a) Write an unbalanced equation for propane (C_3H_8) reacting with oxygen to produce carbon dioxide and water.
(b) Write a balanced equation for the reaction in (a).

2 Formation of Fossil Fuels

The Story of Coal

The story is thought to have started millions of years ago when the Earth was covered in swamps. Over the years the **plants died** and fell into the swamps, where they slowly started to **rot**.

1

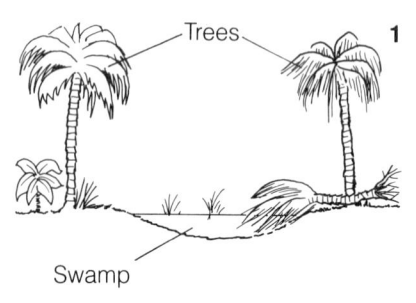

Trees
Swamp

Gradually the rotting vegetation was covered in sand and mud and more plants died, eventually building up **layers** of rotting plants and earth. This sequence may have happened more than once.

2

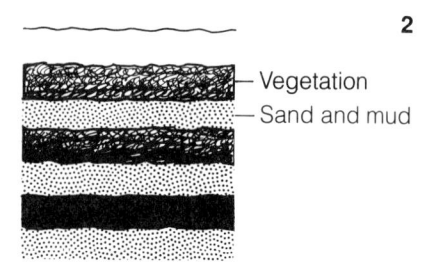

Vegetation
Sand and mud

The weight of the earth was enough to compress the rotting plants into black sticky layers which hardened into seams of solid **coal**.

3

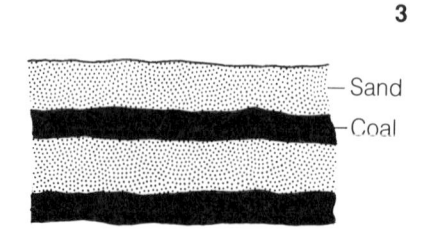

Sand
Coal

These seams are most often found deep underground and some extend out under what is now called the sea. To dig the coal out of these areas, shafts have to be sunk and men and machinery sent down to the seams.

4

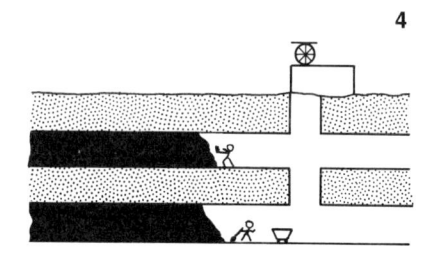

Sometimes the coal is found near the surface, and giant bulldozers can be used to scrape away the surface and expose the coal underneath. Cranes then lift and move the coal. This is called **open-cast** mining. Mining has been going on in Britain for more than a hundred years. We can see the evidence all over the country, especially in the hills of coal waste. These are not only an eyesore, they can be very **dangerous** too. In October 1966 the side of one of these hills in a village called Aberfan in Wales slid down and covered a primary school, killing many pupils and teachers.

In recent years engineers have been levelling off these hills and planting over them to make the environment both safer and more pleasant to live in.

Key Ideas

A *fossil* is the remains of a plant or animal which lived millions of years ago. Fossils are often found trapped in-between layers of rock, like slate and also in coal. They give us a clue as to when our fossil fuels were made and what they are made of. These fuels are vitally important to us but *won't* last for ever – and they *won't* be replaced either!

Coal tip before and after landscaping

FUELS AND HYDROCARBONS 43

The Story of Oil and Gas

Oil and natural gas are thought to have been formed in a similar way to coal. Millions of years ago the seas were filled with microscopic **animals**.

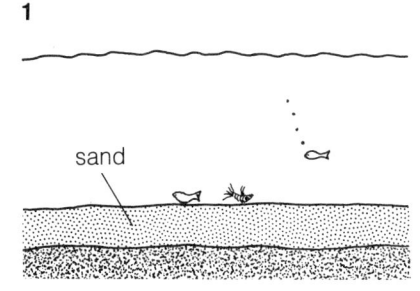

1

sand

When the animals died they sank to the bottom of the sea in enormous numbers. Sand was swept over them and with the pressure of its own weight, the sand turned into rock.

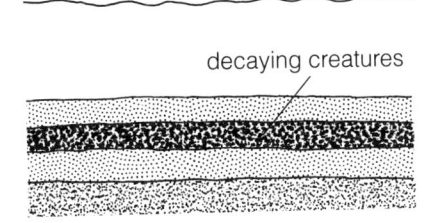

2

decaying creatures

Underneath, the dead creatures were compressed to the point where oil was formed, trapped in sandstone between layers of hard rock. Natural gas and oil are nearly always found together. Vast gas fields may sometimes be found on their own.

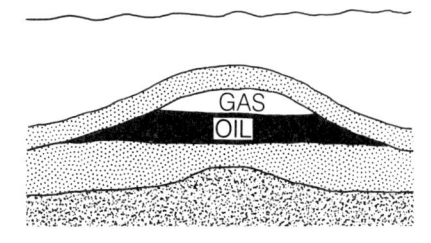

3

GAS / OIL

Many of the seas that existed millions of years ago have now dried up or the sea floor has been raised above sea level. This explains why oil can be found in desert areas like the Middle East and parts of North America.

Major fossil fuel deposits in Britain

▲ Oil fields
--- Oil pipelines
△ Gas fields
— Gas pipelines
● Major coalfields

Locations shown: Brent, Sullom Voe, Frigg, Beryl, Flotta, Beatrice, Tartan, Nigg Bay, St. Fergus, Forties, Cruden Bay, Ekofisk, Grangemouth, NORTH SEA, Barrow, Teeside, Easington, West Sole, Morecambe, Viking, Theddlethorpe, Leman Bank, Bacton

The Perils of Exploration

Exploration of oil and gas and their extraction from the Earth is a **dangerous** and expensive job. Most of Britain's oil and gas is under the bed of the **North Sea** – one of the roughest seas in the world! Once the oil and gas are located, rigs mounted on giant **platforms** have to be towed out and anchored down, so that men can drill through the layers of rock until the precious fuels are reached.

In July 1988 disaster struck one of these rigs when an explosion ripped through the Piper Alpha platform, 200 miles North East of Aberdeen. One hundred and sixty-seven men lost their lives.

The oil and gas are extracted and sent to terminals on land through miles of underwater **pipelines**. Oil can then be transported to processing plants in different parts of the country through land pipes. One such pipeline runs from close to Aberdeen to Grangemouth. You are unlikely to see it though, because it has been buried underground to preserve the environment.

44 FUELS AND HYDROCARBONS

The Problem of Pollution

Britain and the rest of Europe still import a lot of oil from abroad in massive tankers and, although there are strict safety procedures, the danger of pollution from oil **spillages** is ever present. Oil floats on water, so if it spilled in the sea it will **kill marine wildlife** and also be washed onto our shores, spoiling our beaches.

At 12.04 am on Friday 24th March 1989 a huge oil tanker called the *Exxon Valdez* struck a reef off the coast of Alaska. It spilled nearly 50 million litres of crude oil into the sea, and covered more than 850 square miles – that's more than the area of a million football pitches!

The spillage had a disastrous effect on the wildlife in the the area. Sea otters froze to death, because the oil destroyed the warm air gap between the otters' fur and its skin. Birds suffered paralysis and died because their feathers were soaked in oil. Fish and other marine life were also killed.

It is thought that even after the oil is cleaned up it will take more than ten years for the environment to recover.

Detergents can be used to disperse the spillages, but these also damage living things. Chemists at British Petroleum have recently developed a chemical to spray onto the oil which reacts with it and forms a rubber-like solid. This can be rolled up and taken away!

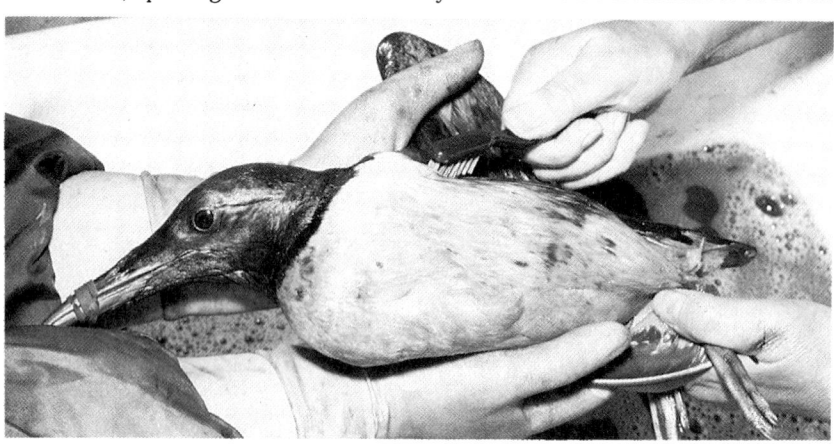

After an oil spillage, many birds die. This more fortunate guillemot is being cleaned of oil by RSPB workers

How Long will our Energy Resources Last?

Britain's vast coal deposits stretch from Scotland, through England, and into Wales. There is also oil and gas under the North Sea. Other areas like the Middle East, North America, Southern Africa and Australia are also rich in fossil fuels. The fuels have taken millions of years to form but they will **not last us for ever**.

The world population continues to increase rapidly and our fossil fuels are being used up very fast. They are a **finite resource**. This means there is only a certain amount of fuel in the ground, and once it is used up it will not be replaced. Estimates vary, but scientists think that even at the present rate of use, oil and gas may run out in approximately 40 years.

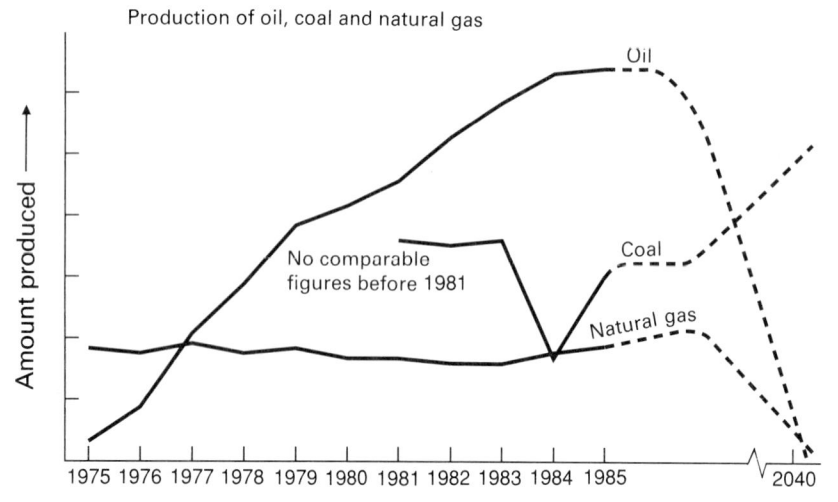

Comparison of British fossil fuel production up to 1985 (solid line) and prediction of what could happen in the next century (broken line)

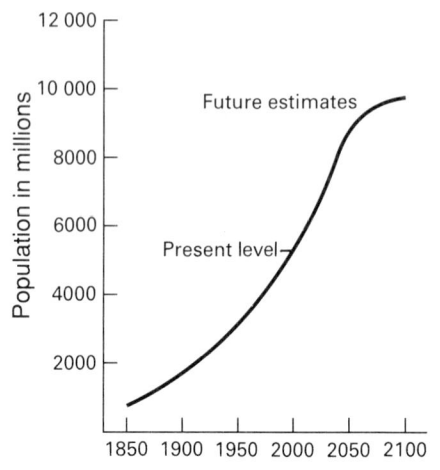

World population growth

FUELS AND HYDROCARBONS

Preparing for Fuel Shortages

Geologists search for fossil fuels in some of the remotest parts of the world – Alaska and the Antarctic for example. But no matter how much is found, these fuels will run out eventually.

Many countries of the world are trying to conserve fuel in order to reduce the **fuel crisis** we are now facing. In Brazil, alcohol made from sugar cane is used as a substitute for petrol. Sugar cane is an example of a **renewable** energy source – it can be grown again and again. Brazil is investigating whether alcohol can be obtained from other crops. They have tried cassava which can be grown in areas where the soil is poor. Although converting cassava into alcohol is difficult, pilot plants already produce over 5000 litres a week.

Collecting sugar cane

Alternative energy source

Alternative energy sources like nuclear-fuelled power stations, solar energy and wind power, are being developed in Britain and other European countries to supplement our fossil fuels. You can help too by switching off lights and fires when they are not needed, and using less hot water when washing!

The Fuel Industry and Jobs

Getting fossil fuels out of the ground is of great **economic** importance to our country. Many **jobs** depend on the fossil fuel industry – not only in extracting the fuels, but in processing them too. The north-east of Scotland and the Shetlands have benefited from oil and gas terminals and from rig construction yards like the one at Nigg Bay.

Oil platform under construction at Nigg Bay

At present the number of pits in the coal industry is declining. But we do have massive coal reserves, enough to last for several hundred years. They can be used some time in the future – coal may well make a comeback next century.

Activities

1. The following extract was taken from a national newspaper: "Although Britain is rich in fossil fuels, we are as a nation suffering a fuel crisis. Our fossil fuel reserves are finite resources, which are the envy of many countries in the world – we must conserve them."
   (a) Give an example of a "fossil fuel" and briefly outline how it was formed.
   (b) In what way are we suffering a "fuel crisis"?
   (c) What is meant by "finite resources"?
   (d) Outline two ways in which countries are helping to conserve fossil fuels.

2. In 1967 the *Torrey Canyon* oil tanker spilled millions of tonnes of oil into the sea off the South coast of Britain. Describe the effects that a spillage of this kind would have on the environment.

3 Using Oil

Key Ideas

The oil that comes out of the ground is known as *crude* oil. It is not pure enough to use for anything on its own because it is a *mixture* of different types of molecules. It has to be *separated* into its different, more useful, components by a process known as *fractional distillation*.

Separating Crude Oil

Although oil all over the world has been formed in the same way, different parts of the globe produce oil having different properties. They can be very thick, black and tar-like, or brown, runny and liquid. Some are foul-smelling, others are not unpleasant. Despite this, these oils all have one important thing in common – they are made up of a **mixture** of many compounds which can be separated to give useful products, many of which are used as **fuels**.

Before separation the oil is known as **crude** oil. Crude oil consists mainly of **hydrocarbons** – these are compounds which contain **hydrogen** and **carbon only**. Each of the hydrocarbon molecules has its own boiling point, depending partly on its size. If the oil is heated, each compound will change into a gas at its particular boiling point, and the gas can be condensed and collected as a liquid. It is very difficult to collect separate, pure compounds because the boiling points are so close. However, we can collect a mixture, or a **fraction** of similar sized compounds over a narrow temperature range. The whole process is called **fractional distillation**.

The separation is done in a huge **fractionating tower** in refineries such as the ones at BP Grangemouth in Scotland and the "Shell Haven" on the river Thames, in England. The diagram of a fractionating tower shows some of the products obtained by distillation of crude oil.

How Does it Work?

The crude oil is heated to above 500°C to produce a mixture of gases which pass up the tower. Each gas condenses when the temperature falls to that of its boiling point.

The fractions towards the top of the tower are the lower boiling fractions and the ones towards the bottom have higher boiling points.

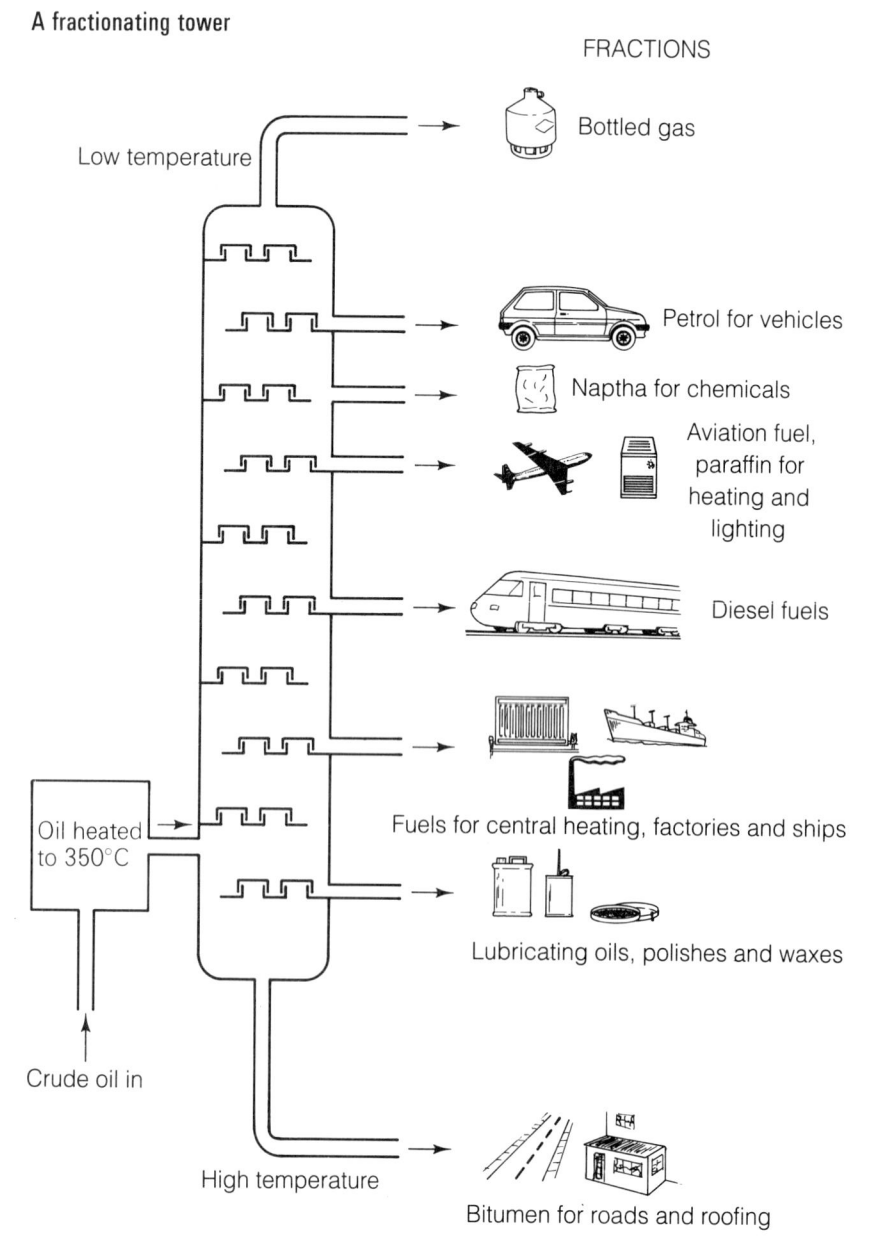

A fractionating tower

FRACTIONS
- Bottled gas
- Petrol for vehicles
- Naptha for chemicals
- Aviation fuel, paraffin for heating and lighting
- Diesel fuels
- Fuels for central heating, factories and ships
- Lubricating oils, polishes and waxes
- Bitumen for roads and roofing

FUELS AND HYDROCARBONS 47

Burning Hydrocarbons

The fractionating tower shows that the most important use of the hydrocarbon fractions produced, is as **fuels**. In the section Energy from Fuels we saw that when methane (a hydrocarbon) is burned efficiently, carbon dioxide and water are the waste products. This is true for **all** hydrocarbon fuels, because they are all made up of carbon and hydrogen only.

The apparatus with the candle burning shows how these combustion products can be collected and identified. Carbon dioxide turns **limewater chalky** (milky), while water **boils at 100 °C, freezes at 0 °C** and turns anhydrous copper(II) sulphate from **white** to **blue**. Often when a hydrocarbon is burned as a fuel there is not enough oxygen present. This causes inefficient combustion, which in turn produces pollutant substances – carbon monoxide for instance.

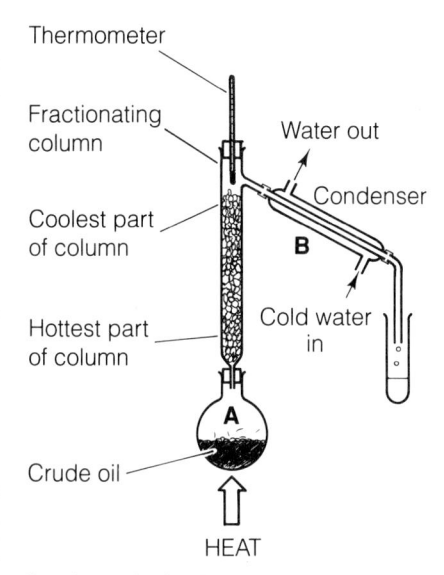

Fractional distillation of crude oil in the laboratory

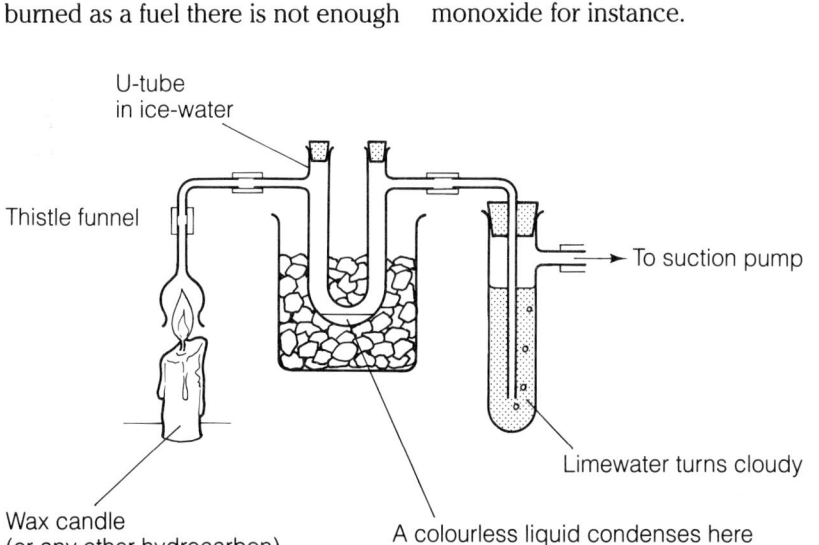

Collecting the combustion products of a hydrocarbon

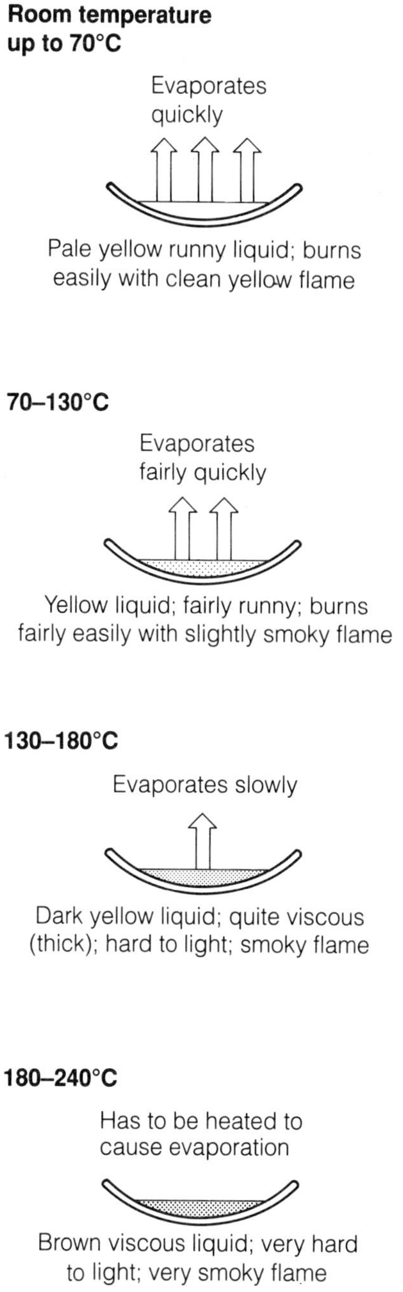

Properties of four fractions obtained from the laboratory distillation of crude oil

Room temperature up to 70°C
Evaporates quickly
Pale yellow runny liquid; burns easily with clean yellow flame

70–130°C
Evaporates fairly quickly
Yellow liquid; fairly runny; burns fairly easily with slightly smoky flame

130–180°C
Evaporates slowly
Dark yellow liquid; quite viscous (thick); hard to light; smoky flame

180–240°C
Has to be heated to cause evaporation
Brown viscous liquid; very hard to light; very smoky flame

The Importance of Molecule Size

Table 2.1 shows the number of carbon atoms in the molecules which make up the fractions in crude oil. Their properties can be linked to the size of the molecules found in the different fractions.

Table 2.1

Product	Number of carbon atoms	Boiling range (°C)
Gas	1–4	<40
Petrol	4–12	40–175
Kerosine	9–16	150–240
Diesel oil	15–25	220–250
Lubrication oil	20–70	250–350
Bitumen residue	>70	>350

48 FUELS AND HYDROCARBONS

Gases (e.g. camping gas)
The gases obtained have **small** molecules with **weak forces** of attraction between them. It doesn't require much energy to separate them from one another so they have low boiling points.

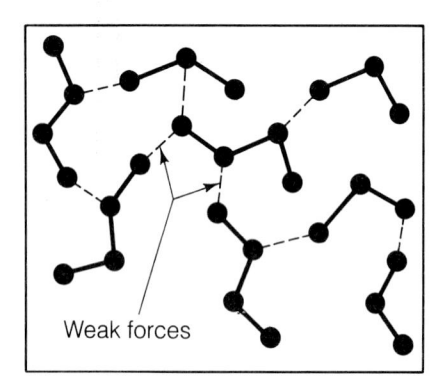

Non-Viscous Liquids
(e.g. kerosine)
The liquid fractions have **bigger** molecules and, although the forces of attraction between them are still weak, there are **more** of them between each molecule. It requires more energy to separate the molecules so they have higher boiling points than the gases.

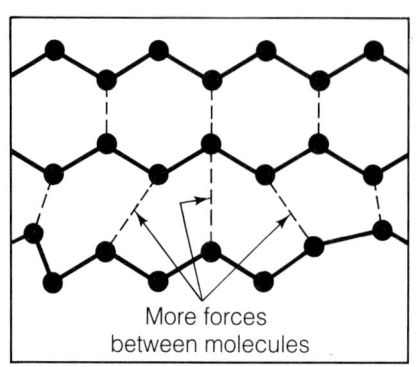

Viscous Liquids
(e.g. lubricating oil)
In the more viscous liquids the molecules are now **long chains** which are tangled together and **very difficult** to separate. They therefore have high boiling points. They do not evaporate easily and are difficult to light. In other words, they are not very good fuels.

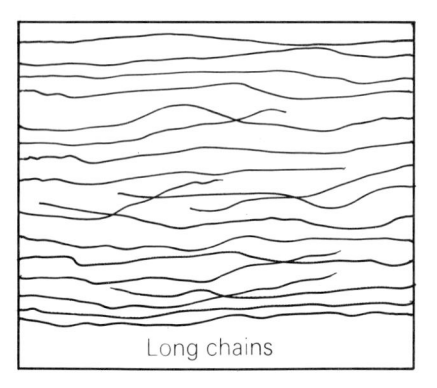

Small number of weak forces between small molecules

Larger number of weak forces between larger molecules

Long chains of very large molecules with many weak forces between them

They are very flammable because they mix easily with air.

These molecules are still small enough to evaporate readily, and burn quite easily.

If heated, they become less viscous, vapourise and eventually catch fire.

The amount of each fraction in a sample of crude oil depends on which oil-producing area of the world it comes from. Some "light" oils, like the British ones, contain a high percentage of non-viscous, flammable fractions, while some of the "heavier" South American oils have more of the viscous fractions. Chemists have developed many processes to change viscous fractions into more useful products.

Activities

○ 1 **Crude** oil is a mixture of **hydrocarbons** which can be separated by **fractional distillation**.
   (a) Explain what the terms in bold print mean.
   (b) Name two fractions and say what they are used for.

○ 2 Look at the earlier diagram showing how a sample of crude oil can be distilled in the laboratory.
   (a) Describe how the properties of the different fractions change as the temperature increases.
   (b) What is happening to the fractions at points A and B?
   (c) Draw a diagram of a fractionating tower used in industry. Indicate on it where you would get a fraction with a boiling range of 220–250 °C and another with molecules of 4–12 carbon atoms.

● 3 Two oil fractions were obtained. One was known to contain molecules with 9–16 carbon atoms, the other 20–50 carbon atoms. Choose the one which would be the better fuel and explain why.

4 Polluting the Air

What Causes Pollution?

The natural composition of air is mainly nitrogen and oxygen. Our bodies need the oxygen and we breathe in thousands of litres of air a day to give us a constant supply of it. Our air is **not pure** however; it sometimes contains harmful substances called **pollutants**, and they arise chiefly from the burning of fossil fuels.

The effects of these pollutants vary. Sometimes doctors are not sure exactly which pollutant causes a particular illness. However, we know that **lung diseases** like cancer and bronchitis are common in areas where air pollution is high. Table 2.2 shows the major air pollutants in Britain. We see that waste products from **vehicle engines** are one of the main causes of air pollution.

Key Ideas

Every year in Britain millions of tonnes of *harmful* substances are released into the atmosphere – these are air *pollutants*. They harm our bodies, our water and our plants. Most of these *pollutants* come from the burning of *fossil fuels*. Chemists and engineers have the means to stop them, but they need our support, as well as the support of governments and industrialists

Table 2.2

Pollutant	Main Source	Effect
Carbon Monoxide	Vehicle engines and industry	Poisonous
Sulphur Dioxide	Burning fossil fuels in power stations	Forms acid rain
Hydrocarbons	Burning fuels in vehicles and factories	Irritating, toxic compounds formed in air
Oxides of Nitrogen	Vehicle engines and power stations	Forms acid rain
Lead	Vehicle engines and lead water pipes	Poisonous

Inside an Engine

Petrol is a mixture of hydrocarbons. When it is burned inside a car engine it produces a lot of energy. This energy drives the wheels of the vehicle. The engine diagrams show the four stages in the combustion of fuel inside an engine – often called the **four-stroke cycle**.

During the induction stroke a mixture of petrol and air is drawn into the engine. Car designers found that engine performance is best when there is a lot more petrol than air. This means the fuel is not burned completely, and instead of carbon dioxide being produced, **carbon monoxide** (CO), **carbon** and **unburnt petrol** are the main components of the exhaust gases.

The Four-Stroke Cycle

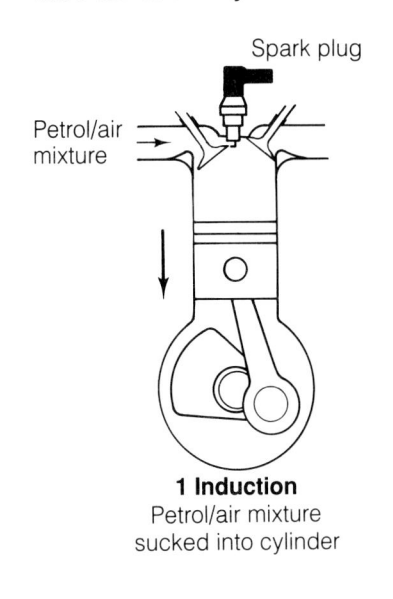

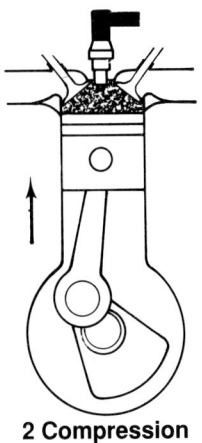

1 Induction
Petrol/air mixture sucked into cylinder

2 Compression
Petrol/air mixture compressed

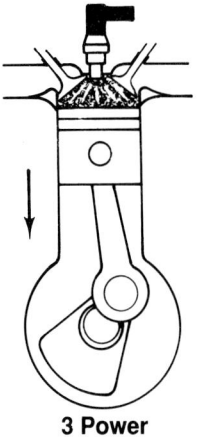

3 Power
Spark plug supplies the energy to ignite petrol/air mixture

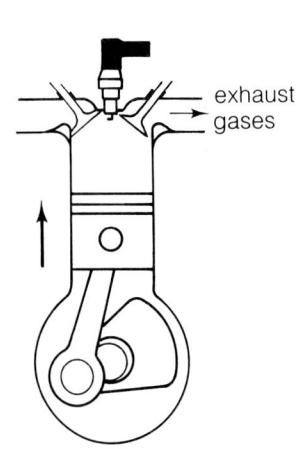

4 Exhaust
Waste gases from combustion are pushed out through exhaust

50 FUELS AND HYDROCARBONS

What Harm does Carbon Monoxide do?

Our blood contains a chemical called **haemoglobin** which gives blood its red colour. Haemoglobin combines with oxygen in our lungs and carries it around our bodies to where it is needed. Carbon monoxide, however, is **200 times better** at combining with haemoglobin than oxygen and so prevents oxygen getting into our bloodstream. As little as 1 per cent carbon monoxide in the air can kill. It is estimated that over 300 million tonnes of carbon monoxide is discharged into the air every year.

What Harm does Unburnt Petrol do?

The air contains petrol and other hydrocarbons in small quantities which are not harmful. However, in cities they are found in **high concentrations**. In the presence of sunlight, the hydrocarbons react with oxygen and oxides of nitrogen to form chemicals which are **toxic** and irritate the lungs. A chemical heat haze over Los Angeles recently produced a fog which was found to be extremely acidic.

Oxides of Nitrogen

Air is a mixture of nitrogen and oxygen. At the **high temperatures** in an engine, there is enough energy to break up the nitrogen and oxygen molecules. The atoms formed can then combine to form nitrogen oxide and nitrogen dioxide.

What Harm do they do?

Nitrogen dioxide is a toxic gas which irritates the breathing passages. In the atmosphere it forms nitric acid (HNO_3), one of the chemicals in **acid rain** (see Acids & Alkalis). Although nitrogen oxide is not nearly as toxic, it reacts quickly with more oxygen in the air to form the dioxide. Oxides of nitrogen are such serious pollutants that the United Nations Economic Commission has plans for an international agreement to reduce nitrogen oxide emissions from motor vehicles and power stations.

nitrogen + oxygen → nitrogen oxide

$N_2(g) + O_2(g) \rightarrow NO(g)$

● $N_2(g) + O_2(g) \rightarrow 2NO(g)$

nitrogen oxide + oxygen → nitrogen dioxide

$NO(g) + O_2(g) \rightarrow NO_2(g)$

● $2NO(g) + O_2(g) \rightarrow 2NO_2(g)$

FUELS AND HYDROCARBONS

Lead

Lead is **deliberately** added to petrol in the form of tetraethyl lead. It helps the engine to **run smoothly** by stopping "knock" or "pinking". "Knock" is caused when the petrol/air mixture burns too quickly, giving a sudden blow or knock to the cylinders. The lead forms oxides which would ruin the engine if they remained inside. With bromine lead forms a gas, so bromine compounds are added to remove the lead in the exhaust gases.

What can be done about the Pollutants?

Unleaded petrol is now widely available

Lead

Since lead is the only polluting material to be deliberately added, the obvious answer is not to add it in the first place! Already the USA has banned lead in petrol, and **unleaded** petrol is now available in many petrol stations throughout Britain. A European Economic Community law states that by 1991 all new cars must be able to run on unleaded petrol. Unleaded petrol contains a mixture of molecules which burn without causing engine "knock".

CO and NO

When a fuel/air mixture is made **less rich** in fuel, lower amounts of carbon monoxide and unburnt petrol is produced. **Special exhaust** systems can also be fitted to convert the carbon monoxide and nitrogen oxide into harmless gases.

How do these Methods Work?

(a) Increased Air Supply

If more air is allowed to mix with the petrol, then there is more oxygen for the petrol to react with. More fuel then burns more completely to form carbon dioxide rather than the monoxide. However, more air also means more nitrogen which produces increased amounts of nitrogen oxides. Chemists are now experimenting with engines which run at lower temperatures, in order to try and reduce the combination of oxygen with nitrogen. Catalysts are being used instead of spark plugs to ensure that the fuel is burned more efficiently. There are two other advantages of using catalysts;
(1) fuels such as paraffin and alcohol can be used instead of petrol;
(2) a car can travel more miles for each litre of fuel used. Computer models predict that soon the average family car will give over 20 miles per litre of fuel used, at speeds of up to 40 miles per hour – twice as efficient as current petrol engines.

(b) Special Exhausts

These exhausts have **catalytic converters** built into them which cause the following reactions:

nitrogen + carbon → nitrogen + carbon
oxide   monoxide   dioxide

$NO(g) + CO(g) \rightarrow N_2(g) + CO_2(g)$

• $2NO(g) + 2CO(g) \rightarrow N_2(g) + 2CO_2(g)$

Various catalysts are used, generally they are **transition metals** such as palladium, platinum or rhodium. You can find these and other transition metals in the periodic table.

The diagram shows a cut-away section of a catalytic converter. One major problem they have is that lead can "**poison**" the catalysts and stop them from working. Once all our cars are running on unleaded petrol this should no longer be a problem.

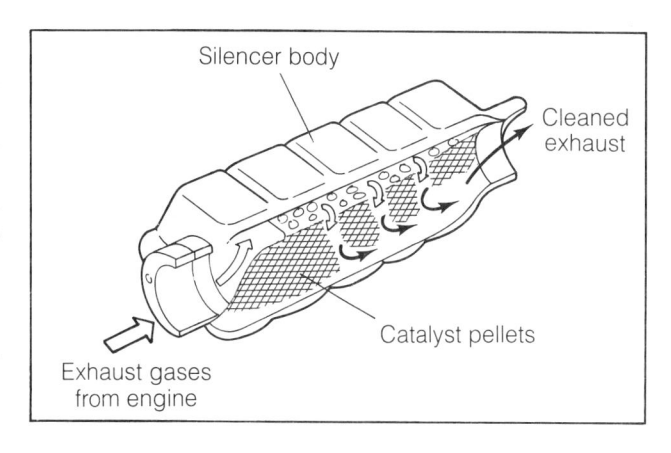

The inside of a catalytic converter

52 FUELS AND HYDROCARBONS

...and we expect it to have a catalytic converter...

£200

Counting the Cost

At present these special exhausts add several hundred pounds to the price of a car and increase the petrol consumption. Cars with converters are therefore more expensive to buy and run. Some people are not happy with the extra expense, and say they cannot afford it. But can we afford to continue to pollute our atmosphere as we are doing now?

Power Stations

Another look at the air pollutant table shows us that **power stations** are the main cause of **sulphur dioxide** pollution. In Europe it is estimated that up to 85 per cent of sulphur dioxide comes from the burning of fossil fuels in power stations.

How is Sulphur Dioxide Formed?

Most of our power stations burn coal and oil to produce energy. Both fuels contain sulphur. Coal can have a sulphur content, of between 0.5 and 5 per cent. When the fuels are burned, the sulphur reacts with oxygen in the air, producing sulphur dioxide:

sulphur + oxygen → sulphur dioxide

$S(s) + O_2(g) \rightarrow SO_2(g)$

It is estimated that in 1988, more than 150 million tonnes of sulphur dioxide was emitted into the atmosphere this way.

What Harm does SO$_2$ do?

Sulphur dioxide is a **poisonous** gas which irritates the lungs, even when present in small quantities. It is very soluble in water and quickly dissolves in moist air to form sulphurous acid:

sulphur + water → sulphurous acid

$SO_2(g) + H_2O(l) \rightarrow H_2SO_3(aq)$

Sulphur dioxide also reacts with oxygen in the air to form sulphur trioxide which then combines with water to form sulphuric acid:

sulphur trioxide + water → sulphuric acid

$SO_3(g) + H_2O(l) \rightarrow H_2SO_4(aq)$

These two acids are the main contributors to the chemical "cocktail" called **acid rain**. Though harmful to the environment, we shall see later that sulphuric acid is a very useful industrial chemical.

What can be done about it?

The problems caused by sulphur dioxide have been known for many years. In Britain it was decided that new power stations would be built away from cities to reduce the pollution problem. By the mid-1970s, chimneys up to 250 metres high were putting more than 5 million tonnes of sulphur dioxide into the air each year.

Some European countries were emitting similar amounts. Siting power stations away from cities had not solved the problem, because sulphur dioxide can travel for thousands of miles in the atmosphere. It was even being carried to non-polluting countries outside Europe!

Coal-fired power station chimneys

A more obvious solution might have been to use a different, non-sulphur-containing fuel, or to **remove** the sulphur before it reached the atmosphere. Nuclear fuel is one alternative, but it could possibly cause pollution problems much more devastating than sulphur dioxide.

Many countries already remove sulphur dioxide: Japan, West Germany and the USA "scrub" the waste gases with chemical absorbants such as lime (calcium oxide) and ammonia. Ammonia forms ammonium sulphate with sulphur dioxide, and this can be sold as a **fertiliser**.

Research is being carried out into mining natural sodium hydrogen carbonate and using it in the burners of power stations. This removes the sulphur dioxide as sodium sulphate (Na_2SO_4). The Central Electricity Generating Board in England plan to spend 500 million pounds over ten years to reduce acid emissions from power stations.

Wasting Sulphur

When chemicals such as lime are used to remove sulphur dioxide, calcium sulphate is formed. This is of limited use and most of it is dumped. However, sulphur is far too precious to lose this way. Sulphur is essential to the manufacture of sulphuric acid, one of our most important industrial chemicals. The pie chart shows uses of sulphuric acid.

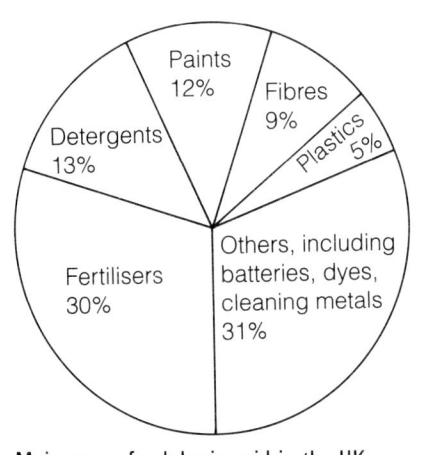

Main uses of sulphuric acid in the UK

Industrial Manufacture of Sulphuric Acid

Most of the sulphur used to make sulphuric acid is sent as rock sulphur from the USA, Poland and Sicily. It is also extracted during the refining of oil and the "cleaning" of natural gas. At BP Grangemouth 50 tonnes of sulphur are obtained every day.

The industrial manufacture of sulphuric acid is known as the **Contact Process**. The flow diagram outlines this process.

Flow diagram to show manufacturing process for sulphuric acid

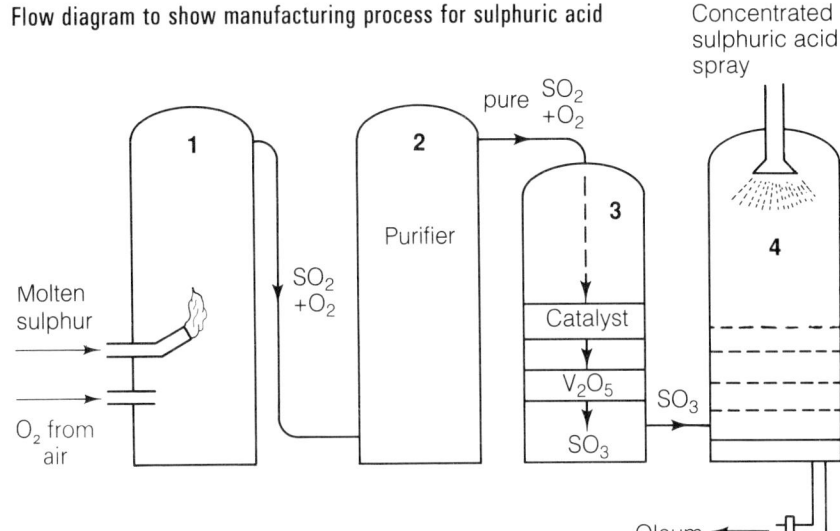

1. Sulphur dioxide (SO_2) is made by burning liquid sulphur in a furnace.
2. The sulphur dioxide and oxygen are cleaned and dried.
3. The SO_2/O_2 mixture is passed over vanadium oxide (V_2O_5) catalyst at about 450 °C. Sulphur trioxide (SO_3) is formed. Modern methods result in more than 99.5 per cent of the SO_2 being converted. This increased efficiency saves money and also cuts down the amount of SO_2 being released into the atmosphere.
4. The SO_3 is absorbed best in concentrated sulphuric acid. This results in a super-concentrated acid called oleum. The oleum is eventually diluted with water to give sulphuric acid.

54 FUELS AND HYDROCARBONS

Carbon Dioxide

So far in this section, carbon dioxide has been referred to as a "harmless gas". It is not toxic and forms an essential part of the plant photosynthesis process (see Carbohydrates). However, its increasing presence in the atmosphere is now causing concern.

Until recently the amount of energy the earth retained and radiated were the same. However, the burning of fossil fuels has produced carbon dioxide. It has been estimated that over 20 thousand million tonnes of carbon dioxide are put into the atmosphere every year, from fossil fuels alone. As the amount of atmospheric carbon dioxide increases, more of the sun's energy is retained, causing the average temperature of the Earth's surface to rise. This is known as the **greenhouse effect**.

At present about 0.035% of the air is carbon dioxide. Some scientists predict that by the year 2080 this figure will have doubled. This may cause the average temperature of the Earth to rise by 2 °C. Scientists still argue about the effect this may have, but some think the weather will change dramatically, causing droughts such as the one experienced in the mid-states of North America in 1988.

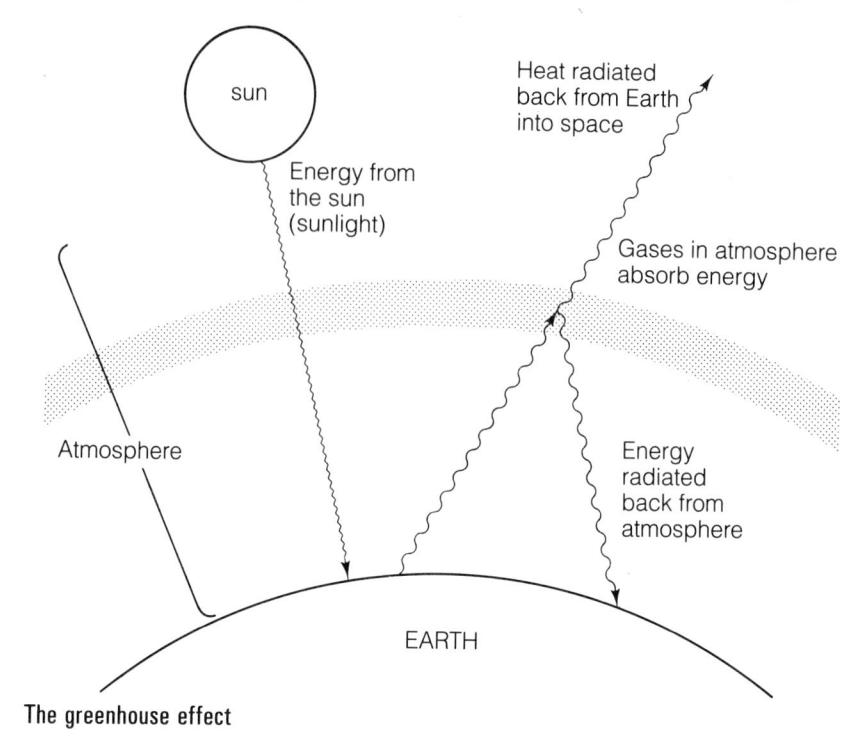

The greenhouse effect

Activities

○ 1 When you are concerned about something happening, what you can do is write to somebody, such as your MP or a government minister. Choose one type of air pollution and in your notebook, write a letter about it to your MP. Outline how the pollution is caused, what effect it has and what you think should be done about it.

○ 2 (a) Leaded petrol contains about 0.15 grams of lead per litre. A family car travels 8 thousand miles in a year and uses 1 litre of petrol for every 8 miles travelled. Work out how much lead is produced by the car engine in a year.

   (b) What happens to the lead produced in the engine?

○ 3 (a) A power station burns 70 thousand tonnes of coal a week. If the coal contains 2 per cent sulphur, how much sulphur will be produced every week?

   (b) Outline a way in which the sulphur produced can be prevented from reaching the atmosphere.

   (c) Why do we want to stop sulphur compounds getting into the air?

● 4 (a) Special exhaust systems can stop some pollutants from reaching the atmosphere. Describe one of these systems and outline what happens to the pollutants inside it.

   (b) One way of reducing the amount of carbon monoxide released into the air, is to increase the amount of air in the fuel/air mixture.

   (i) Explain how the amount of carbon monoxide is reduced.

   (ii) Describe one problem that arises when the amount of air is increased.

   (iii) Explain how the problem in (ii) can be solved.

● 5 (a) Write an equation for sulphur reacting with oxygen to produce sulphur dioxide.

   (b) From the equation in (a), calculate the mass of sulphur dioxide that would be produced in a day, if a factory burned fuel containing 320 kilograms of sulphur each day.

5 The Alkanes

Alkanes from Oil

The **alkanes** are a group or "family" of compounds, the molecules of which are made up of hydrogen and carbon only. They are **hydrocarbons**. The fractions obtained by distilling crude oil contain alkane molecules. Crude oil is our main source of alkanes, and under the right conditions all its fractions will burn to give energy.

Some of the fractions, e.g., petrol and diesel, are liquids. Others like candle wax and bitumen are solid, and camping "Gaz" is a mixture of gases. How can substances which look so different undergo similar reactions? The answer can be found by looking in detail at the **structure** of the alkane molecules.

x = electron from hydrogen
• = electron from carbon

Key Ideas

The hydrocarbon fractions obtained from the distillation of crude oil are made up of *alkane* molecules. They react readily with oxygen to produce a lot of energy and so are good fuels. However, because of the way they are *bonded*, they undergo few other reactions.

Structure of the Alkanes

Methane is the smallest alkane molecule, with just one carbon atom covalently bonded to four hydrogen atoms.

The molecule looks flat when drawn on paper but it is really three-dimensional, like the model shown. The other alkanes are also three-dimensional.

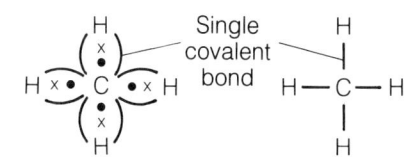

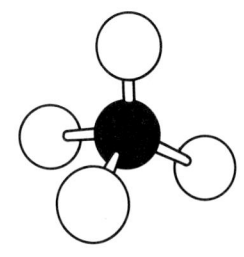

A three-dimensional model of methane

Carbon atoms can bond with other carbon atoms to form chains. Alkane molecules may be more than seventy carbon atoms long. Table 2.3 gives some details about the first eight alkanes.

Table 2.3

Name	Molecular Formula	Full Structural Formula	Shortened Structural Formula
Methane	CH_4		CH_4
Ethane	C_2H_6		CH_3CH_3
Propane	C_3H_8		$CH_3CH_2CH_3$
Butane	C_4H_{10}		$CH_3CH_2CH_2CH_3$
Pentane	C_5H_{12}		$CH_3CH_2CH_2CH_2CH_3$
Hexane	C_6H_{14}		$CH_3CH_2CH_2CH_2CH_2CH_3$
Heptane	C_7H_{16}		$CH_3CH_2CH_2CH_2CH_2CH_2CH_3$
Octane	C_8H_{18}		$CH_3CH_2CH_2CH_2CH_2CH_2CH_2CH_3$

56 FUELS AND HYDROCARBONS

A close look at Table 2.3 reveals three similarities:

(1) Names

All the alkanes have names ending in **-ane**. From pentane onwards, the first part of the name tells us how many carbon atoms are in the molecule, e.g., **Pentane** has 5 carbon atoms, just as a **pent**agon is a 5 sided figure. Similarly for **hex**ane (6), **hept**ane (7) and **oct**ane (8).

(2) Structure

All the molecules are similar in structure. The bonding electrons of all the atoms within the molecules are used to make **single** covalent bonds. Any molecule which is "full" of single bonds is said to be **saturated**. Remember that although they are all drawn flat, the molecules are really three-dimensional, as shown by the models in the photograph.

All the structures shown have one carbon atom following after the other. These are known as **straight chains**.

(3) Formulae

Each compound has a different formula and the difference in the formula of one alkane and the next is always $-CH_2$. The general formula for the alkanes is C_nH_{2n+2} where $n = 1, 2, 3 \ldots > 70$.

e.g., when $n = 1$, substituting a one into the general formula gives:

$$C_1H_{(2\times 1)+2} = CH_4 \text{ methane}$$

when $n = 2$:

$$C_2H_{(2\times 2)+2} = C_2H_6 \text{ ethane}$$

Butane: C_4H_{10}

Pentane: C_5H_{12}

Octane: C_8H_{18}

Three-dimensional models of butane, pentane and octane

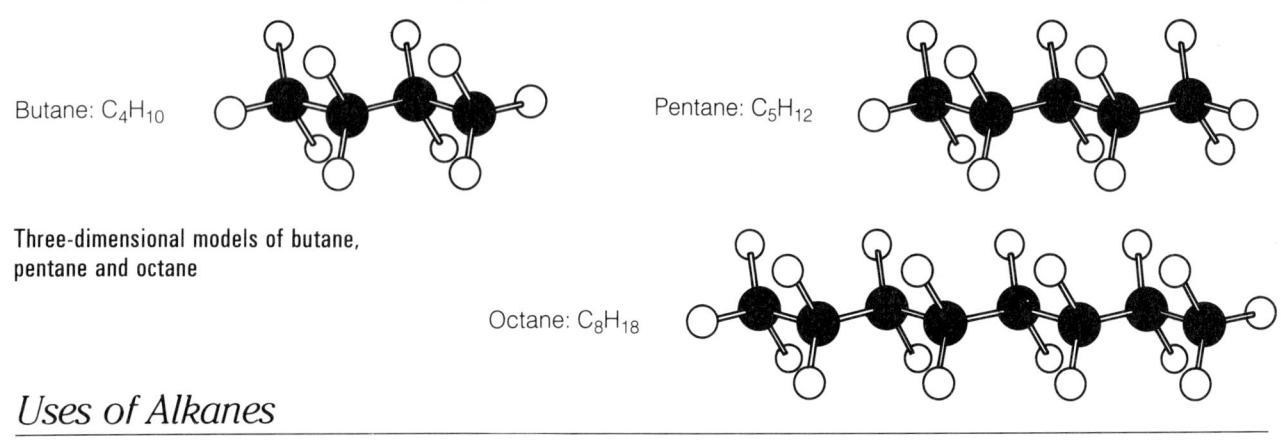

Uses of Alkanes

Many of the alkanes are good **fuels**, both as mixtures obtained from fractional distillation of oil and as individual compounds. **Methane** is the main component of **natural gas**. Table 2.4 shows the gases present in a typical sample of North Sea natural gas.

Table 2.4

Gas	Percentage in North Sea gas
Methane	95.00
Ethane	3.00
Propane	0.50
Carbon dioxide	0.05
Nitrogen	1.00

Natural gas is used in many homes. You may have a cooker or fire which burns it. Bunsen burners in science laboratories also use natural gas. Some power stations use it as a source of energy for making electricity. Methane is the predominant gas in **biogas**. In India and parts of Asia, biogas is produced from animal waste when it decays in the absence of air. The gas is used for heating, cooking and lighting.

It was methane gas which exploded in the Wyredale water tunnel, Lancashire in 1984, killing eleven people. The methane is thought to have formed in stagnant water. There is a danger of methane explosions on sites where cities dump their rubbish. As the rubbish rots, methane is formed. Some firms who operate these sites, pump out the methane and sell it as fuel.

Propane gas is easily liquefied and can be used as bottled gas to fuel domestic gas cookers.

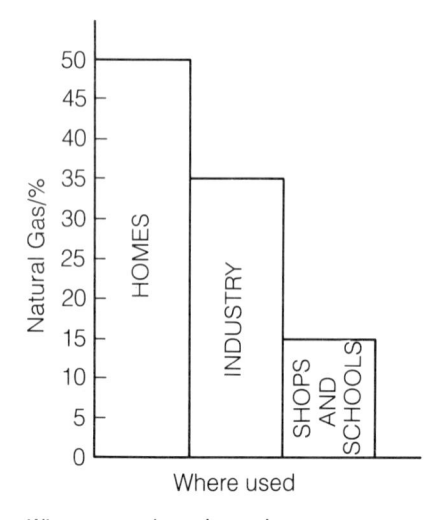

Where natural gas is used

FUELS AND HYDROCARBONS

Reactions of Alkanes

Apart from combustion, alkanes undergo few other reactions. A piece of sodium dropped into petrol will not react. This lack of reactivity is because the alkanes are **saturated** – there are no electrons available to bond with anything else. When they do react, for example with **bromine** solution (orange) the reaction is **very slow**. The bromine solution eventually reacts completely and loses its colour.

$$C_6H_{14}(l) + Br_2(aq) \rightarrow C_6H_{13}Br(l) + HBr(g)$$
hexane   bromine   bromohexane   hydrogen bromide
(clear)   (orange)   (clear)   (white fumes)

Activities

○ 1 For each of the following questions, choose an answer (A–I) from the grid – there may be more than one answer to each question. Which box represents:
  (a) propane?
  (b) butane?
  (c) the sixth alkane in the series?
  (d) the eighth alkane in the series?
  (e) the general formula for the alkanes?
  (f) the alkane that is the main constituent of natural gas?
  (g) a compound which is not an alkane?

○ 2 Use the general formula of the alkanes to work out the formula of:
  (a) the alkane with ten carbon atoms
  (b) the alkane with twenty-four hydrogen atoms
  (c) the ninth alkane

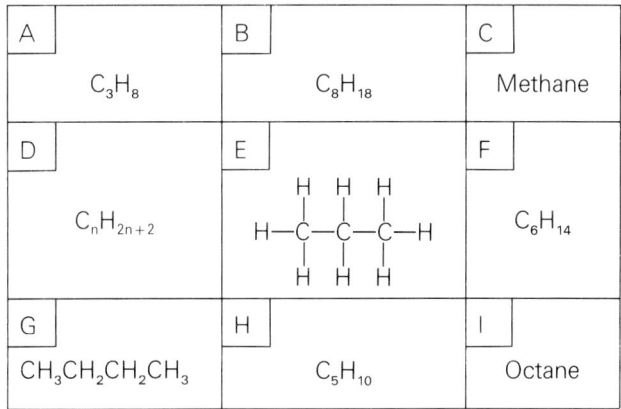

A	B	C
C_3H_8	C_8H_{18}	Methane
D	E	F
C_nH_{2n+2}	H–C–C–C–H (propane structural formula with H atoms)	C_6H_{14}
G	H	I
$CH_3CH_2CH_2CH_3$	C_5H_{10}	Octane

○ 3 (a) Write a word equation for octane reacting with bromine.
  (b) Write a formula equation for the reaction in (a).

6 The Alkenes

Key Ideas

The *alkenes* are a family of hydrocarbons. Their structure differs from the alkanes in a way that makes them reactive. The alkenes are vital as feedstock for the *plastics* industry.

The C=C Bond

Like the alkanes, the **alkenes** are a family of hydrocarbons. What makes them different to the alkanes is the way in which the atoms within the molecules are **bonded**. Alkenes are **not saturated**. Although they do have single bonds, some of the bonding electrons between two adjacent carbon atoms overlap in such a way as to form a **double** covalent bond – represented as **C=C**. Molecules with a double bond are said to be **unsaturated**.

x = electron from hydrogen
• = electron from carbon

The diagram shows how the electrons are shared to form the bonds in **ethene**, the simplest alkene. Ethene does not have a three-dimensional shape – it is flat.

The alkenes, like the alkanes, can form chains of varying length. Table 2.5 gives details of the first six alkenes in the series. Like the alkanes, all the alkenes, except ethene, have a three-dimensional shape.

(1) Naming

The alkenes take their names from the corresponding alkane, ending in **-ene** instead of -ane. Note that there is no methene. Can you work out why?

(2) Formula

Each alkene has two less hydrogen atoms than its corresponding alkane. This is due to the presence of the double bond. The general formula of the alkenes is C_nH_{2n} where n = 2, 3, 4, etc.

Table 2.5

Name	Molecular Formula	Full Structural Formula	Shortened Structural Formula
Ethene	C_2H_4		CH_2CH_2
Propene	C_3H_6		CH_2CHCH_3
Butene	C_4H_8		$CH_2CHCH_2CH_3$
Pentene	C_5H_{10}		$CH_2CHCH_2CH_2CH_3$
Hexene	C_6H_{12}		$CH_2CHCH_2CH_2CH_2CH_3$
Heptene	C_7H_{14}		$CH_2CHCH_2CH_2CH_2CH_3$

FUELS AND HYDROCARBONS

Reactions of Alkenes

(1) Combustion

Like all hydrocarbons, alkenes burn to form carbon dioxide and water. However they are far too useful to be burned as fuels.

ethene + oxygen → carbon dioxide + water

$C_2H_4(g) + O_2(g) \rightarrow CO_2(g) + H_2O(l)$

• $C_2H_4(g) + 3O_2(g) \rightarrow 2CO_2(g) + 2H_2O(l)$

(2) Addition with Bromine Solution

When bromine solution is added to any alkene, it is decolourised **very quickly**. This is because of the C=C double bond. The electrons in the bond are available to form new bonds with other substances.

```
    H  H  H  H  H  H
    |  |  |  |  |  |
H―C=C―C―C―C―C―H     hexene
       |  |  |  |        (colourless)
       H  H  H  H

    +Br―Br
       ↓

    H  H  H  H  H  H
    |  |  |  |  |  |
H―C―C―C―C―C―C―H     dibromohexane
    |  |  |  |  |  |    (colourless)
    Br Br H  H  H  H
```

bromine (orange)

$C_6H_{12}(l) + Br_2(aq) \rightarrow C_6H_{12}Br_2(l)$

The structural formulae show that the bromine atoms have **added** onto the carbon atoms which had the double bond between them. This is an **addition** reaction. The reaction can be used as a test to tell a saturated hydrocarbon (e.g., an alkane) from an unsaturated hydrocarbon (e.g., an alkene).

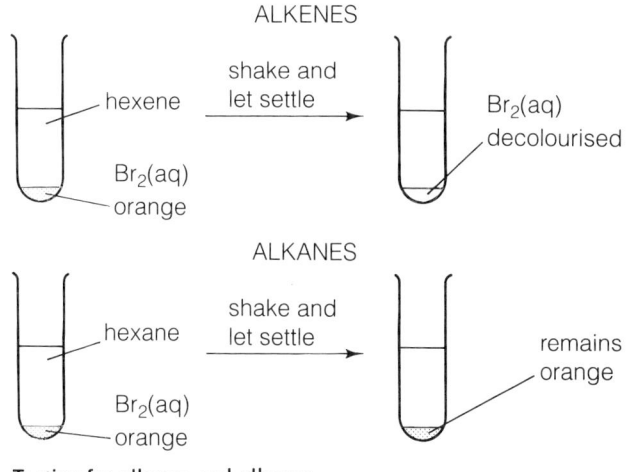

ALKENES

hexene / Br₂(aq) orange — shake and let settle → Br₂(aq) decolourised

ALKANES

hexane / Br₂(aq) orange — shake and let settle → remains orange

Testing for alkenes and alkanes

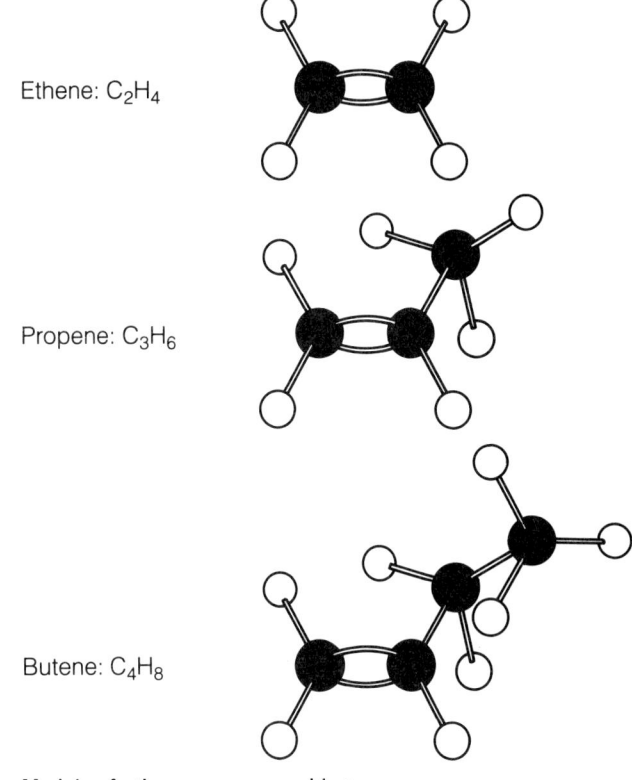

Ethene: C_2H_4

Propene: C_3H_6

Butene: C_4H_8

Models of ethene, propene and butene

Dibromoethane

When ethene reacts with bromine, dibromoethane is formed:

ethene + bromine → dibromoethane

```
 H       H                        H  H
  \     /                         |  |
   C = C     + Br―Br  →      H―C―C―H
  /     \                         |  |
 H       H                        Br Br
```

$C_2H_4(g) + Br_2(aq) \rightarrow C_2H_4Br_2(l)$

Dibromoethane is an important additive to leaded petrol. The lead added to stop "knock" has to be removed from the engine otherwise it will damage the cylinders and spark plugs.

Dibromoethane reacts with the lead to form lead bromide which passes out of the engine with the exhaust gases.

60 FUELS AND HYDROCARBONS

(3) Hydrogenation

Alkenes undergo addition reactions with **hydrogen**. The corresponding **alkane** is formed. Ethene reacts with hydrogen when passed over a nickel catalyst at 150 °C to produce **ethane**.

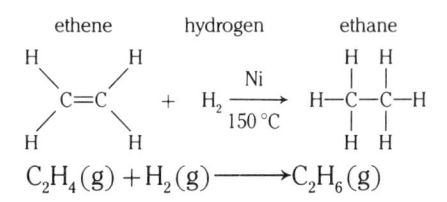

$$C_2H_4(g) + H_2(g) \longrightarrow C_2H_6(g)$$

This is known as **hydrogenation**. It is important in the manufacture of **margarine** from vegetable oils. Vegetable oils like corn oil, are **liquids** which contain unsaturated molecules. During hydrogenation, the hydrogen adds onto the unsaturated molecules to form saturated molecules, which tend to be more **solid**. By controlling the amount of hydrogen added, hard or soft margarine can be produced.

Common vegetable oils and margarines

The Importance of Ethene

Ethene is a very useful molecule, particularly for making other compounds. By far the most important use is in the manufacture of **plastics** and industrial **ethanol** (see Plastics).

Everyday plastics derived from ethene

Activities

1. For each of the following questions, choose an answer (A–F) from the grid – there may be more than one answer to each question. Which box represents:
   (a) pentene?
   (b) propene?
   (c) a molecule which is not unsaturated?
   (d) the fourth alkene?
   (e) the sixth alkene?

2. Collect a set of molecular models.
   (a) Make models of propene and hydrogen, and draw them.
   (b) (i) Make a model of the molecule formed when propene is hydrogenated and draw it.
   (ii) Name the molecule formed.
   (iii) What kind of reaction has taken place?
   (iv) Write a word equation for the reaction between propane and hydrogen.
   (v) Write a formula equation for the reaction in (iv).

3. Collect a set of molecular models.
   (a) Make models of butene and bromine, and draw them.
   (b) (i) Make a model of the molecule formed when butene and bromine react.
   (ii) Name the molecule formed.
   (iii) Would this reaction be slow or fast?
   (iv) Write a word equation for the reaction between butene and bromine.
   (v) Write a formula equation for the reaction in (iv).

A	B	C
CH₂CHCH₃	(structure shown)	C₇H₁₆
D	E	F
Hexene	C₅H₁₀	(structure shown)

7 Cracking Hydrocarbons

Key Ideas

Small hydrocarbons like ethene and those found in petrol are in great demand. They come from crude oil. However, crude oil contains more large hydrocarbon molecules than small ones. Chemists have developed a way of breaking up long chained molecules – it is called *catalytic cracking*.

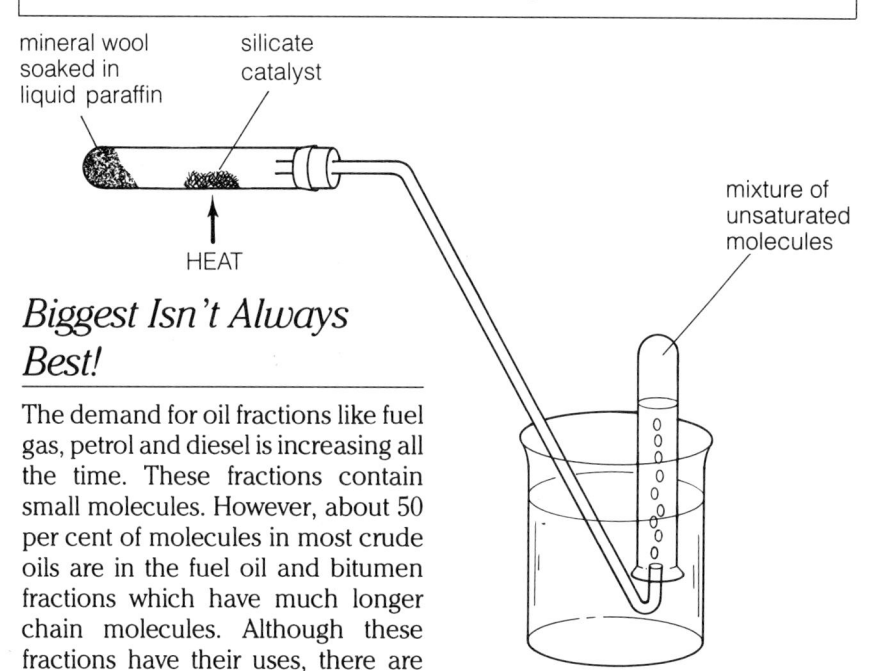

Biggest Isn't Always Best!

The demand for oil fractions like fuel gas, petrol and diesel is increasing all the time. These fractions contain small molecules. However, about 50 per cent of molecules in most crude oils are in the fuel oil and bitumen fractions which have much longer chain molecules. Although these fractions have their uses, there are still millions of tonnes which are not required.

Cracking long chain alkanes in the laboratory

Cracking in the Laboratory

Liquid (medicinal) paraffin can be catalytically cracked in the laboratory using the arrangement shown in the diagram. The mixture of gases collected rapidly decolourise bromine solution showing that it contains some **unsaturated** molecules.

Cracking in Industry

Catalytic cracking in industry is similar to the laboratory method but on a much larger scale. One of the problems with both laboratory and industrial methods is that the catalyst becomes covered in carbon after a while. In the laboratory this causes the cracking to stop – something that must be prevented in industry. Chemical engineers have solved the problem by using a method where the carbon-covered catalyst is continually removed, cleaned and reused. The flow diagram outlines the process.

If we take $C_{22}H_{46}$, a typically long chain alkane, we can see how it might form a **mixture** of small molecules:

$C_{22}H_{46}$ (long chain alkane)
↓ catalytic cracking
$C_8H_{18} + C_3H_8 + C_4H_{10}$ (alkanes)
$+ C_2H_4 + C_3H_6$ (alkenes)
$+ 2C$ (carbon)

Table 2.6

Fraction	Approximate percentage in Crude oil	Approximate percentage in Everyday demand
1 Fuel gas	2	5
2 Petrol	7	22
3 Naphtha	10	5
4 Kerosene	12	9
5 Diesel	19	24
6 Fuel Oil Bitumen	50	35

Table 2.6 shows the approximate percentage of the different fractions in crude oil, and the demand for them.

Rather than waste these fractions, chemists have developed a method for splitting the long chain molecules into more useful smaller molecules – it is called **catalytic cracking**. It not only produces **alkanes**, but also **alkenes**. This method is in fact the main commercial source of alkenes.

62 FUELS AND HYDROCARBONS

Catalytic cracking in industry

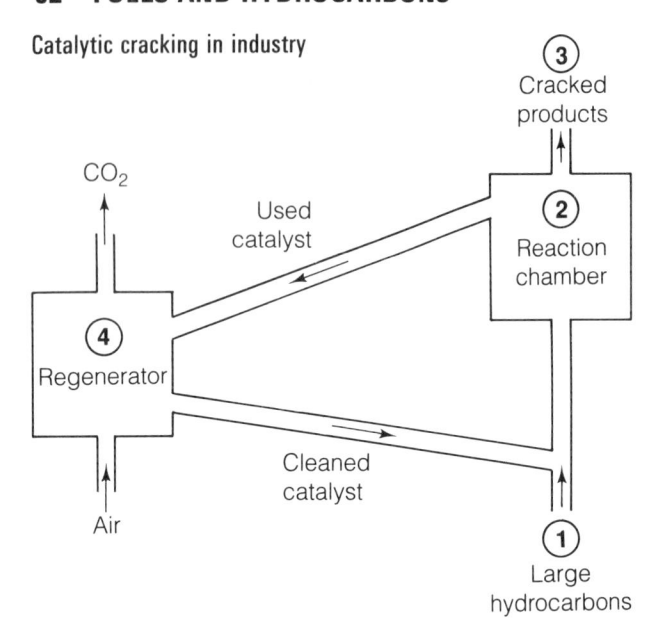

1. The long chain hydrocarbons are fed into the catalytic cracker at a temperature between 350 and 550 °C.
2. Inside the cracker, the hot molecules pass over the **powdered catalyst** at 620–740 °C and are split into **smaller** molecules.
3. The **mixture** of small molecules is extracted and separated by fractional distillation.
4. The carbon-covered (spent) catalyst is fed into the regenerator where air is blown in. The air reacts with the carbon on the catalyst's surface to form carbon dioxide which is emitted into the atmosphere. The cleaned (regenerated) catalyst is fed back into the reaction chamber.

Shell catalytic cracking unit for refining crude oil

Why Use a Catalyst?

When cracking was first used to make petrol, no catalyst was added. The large molecules were broken up by heat alone – this method is known as **thermal** cracking. There are several problems with thermal cracking: very high temperatures are needed, which is very costly; and the petrol produced is not of high enough quality for modern engines. Using a suitable catalyst means that the **temperature** can be **kept down**, so saving energy and money. The **quality** of the petrol fraction is so **high** that it can be blended (mixed) with poorer petrols to improve their quality.

Industrial catalysts

Why a Mixture?

As you have seen, cracking of $C_{22}H_{46}$ gives a **mixture** of alkanes and alkenes. To understand why a mixture is formed during cracking, look at the structure of a simpler molecule, decane, $C_{10}H_{22}$. The equation shows how decane could be cracked.

There are not enough hydrogens on the decane for two alkanes to form when it is split into two. Instead, the hydrogens rearrange themselves and a double bond is formed between two carbon atoms in one of the products.

Cracking decane to produce octane and ethane

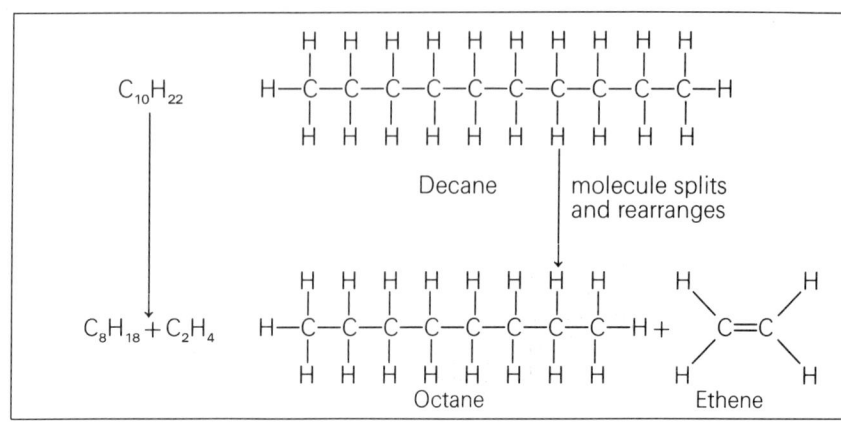

$C_{10}H_{22}$ → Decane → molecule splits and rearranges → $C_8H_{18} + C_2H_4$ (Octane + Ethene)

FUELS AND HYDROCARBONS

Hydrocracking

If chemists wish to crack a large molecule to form alkanes (but no alkenes) then they use the method of hydrocracking. Hydrogen is added to the cracked molecules during the cracking process and this saturates any unsaturated molecules. The long chain molecules from the **wax fraction** of crude oil can be hydrocracked to produce large quantities of the smaller, more useful molecules found in **petrol**. A typical long chain molecule found in wax, could be hydrocracked as follows:

$$C_{26}H_{54}(s) + 3H_2(g) \rightarrow C_8H_{18}(l) + C_7H_{16}(l) + C_6H_{14}(l) + C_5H_{12}(l)$$

High temperature and very high pressure is needed for hydrocracking and this creates many difficult **engineering problems**, both in design and construction of hydrocrackers. The walls of the reactor have to be between 15 and 20 cm thick, to withstand the severe conditions. Large compressors and pumps have to be used. Most hydrocrackers also need their own hydrogen production units. All these special requirements make hydrocracking **very expensive**.

Shell oil refinery hydrocracking unit

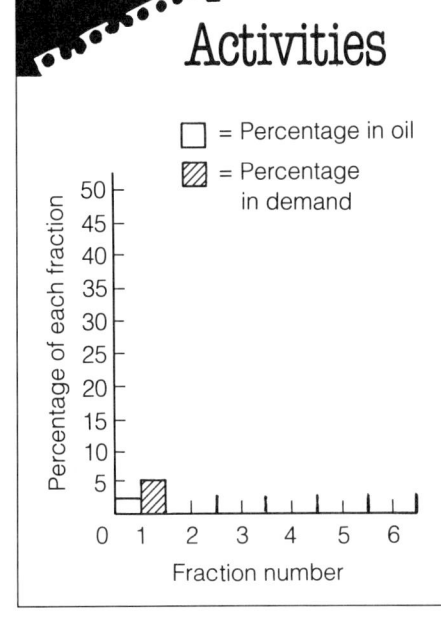

Activities

○ 1 Look at the information in Table 2.6, page 55, and plot both the percentage of each fraction in crude oil, and the everyday demand, on a graph like the one on the left which has been started for you.

○ 2 Collect a set of molecular models and make a model of dodecane ($C_{12}H_{26}$). "Crack" the molecule in two. Draw the molecules formed in your notes and name them. (Remember you will have to rearrange some of the hydrogens.)

● 3 Imagine you are a chemical engineer. What advice would you give an industrialist to persuade him to use a catalyst to crack long-chain alkanes rather than use heat alone.

● 4 Imagine that you are given the job of advising a company about setting up a **hydrocracker**. List some of the advantages and disadvantages of hydrocracking that you think the company should be aware of.

8 Homologous Series and Isomerism

> ## Key Ideas
>
> The alkanes and alkenes are families of hydrocarbons which are chemically similar and can be represented by general formulae. They are examples of *homologous series*, a term which can be applied to any group of compounds with these kinds of similarities. Within a homologous series, some compounds exhibit *isomerism* – they have more than one structural formula.

Homologous Series

Earlier on you saw that the members of the alkane family have very similar structures and as a result undergo very similar chemical reactions. Although they differ slightly in their **physical** properties, such as their state at room temperature and their boiling points, these differences show a regular **pattern** of change, as shown in Table 2.7.

The steady increase in boiling point is due to the gradual increase in size of the molecules. The bigger they get, the stronger the forces are between the molecules and the more energy it takes to separate them. When members of a family of compounds have similar chemical properties, regular changes in physical properties, and can be represented by a general formula, they are said to belong to a **homologous series**. The alkanes are a homologous series of hydrocarbons, and so are the alkenes.

Table 2.7

Name	Formula	Boiling Point (BP) °C	State at Room Temperature
Methane	CH_4	−162	Gas
Ethane	C_2H_6	−87	Gas
Propane	C_3H_8	−42	Gas
Butane	C_4H_{10}	0	Gas
Pentane	C_5H_{12}	36	Liquid
Hexane	C_6H_{14}	69	Liquid
Decane	$C_{10}H_{22}$	174	Liquid
Hexadecane	$C_{16}H_{34}$	280	Solid

The Cycloalkanes

When we looked at the structures of the alkanes and the alkenes, we saw that they are all **open chains**. There are, however, homologous series in which the carbon atoms are joined in a **ring** – one of these series is the **cycloalkanes**. Table 2.8 shows the first four cycloalkanes.

The general formula is C_nH_{2n}, the same as for the alkenes. However, as their name suggests, these molecules are more like alkanes and their structures show they have no double C=C bonds, only single. They are saturated, **cyclic** alkanes.

FUELS AND HYDROCARBONS

Table 2.8

Name	Structural Formula	Molecular Formula
Cyclopropane	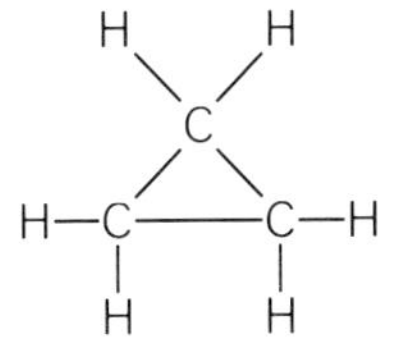	C_3H_6
Cyclobutane	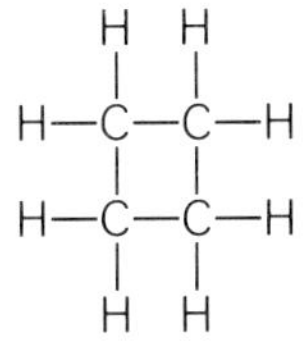	C_4H_8
Cyclopentane	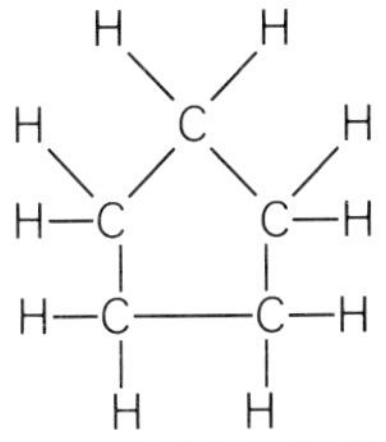	C_5H_{10}
Cyclohexane	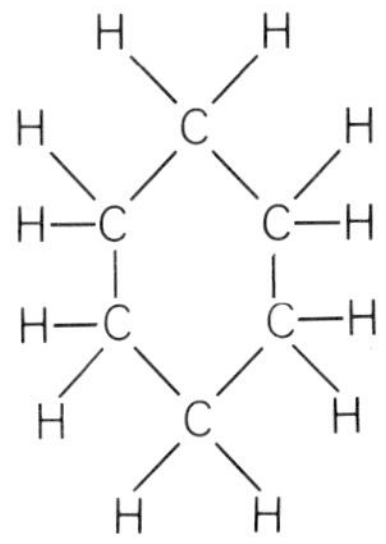	C_6H_{12}

Table 2.9

Name	Molecular Formula	Isomers
Butane	C_4H_{10}	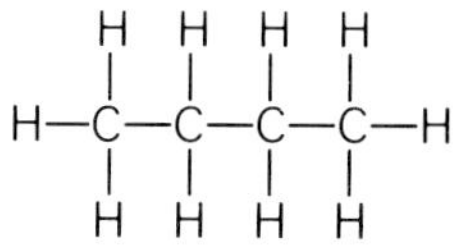 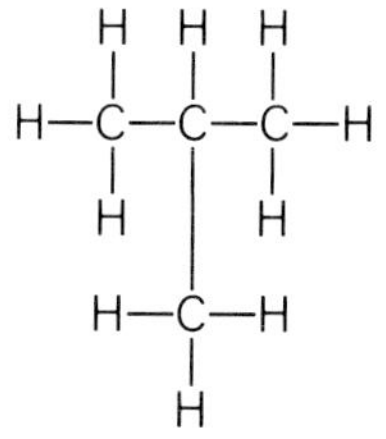
Pentane	C_5H_{12}	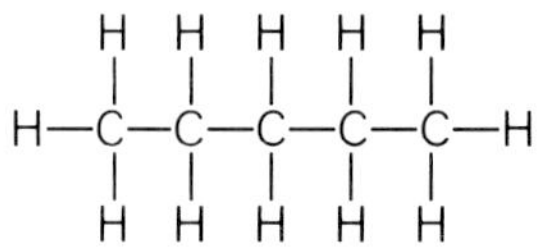 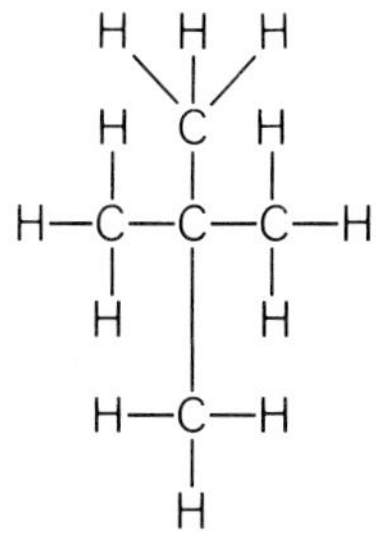 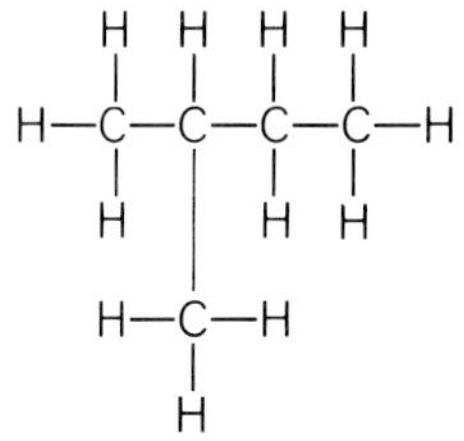
Butene	C_4H_8	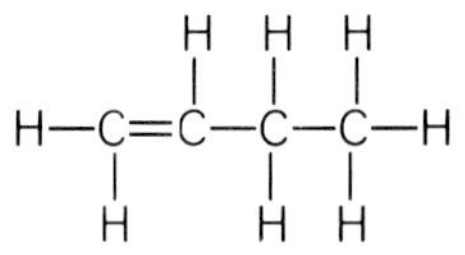 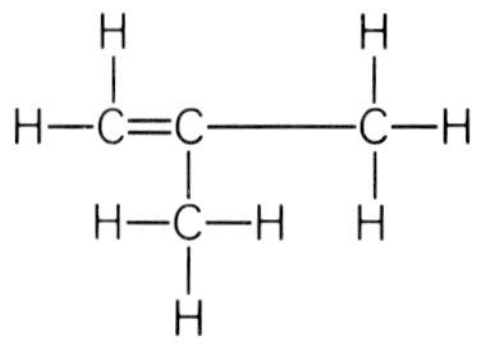 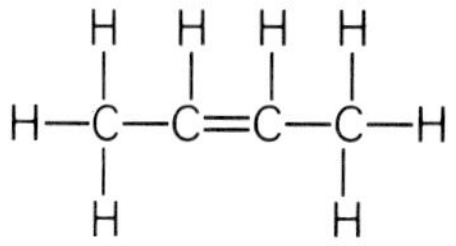

Isomerism

So far alkanes and alkenes have been drawn as compounds which are straight chain molecules. However, the same compounds can exist as molecules in which groups of atoms containing carbon extend from the straight chains. These are **branched** chains.

A compound with a certain molecular formula but more than one possible structural formula is said to show **isomerism** – it has more than one isomer or form. Table 2.9 shows some alkanes and alkenes with their isomers.

Note how in the alkenes the molecules can be branched and the position of the double bond can vary.

As the molecules get bigger the number of possible isomers increases. For example:
pentane (C_5H_{12}) has five isomers
octane (C_8H_{18}) has eighteen isomers
tridecane ($C_{13}H_{26}$) has 802 isomers!

66 FUELS AND HYDROCARBONS

Isomerism does not just occur within a homologous series. We have already seen that the alkenes and the cycloalkanes have the same general formula but that their molecules have completely **different** structures – they are isomers too.

Cyclopropane (C_3H_6)

Propene (C_3H_6)

The Octane Number

Petrol comes in different grades. In petrol stations leaded petrol used to be graded as two, three or four star. This star grading described how good the petrol was at preventing engine "knock" (see Lead, page 45). Nowadays you will usually see only different grades of unleaded petrol. In the petrochemical industry a fuel is also given a number to indicate its quality. These numbers are called **octane numbers**, and the best fuels have high octane numbers. The numbers are calculated by comparing a fuel's anti-knock properties with that of iso-octane, a branched isomer of octane.

iso-octane

Iso-octane has excellent anti-knock properties and is given an octane number of 100. This standard is then used to work out a particular fuel's octane number.

It is generally found that **branched** chain isomers have much higher octane numbers than the corresponding straight chain molecule. A comparison of octane numbers for some straight chain and branched chain isomers is shown in Table 2.10.

Table 2.10

Alkane		Isomer	Octane Number
pentane	straight	$CH_3CH_2CH_2CH_2CH_3$	61.7

	branched	$CH_3CH_2CHCH_3$
		         $\|$
		         CH_3
			92.3

hexane	straight	$CH_3CH_2CH_2CH_2CH_2CH_3$	24.8
	branched	CH_3 $\|$ $CH_3CCH_2CH_3$ $\|$ CH_3	91.8

Petrol is a complicated mixture of molecules with different octane numbers. Lead is added to petrol to help increase its anti-knock properties so that lower octane material can be blended with higher octane material without damaging the engine.

Unleaded petrol doesn't contain lead so its molecules must all have high octane numbers.

Table 2.11 compares the typical compositions of four star and unleaded petrol.

Table 2.11

	Octane Material (%)		
	High	Medium	Low
Four star	45	55	5
Unleaded	60	40	—

Activities

● 1 (a) Look at the boiling points (bp) of the alkanes in the table 2.7 of the homologous series section. Draw a graph of "bp" against number of carbon atoms in the molecules for the first six alkanes and for decane.
   (b) From the graph, predict the boiling points of heptane, octane and nonane (C_9H_{20}).

● 2 Collect a box of molecular models.
   (a) Make a model of pentane and draw it.
   (b) Now make the other two isomers of pentane and draw them.

● 3 (a) Make a model of cyclobutane and draw it.
   (b) Now make at least two isomers of cyclobutane and draw them.

● 4 Cyclopentane is an isomer of pentene. Draw at least three others.

● 5 Information can be presented in pie charts, line graphs, bar charts, etc. Select the **best** way to present the information given in table 2.11. Draw out your graph(s) or chart(s).

9 Spotlight on Industry

Key Ideas

Building a chemical plant of any kind is a complicated and costly business. When choosing a site and designing a plant, a variety of factors have to be considered:
- Is the site close to the materials to be processed?
- Is there enough room to build and expand?
- Is there a workforce available?
- Are the communications good?
- Can the plant be built safely?
- How do the people who live near the site feel?
- Will the environment be affected?

What Happens at Mossmorran?

Mossmorran is located in Scotland, five miles from the Fife coast. There are two separate plants there. One is a **gas fractionation** plant, operated by Shell Expro, which separates **ethane** from other gases found with oil. The other, is the Fife Ethylene (Ethene) Plant operated by Exxon Chemicals. The ethylene plant cracks ethane into ethene. Together these plants are the most modern of their kind anywhere in the world. Around 650 thousand tonnes of ethene are produced every year there. Ethene is used at home and abroad to produce a large range of man-made materials, such as polythene and other plastics (see Plastics), antifreeze, cosmetics and paints.

Mossmorran

The Fife ethylene (ethene) plant at night

Where Does the Story Start?

The Brent Oilfield, jointly operated by Shell and Esso, pipes liquefied gas 278 miles across the seabed to St. Fergus, near Aberdeen. Here, methane is separated out and sold to British Gas who then sell it to us to be used in our homes, schools and factories. The remaining "gas" mixture, known as NGL (natural gas liquids) is then pumped 138 miles through an underground pipeline to Mossmorran.

68 FUELS AND HYDROCARBONS

What Happens to the NGL?

The NGL contains ethane, propane and natural gasoline, which are separated at Shell Expro's Fractionation Plant, by **fractional distillation**. The ethane is piped "next door" to Exxon chemicals where it is **cracked** into ethene. The other products from the separation are not wasted – they are stored in giant tanks, ready for export by ship from the Braefoot Terminal.

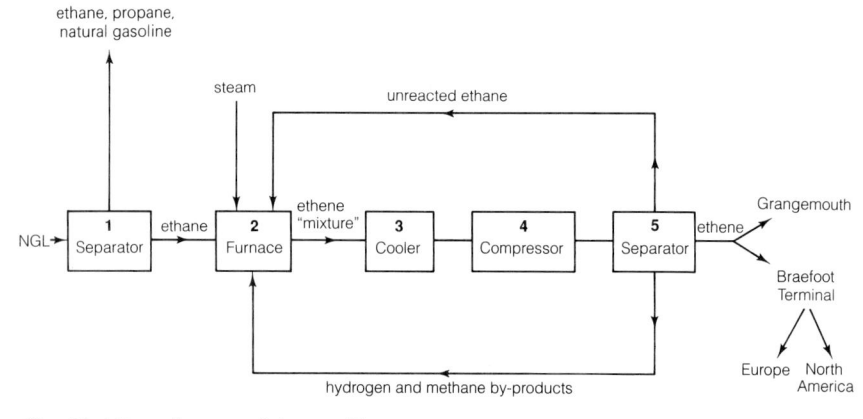

Energy conservation is an important aspect in the running of Mossmorran. The electricity needed for the ethene cracker is greater than that needed by a town of 90 thousand people. The fuel used is more than enough to heat the homes of that town. The plant uses its own by-products as fuel to save money and valuable energy.

Simplifed flow diagram of the cracking process

1 The NGL is separated by fractional distillation.
2 The ethane is mixed with steam and cracked into ethene. Hydrogen and methane are also formed. The steam prevents too many by-products forming.
3 The mixture of gases is cooled by quenching with water.
4 Cracked gas is compressed.
5 The ethene is separated from the other gases by cooling. Unreacted ethane is recycled and cracked. Hydrogen and methane (fuel gas) is used to fuel the furnace.

From Brent to Mossmorran

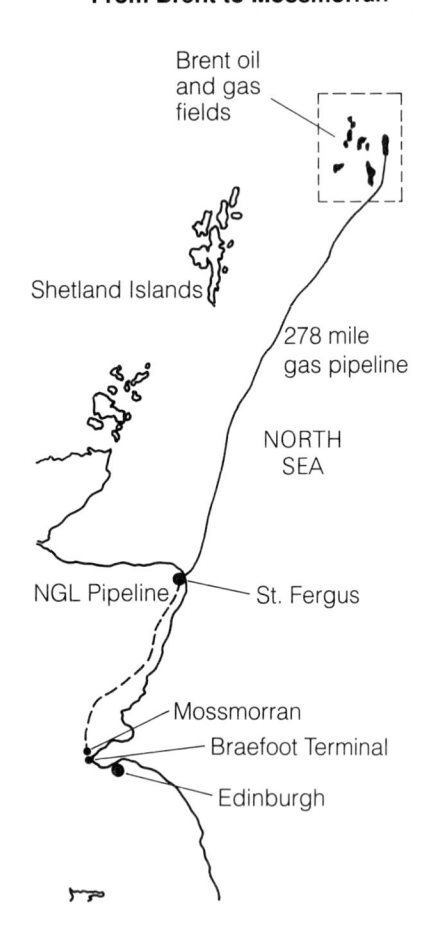

Why Choose Mossmorran?

Shell Expro and Exxon Chemicals decided in the mid-seventies that Mossmorran had a number of advantages over other sites:

- There was enough land for both the NGL separator and the cracker, and still extra land for future development.
- The local authority were keen to encourage companies, because West Fife had a major unemployment problem. There were once eighteen coal mining pits in the area and now they are all closed.
- Fife had good communications by road, rail and air. At Braefoot Bay, the water was deep enough to let tankers anchor and be loaded close to shore. They could transport the ethene easily to North West Europe and North America by sea.

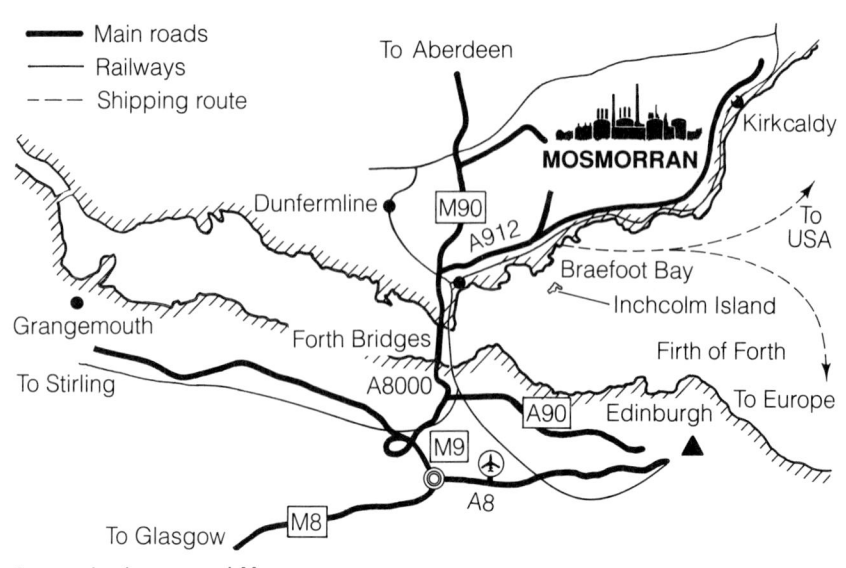

Communications around Mossmorran

Safety

During construction, over 30 million man hours of work was completed without a major accident. Both plants and the marine terminal have built-in safety devices, and the control systems are supervised by computers and highly trained operators. As a back-up, emergency systems are provided to ensure that any failures result in a safe plant shut-down.

Ship loading operations are monitored both on the ships and onshore. Loading can be stopped immediately from either area if necessary. The island of Inchcolm in the Firth of Forth separates the Braefoot Terminal from the main shipping lanes.

The Environment

Close attention has been paid to protecting the environment:
- Waste water is collected in special sewer systems. Any water pumped into the River Forth is carefully checked to make sure it will not harm marine wildlife.
- Waste gases are burned efficiently in a flare to avoid polluting the air.
- Twenty thousand trees have been planted around the site. Eventually they will screen the site so well, it will be difficult to see from land or sea.

The Community

During construction the plants provided greatly needed jobs in the area. Almost half of the labour force came from Fife, and at one stage approximately 750 thousand pounds a week was being paid in wages!

Local businesses benefited immensely during building work. Millions of pounds were spent in Fife on services ranging from lifting gear to office equipment and photography.

At present, 500 people run the ethene cracker and 350 long-term contractors are employed. The chemical companies have also been involved in community projects including sport and education. A Junior Operations Technician Training Scheme (JOTTS) has been set up by Exxon Chemicals and Fife College of Technology – Mossmorran is preparing for future expansion!

Activities

1. Think about where you live and describe the things you think might attract a firm to set up in your area. Also include the things you think might put a firm off your area.
2. Some local residents are worried about a chemical plant being built near them.
   (a) What sort of things do you think they might be concerned about?
   (b) What might you argue would be the benefits of a chemical plant?
3. (a) Collect a box of molecular models. Make a model of ethane and crack it to ethene. Which other molecule is formed?
   (b) Write an equation for the cracking of ethane. Use both molecular and structural formulae.
   (c) How are the by-products of the cracking put to good use?
   (d) What happens to any uncracked ethane?
4. The table below shows the boiling points of the alkane gases separated at Mossmorran:

Alkane	Boiling point (°C)
ethane	−89.0
propane	−42.0
butane	0.5

   Use this information to help you explain how the gases could be separated.

Fuels and Hydrocarbons – Study Questions

1 A molecule of ethane has the formula C_2H_6. Copy and complete the following sentences:
(a) The elements present in ethane are _____ and _____.
(b) The number 2 in the formula means that _____.
(c) The atoms are held together in an ethane molecule by _____. **KU**

2 White spirit (turpentine substitute) is used as a paint thinner. Both saturated and unsaturated hydrocarbons are present in white spirit.
(a) State what is meant by an unsaturated hydrocarbon.
(b) Describe how you would test white spirit to show that it contains unsaturated hydrocarbons. Name the reagent used and give the expected result. **KU**

3 Sulphur compounds are found in some petrols.
(a) Name the poisonous gas which is formed from the sulphur compounds when these petrols are burned.
(b) (i) Name the product formed when this poisonous gas reacts with the water in the atmosphere.
(ii) Give two examples of the effect that this product has on the environment.
(c) Name two other gases which are produced when petrol is burned in a car engine. **KU**

4 The boiling points of some alkanes are given in the table below.

Alkane	Methane	Ethane	Propane	Butane	Hexane
Boiling Point °C	−164	−88	−42	0	69

(a) Draw a bar graph of "Boiling Point/°C" against "Number of Carbon Atoms in the Molecule" for these alkanes.
(b) Use your graph to estimate the boiling point of pentane.
(c) You now have information about six alkanes, including pentane. Name the alkanes which are liquids at −23 °C. **PS**

5 Certain chemicals are added to petrol to prevent "pinking" in car engines. Pinking means that the petrol–air mixture explodes too soon.
It is found that iodine compounds are more effecting in preventing pinking than bromine and chlorine compounds. Compounds of selenium (atomic number 34) and tellurium (atomic number 52) are both more effective than iodine compounds, with tellurium compounds better than selenium compounds.
(a) Using the information above explain why the lead compound, tetraethyl lead, is now added to petrol to prevent pinking. (You may also wish to refer to a periodic table.)
(b) The concentration of tetraethyl lead, $Pb(C_2H_5)_4$, in petrol is $1.5 \times 10^{-4}\,mol\,l^{-1}$. What mass of tetraethyl lead would be dissolved in a car tank containing 40 litres of petrol?
(c) State one problem which results from the addition of tetraethyl lead to petrol. **PS**

6 Copy and complete the following table of information about distillation fractions of crude oil. **KU**

Name of Fraction	Boiling Point Range	Number of Carbon Atoms	Use
Petrol (gasoline)	up to 20 °C	1 to 4	
	20 °C to 230 °C		
	200 °C to 300 °C		fuel for jet aircraft
	280 °C to 360 °C	13 to 25	
Residue	above 350 °C	more than 25	lubricating oil, waxes and bitumen

7 The following reaction shows what happens when an alkene reacts with ozone:

```
  H H H H H
  | | | | |
H-C-C-C=C-C-H  + ozone →
  | |   | |
  H H   H H
```

```
  H H H          H H
  | | |          | |
H-C-C-C=O + O=C-C-H
  | |            | |
  H H            H H
```

(a) Draw the full (extended) structural formulae of the products you would expect from the following reaction.

```
  H H H H H H
  | | | | | |
H-C-C=C-C-C-C-H + ozone → ?
  |   | | | |
  H   H H H H
```

(b) Ozonolysis of another molecule produces only one product. Draw the full (extended) structural formula of an alkene which would react in this way. **PS**

1 Conductors and Insulators

Key Ideas

Substances which conduct electricity are called *conductors*. Because electrons can flow through *metals*, we say metals are *conductors*.

Electrons are unable to flow through some substances and these substances are called *non-conductors*.

All *non-metals*, with the exception of graphite, are *non-conductors*. Some compounds can be made to conduct electricity by melting them or dissolving them in water. These are called *ionic* compounds.

Other compounds cannot be made to conduct, no matter what we do to them. These are called *covalent* compounds.

Electricity power lines

Electricity in Chemistry

ELECTRICITY IN CHEMISTRY

Testing Substances

It is quite easy to find out if a substance will conduct electricity. The circuit shows a simple conduction tester. The unconnected leads from the battery and the bulb are pressed onto the substance. The bulb will light up if it conducts.

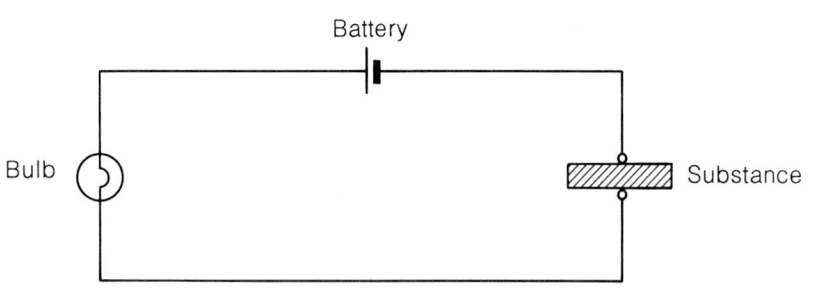

A conduction tester

Substances which cause the bulb to light up are called **conductors**, and those which do not are called **non-conductors** (or **insulators**). The results of testing everyday objects for conduction are shown in table 3.1.

A close look at table 3.1 shows that all the conductors are made of **metal**, except the pencil "lead" which is made of **graphite**, a form of **carbon**. All the non-conductors are made of non-metals.

Table 3.1

Conductors	Non-conductors
Aluminium pot	Rubber tube
Brass key	Plastic handle
Pencil graphite	Wooden spoon
Copper coin	Paper page
Steel ruler	Glass window

Table 3.2

Conductors	Non-conductors
Magnesium	Sulphur
Iron	Silicon
Copper	Iodine
Zinc	Bromine
Carbon (graphite)	Oxygen
Aluminium	Nitrogen

Table 3.2 shows the results obtained when **elements** are tested for conduction. Again we find that **metals conduct** and **non-metals** do **not conduct**. The only exception to this is **graphite**.

Have a look at a piece of electric cable, or at the cable diagram. The electricity travels through the wires which are made of metal, usually copper. If you were to touch the bare metal while an electric current was flowing through it, you would get an electric shock. Mains electricity used at home might even kill you!

To protect you from electric shocks the wire is covered with a non-conducting material such as a plastic. This is called the **insulation**.

The large metal cables which carry electricity around the country at very high voltages use glass or ceramic material as insulators.

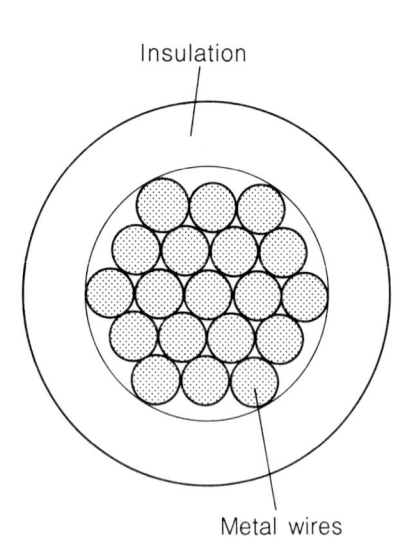

Section through a cable

Why do Metals Conduct?

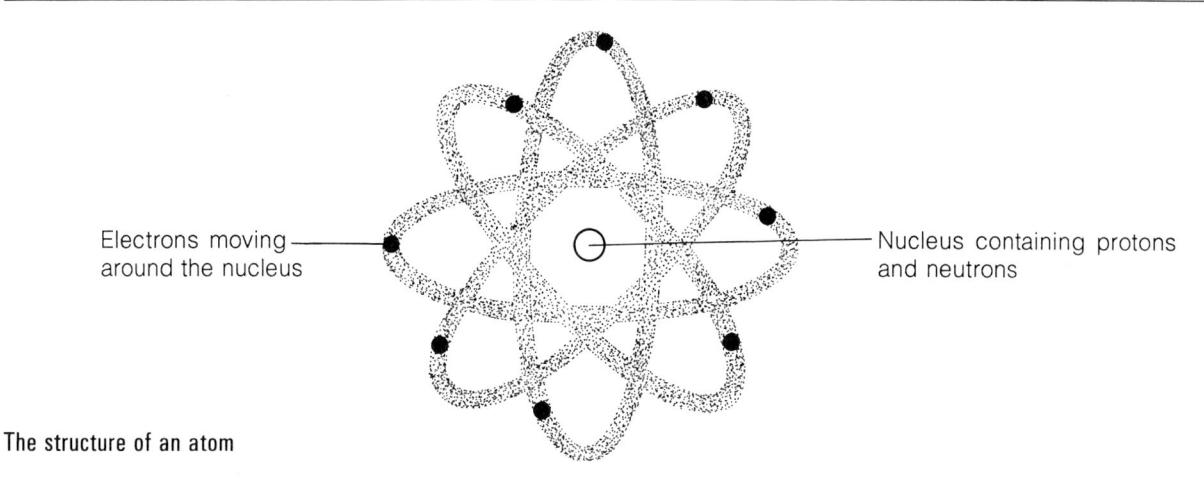

The structure of an atom

We know that an atom of any element is made up of a central nucleus, containing positive protons and neutral neutrons, with negative electrons moving around the nucleus.

In a metal, the atoms are packed so close together that the outer electron levels of neighbouring atoms almost touch each other.

Think about one metal atom. Its outer electrons are in contact with a number of other metal atoms. As a result, these outer electrons can easily drift from one atom to another. At any one time a number of electrons will be drifting around "loose" in the metal.

Over the whole area of a metal, the number of electrons will stay the same, and the metal will still be electrically neutral. When the leads from our conduction tester are connected to a metal, electrons pass from the negative lead of the battery into the metal. The same number of outer electrons, belonging to the metal, are then passed back to the positive lead of the battery.

As long as the leads are connected to the metal there will be a flow of electrons from the negative lead of the battery to the positive. This flow of **electrons** (charged particles) through a **conductor** is called an **electric current**. The metal is unaffected by the passage of electricity.

Some metals are better at conducting electricity than others. Copper is a good electrical conductor. It is relatively cheap to produce, so most electrical cables are made of copper wire. Gold is an even better conductor of electricity, but is very expensive. Only space satellites and some micro-electronic circuits use gold electrical connections.

Non-metal elements (with the exception of graphite) do not have these "free" electrons and so they do not conduct electricity.

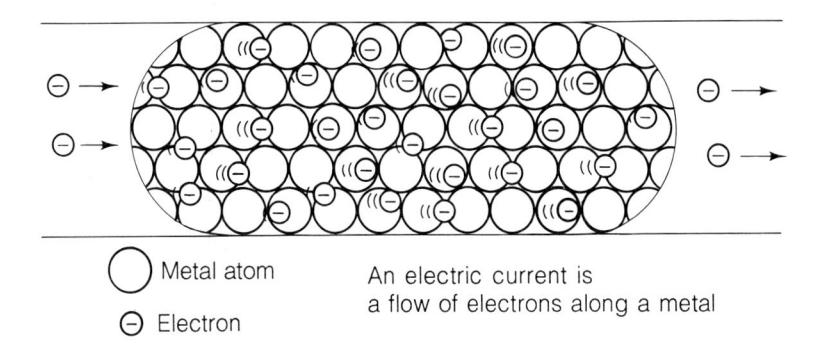

Testing Compounds

If we use our conduction tester on some **solid compounds**, then none of them conduct, even if they contain metal elements. However, if we heat these compounds until they **melt** then those which contain **metals** start to conduct.

We also find that if we dissolve metal compounds in water, the **solutions** formed are able to conduct electricity. Compounds containing only **non-metals** do not conduct, even when molten or in solution.

Table 3.3 (page 74) gives examples of compounds which can be made to conduct, and those which cannot.

Conduction in Melts

When molten lead bromide is tested, using the apparatus shown, the bulb lights up. If the melt is allowed to cool down the bulb dims and finally goes out when the melt has turned solid. This tells us that lead bromide conducts when molten but not when solid.

An electric current is a flow of electrons along a metal

Conduction through a metal

74 ELECTRICITY IN CHEMISTRY

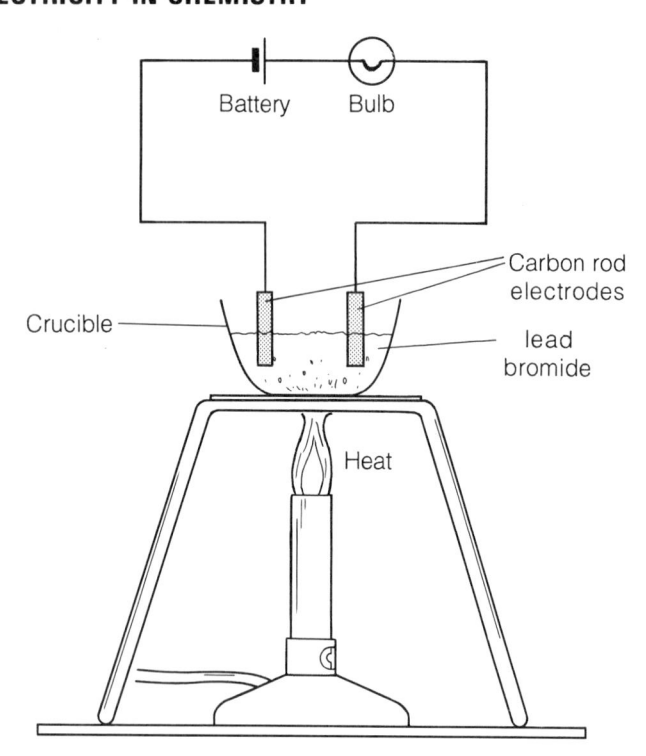

Testing a molten metal compound for conduction

What do we see at the electrodes?

If we examine the electrodes closely we see molten lead metal forming at the negative electrode and brown bromine vapour at the positive electrode. This tells us that the passage of electricity is **chemically changing** the molten ionic compound. This is called **electrolysis**. The positive lead ions are changing into neutral lead atoms and the negative bromide ions into neutral bromine molecules.

When we looked at metallic conduction, we saw that an electric current was a flow of charged particles. This must mean that in a solid compound no charged particles are able to move.

However if a compound conducts when it is molten, some charged particles must be present which could not move in the solid, but can do so when molten. These **charged particles** are called **ions**. Ions are atoms which have become charged (you will see how this happens in the next section).

Metals generally form **positive** ions. **Non-metals** generally form **negative** ions.

In solid lead bromide, all the lead and bromide ions are locked up in a crystal structure, called the **crystal lattice**, and cannot move. However, if we melt the compound, the crystal lattice breaks down and the lead and bromide ions become free to move. As the lead ions are attracted to the negative electrode, and the bromide ions to the positive electrode, we have a flow of charged particles (this time ions). Hence, the **melt conducts and the bulb lights up**.

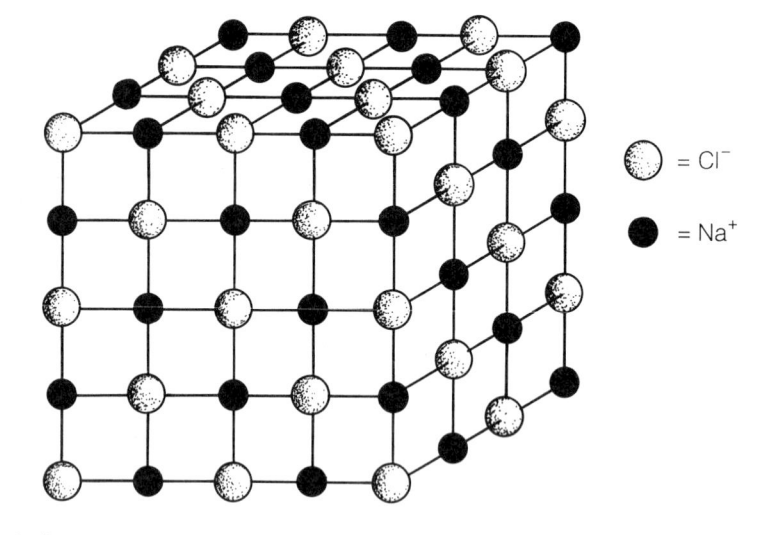

An ionic crystal lattice

○ = Cl⁻
● = Na⁺

Table 3.3

CONDUCTORS			NON-CONDUCTORS		
Substance	State	Formula	Substance	State	Formula
Lead bromide	molten	$PbBr_2$	Sucrose	molten	$C_{12}H_{22}O_{11}$
Potassium iodide	molten	KI	Glucose	molten	$C_6H_{12}O_6$
Aluminium oxide	molten	Al_2O_3	Paraffin wax	molten	$C_{26}H_{54}$
Copper sulphate	solution	$CuSO_4$	Methanol	solution	CH_3OH
Sodium chloride	solution	NaCl	Ethanol	solution	C_2H_5OH
Silver nitrate	solution	$AgNO_3$	Hexanol	solution	$C_6H_{13}OH$

ELECTRICITY IN CHEMISTRY

Conduction in Solutions

When a solid ionic compound dissolves in water, the ions become free to move and it can conduct electricity. Again, the positive ions are attracted to the negative electrode and the negative ions to the positive electrode.

The flow of charged particles, in this case ions, is an electric current, so the solution conducts and the bulb lights up.

As the solid ionic compound does not conduct electricity, dissolving the solid in water must break down the ionic crystal lattice which is holding the ions in fixed positions.

Examination of the electrodes during the electrolysis of copper chloride solution shows brown copper deposits at the negative electrode and chlorine gas at the positive electrode. The **copper ions** must therefore be **positive**, as they are attracted to the negative electrode. The **chloride ions** must be **negative**, as they are attracted to the positive electrode.

The passage of electricity through the solution chemically changes it. A **chemical reaction** must therefore be taking place.

All solutions of ionic compounds will conduct electricity, although some are better conductors than others. Any liquid or solution which conducts electricity is called an **electrolyte**. Note that not all ionic compounds are soluble in water.

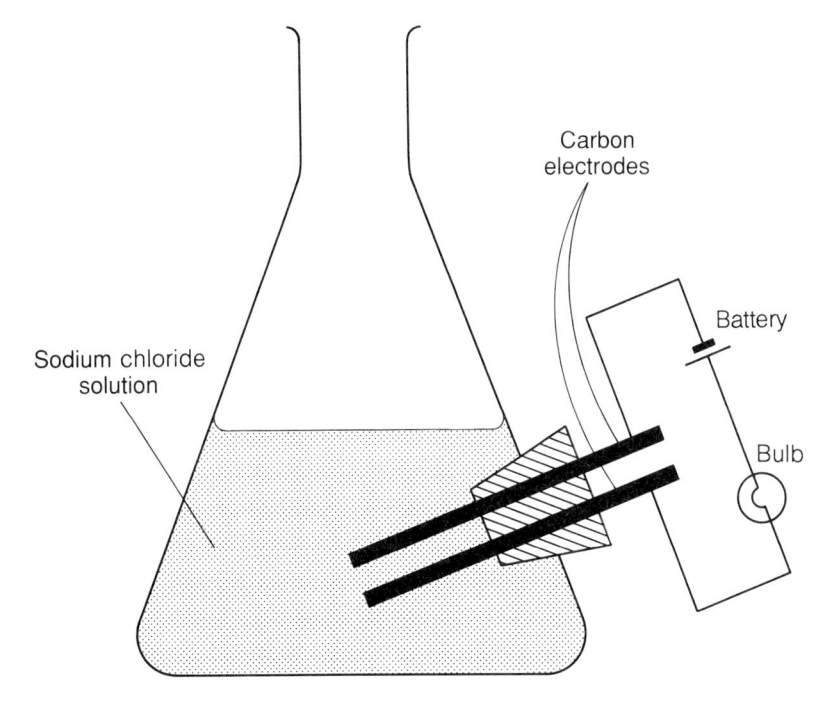

Non-conducting Compounds

The non-conducting compounds in the conductivity table 3.3 will not conduct electricity, whether they are solid, liquid or dissolved in water. These compounds contain only **non-metal** elements and form **covalent** compounds. Covalent compounds have no ions or free electrons and so are unable to conduct electricity.

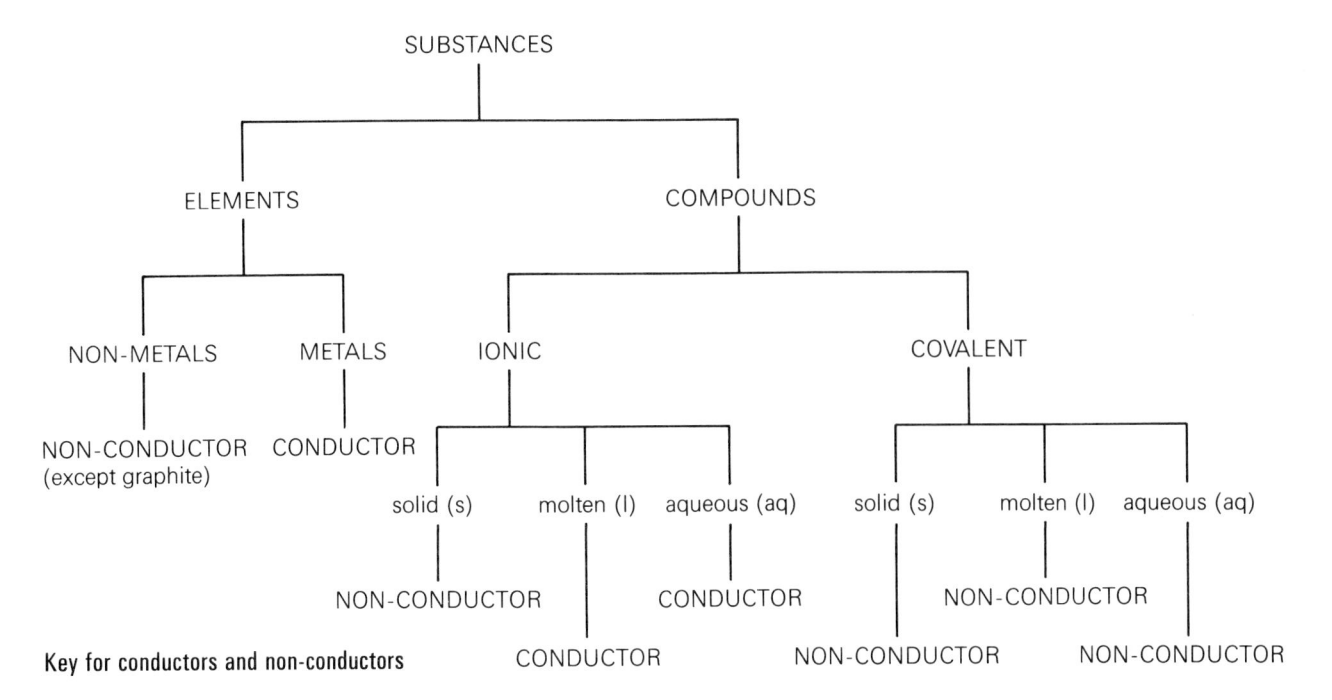

Testing Solutions

Key for conductors and non-conductors

```
                        SUBSTANCES
                       /          \
                 ELEMENTS        COMPOUNDS
                 /      \         /       \
          NON-METALS  METALS   IONIC      COVALENT
              |         |     / | \       / | \
         NON-CONDUCTOR CONDUCTOR solid(s) molten(l) aqueous(aq)  solid(s) molten(l) aqueous(aq)
         (except graphite)          |       |         |            |        |         |
                              NON-CONDUCTOR CONDUCTOR CONDUCTOR NON-CONDUCTOR NON-CONDUCTOR NON-CONDUCTOR
```

76 ELECTRICITY IN CHEMISTRY

Reactions at the Electrodes

As we have seen, the passage of electricity through a molten or aqueous ionic compound, chemically changes the compound.

Molten Lead Bromide

When we pass a current through molten lead bromide, molten lead forms at the negative electrode, and reddish-brown bromine gas is given off at the positive electrode.

What happens at the electrodes?

The positive lead ions move to the negative electrode, where they gain two electrons from the electrode and change from lead **ions** to lead **atoms**. We can write this as an equation:

$$Pb^{2+}(l) + 2e \rightarrow Pb(l)$$

This is called an **ion-electron equation**. The symbol "e" represents an electron.

The negative bromide ions move to the positive electrode. Each bromide ion gives up one electron to the positive electrode and changes into a bromine atom. Two bromine atoms then combine to form a bromine molecule. The overall ion-electron equation for this reaction is:

$$2Br^-(l) \rightarrow Br_2(g) + 2e$$

The two elements present in lead bromide are lead and bromine. The electric current has broken the compound down into its elements. This process is known as **electrolysis**.

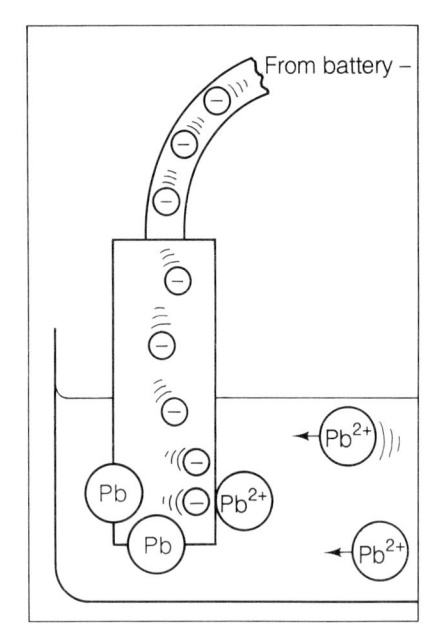

Lead ions at the negative electrode

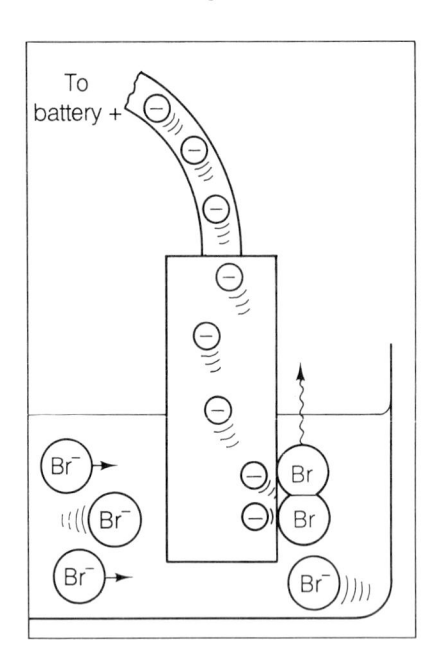

Bromide ions at the positive electrode

Copper Chloride Solution

When an electric current is passed through an aqueous solution of copper chloride, solid copper metal forms at the negative electrode, and bubbles of gas can be seen at the positive electrode. The bleach smell tells us it is chlorine gas.

What happens at the electrodes?

The positive copper ions move to the negative electrode. Here, each copper **ion** gains two electrons and changes into a copper **atom**:

$$Cu^{2+}(aq) + 2e \rightarrow Cu(s)$$

The negative chloride ions move to the positive electrode. Each ion gives away an electron to the positive electrode and changes into a chlorine atom. Two chlorine atoms then combine to form a chlorine molecule:

$$2Cl^-(aq) \rightarrow Cl_2(g) + 2e$$

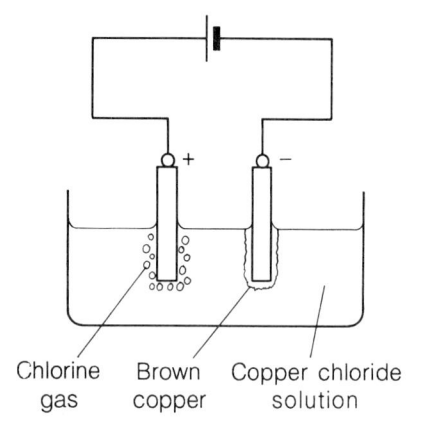

Electrolysis of copper chloride solution

Electrolysis only occurs with ionic compounds which are molten or dissolved in water because these contain free **ions**. The ions are attracted to the electrodes.

A **direct current (d.c.)** must be used if the products of electrolysis are to be identified. With a direct current, one electrode is always positively charged and will always attract negative ions, and the other always negatively charged, always attracting positive ions.

Using Electrolysis in the Manufacture of Calcium

Calcium metal is very reactive. It does not exist in its pure form in the Earth's crust, but it is present in compounds. Calcium is very difficult to extract from these compounds.

To obtain calcium metal, a mixture of calcium chloride and a little calcium fluoride is melted at about 650 °C, in a graphite crucible. The graphite crucible is made the positive electrode (the **anode**). A water cooled negative iron electrode (the **cathode**) is lowered into the melt.

When the iron cathode is just touching the melt (the electrolyte), the electricity supply is switched on. Calcium forms at the cathode and is slowly raised so that a stick of calcium is produced:

$$Ca^{2+}(l) + 2e \rightarrow Ca(s)$$

Chlorine gas is given off at the anode:

$$2Cl^-(l) \rightarrow Cl_2(g) + 2e$$

The crude calcium is further purified by distillation in a vacuum.

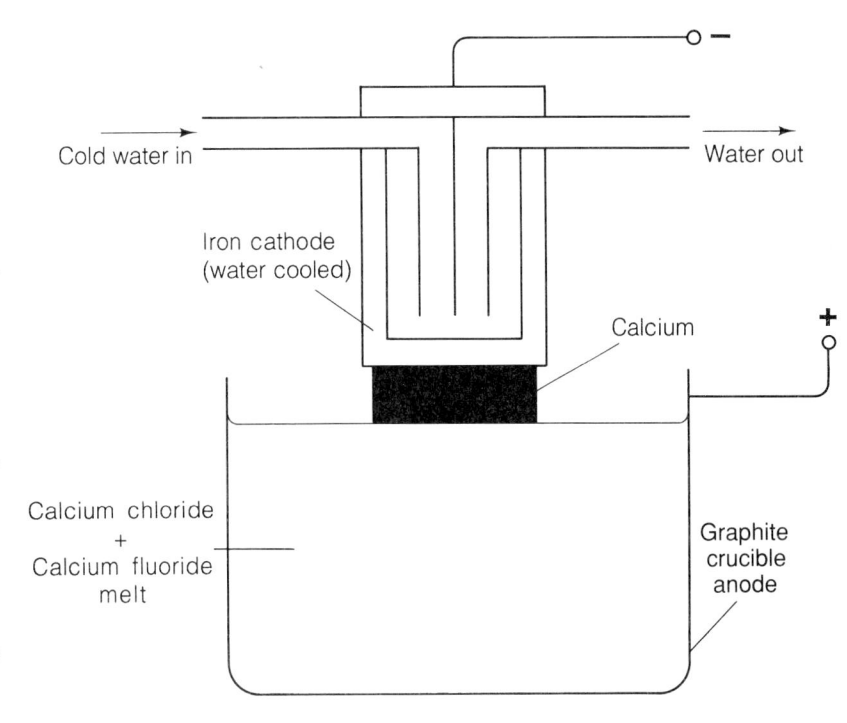

Extraction of calcium

Activities

○ 1 Use a periodic table to help you decide whether the following substances are ionic or covalent:
Potassium bromide (KBr)
Calcium chloride (CaCl$_2$)
Nitrogen iodide (NI$_3$)
Water (H$_2$O)
Aluminium fluoride (AlF$_3$)
Tetrachloromethane (CCl$_4$)

○ 2 Both copper wire and a solution of copper chloride conduct electricity, but they do so in different ways. Explain how conduction takes place in both these substances.

○ 3 (a) Why do solid ionic compounds not conduct electricity?
(b) Give two conditions under which ionic substances will conduct, and explain in each case what has happened to allow conduction to take place.

● 4 (a) Predict the products that would be formed at the positive electrode (the anode) and the negative electrode (the cathode) when an electric current is passed through the following solutions:
(i) Silver bromide Ag$^+$Br$^-$(aq)
(ii) Mercury chloride Hg$^+$Cl$^-$(aq)
(iii) Hydrogen iodide H$^+$I$^-$(aq)
(iv) Glucose C$_6$H$_{12}$O$_6$(aq)
(b) Write down ion-electron equations to show the reaction at each electrode.

● 5 When an electric current is passed through a solution of potassium bromide, a reddish-brown colour appears at one of the electrodes.
(a) At which electrode does the colour appear? Write out the electron half equation for the reaction at this electrode.
(b) What would happen if the terminals on the power supply were switched over?

2 Formation of Bonds

Key Ideas

Atoms can combine in a number of ways to form *compounds*. *Ionic* bonds form when one atom *transfers electrons* to another atom. *Covalent* bonds form when two or more atoms *share* their outer electrons.

Compounds can be *soluble* or *insoluble* in water. Some compounds may be soluble in other *solvents*.

Table 3.4

Name	Formula	State at 20 °C	Melting point/°C	Boiling point/°C
Hydrogen	H_2	gas	−259	−252
Oxygen	O_2	gas	−218	−183
Methane	CH_4	gas	−182	−161
Chlorine	Cl_2	gas	−101	−35
Ammonia	NH_3	gas	−77	−33
Ethanol	C_2H_5OH	liquid	−117	79
Water	H_2O	liquid	0	100
Iodine	I_2	solid	114	184
Silicon	Si	solid	1407	2387
Diamond	C	solid	3547	5827

Why React?

Nearly all atoms will react with other atoms to form compounds. The noble gases (group 0) are exceptions. These elements are very unreactive.

A look at the electron arrangement of the noble gases shows that, with the exception of helium, they all have a **full** outer energy level of eight electrons. Helium also has a full outer energy level, but it only contains two electrons. Both these are very stable arrangements. Atoms are less stable (more reactive) if they have a less than full outer energy level. Atoms react with other atoms in order to form full outer energy levels. Electrons can be **shared** between atoms or **transferred** from one atom to another.

Covalent Bonds

Covalent bonds form when two or more non-metal atoms share their outer electrons. This sharing of electrons allows each atom to obtain a full outer electron level, similar to the nearest noble gas. A **shared pair** of electrons is called a **covalent bond**. A covalent bond is very strong.

When a few atoms are joined, a small molecule is formed. Small molecules are usually liquids or gases at room temperature. Water (H_2O) and methane (CH_4) are examples of small covalent molecules. If we find a substance is a liquid or a gas at room temperature we can predict that it is a covalent substance, as most ionic substances are solid at that temperature.

When this sharing of electrons occurs between a very large number of atoms, a **giant covalent network structure** is formed which will be **solid** at room temperature. Carbon in the form of diamond, and sand (silicon dioxide) are examples of hard, high melting point, giant covalent network solids. Table 3.4 shows some common covalent substances.

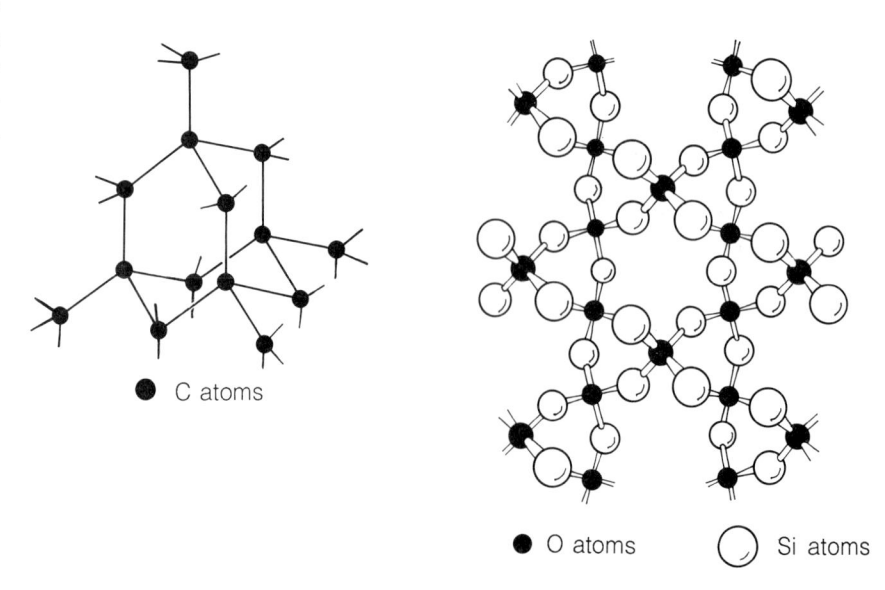

● C atoms

● O atoms   ○ Si atoms

The structure of diamond and silicon dioxide (giant covalent network solids)

Ionic Bonds

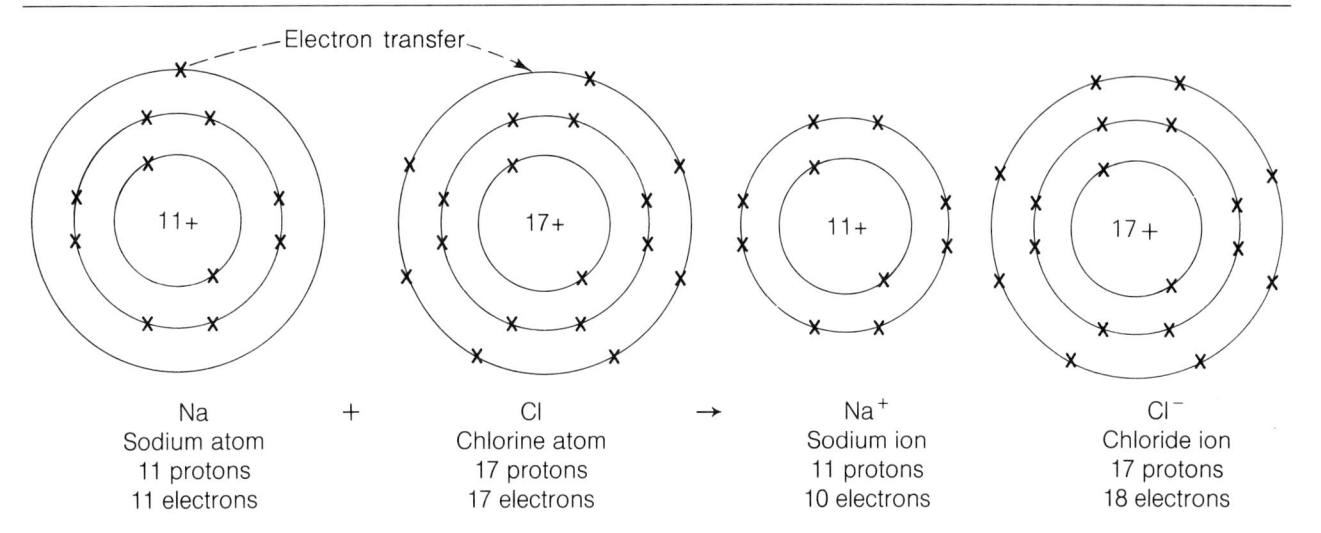

Na — Sodium atom — 11 protons, 11 electrons
Cl — Chlorine atom — 17 protons, 17 electrons
Na⁺ — Sodium ion — 11 protons, 10 electrons
Cl⁻ — Chloride ion — 17 protons, 18 electrons

Ionic bonds are usually formed between metal and non-metal atoms. Some ionic compounds contain non-metals atoms only, e.g., ammonium compounds such as ammonium chloride (NH_4Cl).

When a metal and non-metal react, the metal atom transfers its outermost electrons to the non-metal atom. In doing so the metal loses all its outer electrons, and is left only with completely filled electron levels.

In the neutral metal atom, the number of electrons equals the number of protons. Having lost some electrons, it now has more protons than electrons, and so it is **positively** charged.

The non-metal atom accepts electrons until its outer energy level is full. It then has more electrons than protons and it is **negatively** charged.

The two oppositely charged ions are **strongly** attracted to each other. This is known as **electrostatic** attraction. An **ionic** compound consists of a large number of these positive and negative ions held together in a regular network called the **crystal lattice**.

Ionic compounds form solid crystal lattices at room temperature, and generally have high melting points. Table 3.5 shows the melting points (and boiling points) of some ionic compounds.

Each ion is fixed in place within the lattice and cannot move. If a soluble ionic compound is mixed with water, the water dissolves the crystal lattice, releasing the ions into solution. These ions are then able to move freely around in the solution.

Table 3.5

Name of compound	mp/°C	bp/°C
Barium chloride	963	1560
Calcium oxide	2580	2850
Lithium bromide	547	1265
Magnesium chloride	708	1412
Potassium iodide	686	1330
Sodium chloride	801	1413

Sodium metal consists of atoms and is silver/grey in colour. However many sodium compounds are colourless. This tells us that sodium atoms are not present in the compound, and is explained by the fact that colourless sodium ions are formed.

Similarly, copper metal is brown but many copper compounds are blue. This suggests that copper ions are blue.

80 ELECTRICITY IN CHEMISTRY

Table 3.6

Name	Colour	Name	Colour	Name	Colour
sodium sulphate	colourless	sodium chloride	colourless	sodium nitrate	colourless
calcium sulphate	colourless	calcium chloride	colourless	calcium nitrate	colourless
copper(II) sulphate	blue	copper(II) chloride	blue	copper(II) nitrate	blue
nickel sulphate	green	nickel chloride	green	nickel nitrate	green
cobalt sulphate	pink	cobalt chloride	pink	cobalt nitrate	pink
sodium dichromate	orange	calcium dichromate	orange	lithium dichromate	orange
sodium permanganate	purple	calcium permanganate	purple	cobalt permanganate	purple

If we look at the colours of ionic compounds in table 3.6, we can predict that sodium, calcium, sulphate, chloride and nitrate ions are all colourless, but that copper ions are blue, cobalt ions pink, dichromate ions orange and permanganate ions purple.

Movement of Coloured Ions

A solution of copper dichromate is a muddy green colour. If you put some of this solution into a U-shaped tube and pass an electric current through it, you see a blue colour rising towards the negative electrode.

This is explained by the fact that blue copper ions have a positive charge and are attracted to the negative electrode. The orange dichromate ions are attracted to the positive electrode and so must have a negative charge. Similar experiments provide more evidence for ions and their charges.

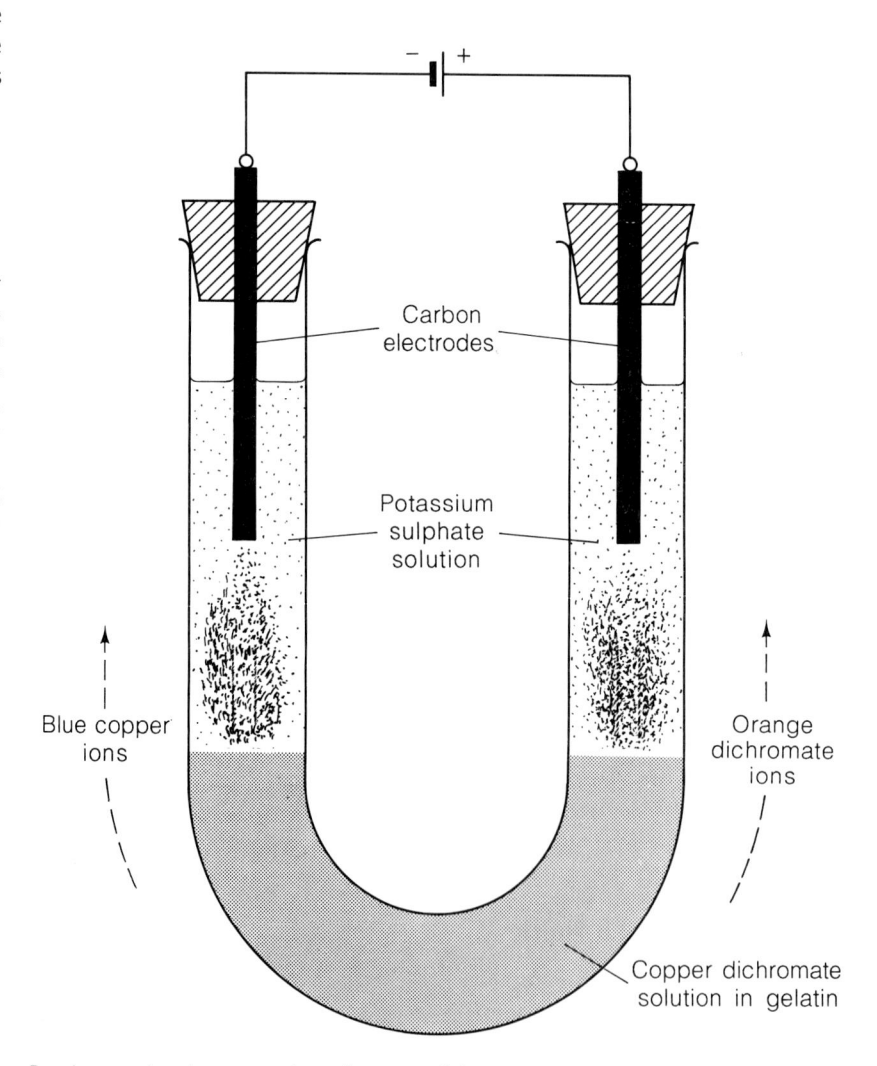

Passing an electric current through copper dichromate solution

Dissolving Substances

1. Ionic Substances

Many ionic substances, such as salt (sodium chloride) and copper sulphate, are **soluble** in water. Some **dissolve** to give clear, colourless solutions, others give coloured solutions. Ionic compounds do not all have the same **solubility**. This can easily be seen in the graph, which shows the solubility of two salts in water, over a range of temperatures.

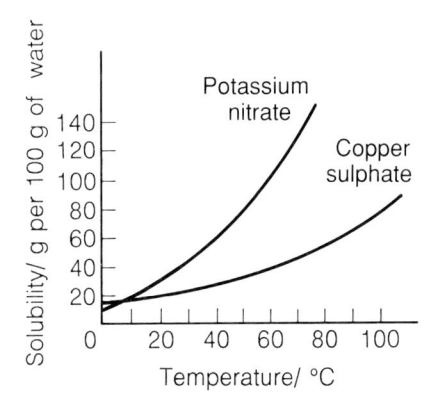

Table 3.7

	carbonate	chloride	hydroxide	nitrate	sulphate
calcium	insol.	vsol.	sol.	vsol.	sol.
copper	insol.	vsol.	insol.	vsol.	vsol.
iron	insol.	vsol.	insol.	vsol.	vsol.
lead	insol.	sol.	insol.	vsol.	insol.
magnesium	insol.	vsol.	insol.	vsol.	vsol.
potassium	vsol.	vsol.	vsol.	vsol.	vsol.
silver	insol.	insol.	insol.	vsol.	sol.
sodium	vsol.	vsol.	vsol.	vsol.	vsol.

insol = insoluble; sol = soluble; vsol = very soluble

There is a change in temperature as an ionic substance dissolves in water. This tells us that a chemical reaction is taking place between the solute and the solvent. This reaction involves the breaking down of the crystal lattice which holds the ions together.

Solubility of copper sulphate and potassium nitrate in water

2. Covalent Substances

Some covalent substances will dissolve in water, for example sugar ($C_{12}H_{22}O_{11}$) and ethanoic acid (CH_3COOH). It is the ability water has to dissolve substances that makes it such an important chemical. It is essential to life on our planet as all living things use **aqueous** (water) solutions in their cells to make them function and keep them alive. When space probes land on other planets, they are often programmed to test for the presence of water. This tells us whether life, as we know it, could exist on the planet.

It is very important to state the temperature of the water when you are describing solubilities, as most substances become more soluble at higher temperatures.

Copper oxide is an example of an ionic compound which is **insoluble** in water.

The dissolving process is speeded up by using a hot solvent and by stirring. When no more solid dissolves we say the solution is **saturated**. The solid being dissolved is called the **solute**, the water is the **solvent** and the final mixture is the **solution**.

solute + solvent → solution

e.g., salt + water → salt solution
varnish + acetone → nail varnish

Table 3.7 shows the solubility of some common ionic compounds.

Consumer products which use covalent solvents

82 ELECTRICITY IN CHEMISTRY

Many covalent solids will also dissolve in other covalent liquids (ionic substances rarely dissolve in covalent solvents). When you spill paint, a covalent substance, you use turpentine, a covalent solvent, to clean it up. You may be wearing nail varnish which is a covalent solid. This will dissolve in acetone (CH_3COCH_3), a covalent liquid.

You might use correcting fluid to cover up your spelling mistakes. Some correcting fluids contain a covalent solvent called trichloroethane.

Many glues use a covalent ester as a solvent. These esters are fruity, sweet smelling compounds.

Most covalent solvents are highly flammable (they catch fire easily), evaporate quickly giving off a characteristic smell and can irritate the skin. Bottles containing such solvents carry warning labels telling you to take care!

Harmful   Flammable

Warning symbols for solvents

Solvent Abuse

If you inhale excessive quantities of these irritant covalent solvents it may permanently affect your liver, kidneys and lungs.

If inhaled, solvents can affect your thinking and you may become "high", believing that nothing can harm you. Some people have died because they thought they could fly, or that moving vehicles would not hurt them, after sniffing these solvents.

Other people died because solvent sniffing left them unconscious, and when they became sick, they choked on their own vomit.

Solvent abuse has become such a serious problem that hardware stores have removed substances containing these solvents from their shelves. They will only sell it to people over eighteen years of age. Manufacturers are always looking for less toxic solvents for their products, but this is not always possible with the newer materials available today.

Soaps and Detergents

The covalent and ionic bonds of some molecules can make them useful. Soaps and soapless detergents (e.g., washing-up liquid) can clean dirty hands and clothes because of the nature of the bonding in their molecules.

When we sweat, an oily film covers our skin, and soon gets onto our clothes. Particles of dirt then stick to this oily layer. We need to wash our skin and clothes to remove the dirt and oil.

Unfortunately, oil and water do not mix, and so washing with water alone does not remove the dirt. Soap overcomes this problem.

Manufacture of Soap

Soap is made by heating a mixture of **fats** and **oils** with an **alkali** such as sodium hydroxide solution. The process is called **saponification**.

A sodium chloride solution, called **brine**, is then added to the mixture and the solid soap forms a crust on the surface of the solution. After further purification, and perhaps the addition of colour and perfume, the soap is ready for use.

A soap "molecule" consists of a long hydrocarbon chain, which is **covalent**, and an **ionic** head:

covalent "tail"   ionic "head"

This is sometimes represented as:

Na^+

ELECTRICITY IN CHEMISTRY

The hydrocarbon chain on the negative ion is so long that the molecule behaves as if one end were ionic and the other end covalent. The **covalent** "tail" is soluble in covalent substances like oil, grease and fats, but is **insoluble** in **water**. The **ionic** "head" is soluble in **water**.

How the Soap Works

When soap is added to an oil/water mixture, it dissolves. The "tail" of the soap molecule dissolves in the oil, and the ionic "head" dissolves in the water.

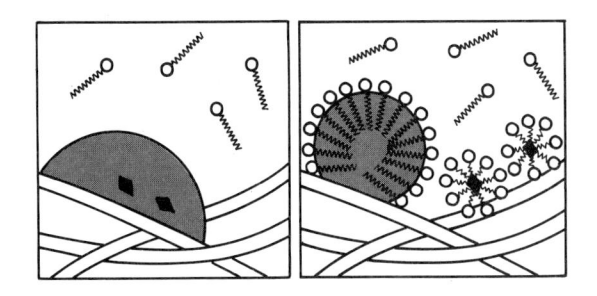

Soap dissolved in an oil/water mixture

If the mixture is shaken, the oil breaks up into small droplets. If these oil droplets try to join together again, the negatively charged "heads" of the soap molecules sticking out of the oil droplets repel one another. The soap has acted as an emulsifying agent, keeping the oil droplets apart and forming an **emulsion**.

The oil can now be easily rinsed away, leaving the article clean.

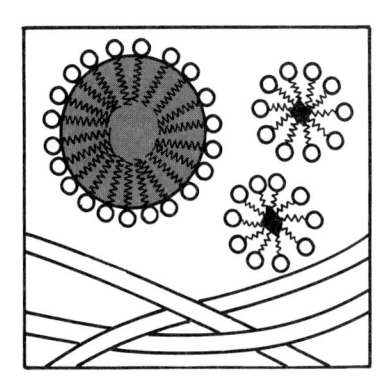

Soapless Detergents

In very chalky areas of the country, the water supply contains a lot of calcium and magnesium ions which dissolve from the chalk as the rain soaks through it. This is called **"hard" water**.

If we use soap with "hard" water, the calcium and magnesium ions react with the ionic "heads" of the soap ions to form an insoluble **scum**, which floats to the top of the water. The soap can no longer work as an emulsifying agent because its ions have been removed from solution.

To overcome this problem, scientists invented a soapless detergent which will not react with the calcium and magnesium ions in hard water.

Most detergents are made from crude oil chemicals. The kerosine fraction is reacted with another hydrocarbon, followed by treatment with sulphuric acid, and finally sodium hydroxide. This produces a molecule similar to soap:

A soapless detergent cleans in the same way as soap.

Protecting the Environment

Soapless detergents used to cause environmental problems. The detergent molecules were not digested by bacteria. When the waste water (**effluent**) from washing machines was discharged into rivers or sewage works, it destroyed essential bacteria, which normally breaks down sewage into harmless material.

Most modern detergents are **biodegradable**. This means they can be broken down by naturally occurring bacteria and are less damaging to the rivers.

Manufacturers of detergents have different "recipes" for different parts of the country, so that the detergent will work efficiently with each regional water supply. In "hard" water areas, like the south of England, phosphates are sometimes added to the detergent to soften the water. Unfortunately, phosphates cause **algae** to grow rapidly in rivers and lakes. Soon a green mat of algae completely covers the surface of the water. The plants under the water do not receive enough sunlight to grow, so they stop producing oxygen and eventually die. Fish then die through lack of oxygen. It is thought that

ELECTRICITY IN CHEMISTRY

phosphates from detergents may play only a minor role in this pollution and that phosphates and nitrates from other sources, like fertilisers, do most damage.

Many washing powders designed for washing machines now contain a mixture of soapless detergents and **enzymes**. The enzymes are able to digest protein stains caused by blood and sweat, and help get the clothes even cleaner. The powders are sold as **biological** washing powders.

When you are doing odd jobs around the house your hands may become very dirty with grease or paint and the soap you use does not clean them properly. If you mix some washing-up liquid with some white spirit (used to thin paint), the mixture turns into a jelly which makes a very effective hand cleaner.

The white spirit is a covalent solvent which easily dissolves the grease or paint. The washing-up liquid emulsifies the solution so it is easily rinsed away.

Activities

1. (a) Name the type of bonding in the following compounds:
   lithium iodide; nitrogen dioxide; magnesium phosphide; hydrogen chloride; aluminium nitride; carbon hydride; barium phosphide; silicon nitride; potassium iodide.
   (b) Describe how you could test these compounds to show the type of bonding present.

2. Look at the labels on some paint tins and glues and see if you can find the name of some covalent solvents.

3. Use the solubility table 3.7 to find out which of the following substances are soluble in water:
   silver chloride; lead sulphate; calcium carbonate; sodium nitrate.

4. Use the solubility table 3.7 to find out which metallic substance has the greatest number of soluble compounds. You should be able to make up a set of rules about solubility from a study of the solubility table.

5. You are examining a series of compounds. By observation of their appearance only, how could you tell which might be ionic and which might be covalent?

6. Explain, with diagrams, how a soapless detergent works to remove an oil stain.

7. The table shows the properties of four substances A, B, C and D.

Substance	Melting Point	Electrical Conductivity solid	molten	solution
A	low	x	x	x
B	high	x	x	x
C	high	x	✓	✓
D	high	✓	✓	insol.

✓ = conductor; x = non-conductor; insol = insoluble

(a) Using the information in the table, state whether the substances A, B, C and D are simple covalent, giant covalent network, metallic or ionic.
(b) C is a compound formed between a group two element and a group six element. Choose and element from these two groups and, by means of a diagram, show what happens to the outer electrons when the bond is formed.
(c) Explain why C is a good conductor when it is molten or in solution, but a non-conductor when it is solid.

3 Ionic Formulae and Equations

Key Ideas

Metal elements form *positive* ions. Non-metal elements form *negative* ions.
Using the number of charges on an ion we can work out the formulae of ionic compounds.
Some ions contain more than one atom. These are *complex* ions.
Formulae and equations can be written using complex ions.

Ion Charges

Because an ionic compound is electrically neutral, the number of positive charges must be equal to the number of negative charges. To find the charge on an ion we must look at the position of the elements in the periodic table.

All the elements are arranged in vertical **groups**. Each element in a vertical group has the same number of outer electrons, and so each will form ions with identical charge.

Elements in groups one, two and three always lose electrons to form positively charged ions. Elements in groups five, six and seven gain electrons to form negatively charged ions.

Elements from groups four and zero rarely form ions.

Look at table 3.8. The amount of charge on a metal ion is the same as its group number.

The value of the charge on a non-metal ion of groups five, six and seven can be worked out by subtracting the group number from eight. For example, the element nitrogen is in group five. The nitride ion will therefore have a charge of $(8-5)=3$ (N^{3-}).

The oxide ion (group six) will have a charge of $(8-6)=2$ (O^{2-}).

The fluoride ion (group seven) will have a charge of $(8-7)=1$ (F^-).

Table 3.8

Group	1	2	3
POSITIVE IONS	Lithium Li^+ Sodium Na^+ Potassium K^+	Magnesium Mg^{2+} Calcium Ca^{2+} Barium Ba^{2+}	Aluminium Al^{3+}
Group	5	6	7
NEGATIVE IONS	Phosphide P^{3-} Nitride N^{3-}	Oxide O^{2-} Sulphide S^{2-}	Fluoride F^- Chloride Cl^- Bromide Br^- Iodide I^-

These charge numbers are the same as the valency numbers previously described in Reactions and the Atom. When writing ionic formulae we must make sure that the total number of positive and negative charges cancel one another out.

Let us examine some examples:

Sodium chloride

Sodium ions have a single positive charge, and chloride ions a single negative charge:

$$Na^+ \quad Cl^-$$

The two charges cancel one another out and so the formula is simply **NaCl**.

Magnesium oxide

The magnesium ion has a double positive charge and the oxygen ion a double negative charge:

$$Mg^{2+} \quad O^{2-}$$

The two charges cancel out and so the formula is **MgO**.

86 ELECTRICITY IN CHEMISTRY

Magnesium chloride

$$Mg^{2+} \quad Cl^-$$

This time only one of the positive charges on the magnesium ion is cancelled by the non-metal ion charge. To balance the charge on the magnesium ion, another chloride ion is required:

$$Mg^{2+} \quad Cl^- \quad Cl^-$$

The charges cancel and the formula is

$$MgCl_2$$

ONE MAGNESIUM ION — TWO CHLORIDE IONS

Aluminium oxide

Aluminium forms a triple positive charged ion and oxygen a double negative ion. To completely cancel the charges on both ions we must have **two** aluminium ions and **three** oxide ions:

$$\underbrace{Al^{3+} + Al^{3+}}_{6+} + \underbrace{O^{2-} + O^{2-} + O^{2-}}_{6-}$$

The formula is

$$Al_2O_3$$

TWO ALUMINIUM IONS — THREE OXIDE IONS

A quicker way of predicting these formulae is to write down the ions with their charges. If the charges do not balance, cross the numbers diagonally over from ion to ion. e.g.,

$$\text{aluminium oxide } Al^{3+} \; O^{2-} \rightarrow Al_2O_3$$

You must remember that the symbol on its own represents one ion and so the number one is never put in. e.g.,

$$\text{sodium phosphide } Na^+ \; P^{3-} \rightarrow Na_3P$$

THREE SODIUM IONS — ONE PHOSPHIDE ION

Relative Formula Mass

In Reactions and the Atom you saw that a molecule of a covalent substance had a **relative molecular mass** (M_r) equal to the sum of the relative atomic masses (A_r) of all the atoms in the molecule.

Since ionic compounds form a large lattice structure of positive and negative ions, we cannot really talk about a "molecule" of ionic substance. We can, however, write a formula which represents a **formula unit** of the compound.

The term **relative formula mass** can be used for ionic **or** covalent compounds and uses the same symbol M_r. It is equal to the sum of the relative atomic masses of all the atoms in a formula unit of the compound.

Examples

Calculate the relative formula mass of magnesium oxide.
Formula   MgO
The relative formula mass is
$M_r = A_r(Mg) + A_r(O)$
    $= 24 + 16$
    $= 40$

Similarly the relative formula mass of aluminium oxide can be found:

Formula Al_2O_3

$M_r = 2A_r(Al) + 3A_r(O)$
   $= (2 \times 27) + (3 \times 16)$
   $= 54 + 48$
   $= 102$

More Complex Ions

Some ions contain several atoms. The ammonium ion (the only positively charged non-metal ion) has the formula NH_4^+. The sulphate ion has the formula SO_4^{2-}. In each of these ions the whole group carries the charge. A sulphate ion must always consist of one sulphur atom and four oxygen atoms combining to give a double negative charge. The formulae for the more complex ions are included in table 3.9.

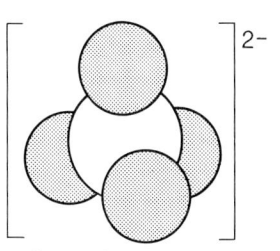

One sulphur atom joined to four oxygen atoms

A sulphate ion

To write formulae with these ions we use the same method as before.

For example:

Sodium carbonate

$Na^+ \quad CO_3^{2-} \rightarrow Na_2CO_3$

Ammonium nitrate

$NH_4^+ \quad NO_3^- \rightarrow NH_4NO_3$

Table 3.9

ONE POSITIVE		ONE NEGATIVE		TWO NEGATIVE		THREE NEGATIVE	
ion	formula	ion	formula	ion	formula	ion	formula
ammonium	NH_4^+	ethanoate	CH_3COO^-	carbonate	CO_3^{2-}	phosphate	PO_4^{3-}
		hydrogencarbonate	HCO_3^-	chromate	CrO_4^{2-}		
		hydrogensulphate	HSO_4^-	dichromate	$Cr_2O_7^{2-}$		
		hydrogensulphite	HSO_3^-	sulphate	SO_4^{2-}		
		hydroxide	OH^-	sulphite	SO_3^{2-}		
		nitrate	NO_3^-				
		permanganate	MnO_4^-				

The Transition Elements

Most of the transition metal elements (between groups two and three in the periodic table) can have ions of different charges. In order that you know the valency of a transition metal ion, it is written in Roman numbers and in brackets, **after** the name of the metal.

The formula copper(I) oxide indicates that the copper has a valency of one and so the ion has a single positive charge:

$$Cu^+ \quad O^{2-} \rightarrow Cu_2O$$

Copper(II) sulphate contains copper with a valency of two, and the ions will have a double positive charge:

$$Cu^{2+} \quad SO_4^{2-} \rightarrow CuSO_4$$

Vanadium(V) oxide tells us that vanadium has a valency of five and its ions will have a five positive charge:

$$V^{5+} \quad O^{2-} \rightarrow V_2O_5$$

Using Brackets

If we try to write the formula for copper(II) nitrate, it is slightly more difficult, because we require a multiple number of nitrate ions:

$$Cu^{2+} \quad NO_3^- \rightarrow Cu(NO_3)_2$$

The nitrate ion must be enclosed by brackets because the number two outside the brackets means that all the atoms in the group are multiplied by two to give the total number present. A bracket is always used when there are multiples of complex ions.

Remember that the brackets are not required for simple ions, so that iron(III) chloride is simply written $FeCl_3$.

Writing Equations Involving Complex Ions

We can use the formulae of compounds to write an equation to describe a chemical reaction. For example, zinc metal reacts with dilute nitric acid to form zinc nitrate. The word equation for this is written:

zinc metal + nitric acid solution → zinc nitrate solution + hydrogen gas

Using formulae we would write:

$$Zn(s) + 2HNO_3(aq) \rightarrow Zn(NO_3)_2(aq) + H_2(g)$$

If magnesium is added to copper(II) nitrate solution, copper and magnesium nitrate are formed:

magnesium + copper(II) nitrate → magnesium(II) nitrate + copper

$$Mg(s) + Cu(NO_3)_2(aq) \rightarrow Mg(NO_3)_2(aq) + Cu(s)$$

Balancing the Equations

In Reactions and the Atom you found out how to balance simple equations. Balancing equations involving complex ions is done in exactly the same way.

Example 1 The sulphate ion is easily tested for because it reacts with barium ions to produce a white precipitate of barium sulphate.

barium hydroxide + sodium sulphate → barium sulphate + sodium hydroxide

$$Ba(OH)_2(aq) + Na_2SO_4(aq) \rightarrow BaSO_4(s) + NaOH(aq)$$

This equation is unbalanced because there are more sodium and hydroxide ions on the left (reactants) than there are on the right (products). This is all made clearer if we add up the individual ions:

Ion	Reactants	Products
barium	1 ion	1 ion
hydroxide	2 ions	1 ion
sulphate	1 ion	1 ion
sodium	2 ions	1 ion

So if we double the amount of sodium and hydroxide ions in the products the equation will balance:

$$Ba(OH)_2(aq) + Na_2SO_4(aq) \rightarrow BaSO_4(s) + \mathbf{2}NaOH(aq)$$

Example 2 Silver nitrate solution reacts with iron(III) chloride to produce a white precipitate of silver chloride

$$\begin{array}{cccc} \text{silver} & + & \text{iron(III)} & \rightarrow & \text{silver} & + & \text{iron (III)} \\ \text{nitrate} & & \text{chloride} & & \text{chloride} & & \text{nitrate} \end{array}$$

$$AgNO_3(aq) + FeCl_3(aq) \rightarrow AgCl(s) + Fe(NO_3)_3(aq)$$

Totalling up the ions we get:

Ions	Reactants	Products
silver	1 ion	1 ion
nitrate	1 ion	3 ions
iron	1 ion	1 ion
chloride	3 ions	1 ion

Notice that the nitrate ions have increased by three times as we move from reactants to products. This suggests that the number of nitrate ions in the reactants needs to be multiplied by three. The consequence of doing this means that three silver ions are then needed on the product side. This now balances the chloride ions.

$$\mathbf{3}AgNO_3(aq) + FeCl_3(aq) \rightarrow \mathbf{3}AgCl(s) + Fe(NO_3)_3(aq)$$

If you check the numbers of ions on each side, you will find they all balance.

Calculations from Equations

For the reaction between barium hydroxide and sodium sulphate the balanced equation is:

$$Ba(OH)_2(aq) + Na_2SO_4(aq) \rightarrow BaSO_4(s) + 2NaOH(aq)$$

A number of calculations can be made from this equation. We can calculate the amount of reactant required to produce a specified amount of product, or the amount of product formed using a specific amount of reactant. This proves very useful in industrial processes.

For example, cement is made by roasting limestone (calcium carbonate) in a furnace. Lime (calcium oxide) is formed and carbon dioxide gas is given off. We might be asked to make a number of calculations, based on this reaction. The first three steps are the same for any calculation:

Step 1 Write the balanced equation, in this case:

$$CaCO_3(s) \rightarrow CaO(s) + CO_2(g)$$

Step 2 Write out the number of moles of each reactant and product from the balanced equation:

i.e. 1 mole of calcium carbonate produces 1 mole of calcium oxide and 1 mole of carbon dioxide

Step 3 Calculate the relative formula mass for each substance in grams:

$$\begin{array}{ccc} CaCO_3 & \rightarrow CaO & + & CO_2 \\ 40 + 12 + (16 \times 3) & \rightarrow 40 + 16 & & 12 + (16 \times 2) \\ 100\,g & \rightarrow 56\,g & & 44\,g \end{array}$$

So, 100 g of calcium carbonate produces 56 g of calcium oxide and 44 g of carbon dioxide.

Step 4 Carry out the required calculation. All the masses reacting and being produced are proportional to each other,

so if 100 g of calcium carbonate produces 56 g of calcium oxide and 44 g of carbon dioxide,
200 g of $CaCO_3$ will produce 112 g of CaO and 88 g of CO_2
and 50 g of $CaCO_3$ produces 28 g of CaO and 22 g of CO_2
and 1 g of $CaCO_3$ produces 0·56 g of CaO and 0·44 g of CO_2 etc.

Example 2 Calculate the amount of barium sulphate formed when 60 g of barium hydroxide is reacted with an excess amount of sodium sulphate solution. (Excess means that there is more than enough sodium sulphate for complete reaction with the barium hydroxide).

Step 1 Write the balanced equation:

$$Ba(OH)_2(aq) + Na_2SO_4(aq) \rightarrow BaSO_4(s) + 2NaOH(aq)$$

Step 2 Write out the number of moles of reactant and product from the equation which are needed for the calculation:

i.e. 1 mole of $Ba(OH)_2$ produces 1 mole of $BaSO_4$

Step 3 Calculate the relative formula mass of each substance, in grams:

$$\begin{array}{cc} 1 \text{ mole of } Ba(OH)_2 & \rightarrow 1 \text{ mole of } BaSO_4 \\ 137 + 2 \times (16+1) & 137 + 32 + (4 \times 16) \\ 171\,g & \rightarrow 233\,g \end{array}$$

so 171 g of $Ba(OH)_2$ produces 233 g of $BaSO_4$

90 ELECTRICITY IN CHEMISTRY

Step 4 The calculation:

If 171 g of $Ba(OH)_2$ produces 233 g of $BaSO_4$

then 1 g of $Ba(OH)_2$ will produce $\frac{233}{171}$ g of $BaSO_4$

so 60 g of $Ba(OH)_2$ produces $\frac{233 \times 60}{171}$ g

= **81.75 g of $BaSO_4$**

Example 3 Iron ore consists mainly of iron(III) oxide. In a blast furnace the ore is reacted with carbon monoxide to produce iron metal and carbon dioxide. Calculate the amount of ore required to produce 1000 kg of iron metal.

Step 1 Write the balanced equation:

$$Fe_2O_3(s) + 3CO(g) \rightarrow 2Fe(l) + 3CO_2(g)$$

Step 2 Write out the number of moles of iron ore (Fe_2O_3) producing iron metal:

i.e. 1 mole of Fe_2O_3 produces 2 moles of Fe metal

Step 3 Calculate the relative formula mass of each substance, in grams:

1 mole of Fe_2O_3 → 2 moles of Fe
$2 \times 56 + 3 \times 16$ → 2×56
160 g → 112 g

so, 160 g of Fe_2O_3 produces 112 g of Fe

Step 4 If 160 g of Fe_2O_3 produces 112 g of Fe

then $\frac{160}{112}$ g of Fe_2O_3 produces 1 g of Fe

so $\frac{160 \times 1000}{112}$ kg of Fe_2O_3 produces 1000 kg of Fe

Therefore 1428.57 kg of iron ore must be used to produce 1000 kg of iron metal.

Activities

1. Write the formulae for the following compounds:
   lithium sulphide   calcium chloride
   boron nitride   potassium iodide
   magnesium oxide   aluminium phosphide
   sodium carbonate

2. Write equations for the following reactions; they need not be balanced:
   (a) Silver nitrate solution reacts with calcium metal to produce a precipitate of silver and a calcium nitrate solution.
   (b) Hydrogen gas is given off when zinc metal reacts with hydrogen chloride solution (hydrochloric acid) to produce a solution of zinc chloride.
   (c) When magnesium metal is heated in oxygen gas, magnesium oxide is formed.

3. Write the formulae for the following compounds:
   strontium nitrate   iron(III) bromide
   ammonium sulphate   barium phosphate
   copper(II) ethanoate

4. Write balanced chemical equations for the following reactions:
   (a) When a silver nitrate solution is mixed with a magnesium chloride solution a white precipitate of silver chloride, and a solution of magnesium nitrate are formed.
   (b) Copper sulphate solution reacts with sodium hydroxide solution to form a gelatinous precipitate of copper(II) hydroxide, and a solution of sodium sulphate.
   (c) Silver(I) carbonate decomposes on heating to form silver metal, oxygen and carbon dioxide.

5. Calculate the relative formula mass of the following compounds:
   copper(II) permanganate
   potassium dichromate
   iron(II) hydroxide
   lithium carbonate
   beryllium nitrate
   aluminium hydrogensulphate

6. Calculate the mass of calcium oxide that would be produced if 1500 kg of calcium carbonate were heated in a furnace.

7. A solution containing lead(II) nitrate was mixed with excess potassium iodide solution. The yellow precipitate of lead(II) iodide was filtered off, dried and weighed. If the mass of the precipitate was 9.22 g, calculate the mass of lead(II) nitrate in the original solution.

4 Electricity from Chemicals

A selection of batteries

Key Ideas

We use batteries as portable forms of electricity. Batteries are also known as *cells*. A battery changes *chemical energy* into *electrical energy*. Most commercial batteries contain *metals* and an *electrolyte* to complete the circuit. Once the chemicals in the battery are used up, the battery goes "flat" and stops producing electricity. Some batteries are *rechargeable* and can be used again.

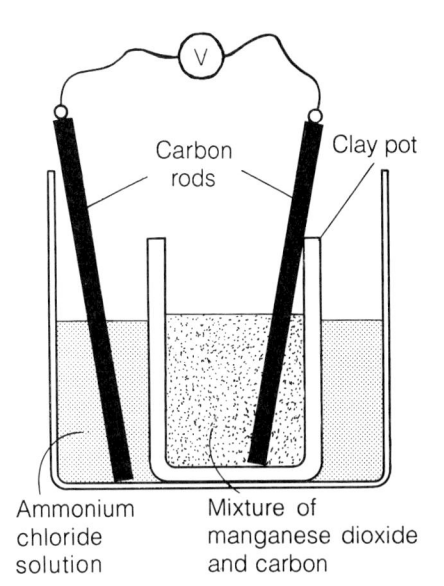

A Leclanche Cell — Carbon rods, Clay pot, Ammonium chloride solution, Mixture of manganese dioxide and carbon

The Development of Batteries

In 1790, Luigi Galvani, an Italian professor, was carrying out some experiments on frogs. In one experiment, he hung a dead frog over an iron balcony railing using a copper hook, and immediately the dead frog began to twitch! Galvani thought that the twitching was caused by natural electricity coming from the frog, and he published a paper describing his experiments.

Alessandro Volta, an Italian Professor of Physics, read this paper but disagreed with Galvani's conclusions. Volta showed that the presence of two different metals was the cause of the electricity, and that the frog only acted as an electrolyte to complete the circuit! Galvani had made a **chemical cell**.

Volta also showed that in a **cell** consisting of a sheet of zinc and a sheet of copper, separated by discs of moist pasteboard, a current was produced.

In 1800 Volta constructed the first **battery** by building a pile of zinc and copper discs separated by pasteboard soaked in a salt solution. A steady current of electricity was produced. This battery was known as a **voltaic pile**. Cells are often called batteries.

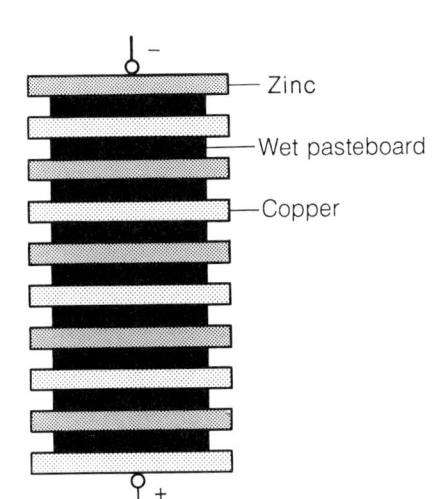

A Voltaic Pile — Zinc, Wet pasteboard, Copper

Volta's battery, or cell, was not very efficient, and was incapable of giving large currents for any length of time. The actual chemistry of the battery was not fully understood at that time, but we now know that **electrons** were being produced as the result of a **chemical reaction**.

In 1868, a French scientist called Leclanche, invented a more efficient cell, capable of producing a current over a longer period of time. Leclanche put a mixture of manganese dioxide and carbon powder into a clay pot, with a carbon rod pushed into the mixture to form the positive electrode. The clay pot was placed in a solution of ammonium chloride, and a carbon rod in the chloride solution acted as the negative electrode.

Although the battery was more successful, it was heavy and the solution was easily spilled. Leclanche cells were manufactured up until 1970.

ELECTRICITY IN CHEMISTRY

The Zinc-Carbon Cell

The battery that you use in a torch is the modern equivalent of the Leclanche cell. It has a zinc case which acts as the negative terminal of the battery, and the metal case is in contact with paper. The paper is soaked in ammonium chloride solution, which is the electrolyte, and is there to complete the circuit.

A mixture of manganese dioxide and carbon powder separates the paper from a central carbon rod which is the positive terminal. This battery produces 1.5 volts, and is known as a zinc-carbon cell. It is one of the cheapest batteries you can buy and is suitable for low powered electrical equipment which is only used occasionally.

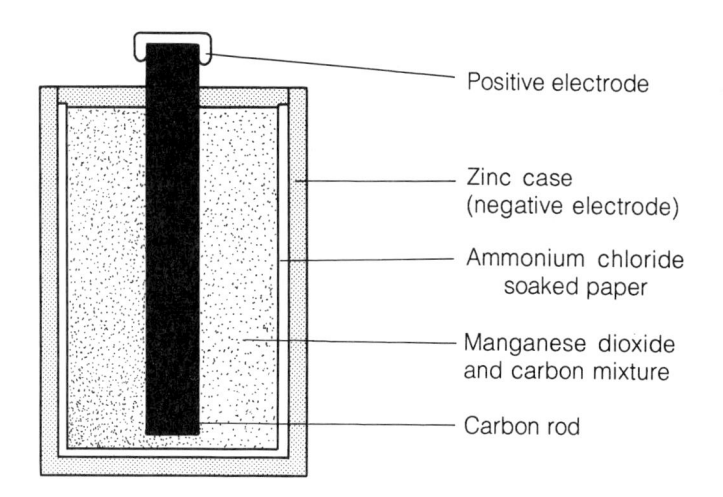

The modern zinc-carbon cell

The Alkaline Manganese Cell

When higher currents are required or if low powered systems are to be run for long periods, then an alkaline battery is better (though more expensive) than a zinc-carbon battery.

The alkaline cell has the same electrodes as the zinc-carbon cell, but the electrolyte is the alkali potassium hydroxide. A potassium hydroxide solution conducts better than the same concentration of an ammonium chloride solution, and allows a higher current to be produced.

The Silver Oxide Cell

An even more expensive cell is the silver oxide cell. This type is often found in watches or calculators, and looks like a small button. It still uses a zinc case and potassium hydroxide electrolyte, but the positive electrode is made of silver oxide. The cell can produce small currents continuously for long periods of time, some times up to one or two years.

The Lithium Cell

In some cases of heart disease, the patient's heart beats irregularly. In order to make the heart beat regularly a pacemaker can be implanted into the chest.

The pacemaker requires a small battery to operate it. The battery has to be non-toxic, leak proof and small enough to go inside the human body.

The first batteries used in pacemakers lasted for about two years, and so the patient then had to undergo another operation to replace the battery. It was thought that the element lithium might produce a longer lasting battery. The problem with lithium was it reacted with both air and water, and all the electrolytes available had water in them. Fortunately chemists discovered that solid iodine could be used as an electrolyte, and so the lithium battery was developed.

Such a battery can power a pacemaker for up to ten years before needing to be replaced. Research still goes on to find other batteries which might extend this period, and also to build a rechargeable version which would avoid the need for replacement operations.

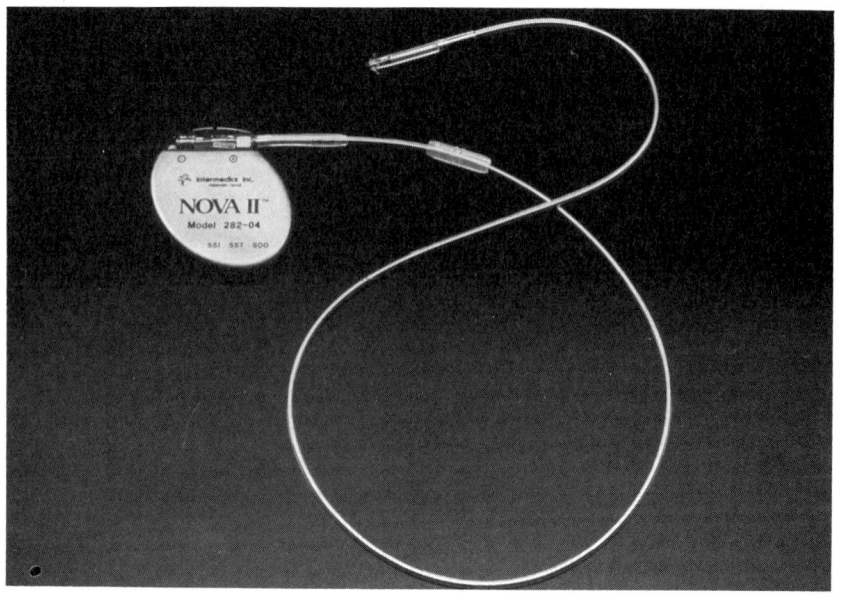

A heart pacemaker

ELECTRICITY IN CHEMISTRY

Rechargeable Batteries

As the chemicals in a zinc-carbon battery run out, the battery goes **flat**. You can buy batteries now that are rechargeable. By passing the correct current and voltage of electricity into the flat, rechargeable battery you can reverse the chemical process and recharge the battery.

The most common rechargeable battery is the lead-acid battery. When two lead plates are put into a fairly concentrated solution of sulphuric acid and a current is passed between the two plates, the cell becomes charged. The cell stores up some of the energy that passes through it.

If the charging current is removed, and a bulb is connected between the plates, it lights up. Some time later the bulb will dim and then go out. The battery is flat. If a current is again passed between the plates the battery will recharge and can be used again.

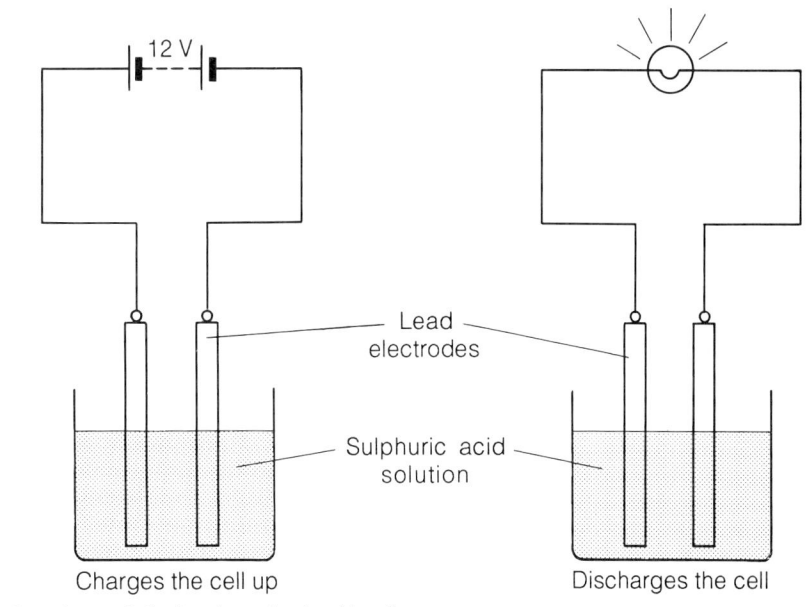

The lead-acid battery is used in motor vehicles. The battery consists of a number of lead plates connected together inside a plastic container filled with sulphuric acid. Each battery contains six, two-volt cells connected together to produce twelve volts. When the battery turns the starter motor it uses up a lot of the chemical energy. However, when the engine is running, an alternator recharges the battery so that it is at full power when it is required to turn the starter motor again. The battery is not used to keep the engine running. The alternator provides the electricity for this.

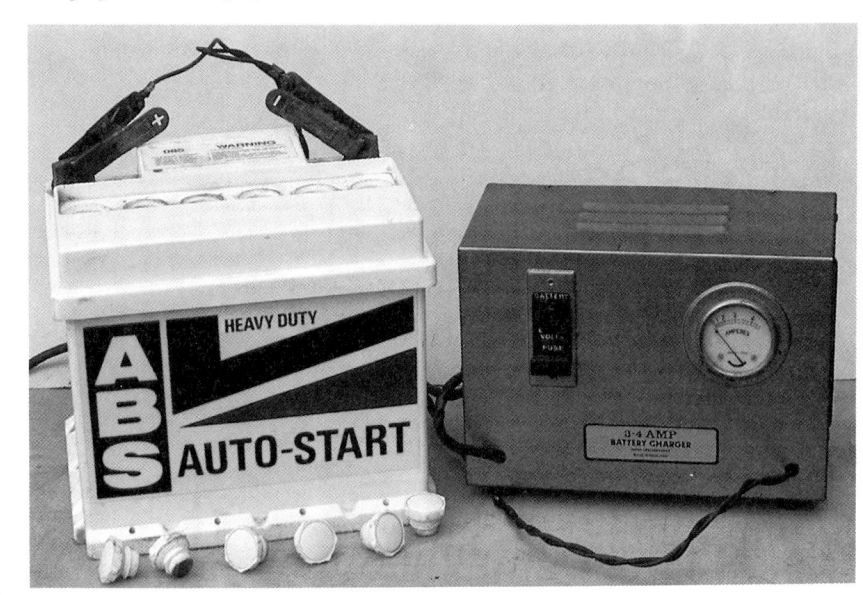

Charging and discharging a lead-acid cell

Charging a battery

A car engine

In some car batteries, water is used up during the discharge and charge cycles, so that the acid becomes more concentrated. The acid level needs to be checked regularly and topped up with distilled water.

The very latest car batteries are often sealed for life and never need topping up.

If a car battery has been "flattened" trying to start the car it can be removed and charged using a charger. The charger operates from the mains supply, and consists of a transformer which changes the 240 volt alternating current supply (a.c.) to twelve or six volts direct current (d.c.).

94 ELECTRICITY IN CHEMISTRY

The red wire from the charger is attached to the positive terminal and the black wire to the negative terminal of the battery. To prevent permanent damage to the battery, it is very important to use the correct voltage, d.c. supply, and to connect the correct coloured wires to the terminals.

One word of warning: the acid in car or motorcycle batteries is very concentrated and will damage clothes or paint work if it is spilled.

The Nickel-Cadmium Battery

A smaller rechargeable battery which can be used in portable radios or personal stereos is the nickel-cadmium battery. This has a positive electrode made from a nickel compound and a negative electrode of cadmium. It is at least ten times more expensive than the zinc-carbon battery, but it can be recharged and used again and again.

Great care must be taken in recharging these batteries. The correct type of charger must be used, because if too great a voltage is used hydrogen gas is produced. Because the cell is sealed, this might cause an explosion.

Most batteries produced today are sealed and should never be thrown onto a fire, because of the risk of explosion. Metals such as cadmium can be very poisonous if they get into the food chain. In Sweden they have banned cells containing cadmium, as they consider their disposal a public risk.

Using Solar Energy

You may have a calculator or a watch which is powered by sunlight. The watch not only works in the light, but it continues to function in the dark. This is because the watch has a rechargeable battery, charged by photocells. The photocells convert light energy into electrical energy. This is **not** a chemical reaction as chemicals are not changed in the photocell.

As oil supplies continue to run out, the cars of the future may have to use solar power, with the sun's energy recharging the batteries as the car moves along the road.

Such cars have already been built, but research is going on to find lighter, higher powered and more efficient batteries so that the cars can run for longer periods.

Spacecraft and satellites use solar powered rechargeable batteries.

A "solar" camel

A solar powered car

A novel use of solar power concerns itself with the transport of medicines in very hot countries. Often the only route to remote villages is across the desert by camel. The journey takes a long time, and the heat can affect many drugs, making them unusable when they reach their destination. Small refrigerators which use solar powered rechargeable batteries were developed. They are strapped onto the camel's back, and the sun keeps the batteries "topped up" so that the medicine is kept cool. The next time you see a camel with a solar panel, you'll know what it is doing!

Comparing Batteries and Mains Electricity

Table 3.10 compares the use of electricity from batteries with mains electricity.

Table 3.10

Batteries	Mains Electricity
An individual battery is cheap to manufacture, but if we try to match the production of a power station with batteries alone, it is expensive	Power stations are very expensive to build
Can provide power anywhere, even in space or under the sea	Can only be used where power lines are present
Low risk of lethal electric shock as they tend to be of low power (although larger, higher voltage batteries are available)	High currents and voltages present a greater risk of harm
Elements like lithium and cadmium can damage the environment	Air pollution from fossil fuel burning power stations Radioactivity hazards from nuclear power stations
Use up finite supply of metals	Use of finite supply of fossil fuels
Frequent replacement or recharging of batteries is necessary	Power is available at the flick of a switch
	High currents and voltages are needed to run industrial machinery

Activities

1. Look back through this section and make out a list of all the chemicals which can be used in batteries. Write out their chemical formulae.
2. Some car batteries need to be topped up from time to time with distilled water. Why is distilled water preferred to tap water (especially in hard water areas)? Write an equation for the reaction between calcium carbonate and sulphuric acid to produce calcium sulphate, water and carbon dioxide.
3. Make a list of all the different types of batteries mentioned in this section and state their advantages and disadvantages.

5 The Chemistry of the Cell

The Electrochemical Series

When a piece of wet filter paper, soaked in a solution of salt, is placed between two **different** metals, a chemical reaction takes place and a current is produced. The wet filter paper acts as an **electrolyte**, completing the circuit.

Table 3.11 shows typical results obtained when copper is connected, through a wet filter paper, to other metals.

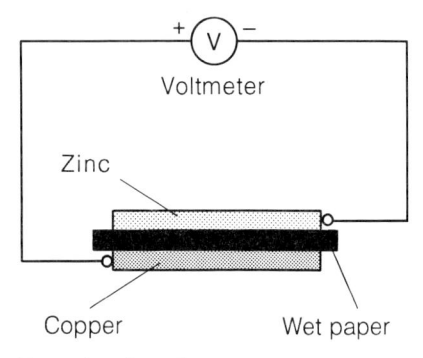

Measuring the voltage

Table 3.11

Metal	Voltage/V
Magnesium	2.0
Zinc	1.0
Iron	0.7
Tin	0.5
Lead	0.4

Volta's cell contained zinc and copper, and this gives a voltage of 1.0 V. The current produced by any of these cells is usually very low. They do, however, have practical uses.

It has been found that massaging skin muscles speeds up the healing of small cuts. One particular manufacturer has incorporated tiny particles of zinc and copper into the adhesive part of wound dressings. The sweat on the surface of the skin contains salt which acts as an electrolyte. This sets up a lot of small cells. The current produced causes the muscles to twitch thus massaging the skin and speeding up the healing process.

Statoil, the Norwegian oil company, is researching the possibility of developing a sea battery. One electrode is to be made of aluminium, magnesium or zinc and the other from copper. Sea water and dissolved oxygen forms the electrolyte. It is hoped to install all this 1000 feet under the sea, and produce a 24 V direct current supply.

The blocks of metal will need replacing every three years, but this would be relatively cheap compared to laying power cables from the shore, at a cost of around 200 thousand pounds per kilometre.

Key Ideas

When *two metals* are connected through an *electrolyte*, a voltage is produced. Different metal pairs give rise to different voltages, and the voltages can be used to work out the *electrochemical series*. The electrochemical series can be used to explain why *displacement* reactions occur.

Sea-water battery proves to be well worth its salt

STATOIL, Norway's state oil company, is stepping up experiments into a novel form of sea power which could aid the development of oil and gas fields in deep and remote waters.

At the opening session of the Offshore Northern Sea conference in Stavanger yesterday, the company announced it had developed a sea-water battery system which could provide a flow of electric current to operate subsea wellhead installations located far from production platforms or shore-based generating plants.

As part of a research and development programme into underwater power and communication systems, Statoil has already carried out tests on prototypes of the battery at water depths of about 150 feet.

It now plans to use the concept to power an underwater navigational station at the Haltenbanken oilfield, in nearly 1,000 feet of water, in the Norwegian sector of the North Sea.

Statoil said that the longer-term aim of the experiment was to provide a subsea power source to operate oil and gas wells situated on the sea bed.

Power from the sea bed: An artist's impression of a seawater battery pack surrounding an underwater oil well

If the voltages of a large number of pairs of metals are measured, a pattern is seen. If one of the metals in the pair is always kept the same, it acts as a standard, and we can then arrange the other metals in the order of the voltages produced. The metals so arranged, are called **the electrochemical series**:

Lithium	Li
Potassium	K
Calcium	Ca
Sodium	Na
Magnesium	Mg
Aluminium	Al
Zinc	Zn
Iron	Fe
Tin	Sn
Lead	Pb
Copper	Cu
Silver	Ag
Gold	Au

Displacement Reactions

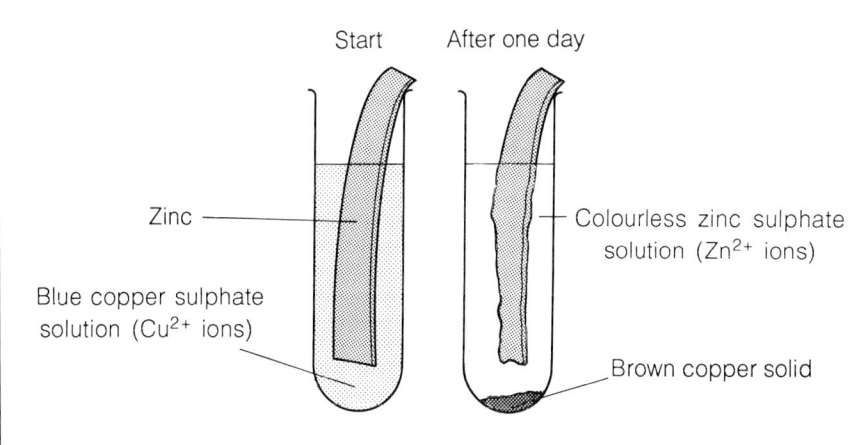

Displacing copper ions with zinc

When a piece of zinc is put in a solution of copper(II) sulphate, the zinc becomes coated in dark brown copper. After a while the zinc will completely dissolve, and brown copper metal is left in the beaker. The original blue colour of the solution slowly fades until it is completely colourless. The zinc has **displaced** the copper ions from solution.

If we make a number of solutions containing metal ions, then add solid metals to them, we can watch for signs of displacement reactions. In some cases the displacement is signalled by a discolouration of the metal and in others by the solution losing its colour. The results of such an experiment are shown in table 3.12.

Notice that the metal higher in the electrochemical series displaces the lower metals from solution.

The table indicates that these experiments could also have been used to build up our electrochemical series. The metal which displaces all the other metal ions would be placed at the top, and the metal which failed to displace any of the other ions at the bottom of the series.

Table 3.12

	Magnesium sulphate	Zinc sulphate	Iron sulphate	Tin sulphate	Copper sulphate
Magnesium	0	✓	✓	✓	✓
Zinc	0	0	✓	✓	✓
Iron	0	0	0	✓	✓
Tin	0	0	0	0	✓
Copper	0	0	0	0	0

0 = no displacement; ✓ = displacement occurs

ELECTRICITY IN CHEMISTRY

Predicting Reactions

We can predict whether a displacement reaction will occur by looking at the position of the metals involved, in the electrochemical series. We can also predict what will be seen during an experiment.

Example 1
What will be seen when copper metal is added to silver sulphate solution?

Prediction: copper is **higher** in the electrochemical series than silver. Copper **should** displace the silver from solution, forming blue copper(II) sulphate solution.

Experiment: A reaction is seen but silver metal forming at the surface of the copper slows the reaction down. Eventually a light blue colour appears.

Example 2
What will be seen when gold is added to sodium chloride solution?

Prediction: Gold is **lower** in the electrochemical series than sodium. There should be no displacement, and no evidence of reaction seen.

Experiment: A gold ring left in sodium chloride solution shows no sign of reaction. Similarly, ancient gold coins and ornaments lost under the sea (mainly sodium chloride) for hundreds of years, show no signs of a displacement reaction occurring.

Hydrogen in the Electrochemical Series?

An acid is a hydrogen ion solution. When metals like magnesium, zinc and lead are added to hydrochloric acid, **hydrogen** is **displaced** from solution. Metals like gold and copper, however, don't react – hydrogen is not displaced. This suggests that hydrogen lies **between lead** and **copper** in the electrochemical series (see table 3.13).

Table 3.13

Metal	Reaction
lithium	$Li^+(aq) + e \rightarrow Li(s)$
potassium	$K^+(aq) + e \rightarrow K(s)$
calcium	$Ca^{2+}(aq) + 2e \rightarrow Ca(s)$
sodium	$Na^+(aq) + e \rightarrow Na(s)$
magnesium	$Mg^{2+}(aq) + 2e \rightarrow Mg(s)$
aluminium	$Al^{3+}(aq) + 3e \rightarrow Al(s)$
zinc	$Zn^{2+}(aq) + 2e \rightarrow Zn(s)$
iron	$Fe^{2+}(aq) + 2e \rightarrow Fe(s)$
nickel	$Ni^{2+}(aq) + 2e \rightarrow Ni(s)$
tin	$Sn^{2+}(aq) + 2e \rightarrow Sn(s)$
lead	$Pb^{2+}(aq) + 2e \rightarrow Pb(s)$
hydrogen	$2H^+(aq) + 2e \rightarrow H_2(g)$
	$SO_4^{2-}(aq) + 2H^+(aq) + 2e \rightarrow SO_3^{2-}(aq) + H_2O(l)$
copper	$Cu^{2+}(aq) + 2e \rightarrow Cu(s)$
	$I_2(s) + 2e \rightarrow 2I^-(aq)$
	$Fe^{3+}(aq) + e \rightarrow Fe^{2+}(aq)$
silver	$Ag^+(aq) + e \rightarrow Ag(s)$
mercury	$Hg^{2+}(aq) + 2e \rightarrow Hg(l)$
	$Br_2(l) + 2e \rightarrow 2Br^-(aq)$
	$Cl_2(aq) + 2e \rightarrow 2Cl^-(aq)$
gold	$Au^+(aq) + e \rightarrow Au(s)$

Activities

- 1 Which of the following metals would react with dilute hydrochloric acid (HCl(aq)) to give off hydrogen gas?
  Copper; zinc; magnesium; silver
  Write a balanced equation for any reaction which occurs.

- 2 Which of the following sets of chemicals would produce a displacement reaction?
  Zinc metal in magnesium chloride solution;
  Iron metal in lead nitrate solution;
  Magnesium metal in copper sulphate solution.
  Write balanced equations for those reactions where a displacement occurs.

- 3 A voltage is produced when two metals, separated by some moist filter paper, are connected by a wire. Which pair of the following pairs would give the largest voltage, and which the smallest voltage?
  Zinc/copper   Magnesium/silver   Aluminium/gold
  Copper/silver.
  Explain your answer.

6 Electrochemical Cells

Making a Cell

We have already seen that when filter paper soaked in sodium chloride solution is "sandwiched" between two different metals, an electric current flows. An electrochemical **cell** is formed. We can also produce electricity using a cell made from two metals dipped into a solution of their own ions.

Each metal in its solution is a **half cell**. It cannot produce any electricity by itself.

Even if two half cells are connected by wires through a voltmeter, no electricity is produced. The circuit is incomplete. However, when a paper towel soaked in salt solution is dipped into both solutions a reading is immediately seen on the voltmeter. The salt soaked paper has **completed the circuit**. This connection is called an **ion bridge** (or salt bridge) as it allows ions to move between the two solutions.

A more permanent ion bridge can be made by filling a U-tube with a hot solution of potassium chloride and gelatine. When the solution has cooled down, the gelatine sets to form a salty jelly which then acts as the ion bridge.

Key Ideas

We can produce electricity by connecting two **different metals** each in a solution of their *ions*.

The solutions are connected by wires and an *ion bridge*. The bridge completes the circuit, by allowing ions to move across from one solution to the other.

It is possible to produce electricity from a cell in which one half of the cell does not involve metal atoms.

Oxidation and *reduction* reactions take place at the *electrodes*.

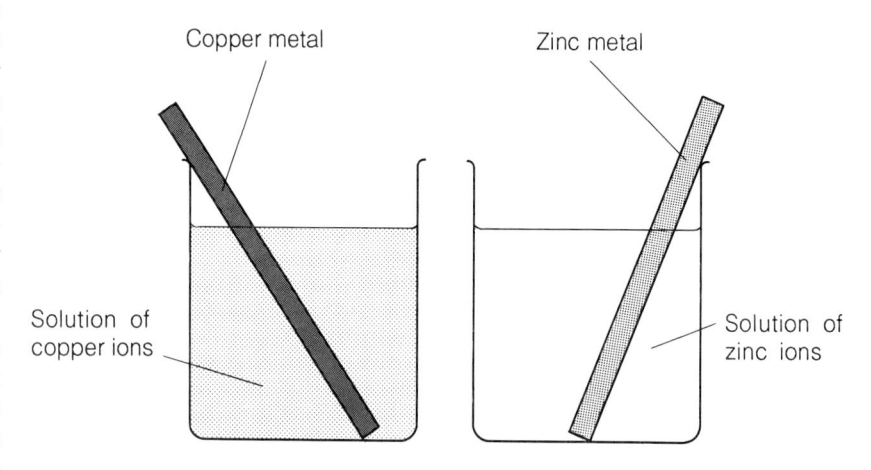

Two half cells

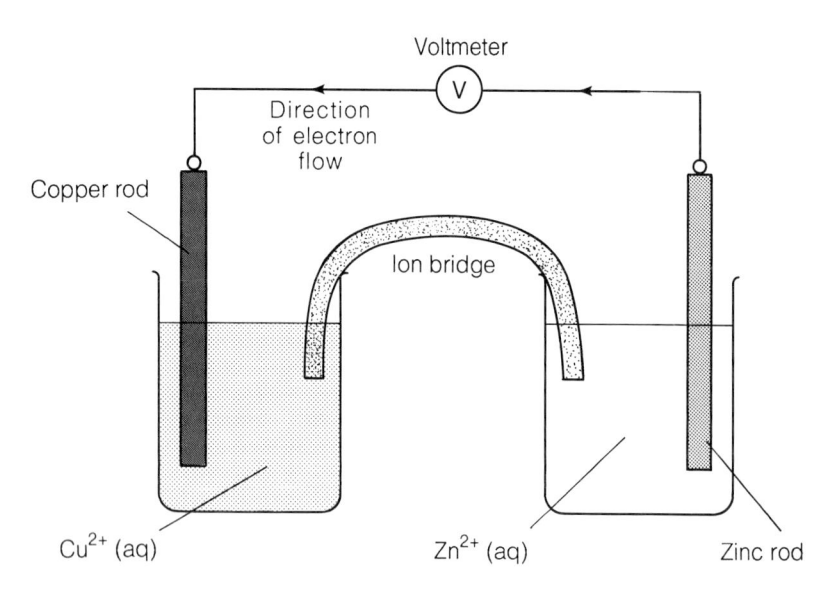

The electrons move through the wires (the **external circuit**) connecting the metals together. The electrons always flow from a metal high in the electrochemical series to one lower down the series.

Two half-cells connected to produce an electric current

What's Happening at the Electrodes?

In the zinc/copper cell shown, electrons flow through the wire **from** zinc **to** copper. The zinc **loses** two electrons and forms the Zn^{2+} ion. The ion–electron equation is:

$$Zn(s) \rightarrow Zn^{2+}(aq) + 2e$$

This **loss** of electrons is known as **oxidation**. The electrons are gained by the Cu^{2+} ions in the copper half cell. The ion–electron equation for this is:

$$Cu^{2+}(aq) + 2e \rightarrow Cu(s)$$

This **gain** of electrons is known as **reduction**.

Table 3.13 is a more detailed electrochemical series than the one shown earlier (page 97). It clearly shows the position of hydrogen and includes ion–electron equations for some common reduction reactions. These equations can be **reversed** to get the oxidation equation.

A memory aid to help you remember what happens to electrons during oxidation and reduction is:

```
O    I    L       R    I    G
x    s    o       e    s    a
i         s       d         i
d         s       u         n
a                 c
t                 t
i                 i
o                 o
n                 n
```

A Closer Look at Oxidation and Reduction

Oxidation and reduction don't just occur in chemical cells. Oxidation and reduction occur in any reaction in which reactants gain or lose electrons.

Displacement reactions involve oxidation and reduction. When magnesium metal displaces copper ions from a solution of copper(II) sulphate, copper metal and magnesium sulphate are formed:

$$Mg(s) + CuSO_4(aq) \rightarrow Cu(s) + MgSO_4(aq).$$

Showing the ions present we have:

$$Mg(s) + Cu^{2+}(aq) + SO_4^{2-}(aq)$$
$$\rightarrow Cu(s) + Mg^{2+}(aq) + SO_4^{2-}(aq)$$

The ionic equation shows that during the reaction magnesium **loses electrons**:

$$Mg(s) \rightarrow Mg^{2+}(aq) + 2e \quad \textbf{oxidation}$$

Copper ions **gain** electrons:

$$Cu^{2+}(aq) + 2e \rightarrow Cu(s) \quad \textbf{reduction}$$

Notice that the sulphate ions (SO_4^{2-}) neither gain nor lose electrons. They are called **spectator** ions.

Burning a metal in oxygen also involves oxidation and reduction. Using calcium as an example:

$$2Ca(s) + O_2(g) \rightarrow 2CaO(s)$$

showing the ions present we have:

$$2Ca(s) + O_2(g) \rightarrow 2Ca^{2+}O^{2-}(s)$$

The ionic equation shows that during the reaction, calcium **loses** electrons:

$$2Ca(s) \rightarrow 2Ca^{2+}(s) + 4e \quad \textbf{oxidation}$$

and each oxygen atom in the molecule **gains** electrons:

$$O_2(g) + 4e \rightarrow 2O^{2-}(s) \quad \textbf{reduction}.$$

Reactions in which reduction and oxidation occur are called **redox** reactions. The word comes from **red**uction and **ox**idation. As the examples show, reduction and oxidation **always** occur together.

Cells with Non-Metals

The half cells in a chemical cell need **not** involve **metal atoms**. A cell can be set up using a sodium sulphite solution $(Na_2SO_3(aq))$ as one half cell and iron(III) chloride solution $(FeCl_3(aq))$ as the other. Carbon electrodes can be used in both half cells. They will not react with the solutions.

The ion–half equations can be obtained from table 3.13:

$$SO_3^{2-}(aq) + H_2O(l) \rightarrow SO_4^{2-}(aq) + 2H^+(aq) + 2e$$
oxidation
$$Fe^{3+}(aq) + e \rightarrow Fe^{2+}(aq) \quad \textbf{reduction}$$

The half equations show that the sulphite ions lose electrons and the iron(III) ions gain an electron. The flow of electrons must be **from** the sodium sulphite solution **to** the iron(III) chloride solution (through the connecting **wire**).

Activities

- 1 State which reactant in the following reactions is oxidised, and which is reduced:
  - (a) $Mg(s) + 2H^+(aq) \rightarrow Mg^{2+} + H_2(g)$
  - (b) $Zn(s) + 2Ag^+(aq) \rightarrow 2Ag(s) + Zn^{2+}(aq)$
  - (c) $2Fe^{2+}(aq) + Br_2(aq) \rightarrow 2Fe^{3+}(aq) + 2Br^-(aq)$

- 2 Draw a labelled diagram to show a magnesium half cell connected to a lead half cell. Indicate on your diagram the direction of the flow of electrons in the external circuit.

- 3 You are given two carbon rods, an ion-bridge, a solution of bromine, a solution of iron(II) sulphate and any other apparatus you need.
  - (a) Draw a labelled diagram for the $Br_2(aq)/Fe^{2+}(aq)$ cell you could make.
  - (b) What is the purpose of the ion bridge?
  - (c) Write oxidation and reduction ion half equations for the reactions occurring in each half cell. (Table 3.13 may help you.)
  - (d) Show the direction of electron flow on your diagram.

7 Spotlight on Industry

Key Ideas

Sodium chloride (salt) is a very useful chemical for making other compounds. Britain has large reserves of underground salt. Most of the salt used in the chemical industry is for *electrolysis* processes. Products from these processes include *hydrogen*, *sodium hydroxide* and *chlorine* – this is known as the chlor-alkali industry. Over the past one hundred years the electrolysis processes have developed, making them more *economical*, more *efficient* and *safer*.

The Chlor-alkali Industry

Chlorine and sodium hydroxide are two very important raw materials for the chemical industry.

Over 35 million tonnes of chlorine are produced each year by 250 chemical plants in around seventy countries.

In 1986, for each tonne of chlorine produced, 1.130 tonnes of sodium hydroxide and 0.028 tonnes of hydrogen were also produced.

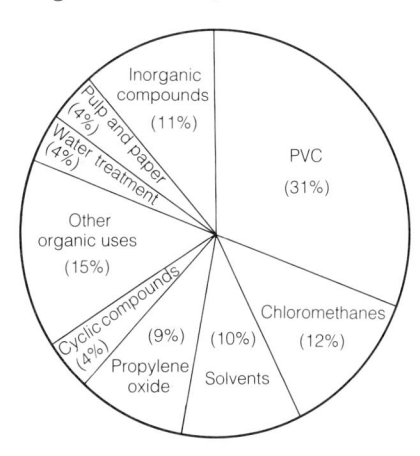

Uses of chlorine

In the Past

During the nineteenth century the cotton industry underwent immense change as the introduction of steam power gradually mechanised the looms. This in turn caused a huge expansion in the chemical industry because the manufacture of cotton materials required large quantities of bleach.

The raw materials required to make bleach were coal, limestone and salt. All of these were found in large quantities around Cheshire and so chemical plants were sited there. Cheshire is still one of the major industrial chemical areas in the UK today.

In 1897, the Castner–Kellner Company developed a process for the electrolysis of **brine** (sodium chloride solution) which produced chlorine, hydrogen and sodium hydroxide solution. Since chlorine and sodium hydroxide are produced together, this section of the chemical industry is known as the **chlor-alkali** industry.

Simple Electrolysis of Brine

If an electric current is passed through a solution of brine, hydrogen is formed at the negative electrode (cathode):

$$2H^+(aq) + 2e \rightarrow H_2(g) \quad \text{reduction}$$

Chlorine gas is formed at the positive electrode (anode):

$$2Cl^-(aq) \rightarrow Cl_2(g) + 2e \quad \text{oxidation}$$

The hydrogen ions are removed from solution as hydrogen gas, leaving hydroxide ions, from the water, behind. The removal of chlorine gas leaves sodium ions from the sodium chloride solution. The solution thus becomes rich in sodium and hydroxide ions, forming sodium hydroxide solution.

Two problems arise in this process:

1 Hydrogen and chlorine gases form an explosive mixture which could react as follows:

$$H_2(g) + Cl_2(g) \rightarrow 2HCl(g)$$

2 The chlorine coming off at the anode, reacts with the sodium hydroxide solution to form sodium chlorate. This contaminates the sodium hydroxide:

$$2NaOH(aq) + Cl_2(g)$$
$$\rightarrow NaClO(aq) + NaCl(aq) + H_2O(l)$$

Solving the Problem

The Castner–Kellner process separated the products of electrolysis to overcome these problems.

Liquid mercury was used as the cathode and titanium as the anode.

This is known as the **mercury cell**.

When a current is passed through the brine, chlorine gas is given off at the anode. The chlorine is collected and liquified for transportation.

Sodium is formed at the mercury cathode. It forms a liquid alloy with the mercury called an **amalgam**. The mercury amalgam is pumped into a separate reaction vessel where only the sodium reacts with water to produce sodium hydroxide solution and hydrogen gas:

$$2Na/Hg\,(l) + 2H_2O\,(l) \rightarrow 2NaOH\,(aq) + H_2\,(g) + 2Hg\,(l)$$

The mercury is recycled back to the electrolysis cell. The cell produces pure hydrogen, chlorine and sodium hydroxide, but it is expensive to install and run. Mercury is also a very toxic element and further expense is required to ensure that none escapes to pollute the environment.

The Mercury Cell

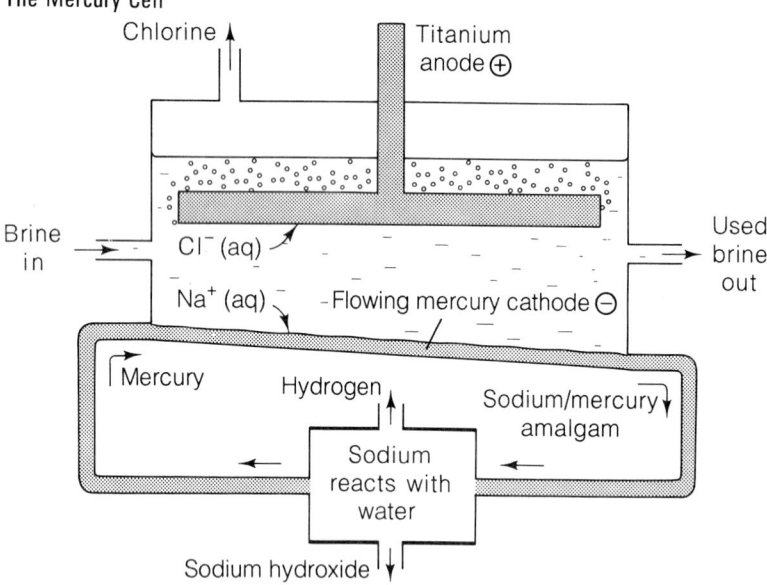

The Diaphragm and Membrane Cells

More recent production of chlorine and sodium hydroxide uses a **barrier** to separate the anode and cathode compartments and prevent unwanted mixing of chemicals.

The **diaphragm** process uses a porous asbestos barrier between the two components. Since ions can pass through the porous diaphragm, electrolysis can take place. Chlorine is produced at the titanium anode and hydrogen at the steel cathode.

The solution left behind contains sodium ions, chloride ions and hydroxide ions. The solution is evaporated until sodium chloride crystallises out, leaving an only slightly impure solution of sodium hydroxide. The diaphragms need to be replaced at frequent intervals.

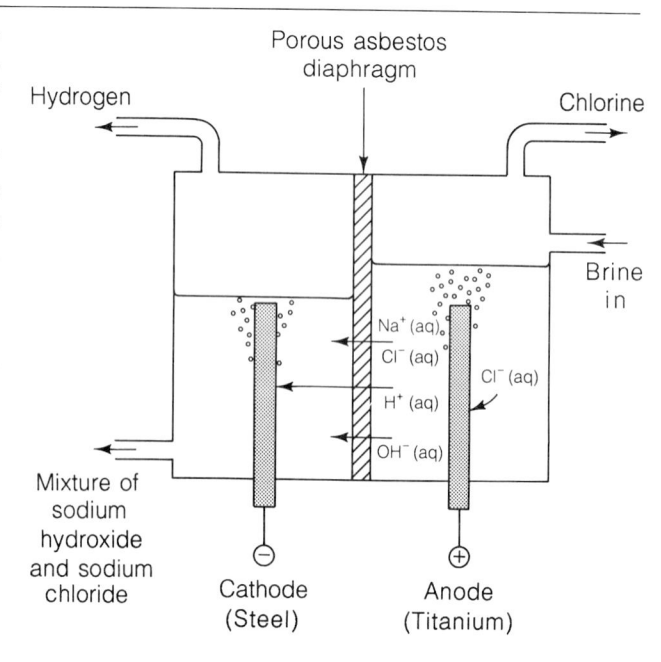

The Diaphragm Cell

The Membrane Cell

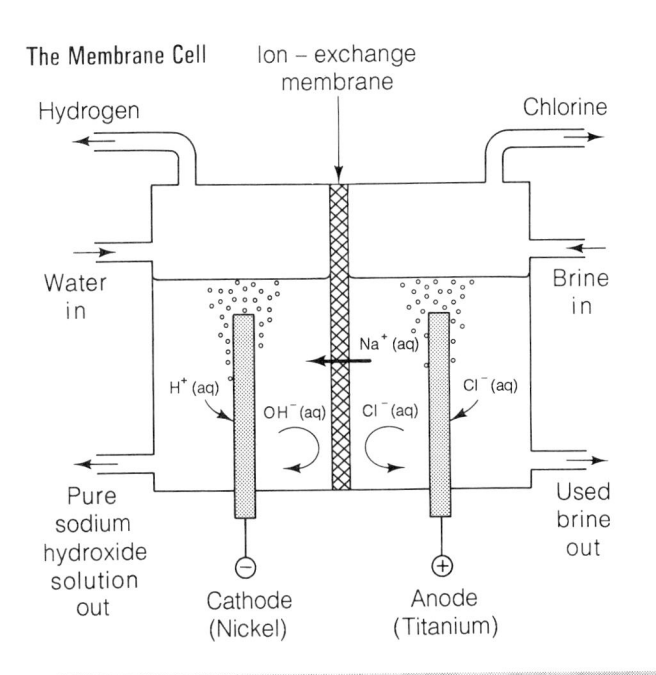

[Diagram of the Membrane Cell showing: Hydrogen out and Water in on the left side connecting to the Cathode (Nickel) with Pure sodium hydroxide solution out at the bottom; Chlorine out and Brine in on the right side connecting to the Anode (Titanium) with Used brine out at the bottom; Ion-exchange membrane in the centre with Na⁺ (aq) passing through it; H⁺ (aq) and OH⁻ (aq) shown in cathode compartment; Cl⁻ (aq) shown in anode compartment.]

The most recent cell is called the **membrane** cell. The membrane is made of special chemicals which only allow the passage of positive ions through it, and not negative ions.

Again, hydrogen is given off at the cathode and chlorine at the anode. The solution in the cathode compartment contains only sodium and hydroxide ions since the negative chloride ions are unable to pass through the membrane. The pure sodium hydroxide is concentrated by evaporation. Care has to be taken to ensure the brine is very pure, as other positive ions might pass through the membrane and contaminate the sodium hydroxide. The membrane needs to be replaced every two to three years.

Activities

- 1 Use the information in the passage to explain why the membrane cell is gradually replacing the diaphragm and mercury cells.
- 2 Using the information in the passage, calculate the mass of chlorine, hydrogen and sodium hydroxide solution produced in 1986.
- 3 Draw a flow diagram to show the production of chlorine, hydrogen and sodium hydroxide from solid salt.

Electricity and Chemistry – Study Questions

1 (a) Copy and complete the following table.

	Conducts electricity	
Substance	when solid	when molten
Zinc		yes
Sulphur		
Zinc sulphide	no	

(b) Explain why solid zinc sulphide does not conduct electricity. **KU**

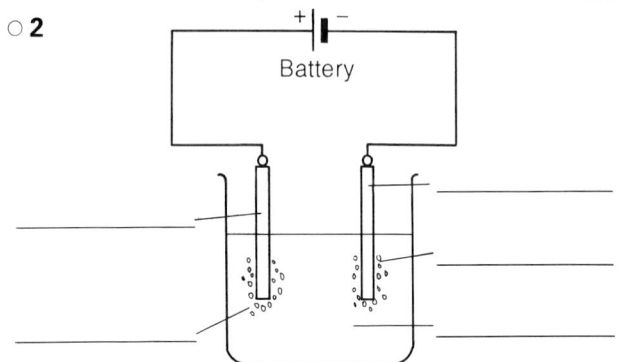

2

With a battery as a power supply, hydrochloric acid can be electrolysed using carbon electrodes. During the electrolysis chlorine gas is given off at the positive electrode and hydrogen gas is given off at the negative electrode.
(a) Copy and complete the labelling in the diagram.
(b) Give a reason why chlorine gas is given off at the positive electrode.
(c) Give a reason why the electrodes are not made of iron. **KU**

3 Three metals were tested as shown in the diagram. The results are shown in the table.

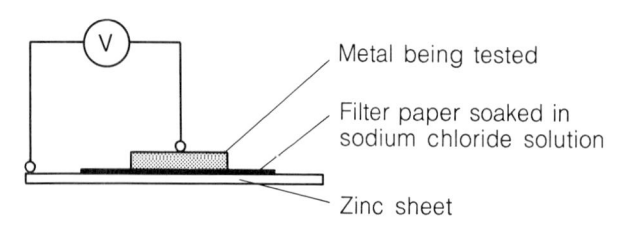

Metal Tested	Voltage/V	Direction of Electron Flow
R	0.3	zinc to metal R
S	0.4	metal S to zinc
T	1.0	zinc to metal T

(a) State which **one** of the four metals (R, S, T, zinc) is the highest in the electrochemical series.
(b) Arrange the **four** metals in order of their position in the electrochemical series, with the highest first. **PS**

4 Copper can be purified by electro-refining. This process is illustrated in the diagram.

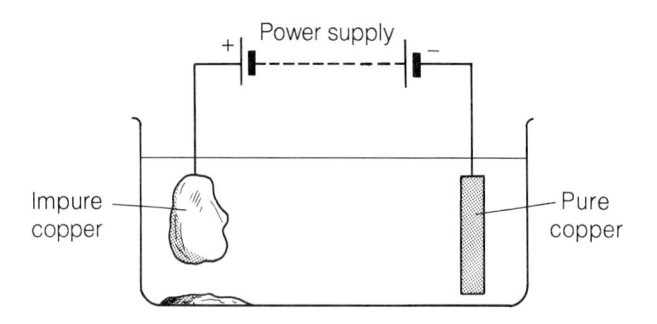

The ion-electron equation for the process occurring at the **impure** positive electrode is:

$$Cu(s) \rightarrow Cu^{2+}(aq) + 2e$$

(a) During the electro-refining, what happens to the mass of the **pure** copper electrode?
(b) Explain why the pure copper electrode must be negative. **PS**

5 Over 150 years ago, one of the first cells was invented by a scientist called J. Daniell. For many years, door bells in houses were powered by Daniell cells. Here is a diagram of one with a voltmeter connected across its terminals.

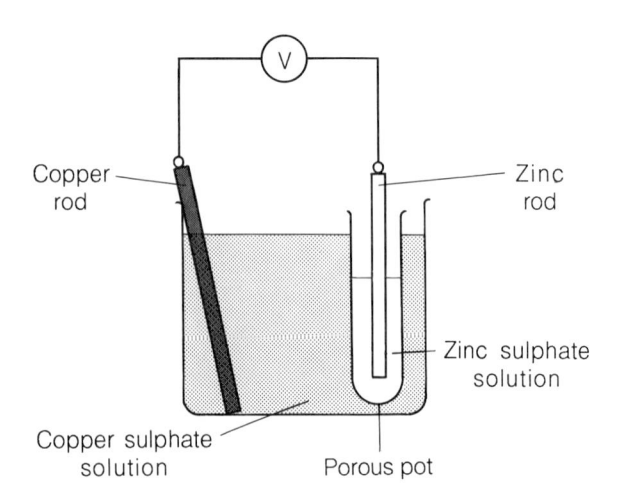

(a) In which direction will the electrons flow?
(b) State what difference there would be in the reading on the meter, if the zinc and zinc sulphate solution were replaced by magnesium and magnesium sulphate solution. **PS**

ELECTRICITY IN CHEMISTRY

6 (a) Explain why sodium chloride has a high melting point.
(b) Copper(II) chloride solution is electrolysed in the apparatus shown.

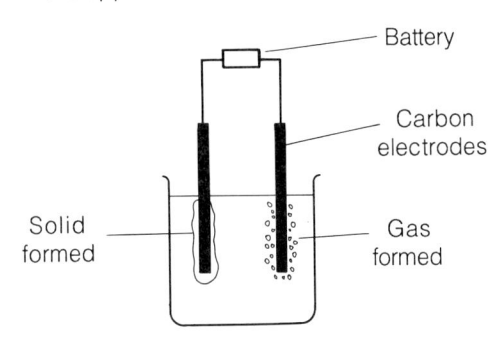

Write ion–electron equations for the formation of:
(i) the solid; (ii) the gas. **KU**

7 Each box in the grid shows a diagram of a cell.

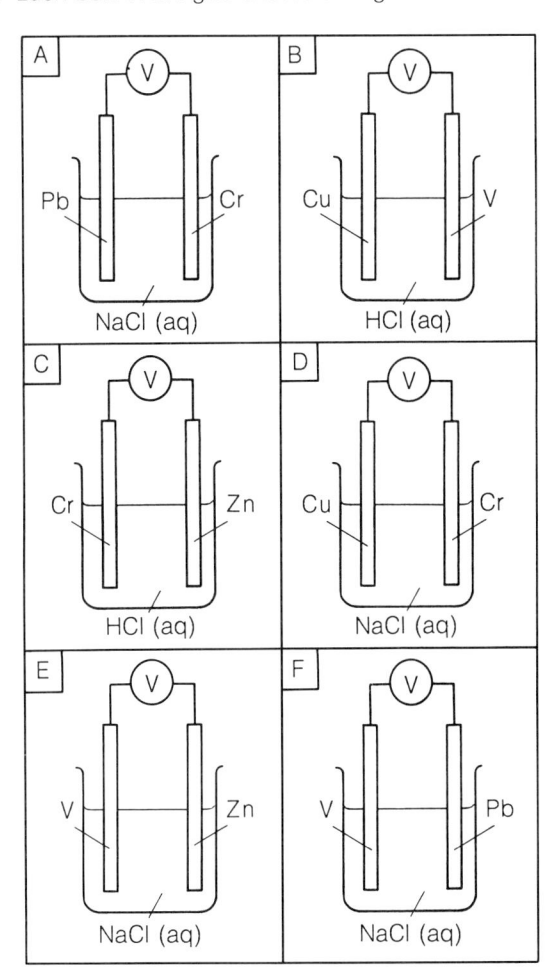

You have been asked to investigate whether vanadium or chromium is higher in the electrochemical series.
Which **two** boxes show cells which could be compared in a fair test to provide this information? **KU**

8 You are given a number of bottles containing solutions of ionic substances. You note that some of the solutions are coloured, and make up this list.

chromium(III) sulphate	green
iron(III) nitrate	red–brown
nickel(II) sulphate	green
potassium sulphate	colourless
potassium chromate	pale yellow
chromium(III) chloride	green
iron(II) sulphate	green
caesium chloride	colourless
barium chromate	pale yellow
chromium(III) nitrate	green

Using **only** the information in this list, suggest a general rule (hypothesis) about the colour of one particular ion. **PS**

Acids and Alkalis

1 Acids and Alkalis all Around

Key Ideas

Acids and *alkalis* play an important part in our lives. We find them in our food and they occur in our bodies.

They are important industrially for making other chemicals.

Acids produce *hydrogen ions* in solution. Alkalis produce *hydroxide ions* in solution.

We can use coloured *indicators* to tell acids and alkalis apart.

Many bathroom and kitchen cleaning fluids contain **alkalis** to help clean greasy surfaces.

Look in your kitchen cupboards at home and you will find **acids** are present in jams, fruit juices and sauces.

In industry, many millions of tonnes of **acids** are produced every year to make other useful chemicals, such as detergents and fertilisers.

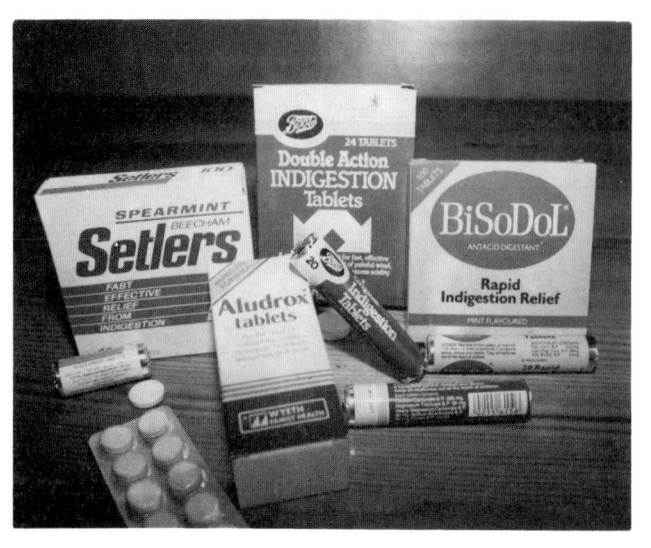

Acids in our stomach help to break down food. Sometimes we have too much **acid** in our stomach (indigestion) and we take medicine containing an **alkali** to reduce it.

What is an Acid?

Many elements burn in oxygen to form oxides. **Non-metal oxides** form **acidic** solutions when they dissolve in water.

Sulphur is a non-metal which burns in oxygen to produce sulphur dioxide, a choking gas. Sulphur dioxide is very soluble in water, forming sulphurous acid:

$$S(s) + O_2(g) \rightarrow SO_2(g)$$
sulphur dioxide

$$SO_2(g) + H_2O(l) \rightarrow H_2SO_3(aq)$$
sulphurous acid

A close look at table 4.1 shows that all acids contain **hydrogen**.

When an electric current is passed through an acidic solution, bubbles of the same gas always come off at the negative electrode.

The gas **'pops'** when a **lighted splint** is held at the mouth of the test tube. This is a positive test for **hydrogen** gas. The hydrogen has reacted with oxygen to produce water.

The negative electrode attracts only positive particles, so the hydrogen must have had a positive charge when it was in solution.

The positively charged hydrogen is called a **hydrogen ion (H^+)**. It is often written H^+ **(aq)**. The plus sign shows that it is positive, and the (aq) shows that it is dissolved in water. **All acids produce hydrogen ions in solution**.

Table 4.2 shows the ions present in some common acids.

Table 4.1

Oxide	Formula	Solution formed	Formula
Sulphur dioxide	$SO_2(g)$	Sulphurous acid	$H_2SO_3(aq)$
Sulphur trioxide	$SO_3(g)$	Sulphuric acid	$H_2SO_4(aq)$
Carbon dioxide	$CO_2(g)$	Carbonic acid	$H_2CO_3(aq)$
Nitrogen dioxide	$NO_2(g)$	Nitric acid	$HNO_3(aq)$
Phosphorus (V) oxide	$P_2O_5(s)$	Phosphoric acid	$H_3PO_4(aq)$

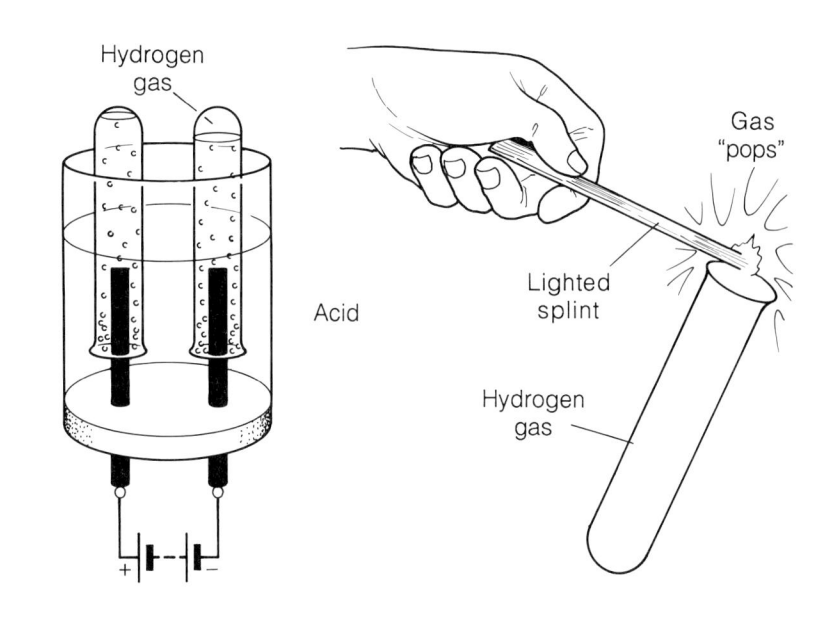

Testing for hydrogen

Table 4.2

Acid solution	Formula	Positive ion	Negative ion	
Hydrochloric	$HCl(aq)$	$H^+(aq)$	$Cl^-(aq)$	chloride
Nitric	$HNO_3(aq)$	$H^+(aq)$	$NO_3^-(aq)$	nitrate
Ethanoic	$CH_3COOH(aq)$	$H^+(aq)$	$CH_3COO^-(aq)$	ethanoate
Sulphuric	$H_2SO_4(aq)$	$2H^+(aq)$	$SO_4^{2-}(aq)$	sulphate
Sulphurous	$H_2SO_3(aq)$	$2H^+(aq)$	$SO_3^{2-}(aq)$	sulphite
Carbonic	$H_2CO_3(aq)$	$2H^+(aq)$	$CO_3^{2-}(aq)$	carbonate
Phosphoric	$H_3PO_4(aq)$	$3H^+(aq)$	$PO_4^{3-}(aq)$	phosphate

110 ACIDS AND ALKALIS

Using Acids

We are familiar with acids in the laboratory and know how dangerous they can be, causing burns to skin and making holes in clothes.

Acids are also familiar at home. It is acids that give some foods their sharp taste, and our stomachs contain hydrochloric acid to help digest our food. Table 4.3 shows some acids found in foods.

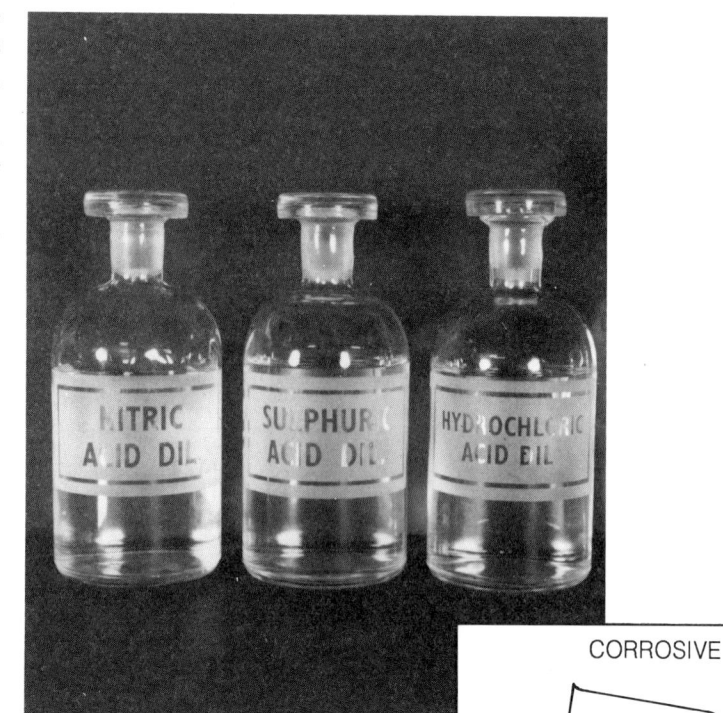

Table 4.3

Acid	Food
Ethanoic	Vinegar
Citric	Lemons
Oxalic	Rhubarb
Tartaric	Grapes
Lactic	Yoghurt

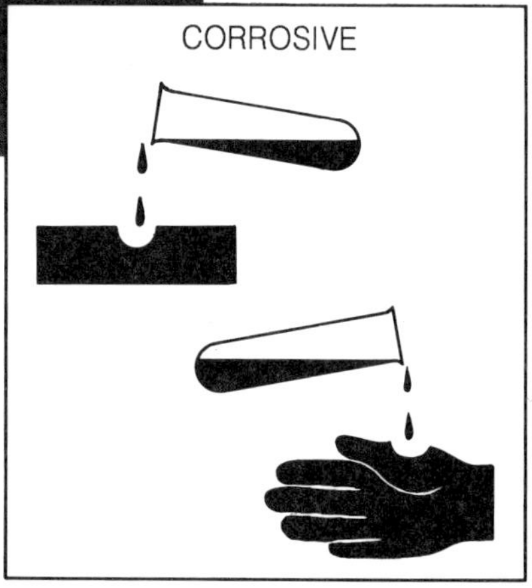

Acids are used in industry to make fertilisers and explosives, to treat metals and in the manufacture of batteries.

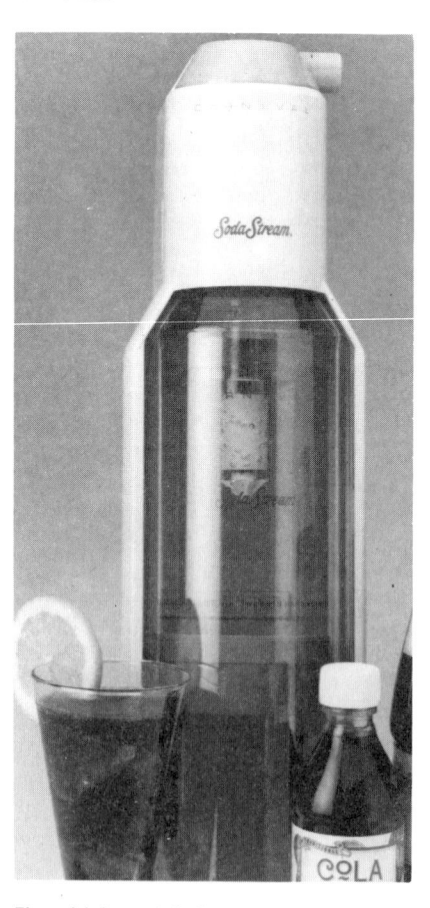

Lemonade

Many lemonades, and other fizzy drinks, are made by adding sweetener, colouring and flavouring to water. The flavouring often contains citric acid. The mixture is carbonated by bubbling carbon dioxide gas through, under pressure. You may have a machine for doing this at home. Some of the gas dissolves in the water, forming carbonic acid:

$$CO_2(g) + H_2O(l) \rightarrow H_2CO_3(aq)$$
carbonic acid

Vinegar

Many vinegars are made by blowing air into wine or fermented malt. The oxygen in the air changes the alcohol (ethanol) into ethanoic acid. The final solution is sold as malt or wine vinegar.

It is also possible to make white vinegar by diluting concentrated ethanoic acid with large amounts of water.

Fizzy drinks and Sodastream

Foods containing vinegar

What is an Alkali?

Soluble **metal oxides** and **metal hydroxides** dissolve in water to form **alkaline** solutions. Table 4.4 shows some common alkalis. Like the acids, they form ionic solutions, but they contain the **hydroxide ion (OH⁻)**. This is often written as **OH⁻(aq)** to show that it is dissolved in water. Table 4.5 shows the ions found in some common alkaline solutions. Notice that ammonia solution is the exception to the rule that alkalis always contain a positive metal ion.

Ammonia contains the non-metal elements nitrogen and hydrogen. When it dissolves in water, it produces **some** hydroxide ions, so the solution is alkaline.

Laboratory alkalis

Table 4.4

Oxide	Formula	Alkaline solution formed	Formula
Sodium oxide	Na_2O	Sodium hydroxide	$NaOH(aq)$
Potassium oxide	K_2O	Potassium hydroxide	$KOH(aq)$
Magnesium oxide	MgO	Magnesium hydroxide	$Mg(OH)_2(aq)$
Calcium oxide	CaO	Calcium hydroxide	$Ca(OH)_2(aq)$

Table 4.5

Solution	Positive ion	Negative ion
Sodium hydroxide	$Na^+(aq)$	$OH^-(aq)$
Potassium hydroxide	$K^+(aq)$	$OH^-(aq)$
Calcium hydroxide	$Ca^{2+}(aq)$	$2OH^-(aq)$
Ammonia (NH_3) (not completely ionised)	$NH_4^+(aq)$	$OH^-(aq)$

Uses of Alkalis

In 1986, almost 40 million tonnes of sodium hydroxide were produced from 250 industrial plants in around 70 countries, worldwide. Table 4.6 shows how the sodium hydroxide is used in Western Europe.

Alkalis are able to combine with fats and oils. This makes them good for **cleaning** greasy surfaces. Many commercial window cleaners contain ammonia to remove oily smears from the glass.

Oven cleaners and paint strippers are fairly concentrated alkalis and you need to wear rubber gloves when you work with them, so you do not burn your hands.

Table 4.6

Field in which sodium hydroxide used	Proportion of total sodium hydroxide (%)
Chemicals	51
Pulp and paper	13
Soap and cleaning agents	7
Textiles	6
Aluminium and other metals	5
Water treatment	3
Food industries	2
Others	13

You may have seen adverts offering to **strip paint** off doors, and return them to their natural wood finish. Such firms dip the doors (or furniture) into tanks of sodium hydroxide, which dissolves away all the layers of paint and varnish.

To make **soap**, vegetable oils are heated and reacted with sodium or potassium hydroxide. After purification and the addition of scent and perhaps colour, the soap is ready to use. (See Electricity in Chemistry page 82.)

ACIDS AND ALKALIS

Testing for Acids and Alkalis

We can tell whether a solution is acidic or alkaline in a number of ways. The simplest is to use an **indicator paper** or an **indicator solution**. Indicators are made from dyes which are one colour in an acid solution and another colour in an alkaline solution.

In table 4.7 the colour changes of some common indicators are shown. Universal Indicator is made from a mixture of dyes, and can be used to find the acidity (or alkalinity) of a solution, over a wide range. Moist indicator paper is dipped in the solution and the resulting colour is compared with a colour chart. Each colour represents a different degree of acidity or alkalinity, and is given a **pH number**.

Table 4.7

Indicator	Colour in acid	Colour in alkali
Litmus	Red	Blue
Phenolphthalein	Colourless	Pink
Methyl orange	Red	Yellow

Table 4.8

pH	Colour of Universal Indicator	Some common solutions
1	red	hydrochloric acid
2		
3 (increasing acidity)	orange	lemon juice
4		vinegar
5		black coffee
6	yellow	
		milk
7 (neutral)	green	pure water
8		
9	blue	baking soda
10		
11 (increasing alkalinity)	indigo	oven cleaner
12		
13	violet	caustic soda
14		

The pH Scale

The pH scale is a continuous numbered scale.

When a solution has a pH **less than 7**, it is an **acid**.

A solution with a pH **greater than 7** is an **alkali**.

A pH of **exactly 7** is neither acid nor alkali, and is said to be **neutral**.

Water and alcohol are examples of **neutral** substances.

Table 4.8 shows the colour of Universal Indicator at different pHs. Notice that a very low pH number indicates a very acidic solution, but that as the pH approaches 7, the solution becomes less acidic. Similarly a high pH number indicates a very alkaline solution, the alkalinity decreasing as the pH drops towards pH 7.

An acid, such as hydrochloric acid, can have any pH value below 7, depending on the **concentration** of the hydrogen ions in the solution. A very dilute solution of the acid (lots of water, few acid ions) could have a pH around 5 or 6, whereas a more concentrated acid solution (less water, more ions) could have a pH of 1 or 2. Alkaline solutions follow a similar pattern, concentrated solutions having a pH nearer 14 and more dilute solutions a pH nearer 7. The use of indicators is limited to your skill at observing small changes in colour, and if the original solution is coloured the indicator colour may be "hidden". A more accurate way of measuring pH is to use a **pH meter**.

The pH Meter

The pH meter has a special electrode which, when dipped into a solution, can measure the number of hydrogen ions present. The pH value of the solution is read off from the scale.

Not only is a meter more accurate than an indicator, it also measures the pH without affecting the solution being tested (indicators leave the solution coloured).

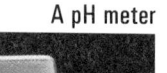

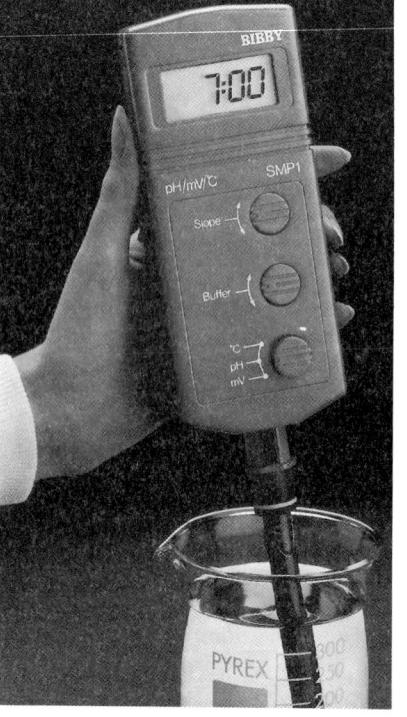

A pH meter

Diluting Acids and Alkalis

When we add water to a solution of ions, the same number of ions are spread through more liquid. We say the solution has been **diluted**. It is like diluting orange squash. If we quarter fill a glass with the squash and then top up with water, we have a diluted solution. The glass contains as much orange squash as before, but it is now spread through a larger volume.

In the same way, 10 cm³ of concentrated acid can spread through 100 cm³ or 1000 cm³ of solution, simply by adding the appropriate amount of water. Each solution contains the same number of acid ions, but the **concentration** of the ions **decreases** as the volume of the solution **increases**.

As the acid solution becomes more and more **dilute**, the concentration of acid ions is less. This has the effect of **raising the pH**. The pH is related to the **concentration of hydrogen ions**. As the acidity of the solution decreases, the pH of the solution increases towards pH 7. In a similar way, diluting an alkaline solution decreases the alkalinity and the pH decreases towards pH 7.

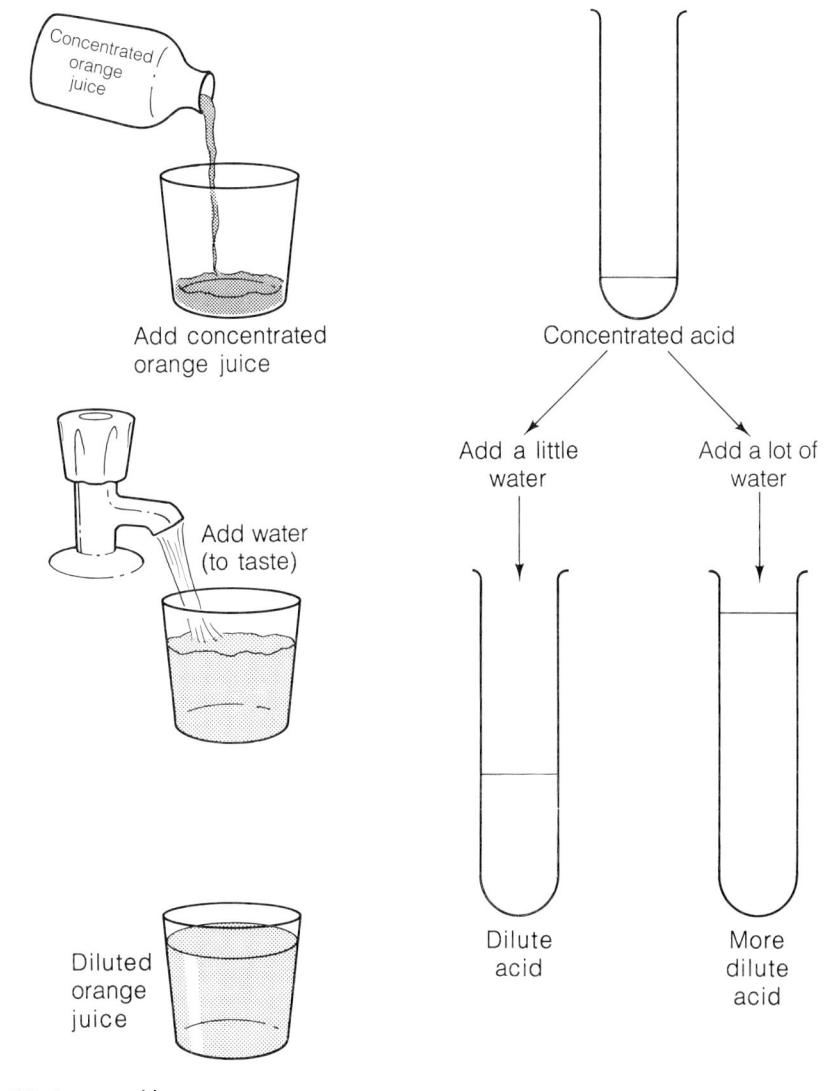

Diluting an acid

Ions in Solution

Water is a covalent liquid at room temperature. It should not conduct electricity. However, if a very sensitive conductivity meter is used, a small current can be detected.

Only ionic solutions can conduct electricity, so this suggests that **some ions** must be present in water. They are hydrogen and hydroxide ions, produced when **some** of the molecules ionise.

$$H_2O(l) \xrightarrow{some} H^+(aq) + OH^-(aq)$$

As the conductivity of water is very low, only a **few** of these ions must be present. In fact, for every hydrogen or hydroxide ion present in water, there are about 555 million water molecules!

From the equation it can be seen that there are equal numbers of hydrogen and hydroxide ions. When an acidic substance is added to water, a reaction occurs and causes a large **increase** in **hydrogen** ions.

An alkaline substance reacts with water to cause a large **increase** in **hydroxide** ions.

Acids, then, are substances which dissolve in water to produce an **excess** of **hydrogen ions**. **Alkalis** are substances which dissolve in water to produce an **excess** of **hydroxide ions**. A **neutral** solution contains **equal numbers** of **hydrogen ions** and **hydroxide ions** (or none at all).

ACIDS AND ALKALIS

Activities

1. (a) When you are at home, ask if you can look at bottles and cans in your food cupboard. Read the list of ingredients on the labels and find out if they contain any acid or alkali. Make a short report about your findings.
   (b) Do the same with cleaning materials and other household items.
   (c) Your teacher may let you test the pH of some of these household substances.

2. You are given three colourless liquids and told that one is acid, one alkali and one water. Describe tests you would carry out to tell them apart.

3. Electricity is passed through an acidic solution. What would be given off at the negative electrode? How would you test for this substance?

4. From the grid, choose answers to the following questions. (There may be more than one correct answer.)

A acidic	B sodium oxide	C contains $OH^-(aq)$ ions
D pH 12	E contains $H^+(aq)$ ions	F alkaline
G sulphur dioxide	H pH 7	I pH 2

(a) Which box(es) gives correct information about the solution formed when nitrogen dioxide dissolves in water?
(b) Which box(es) gives correct information about the solution formed when potassium oxide dissolves in water?
(c) Which box(es) shows an acidic oxide?
(d) Which oxide forms an alkaline solution?
(e) Which box(es) shows the pH of pure water?

5. The uses of sodium hydroxide (see table 4.6 in Uses of Alkalis) can be presented in a pie chart, bar graph, line graph etc. Choose a way to present the information and sketch your graph, or chart, in your notebook.

6. A laboratory technician poured 100 cm³ of an alkali into a beaker, labelled A. She then placed 50 cm³ of the same alkali into a second beaker, labelled B, and mixed this with 50 cm³ of water.
   (a) How will the pH of the solutions in each beaker, A and B, differ?
   (b) Which solution will be the most alkaline?
   (c) How would the number of $OH^-(aq)$ ions compare?

7. (a) How will the number of $H^+(aq)$ and $OH^-(aq)$ ions compare in the following solutions?

   A: pH 10
   B: pH 7
   C: hydrochloric acid

   (b) Suggest what solutions A and B might be.
   (c) What sort of pH might C have?

2 Reactions of Acids

Neutralisers

A substance which reacts with an acid and causes its pH to **rise** towards pH 7 (neutral) can be called a **neutraliser**. Similarly, the word neutraliser can be used to describe a substance which causes the pH of an alkali to **fall** towards pH 7. The following reactions show acids reacting with neutralisers.

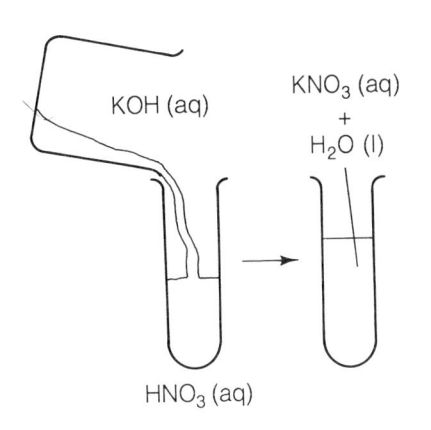

Key Ideas

A *neutraliser* is a chemical which causes the pH of an *acidic* solution to *rise* towards *pH 7*, or the pH of an *alkaline* solution to *fall* towards *pH 7*.

Alkalis, metal oxides, metal carbonates and some metals can all neutralise acids.

A neutralisation reaction always forms a *salt*, and the H^+ (aq) ion is always *removed* as *water*.

Metal oxides, hydroxides, and ammonia are known as *bases*.

Acid plus Alkali

An **acid** always reacts with an **alkali** to form a **salt** and **water**:

Acid + Alkali → Salt + Water

It is a **neutralisation** reaction. The alkali sodium hydroxide reacts with hydrochloric acid to form sodium chloride (the **salt**) plus water. As the alkali is added, the pH of the acid rises towards 7:

NaOH(aq) + HCl(aq) →
$\quad$ NaCl(aq) + H_2O(l)

Nitric acid reacts with the alkali potassium hydroxide, to form potassium nitrate and water:

HNO_3(aq) + KOH(aq)
$\quad$ → KNO_3(aq) + H_2O(l)

Acid plus Metal Carbonate

An **acid** always reacts with a **metal carbonate** to produce a **salt**, **carbon dioxide** and **water**. Copper carbonate reacts with sulphuric acid to produce copper sulphate, carbon dioxide and water.

Acid + Metal carbonate → Salt + Water + Carbon dioxide
H_2SO_4(aq) + $CuCO_3$(s) → $CuSO_4$(aq) + H_2O(l) + CO_2(g)

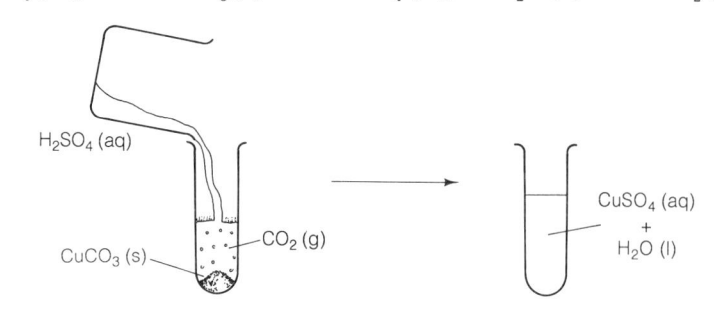

When the acid is first added to the copper carbonate, carbon dioxide gas is given off and the mixture fizzes (it effervesces).

Can you remember the test for carbon dioxide? **Carbon dioxide turns limewater cloudy.**

Metal carbonates neutralise the hydrogen ions from the acid to form water.

When you spill acid on the laboratory bench, the usual procedure is to dilute the acid with water first, and then pour a solution of sodium carbonate onto the acid. This neutralises the acid.

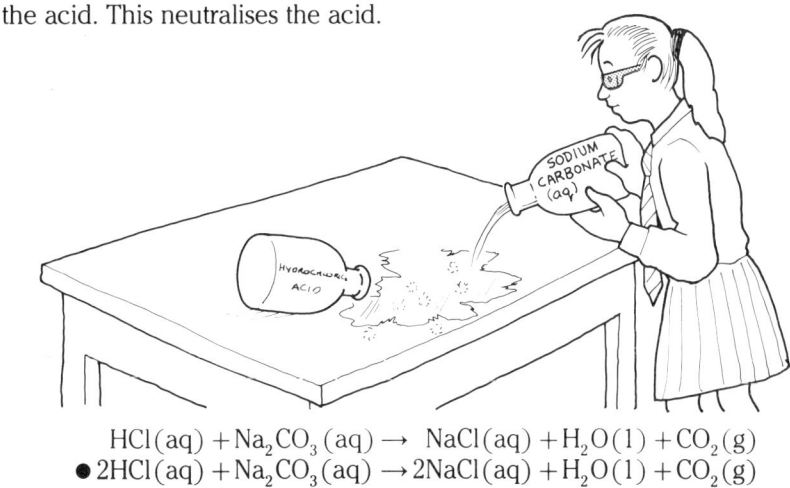

HCl(aq) + Na_2CO_3(aq) → NaCl(aq) + H_2O(l) + CO_2(g)
● 2HCl(aq) + Na_2CO_3(aq) → 2NaCl(aq) + H_2O(l) + CO_2(g)

116 ACIDS AND ALKALIS

Acid plus Reactive Metal

When an acid reacts with a metal, the hydrogen ions from the acid form neutral hydrogen gas. This always happens when a **reactive metal** reacts with an acid. A **salt** and **hydrogen** are formed:

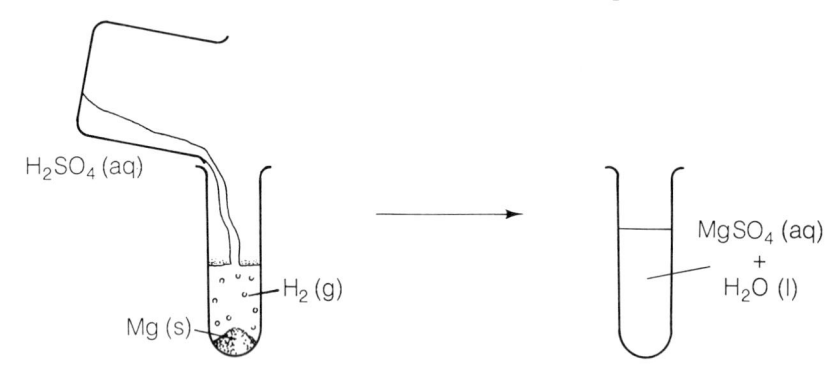

Reactive metal + Acid → Salt + Hydrogen
$Mg(s)$ + $H_2SO_4(aq)$ → $MgSO_4(aq)$ + $H_2(g)$

Fruits and fruit juices can be quite acidic. If these products are canned, the acidic juices can react with the tin to produce hydrogen gas. The gas could cause the can to swell, and even explode! Even if it is opened before this stage, the fruit can still be spoiled by contamination from dissolved metal.

To prevent all this, the inside of the can is coated with a special lacquer which protects the tin from the acid. Next time you open a can of fruit in the house, look inside; you may be able to see the golden lacquer coating.

Zinc reacts with hydrochloric acid to produce hydrogen gas and zinc chloride solution:

$Zn(s)$ + $HCl(aq)$ → $ZnCl_2(aq)$ + $H_2(g)$
• $Zn(s)$ + $2HCl(aq)$ → $ZnCl_2(aq)$ + $H_2(g)$

What do these Reactions have in Common?

(a) **Salts are formed**
All three types of reaction form a **salt**.

(b) **H^+ (aq) ions are removed**
All three types of reaction **remove H^+ ions**.

(i) **With any alkali**
$H^+(aq)$ + $OH^-(aq)$ → $H_2O(l)$
from   from   water
acid   alkali   (neutral)

(ii) **With any carbonate**
$2H^+(aq)$ + $CO_3^{2-}(s)$ → $H_2O(l)$ + $CO_2(g)$
from   from   water   carbon
acid   carbonate   dioxide

(iii) **With any reactive metal**
$2H^+(aq)$ + $M(s)$ → $H_2(g)$ + $M^{2+}(aq)$
from   reactive   hydrogen   metal
acid   metal   ion

These equations only show the ions which react to form new products. The ions which don't react are called **spectator ions**.

Example
$NaOH(aq) + HCl(aq) \rightarrow NaCl(aq) + H_2O(l)$
Showing ions
$Na^+(aq) + OH^-(aq) + H^+(aq) + Cl^-(aq)$
$\rightarrow Na^+(aq) + Cl^-(aq) + H_2O(l)$

Only the **H^+ (aq)** and **OH^- (aq)** ions are reacting to form water. The spectator ions are **Na^+ (aq)** and **Cl^- (aq)** which have not reacted.

Bases

Some neutralisers are called **bases**. A base is chemically the opposite of an acid:

Acids produce H^+ (aq) ions
Bases accept H^+ (aq) ions

Metal oxides and **hydroxides** are **bases**. When they react with acid the oxide ion (O^{2-}) or hydroxide ion (OH^-) combine with the hydrogen ion (H^+) to form **water**. The base in each reaction takes a hydrogen ion from the acid, thus neutralising the acid.

$Na^+_2 O^{2-} (s) + 2H^+ (aq) + SO_4^{2-} (aq) \rightarrow 2Na^+ (aq) + SO_4^{2-} (aq) + H_2O(l)$

$K^+OH^- (s) + H^+ (aq) + Cl^- (aq) \rightarrow K^+ (aq) + Cl^- (aq) + H_2O(l)$

When a base is soluble in water, it forms an **alkaline** solution. Sodium oxide and potassium hydroxide are both soluble bases and so form alkaline solutions.

$Na_2O(s) + H_2O(l) \rightarrow 2Na^+ (aq) + 2OH^- (aq)$

$KOH(s) \xrightarrow{H_2O(l)} K^+ (aq) + OH^- (aq)$

Ammonia is another example of a soluble base, reacting with water to produce **some** ammonium and hydroxide ions.

$NH_3(g) + H_2O(l) \rightarrow NH_4^+ (aq) + OH^- (aq)$

Copper(II) oxide is a base which is insoluble in water, and so cannot form alkaline solutions. The insoluble bases can, however, still be used as neutralisers, because they react with acids.

Table 4.9

metal	oxide	hydroxide
aluminium	insol.	insol.
barium	reacts	vsol.
calcium	reacts	sol.
copper(II)	insol.	insol.
iron(II)	insol.	insol.
lead(II)	insol.	insol.
lithium	reacts	vsol.
magnesium	insol.	insol.
nickel	insol.	insol.
potassium	reacts	vsol.
silver	insol.	insol.
sodium	reacts	vsol.
tin(II)	insol.	insol.
zinc	insol.	insol.

How some metal oxides and hydroxides behave in water (insol. = insoluble; sol. = soluble; vsol. = very soluble)

Using Insoluble Bases and Carbonates

We can use insoluble bases and carbonates to make **soluble salts**.

To make iron(II) sulphate, we could react a base containing iron(II) ions with sulphuric acid. Both iron(II) oxide and iron(II) hydroxide are insoluble in water, so we simply need to add the solid base to sulphuric acid until no more reacts. Any excess base can be filtered off, leaving an exactly neutral solution. The solution is evaporated to leave crystals of iron(II) sulphate.

Acid + Insoluble base → Salt + Water
$H_2SO_4(aq) + FeO(s) \rightarrow FeSO_4(aq) + H_2O(l)$

Copper(II) carbonate is insoluble in water, but if the carbonate is added to hydrochloric acid, it will react to give off carbon dioxide. The remaining solution contains the salt copper(II) chloride, which can be recovered by evaporation.

Acid + Carbonate → Salt + Carbon dioxide + Water
$2HCl(aq) + CuCO_3(s) \rightarrow CuCl_2(aq) + CO_2(g) + H_2O(l)$

Table 4.10 (page 118) shows that salts can be thought of as simply acids which have had their H^+ (aq) ions replaced by **metal ions**, or by the **ammonium ion**.

Table 4.10

Base	Acid	Salt formed
Copper(II) oxide $Cu^{2+}O^{2-}$	Sulphuric $2H^+SO_4^{2-}$	Copper(II) sulphate $Cu^{2+}SO_4^{2-}$
Magnesium carbonate $Mg^{2+}CO_3^{2-}$	Hydrochloric H^+Cl^-	Magnesium chloride $Mg^{2+}(Cl^-)_2$
Aluminium hydroxide $Al^{3+}(OH^-)_3$	Nitric $H^+NO_3^-$	Aluminium nitrate $Al^{3+}(NO_3^-)_3$
Ammonium hydroxide $NH_4^+OH^-$	Sulphuric $2H^+SO_4^{2-}$	Ammonium sulphate $(NH_4^+)_2SO_4^{2-}$

Activities

1. A motorcyclist has removed the battery from his motorbike for recharging. During the process he accidentally spills some of the concentrated sulphuric acid, which is in the battery, onto the kitchen table. What household chemicals would you suggest he could use to neutralise the acid and so prevent damaging the table?

2. Look up the solubility table in a data book, or use table 4.9. Select six compounds, three of which would form alkaline solutions and three which would not.

3. Describe **four** different chemical tests you could use to show that a clear solution is an acid.

4. A diver exploring an old shipwreck finds some gold coins partly encrusted with limestone ($CaCO_3$). Explain how he could chemically get rid of the limestone without damaging the coins.

5. (a) Place the following substances into one of three columns, headed, acid, base and salt:

   $CuCl_2$ H_2SO_4 KOH
   HCl $BaSO_4$ $Ca(OH)_2$
   $NaCl$ K_2SO_4 $Fe(OH)_2$

   (b) From the list, which two substances could be used to form iron(II) sulphate?
   (c) Write a balanced equation for the reaction in (b).

6. (a) Write down the **spectator ions** in each of the following equations:
   (i) $KOH(aq) + HNO_3(aq) \rightarrow KNO_3(aq) + H_2O(l)$
   (ii) $AgNO_3(aq) + NaCl(aq) \rightarrow AgCl(s) + NaNO_3(aq)$

   (b) Rewrite the above equations without the spectator ions. (Show only the ions reacting.)

3 Neutralisers in Action

Key Ideas

Neutralisers are not just used inside the laboratory – they are part of our everyday lives. Acid indigestion, and the pain caused by acid or alkaline stings from insects and nettles, can be relieved by neutralisers. Farmers reduce the acidity of soil by adding a neutraliser. Salts formed in neutralisation reactions have a variety of uses.

Indigestion

The stomach contains **hydrochloric acid** to help us to digest our food. The walls of the stomach are coated with a mucus to prevent damage by the acid.

When we eat food quickly, some of the stomach acids are pushed up into our gullet. The gullet is not protected like our stomach and a strong burning sensation (known as **indigestion**) can be felt. Some stomach disorders interfere with the protective lining of the stomach, and acid will cause pain there.

Indigestion is caused by too much acid in the stomach. Indigestion tablets, or powders, contain a neutraliser which causes the pH to move towards 7, and so less acidic. Indigestion remedies can contain either sodium hydrogen carbonate ($NaHCO_3$), magnesium hydroxide ($Mg(OH)_2$) or aluminium hydroxide ($Al(OH)_3$).

Bee and Wasp Stings

When you are stung by a bee, it injects methanoic acid under your skin. This causes swelling and pain.

The sting can be neutralised by washing the area with a solution of sodium bicarbonate ($NaHCO_3$) or dilute household ammonia (NH_3). Stinging nettles also contain methanoic acid, and the sting can be neutralised in a similar way.

A wasp sting is alkaline, so an acid is needed to neutralise it. Household acids which might be used are lemon juice or vinegar.

The sting of a bee

Soil Acidity

Plants depend on the chemicals in the soil for their growth. The chemicals have to be soluble in water so that the plant can take them up in solution through their roots. The solubility of these chemicals depends on the pH of the water. Chemicals containing nitrogen, phosphorus, potassium or sulphur are most soluble over a pH range of 6 to 7, but are less soluble as the pH becomes more acid. Chemicals containing iron and manganese are more soluble in acidic soils.

The farmer has to know what chemicals are best for the particular crop he intends to plant in a field. He adjusts the pH of the soil to make the chemicals and nutrients soluble for plant growth.

The exact pH of the soil is measured and if it is too acidic, the correct amount of **lime** (neutraliser) is spread over the field to adjust the pH to the required level. Lime is the common name given to calcium oxide. It will neutralise any acids in the soil.

You can buy a soil testing kit which

Indigestion remedies

120 ACIDS AND ALKALIS

allows you to measure the pH of the soil in your garden. It contains a small beaker in which you mix some soil with water. The mixture is tested with pH paper, and the instructions are used to work out whether a neutraliser needs to be added to your soil.

Farmer liming field

Manufacture of Fertilisers

Nearly 30 per cent of all the sulphuric acid produced in the world (and 80 per cent of all ammonia) is used to manufacture fertilisers.

One such fertiliser is **ammonium sulphate**. It is made by neutralising sulphuric acid with ammonia solution:

$$H_2SO_4(aq) + NH_3(aq) \rightarrow (NH_4)_2SO_4(aq)$$
$$\bullet H_2SO_4(aq) + 2NH_3(aq) \rightarrow (NH_4)_2SO_4(aq)$$

Water is evaporated off to leave the solid ammonium sulphate.

Another fertiliser is **ammonium nitrate**, also formed by a neutralisation reaction. Nitric acid and ammonia are the reactants this time.

$$HNO_3(aq) + NH_3(aq) \rightarrow NH_4NO_3(aq)$$

SAI fertiliser plant in Leith

Manufacture of Aluminium Sulphate

The manufacture of aluminium sulphate involves a neutralisation reaction. The most common ore of aluminium is bauxite, a red coloured rock consisting mainly of aluminium oxide.

Bauxite is imported into the UK, and initially processed to give pure aluminium oxide. This aluminium oxide is the starting point for the manufacture of aluminium and its compounds. When the oxide is reacted with sulphuric acid, aluminium sulphate is formed:

$$Al_2O_3(s) + 3H_2SO_4(aq) \rightarrow Al_2(SO_4)_3(aq) + 3H_2O(l)$$

The solution formed can be evaporated to give solid aluminium sulphate. However, many customers prefer to buy their aluminium sulphate as a solution and so complete evaporation of the water is not required. This helps to reduce the cost of producing the compound.

Using Aluminium Sulphate

1 Water Treatment

Aluminium sulphate is used in water treatment plants to help clean up dirty water. Most of the solid particles in the water can be removed by filtration, but often the water remains cloudy due to extremely small particles which can pass through the filter.

Aluminium sulphate solution is mixed with the cloudy water, and the mixture is pumped into large settling tanks.

The tiny particles which caused the cloudiness are attracted to the aluminium ions, and when they join together they sink slowly to the bottom of the tank. This is called **sedimentation**. The sediment can be removed by **filtration**. The clear water can then be released into the public supply.

In 1988 a large quantity of aluminium sulphate solution at a water treatment plant was accidently released into the public drinking supply.

This is what happened: the water from the reservoir was slightly acidic (pH6). A pH meter measured the pH of the water as it passed from the reservoir and along a pipe. The meter controlled a machine which **should** have added lime to the water to raise the pH up to 9. A tanker delivering 20 tonnes of aluminium sulphate solution to the treatment plant unloaded the solution into the wrong tank (it was actually fed straight into the water supply). At about the same time the machine for adding the lime developed a fault, and the water became **more** acidic reaching pH 4.

People who drank the water felt a burning sensation in their mouths and began to feel sick. Their lips and fingers felt sticky after washing and milk put into tea curdled. Others, with bleached hair, found that their hair turned green. Some hot water supplies turned blue. The acidic water dissolved copper from the water supply pipes, and this had turned hair green, and hot water blue.

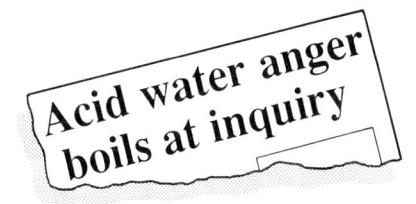

Acid water anger boils at inquiry

2 Paper Treatment

Aluminium sulphate has been used in paper making since 1850 to prevent printing ink from spreading on the paper. Unfortunately the sulphate combines with moisture in the air to form sulphuric acid. This attacks cellulose in the paper and breaks it down, turning it yellow and eventually into dust. Millions of old books are lost each year as a result of this process.

Activities

o 1 Examine some indigestion remedies or toothpastes you have at home and by looking at the list of ingredients try to identify the alkalis used. Present your results in a table.

o 2 Collect some soil from your school grounds or from home and test a solution of the soil and pH paper. Does it need any lime?

o 3 Some fertilisers contain phosphates. Sodium phosphate and ammonium phosphate are both salts of phosphoric acid (H_3PO_4). Write word equations for the reaction of the acid with suitable alkalis to make these salts.

• 4 Write balanced chemical equations for the above reactions.

• 5 The EEC are to prosecute the UK for failing to bring some of our water supplies up to EEC standards. The main problem lies in East Anglia where some water supplies have been contaminated with soluble nitrates, which get into rivers and fields spread with nitrate fertilisers.
  (a) How does the nitrate get from the fields to the rivers?
  (b) Write balanced chemical equations for possible methods of producing ammonium nitrate, potassium nitrate and calcium nitrate.

4 Acid Rain

Key Ideas 🔑

The acidic gases being released into the atmosphere are making rainwater very *acidic*. This is known as *acid rain*. These gases come from industry, power stations and cars. Acid rain attacks metals, stone structures and living things. Acidic water can be neutralised, but it would be better to stop it altogether.

The Changing pH of Rain

Rain has always been slightly acidic since carbon dioxide dissolves in moist air to form carbonic acid. This gives rain water a pH of about 6.

$$CO_2(g) + H_2O(l) \rightarrow H_2CO_3(aq)$$
carbonic acid

In chalk and limestone areas of the country, the action of acid rain over the centuries has carved out caves. Often these caves have stalactites hanging from the roof and stalagmites rising from the floor.

Stalagmites and stalactites

The small amount of carbonic acid in the rain water is sufficient to react with the limestone to form soluble calcium hydrogencarbonate.

$$CaCO_3(s) + H_2CO_3(aq) \rightarrow Ca(HCO_3)_2(aq)$$
calcium hydrogencarbonate

As the rainwater seeps deeper into the limestone, the limestone slowly dissolves and caves are formed. Drips of calcium hydrogencarbonate solution fall to the floor of the cave, and others hang from the roof. Evaporation occurs leaving small deposits of solid calcium carbonate, which gradually increase in size.

These deposits grow slowly to form stalagmites and stalactites.

$$Ca(HCO_3)_2(aq) \rightarrow CaCO_3(s) + CO_2(g) + H_2O(l)$$
calcium carbonate

In recent years the rain has become more acidic. In central Europe, rain with a pH of 4 is quite common (this is more than one hundred times as acidic as pH 6).

A pH of less than three has been recorded in some rain, and fog can be even more acidic than this. In London in 1952 there was a particularly bad **smog** (a mixture of smoke and fog) which had a pH below 2. An estimated four thousand people died that year as a result of illnesses brought on by the poisonous fog.

London smog of 1952

ACIDS AND ALKALIS

What has made the Rain more Acidic?

The widespread combustion (burning) of non-metals has led to atmospheric pollution, which in turn produces acid rain.

Industrial countries throughout the world have an acid rain problem, but it is most serious in Europe. One cause of acid rain is sulphur. Sulphur is present in coal, and when coal is burned, one of the waste gases is **sulphur dioxide**:

$$S(s) + O_2(g) \rightarrow SO_2(g)$$

Once in the air, the sulphur dioxide will remain unchanged in dry weather, and react with oxygen in the air to form sulphur trioxide:

$$SO_2(g) + O_2(g) \rightarrow SO_3(g)$$
- $2SO_2(g) + O_2(g) \rightarrow 2SO_3(g)$

Both these sulphur oxides dissolve in water droplets to form very dilute acids, which fall to the ground as **acid rain**.

$$SO_2(g) + H_2O(l) \rightarrow H_2SO_3(aq)$$
sulphurous acid

$$SO_3(g) + H_2O(l) \rightarrow H_2SO_4(aq)$$
sulphuric acid

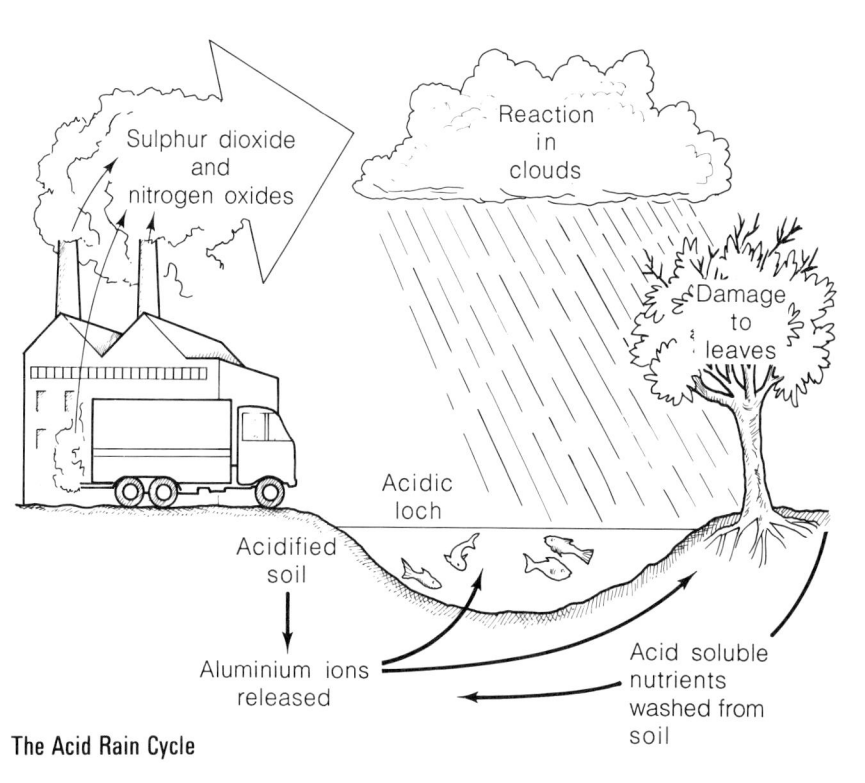

The Acid Rain Cycle

Another cause of acid rain is atmospheric nitrogen.

Air is about 80 per cent nitrogen, and at high combustion temperatures, e.g., in car engines or large furnaces, this nitrogen combines with oxygen to form oxides:

$$N_2(g) + O_2(g) \rightarrow NO(g)$$
$$NO(g) + O_2(g) \rightarrow NO_2(g)$$
- $N_2(g) + O_2(g) \rightarrow 2NO(g)$
$2NO(g) + O_2(g) \rightarrow 2NO_2(g)$

Nitrogen dioxide is soluble in moist air and forms nitric acid (HNO_3).

The Effects of Increased Acidity

1 Releasing Aluminium

The most plentiful metal element in the Earth's crust is aluminium, but it usually occurs combined with other elements in compounds (minerals).

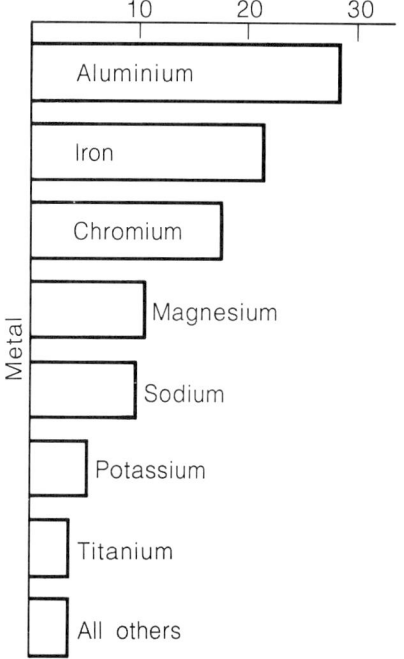

Metals in the Earth's crust

These aluminium compounds are soluble in dilute acid. Acid rain dissolves the aluminium compounds and aluminium ions find their way into living systems.

124 ACIDS AND ALKALIS

Fish
Many lakes in southern Scandinavia, Scotland and Canada are now without fish. Aluminium ions washed from the soil have contaminated the rivers and lakes. These affect the gills of fish, reducing the amount of oxygen which reaches their blood. Subsequently the fish have all died.

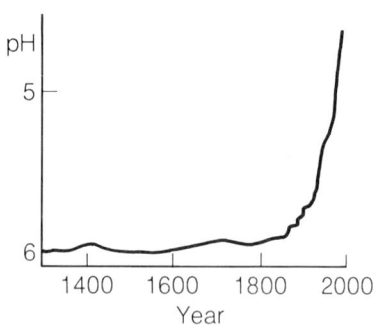

Acidification of a loch

More algae and moss grow on the surface of poisoned lakes and this in turn cuts down the food available for other plants and animals – they too slowly die off.

A Greenpeace survey in 1988 showed that of twenty lochs already acidified in Scotland, six of them had no fish left (five of these lochs are in one region alone).

Trees
Trees take up nutrients from the soil through their root system. These nutrients dissolve slowly in normal rain, but very rapidly in acid rain. Heavy acid rainfalls wash the useful nutrients out of the ground, and at the same time release aluminium ions into the soil. It is thought that the aluminium ions prevent the roots from absorbing water and nutrients. Trees die due to a combination of starvation and disease.

A House of Commons Committee concluded in May 1988 that only 40 per cent of British trees could be considered healthy.

Humans
Premature senility in humans (Alzheimer's disease) has been linked with aluminium ions in drinking water. Aluminium sulphate is added directly to water at the reservoir to make it clear. The metal also dissolves from aluminium pots and pans, into acidic foods, such as fruit.

We do not yet fully understand the causes of Alzheimer's disease but there are increasing numbers of people suffering from this illness.

A dying forest

2 Damaging Buildings
We saw how caves were formed in limestone areas. Any structure made from a carbonate containing mineral (e.g., marble, limestone) will react in the same way. If the rain falling on these buildings is more acidic, the erosion process is much quicker because of the increased acidity.

The process is particularly noticeable on areas where drips of water hang or gather. The cement which joins most stone and brickwork also contains calcium carbonate and it too is eroded away. Buildings can be rendered dangerous.

At Westminster Abbey, 5 million pounds has been spent repairing acid rain damage to limestone carvings, which had been in place only 90 years.

3 Steel Structures
Iron and steel rust in the presence of oxygen and water. If the water is acidic, the rate of rusting increases. Steel structures like the Forth Rail Bridge have to be constantly painted in an attempt to prevent rain attacking the bare metal.

Building damaged by acid rain

Solving the Problem

1 Power Stations

The causes and effects of acid rain have become a major political issue. To complicate the situation, scientists disagree about some effects, and much research still needs to be done. The EEC agreed that power stations over a certain size must use chemical **scrubbers** to remove harmful gases before they enter the atmosphere.

Drax Power Station, near Selby in Yorkshire, is to be fitted with such a scrubber. It burns 33 thousand tonnes of coal (thirty train loads) and emits 250 thousand tonnes of sulphur dioxide gas into the atmosphere – every day. According to Sir John Mason, in his lecture to the British Association for the Advancement of Science in 1988, the UK is only fifth in the European league of sulphur dioxide polluters, producing nearly 10 per cent of European pollution, and nearly 2 per cent of world pollution. The three worst polluters are Czechoslovakia, Poland and East Germany.

Preventing sulphur dioxide getting into the atmosphere costs a lot of money and in the long term will put up the cost of electricity. Scrubbers use the mineral gypsum to extract the harmful gases. Huge quantities will have to be mined each year. After use, the spent gypsum will have to be dumped somewhere, raising yet another environmental issue.

The UK has agreed to cut pollution by 35 per cent by the year 2000. In fact, only six out of the UK's forty power stations will have reduced emissions by then. Greenpeace estimate that a 78 per cent drop in emissions is required to protect the environment for the future.

2 Car Exhausts

In the USA all vehicles must have a catalytic converter fitted to their exhaust system to remove harmful gases.

The system is checked each year and inefficient vehicles are banned from the road. The catalytic converter adds a few hundred pounds to the price of a car and is equally expensive to replace.

Meanwhile, some European countries try to reduce the effects of acid rain by spreading limestone powder over land, rivers and lakes.

In the long term the prevention of gases being released into the atmosphere is the sole solution, and will be very expensive to implement.

Spreading lime from a helicopter

Activities

1. Give two examples of how acid rain can effect:
   (a) living things
   (b) non-living things.

2. Give two examples of gases which can form acid rain, and write equations for the reaction of these gases with water.

3. (a) What action can countries take to reduce the amount of acid rain?
   (b) Why is progress in reducing acid rain so slow?
   (c) Using the graph on page 124 predict how the graph would continue up until 2050 if:
   (i) no action was taken to stop acid rain pollution
   (ii) acid rain pollution was reduced in the next ten years to almost nothing.

5 Making Salts

Soluble Salts

Every neutralisation reaction results in the formation of a **salt**.

The salt is an ionic compound consisting of two ions – a positive metal ion from the base and a negative ion from the acid. The positive ion can sometimes be the ammonium ion (NH_4^+).

Before deciding on the best method of preparing a salt, we need to know whether the salt is **soluble** or **insoluble**.

Table 4.11 shows the solubilities of some salts in water.

Making a soluble salt by reacting an alkali with an acid

Key Ideas

Soluble and *insoluble* salts can be made in the laboratory. Soluble salts are made by reacting an acid with a *neutraliser*. The final solution contains the salt *dissolved* in water. The salt is recovered by *evaporating* off the water. Insoluble salts are prepared by *mixing* solutions containing the *ions* required in the salt. The insoluble salt forms a *precipitate* which can be filtered off.

Making a Soluble Salt

The chemical name for the salt we put on our food is **sodium chloride**. It is an example of a **soluble salt**. Soluble salts can be made by reacting an **alkali** with an **acid**.

Sodium hydroxide solution contains **sodium** ions and hydrochloric acid **chloride** ions. These chemicals would be suitable starting materials for making sodium chloride:

(1) Hydrochloric acid and sodium hydroxide solutions, of known concentration, are carefully added together, and an indicator is used to tell when the solution is exactly neutral. This is known as **titration**.

(2) The experiment is then repeated **without the indicator**, but using the same volumes of acid and alkali solutions. This produces a solution of the salt.

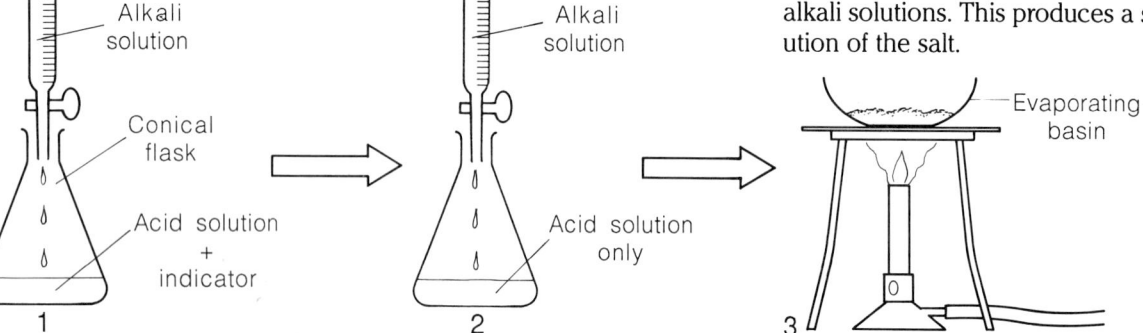

Table 4.11

	bromide	carbonate	chloride	iodide	nitrate	phosphate	sulphate
aluminium	vsol.	insol.	vsol.	vsol.	vsol.	insol.	vsol.
ammonium	vsol.	vsol.	vsol.	vsol.	vsol.	vsol.	vsol.
barium	vsol.	insol.	vsol.	vsol.	vsol	insol.	insol.
calcium	vsol.	insol.	vsol.	vsol.	vsol.	insol.	sol.
copper(II)	vsol.	insol.	vsol.	—	vsol.	insol.	vsol.
iron(II)	vsol.	insol.	vsol.	vsol.	vsol.	insol.	vsol.
lead(II)	sol.	insol.	sol.	insol.	vsol.	insol.	insol.
lithium	vsol.	vsol.	vsol.	vsol.	vsol.	insol.	vsol.
magnesium	vsol.	insol.	vsol.	vsol.	vsol.	insol.	vsol.
nickel	vsol.	insol.	vsol.	vsol.	vsol.	insol.	vsol.
potassium	vsol.	vsol.	vsol.	vsol.	vsol.	vsol.	vsol.
silver	insol.	insol.	insol.	insol.	vsol.	insol.	sol.
sodium	vsol.	vsol.	vsol.	vsol.	vsol.	vsol.	vsol.
tin(II)	vsol.	insol.	vsol.	sol.	—	insol.	vsol.
zinc	vsol.	insol.	vsol.	vsol.	vsol.	insol.	vsol.

vsol = very soluble (solubility greater than 10 gl^{-1}); sol = soluble (solubility between 1 and 10 gl^{-1});
insol = insoluble (solubility less than 1 gl^{-1}); — = data unavailable

ACIDS AND ALKALIS

(3) The water is **evaporated** off, leaving solid sodium chloride crystals behind.

Another way of producing a soluble salt is to add a solid **metal oxide** or **metal carbonate** to a solution of an **acid**:

(1) A quantity of acid is put into a beaker. Solid metal oxide or metal carbonate is added to the acid, until no more reacts.

Sometimes the mixture needs to be heated to speed up reaction.

(2) The excess solid is filtered off, leaving a clear **neutral** solution of the salt.

(3) The solution is then evaporated, leaving crystals of the salt behind.

The size of the crystals formed depends on the rate of evaporation of the solution. If the salt solution is evaporated rapidly, the crystals will be very small.

If the salt solution is only partly evaporated and then left to stand in a warm place, the remaining water evaporates more slowly, and larger crystals are formed.

The crystals can be dried by pressing them between dry filter papers or placing them in an oven.

Making a soluble salt from a metal oxide or carbonate

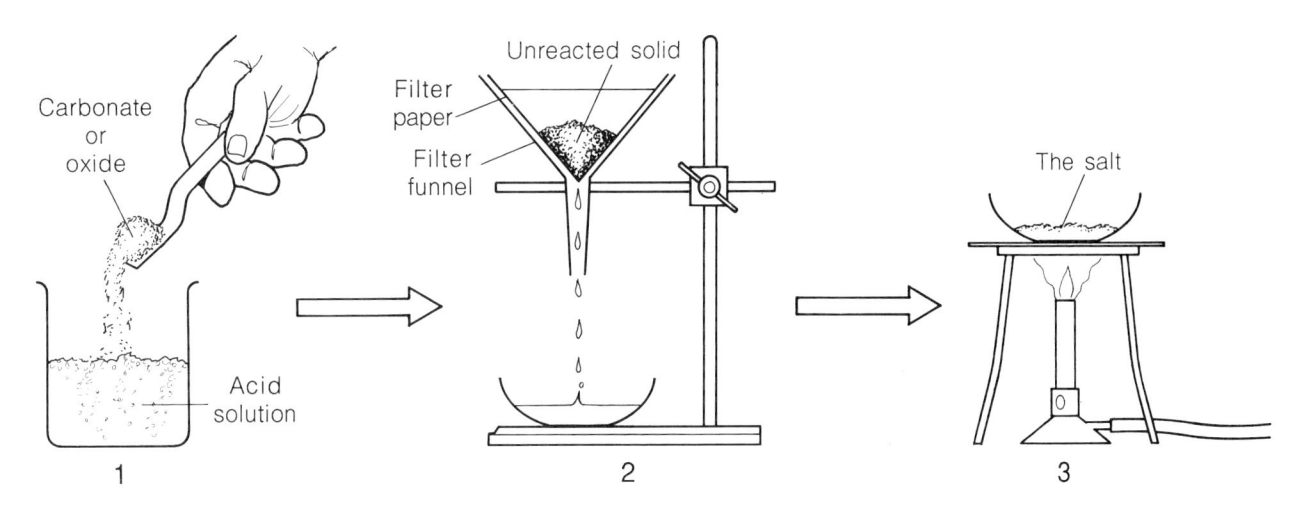

Sodium chloride crystals

Naming Soluble Salts

When naming soluble salts the metal ion from the alkali, oxide or carbonate is always written first, followed by the negative ion from the acid.

Sulphuric acid forms salts called **sulphates**:

sodium sulphate	Na_2SO_4
ammonium sulphate	$(NH_4)_2SO_4$
calcium sulphate	$CaSO_4$

Hydrochloric acid forms salts called **chlorides**:

sodium chloride	NaCl
copper(II) chloride	$CuCl_2$
barium chloride	$BaCl_2$

Nitric acid forms salts called **nitrates**:

potassium nitrate	KNO_3
magnesium nitrate	$Mg(NO_3)_2$
aluminium nitrate	$Al(NO_3)_3$

ACIDS AND ALKALIS

The Importance of Common Salt

Sodium chloride is an important ingredient in our diet. We each contain about 250 grams of salt, which:
1 Helps regulate the flow of water, food and waste in and out of cells.
2 Helps muscles and nerves control body movements.
3 Assists the digestion of proteins.

We lose salt when we sweat so we need to eat food to replace any salt lost.

A daily intake of 5 grams of salt is recommended.

High intakes of salt are thought to be linked to high blood pressure, which can lead to heart disease and strokes. However, we must have some salt in order to live!

Salt is also an important raw material for industry.

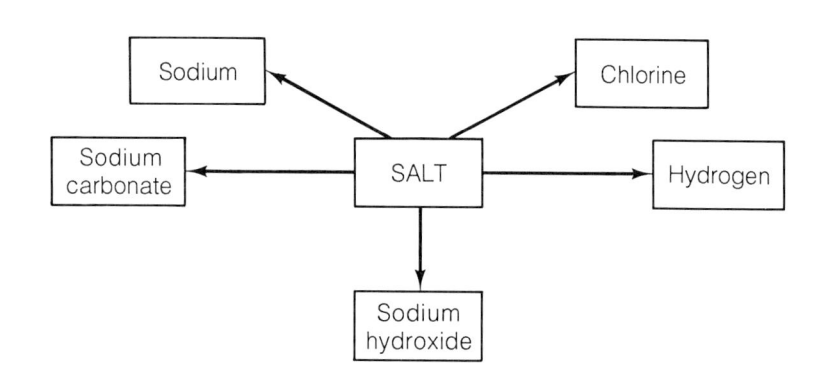

Industrial uses of salt

Industrial Preparation of Salt

Salt from the Sea

Each litre of sea water contains about 26 grams of sodium chloride. In countries with hot, dry climates, the sea is allowed to flow into man-made lagoons. The entrance to the lagoon is then sealed off, and the heat of the sun slowly evaporates the water, leaving a mass of salt crystals.

Salt pans

This salt is often called **solar salt**, and has larger crystals than the table salt we use. Can you work out why?

Salt under our Feet

Millions of years ago, the middle part of the UK was covered by sea water. The water became trapped, forming an inland sea, and the heat of the sun gradually evaporated the water away. This left deep beds of salt.

Dissolving underground salt (solution mining)

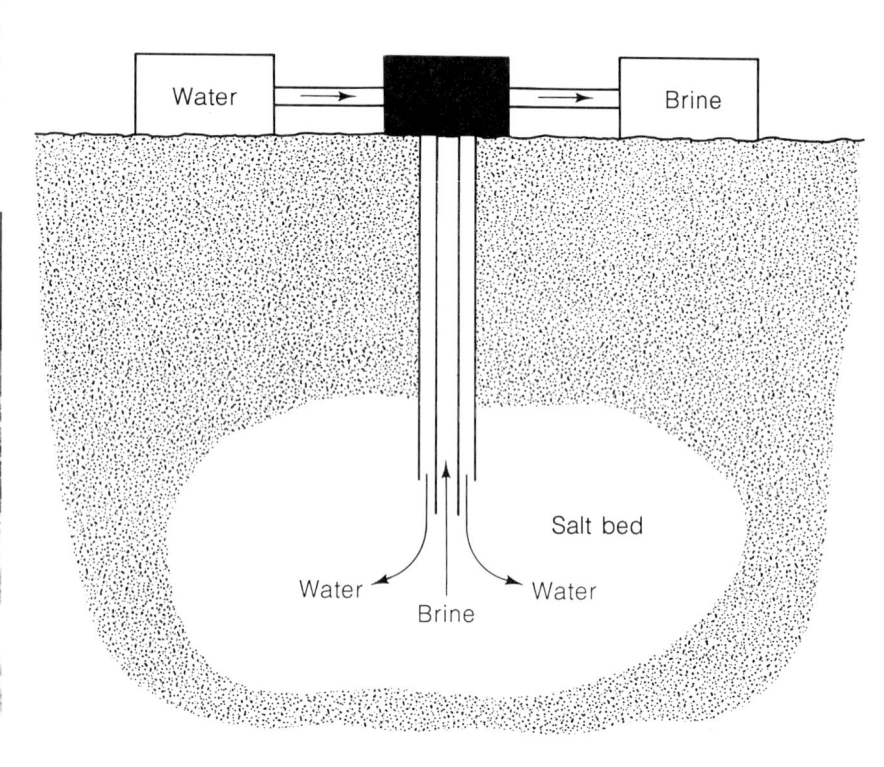

The salt beds were gradually covered in dust and soil, and now lie deep underground. The largest salt beds are found in the Cheshire area, and the salt is called **rock salt**.

Rock salt can be mined in a similar way to coal. The rock salt contains sand and other minerals, and after crushing, it can be used for road

Extracting salt at a commercial brinefield

A salt mine

gritting. Gritting helps to melt ice and snow and allows vehicle tyres to grip on the slippery surface.

Another method of extracting salt from the underground beds, is by drilling holes from the surface into the deposits. Two pipes are then lowered down each hole.

Water is pumped down one pipe, and dissolves the salt to form a solution called **brine**. The brine is pumped up the other pipe and then evaporated to produce solid salt.

The removal of the salt often leaves huge underground caves which can collapse causing subsidence at the surface. To prevent this the caves are filled with water after the salt supply is exhausted.

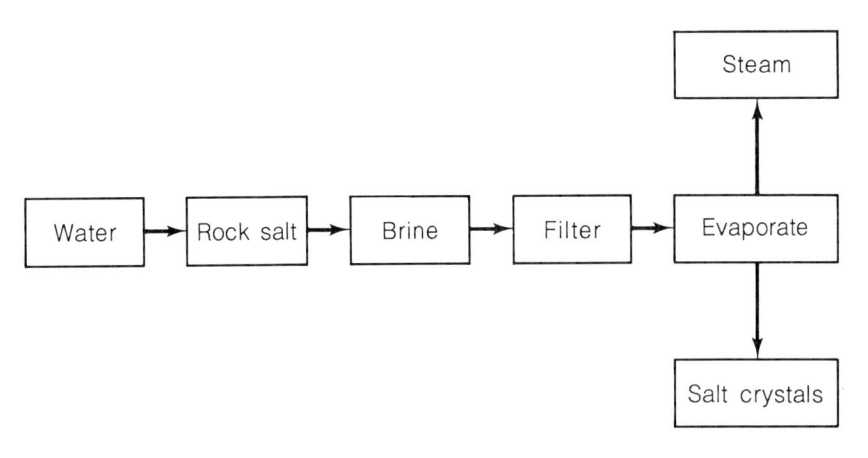

Flow diagram for purifying salt.

The Evaporation of Brine

Rock salt and sea salt are both **impure** as they contain many other soluble salts.

Pure sodium chloride can be obtained from either source by a process called **fractional crystallisation**.

The brine is first filtered to remove any insoluble material. The solution is heated and evaporation begins. Each soluble salt present in the solution crystallises out at a different concentration.

When the concentration for sodium chloride is reached, the salt begins to crystallise out, leaving other soluble salts behind.

Some magnesium carbonate is added to ensure that the salt does not form lumps when it is stored in damp conditions.

Insoluble Salts

Insoluble salts can be prepared in the laboratory by **mixing** two solutions of soluble salts. One solution must contain the **positive ion** required in the salt, and the other solution must contain the **negative ion**. As the positive and negative ions meet, they lock together to form a solid (known as the **precipitate**).

The other product must be a soluble salt. The precipitate can be separated from the solution by **filtration**. The filtered precipitate is then washed with more water and left to dry in air.

Making an Insoluble Salt

Both lead nitrate and potassium iodide are soluble salts. If solutions of these two chemicals are mixed together, insoluble **lead iodide** forms as a yellow precipitate. The solution will also contain the soluble salt potassium nitrate.

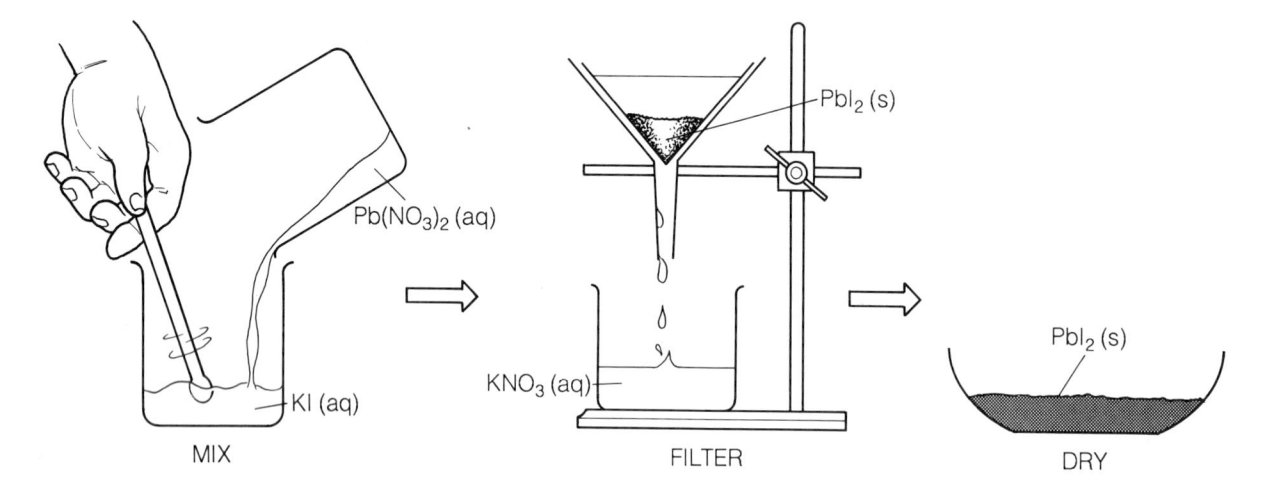

$$Pb(NO_3)_2 (aq) + KI(aq) \rightarrow PbI_2 (s) + KNO_3 (aq)$$
$$\bullet\, Pb(NO_3)_2 (aq) + 2KI(aq) \rightarrow PbI_2 (s) + 2KNO_3 (aq)$$

Making lead(II) iodide

When the mixture is filtered, the potassium nitrate will pass through the filter paper, leaving the insoluble lead iodide as residue.

Using an Insoluble Salt

Magnesium oxide is a useful chemical which can be made from an **insoluble salt**. It withstands high temperatures and so it is used to line furnaces and make refractory bricks.

Magnesium is also an essential trace element for plants, and without it the leaves will "yellow".

Lack of magnesium in grass can affect milking cows. Without magnesium the cows fall unconscious and die unless they are quickly injected with a magnesium salt.

For these reasons, magnesium oxide is often added to both fertiliser and animal feed.

Magnesium oxide is also used in cements, flame proof building boards, electric heating element cores and as filler for plastics.

Water treatment and leather tanning industries also make use of magnesium oxide.

Magnesium oxide can be made from an ore called **magnesite**. Magnesite is mainly **magnesium carbonate** (an insoluble salt). When this is heated to between 700 and 1000 °C, it forms magnesium oxide:

$$MgCO_3 (s) \xrightarrow{[heat]} MgO(s) + CO_2 (g)$$
insoluble salt

Activities

1. Copper sulphate crystals ($CuSO_4.5H_2O$) can be made by adding excess copper oxide (CuO), which is insoluble in water, to dilute sulphuric acid.
   (a) Why is the copper oxide added in excess to the acid?
   (b) How could you tell that a reaction had taken place just by looking at the mixture?
   (c) The following apparatus is used to separate the excess copper oxide from the solution. Copy and label the diagram.

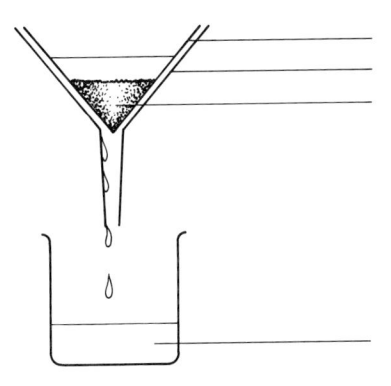

   (d) After the copper oxide has been removed, the solution is split into two. One sample is evaporated to dryness, the other is only partly evaporated, then set aside. Describe the difference in the two products.

2. Using table 4.11 decide the best way to make the following salts:
   (a) iron(II) carbonate
   (b) barium chloride.
   Describe how you would obtain a pure, dry sample of each salt.

A	B	C
NaCl(aq)	$AgNO_3$(aq)	HCl(aq)
D	E	F
$Ba(OH)_2$(aq)	H_2SO_4(aq)	$CuSO_4$(aq)
G	H	I
NaOH(aq)	$MgCO_3$(s)	Zn(s)

3. Using the chemicals in the boxes A to I, and the solubility table (4.11):
   (a) Write a balanced equation for a reaction which would produce a soluble salt.
   (b) Write a balanced equation for a reaction which would produce an insoluble salt.
   (c) Give the letters of two boxes only, which, when reacted together, would produce hydrogen gas and a soluble salt.
   (d) Give the letters of two boxes only, which, when reacted together, would produce carbon dioxide gas and a soluble salt.

6 Spotlight on Industry

Key Ideas

Building a chemical plant is a complicated and costly business. When choosing a site for the plant, a number of factors have to be taken into account:
- Is the site close to the materials to be processed?
- Is fuel readily available?
- Are road and rail communications good?

Steetley's plant at Hartlepool

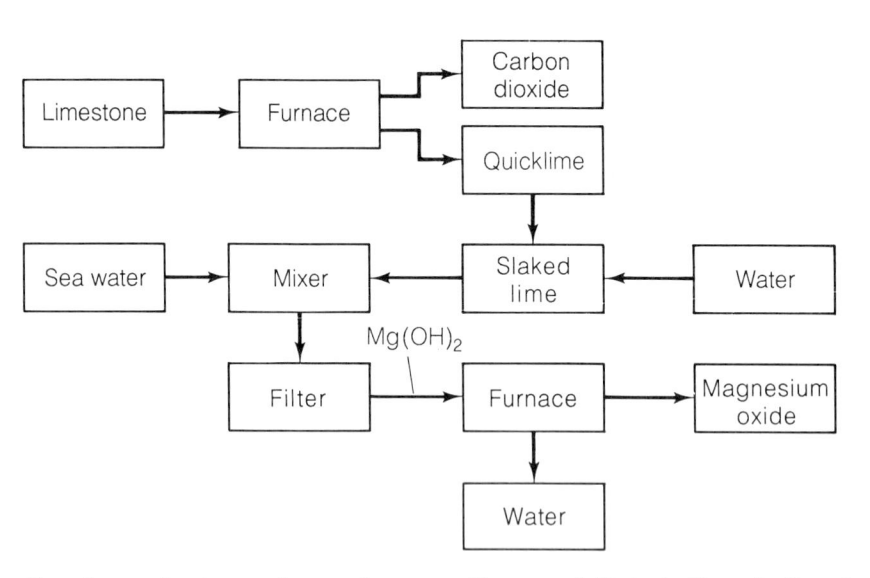

Making Magnesium Oxide in Britain

Unfortunately Britain has no natural magnesite deposits which it can use to make magnesium oxide.

However sea water contains about 0.13 per cent magnesium ions and we have plenty of sea water around our coasts.

A process was developed by a company called Steetley to extract magnesium ions from the sea.

The world's first commercially viable extraction of magnesium from sea water was carried out at Hartlepool in 1937.

Steetley still operate a plant at that site today, and about 60 per cent of its magnesium oxide output is used as a feed additive for cattle food and in fertilisers.

During the first stage of this process, limestone ($CaCO_3$) is heated in a furnace, and is changed into quicklime (CaO).

$$CaCO_3(s) \xrightarrow{[heat]} \underset{\text{quicklime}}{CaO(s)} + CO_2(g)$$

When the quicklime is mixed with water, slaked lime ($Ca(OH)_2$) is produced:

$$CaO(s) + H_2O(l) \rightarrow \underset{\text{slaked lime}}{Ca(OH)_2(aq)}$$

Flow diagram for the manufacture of magnesium oxide

In the Steetley plant sea water is drawn from the North Sea and mixed with the slaked lime. (Over 300 tonnes of sea water are needed to produce 1 tonne of magnesium oxide). An insoluble precipitate of magnesium hydroxide is produced:

$$Mg^{2+}(aq) + Ca(OH)_2(aq) \rightarrow \underset{\text{magnesium hydroxide}}{Mg(OH)_2(s)} + Ca^{2+}(aq)$$

The **precipitate** is filtered off and passed through a high temperature rotary furnace to eliminate water. Magnesium oxide is formed:

$$Mg(OH)_2(s) \xrightarrow{[heat]} MgO(s) + H_2O(l)$$

The plant is one of the largest of its kind in the world and can produce some 200 thousand tonnes of magnesium oxide every year. Steetley sell their magnesium oxide under the trade name Britmag.

Why Build a Site in Hartlepool?

Steetley's plant is a good example of building a chemical factory close to its supply of raw materials:

- The sea off Hartlepool does not receive fresh water from rivers which could otherwise dilute the salt content.
- High quality dolomite (a rock made of magnesium oxide and calcium carbonate) from which slaked lime can be made is mined close by, near Durham. The fact that it contains magnesium oxide also helps improve the final magnesium oxide yield.
- Low ash coal (for the furnaces) is mined around Middlesborough. Oil for the newer furnaces is obtained from the petrochemical works on Teesside.
- Good road and rail links connect the plant with all these suppliers of raw materials.

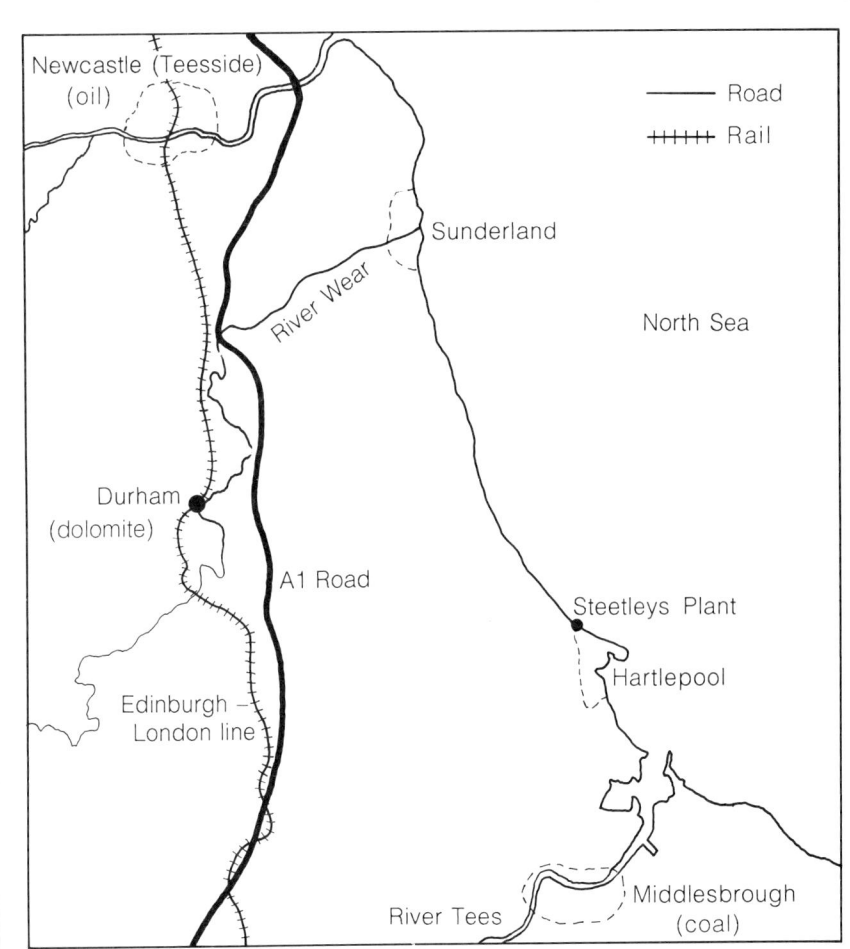

Map of area around Hartlepool

Activities

1. Outline the main reasons why Steetley built a magnesium oxide plant at Hartlepool.

2. Try to find out why calcium oxide is called quicklime and calcium hydroxide is called slaked lime.

3. Britmag is a trade name for magnesium oxide. What is a trade name?
   Some everyday chemicals used in your home are sold under trade names. Make a table showing the trade name and the chemical name of some of these substances (the ingredients list might help you).

7 Concentration

Key Ideas 🔑

The *concentration* of a solution depends on the *amount* of solute and the *volume* of solvent. The concentration of an acid or alkali can be calculated from a *neutralisation* reaction.

The volume of acid needed to neutralise an alkali of known volume and concentration is obtained from the *end-point*, during a *titration*. The end-point can be detected using *indicators*, or conductivity readings.

Preparing Solutions

The **concentration** of a solution can be measured in grams per litre (gl^{-1}) or moles per litre ($mol\, l^{-1}$).

Moles per litre can be written as $mol\, l^{-1}$ or mol/l.

One **mole** of a substance is its **formula mass** expressed in **grams**. When **one mole** of a chemical is dissolved in water and made up to exactly one litre of solution, the solution has a **concentration** of $1\, mol\, l^{-1}$.

For example, if you were asked to prepare a $1\, mol\, l^{-1}$ solution of sodium hydroxide, you would first have to find the formula mass of sodium hydroxide:

$$NaOH = 23 + 16 + 1 = 40$$

One mole is the formula mass expressed in grams, so one mole of sodium hydroxide will be 40 grams.

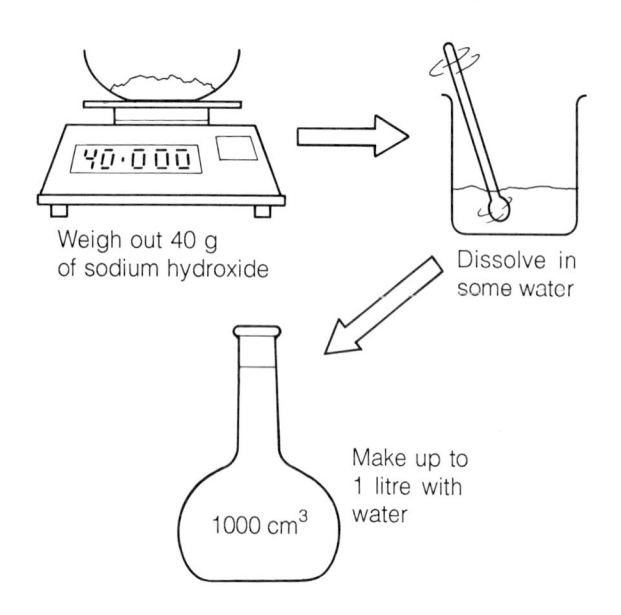

Weigh out 40 g of sodium hydroxide

Dissolve in some water

Make up to 1 litre with water

1000 cm³

Preparing a $1\, mol\, l^{-1}$ sodium hydroxide solution

You would then weigh out 40 grams of sodium hydroxide, dissolve it in some water, and make it up to exactly one litre. The solution would then have a concentration of $1\, mol\, l^{-1}$.

Concentration is sometimes called **molarity (M)**. For example, a 2M (two molar) solution of hydrochloric acid has a concentration of $2\, mol\, l^{-1}$. You may see solutions in the laboratory labelled with their concentration in molarity.

Calculating Concentration

Calculations involving concentration are usually concerned with three factors:
(1) **c** the **concentration** of the solution
(2) **V** the **volume** of the solution in litres
(3) **m** the number of **moles** of substance dissolved in volume **V**.

It is easy to work out their relationship if you remember this triangle:

so $c = \dfrac{m}{V}$ or $V = \dfrac{m}{c}$ or $m = cV$

Let's try out a few examples and find out how the triangle works:

1 Find the **concentration** (in $mol\, l^{-1}$) of a potassium hydroxide solution containing 14 g of potassium hydroxide in 500 cm³ of solution.

From the triangle $c = \dfrac{m}{V}$

First we need to find the value of m, the number of moles of KOH in the solution.

Formula mass of $KOH = 39 + 16 + 1 = 56$

Number of moles $= \dfrac{\text{actual mass}}{\text{formula mass}} = \dfrac{14}{56} = 0.25\, mol$

Substituting this value into our equation, and remembering that volume must be in litres, we get

$$c = \dfrac{m}{V} = \dfrac{0.25\, mol}{0.5\, l}$$

$$= 0.5\, mol\, l^{-1}$$

2 How many **moles** of nitric acid are there in 350 cm³ of a $0.4\, mol\, l^{-1}$ solution?

From the triangle $m = cV$
$= 0.4\, mol\, l^{-1} \times 0.35\, l$
$= 0.14\, mol$

Calculating an Unknown Concentration

Earlier in the chapter you saw how an alkali could be neutralised by titrating it with an acid. The point at which neutralisation is just complete is called the **end-point** of the reaction.

If you know the concentration of one of the solutions, and the exact volume of each solution needed to reach the end-point, then the concentration of the second solution can be calculated.

A set volume of one solution (of known concentration), say the alkali, is put into a conical flask, and a few drops of indicator solution added.

The acid, of **unknown concentration**, is put into a burette and then slowly run into the conical flask. The flask is constantly shaken to ensure that the reactants are mixed well together. The indicator changes colour when the solution is neutral and the volume of acid used to reach the end-point is noted.

The titration is usually repeated a number of times and an averaged value is used for calculation.

Example 1

You are asked to find the **concentration** of acid in a bottle marked HYDROCHLORIC ACID.

The first step is to transfer 25 cm³ of an alkali of **known concentration** into a flask using a pipette. A few drops of indicator are added to the alkali. The acid is put into a burette and the alkali titrated with the acid until the indicator changes colour.

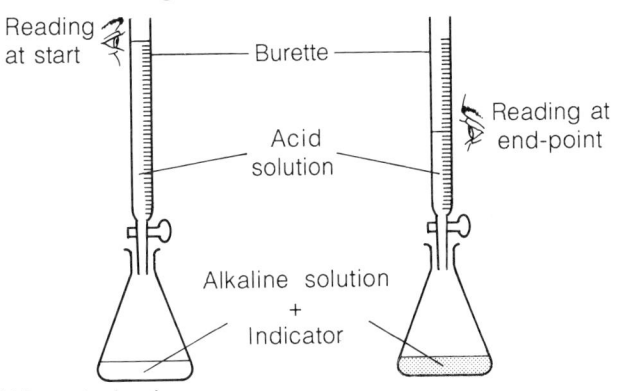

Volumetric titration

Suppose you found out that 25 cm³ of a 1 mol l⁻¹ solution of sodium hydroxide was exactly neutralised by 20 cm³ of the hydrochloric acid solution. You would calculate the concentration of acid as follows:

Step 1 Always start by writing a **balanced equation** for the reaction:

sodium   + hydrochloric →   sodium   + water
hydroxide   acid   chloride
NaOH(aq) +   HCl(aq) → NaCl(aq) + H_2O(l)
1 mol   1 mol   1 mol   1 mol

This tells us that **1 mole of NaOH** neutralises **1 mole of HCl**.

Step 2 Now we can calculate the number of **moles of sodium hydroxide** in the original 25 cm³.

$$m = cV = 1 \times 0.025 = \mathbf{0.025 \, mol}$$

Step 3 From the balanced chemical equation, the number of moles of alkali in the flask must be equal to the number of moles of acid added from the burette.

If 25 cm³ of the alkali contained 0.025 mol then **20 cm³** of acid also contains **0.025 mol**. We can now calculate the concentration of the acid.

$$c = \frac{m}{V}$$
$$= \frac{0.025 \, \text{mol}}{0.02 \, \text{l}}$$
$$= 1.25 \, \text{mol} \, l^{-1}$$

The **concentration** of HCl is $\mathbf{1.25 \, mol \, l^{-1}}$.

Example 2

25 cm³ of a 1.5 mol l⁻¹ solution of sulphuric acid requires 15 cm³ of a potassium hydroxide solution to exactly neutralise it. Calculate the **concentration** of the potassium hydroxide solution.

Step 1 The balanced equation.

sulphuric acid + potassium → potassium + water
                 hydroxide   sulphate
H_2SO_4(aq)   + 2KOH(aq) → K_2SO_4(aq) + $2H_2O$(l)
1 mol   2 mol   1 mol   2 mol

So **1 mole of H_2SO_4** neutralises **2 moles of KOH**.

Step 2 Number of moles in **known** solution (H_2SO_4).

From the triangle m = cV
$$= 1.5 \times 0.025$$
$$= \mathbf{0.0375 \, mol}$$

Step 3 Concentration of KOH solution.

From the balanced equation the number of moles of KOH is equal to **twice** the number of moles of H_2SO_4.

Since 25 cm³ of the acid contains 0·0375 mole, **15 cm³** of the alkali must contain 2 × 0.0375 mol = **0.075 mol**

We can now calculate the concentration of the alkali:

$$c = \frac{m}{V}$$
$$= \frac{0.075 \, \text{mol}}{0.015 \, \text{l}}$$
$$= 5 \, \text{mol} \, l^{-1}$$

The **concentration** of sodium hydroxide solution is $\mathbf{5 \, mol \, l^{-1}}$.

136 ACIDS AND ALKALIS

Conductivity Titrations

It is possible to detect the end point in an acid/alkali titration by continually measuring the conductivity of the solution during the titration process.

The neutral point in a conductivity titration can often be measured more accurately than in a titration using an indicator, where the change of colour at the end-point is often difficult to judge. This is particularly so when you are trying to determine the end-point in a solution which is already coloured, e.g., blackcurrant juice.

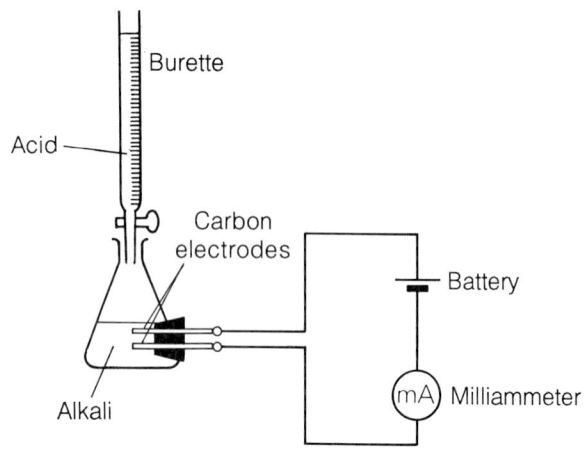

Conductivity titration apparatus

A graph is plotted of the volume of solution added against the conductivity. The graph is V-shaped, with the neutral point at the lowest point in the V (lowest conductivity).

The volume of acid or alkali required for the neutralisation can be obtained from the graph. The unknown concentration is calculated as before.

Example A bottle is known to contain a solution of nitric acid. The acid neutralises 25 cm³ of a 0.5 mol l⁻¹ sodium hydroxide solution, and the following conductivity graph is obtained.

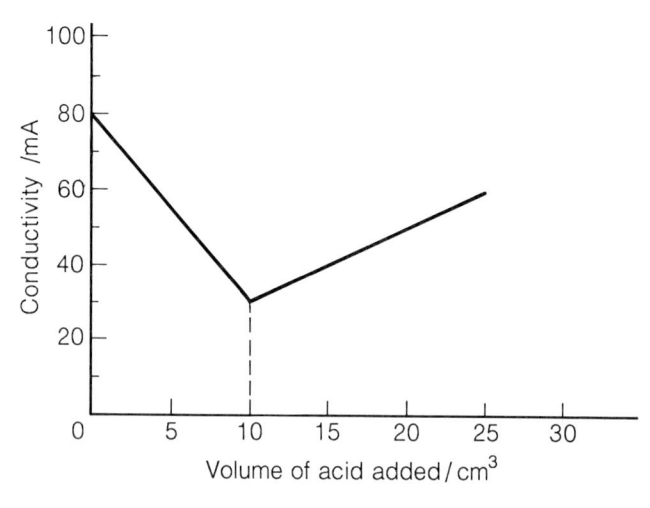

Calculate the **concentration** of the nitric acid.

Answer
From the graph, **10 cm³** of HNO_3 (aq) exactly neutralises 25 cm³ of 0·5 mol l⁻¹ NaOH(aq).

Step 1 The balanced equation.

$$NaOH(aq) + HNO_3(aq) \rightarrow NaNO_3(aq) + H_2O(l)$$
$$\text{1 mol} \quad\quad \text{1 mol} \quad\quad \text{1 mol} \quad\quad \text{1 mol}$$

1 mole of NaOH neutralises **1 mole of HNO_3**

Step 2 Number of **moles** in the **known solution** (NaOH).

$$m = cV = 0.5 \times 0.025$$
$$= \mathbf{0.0125\,mol}$$

Step 3 Concentration of the unknown solution (HNO_3).

$$c = \frac{m}{V} = \frac{0.0125}{0.01} = \mathbf{1.25\,mol\,l^{-1}}$$

The concentration of the nitric acid is 1.25 mol l⁻¹.

ACIDS AND ALKALIS

Activities

1. What mass of chemical needs to be weighed out to prepare one litre of the following 1 mol l^{-1} solutions?

    (a) NaOH (b) KCl (c) AgNO$_3$ (d) K$_2$SO$_4$

2. How many moles of substance are in the following solutions?
    (a) 200 cm³ of 0.5 mol l^{-1} potassium hydroxide solution.
    (b) 25 cm³ of 1·5 mol l^{-1} sulphuric acid.
    (c) 2 litres of 0.1 mol l^{-1} sodium chloride solution.

3. What is the concentration in mol l^{-1} of the following solutions?
    (a) 24 g of sodium hydroxide in 400 cm³ of solution.
    (b) 138 g of magnesium nitrate in 2.5 litres of solution.
    (c) 37 g of sodium nitrate in 0.7 litres of solution.

4. 25 cm³ of hydrochloric acid solution is neutralised by 30 cm³ of a 0.3 mol l^{-1} solution of sodium hydroxide. Calculate the concentration of HCl in the solution.

5. What volume of 0.5 mol l^{-1} sulphuric acid will be required to exactly neutralise 100 cm³ of 0.6 mol l^{-1} potassium hydroxide solution?

6. The following table refers to the results obtained when 20 cm³ of a 1 mol l^{-1} solution of barium hydroxide (Ba(OH)$_2$) is titrated with sulphuric acid (H$_2$SO$_4$).

Volume of acid cm³	Conductivity mA
0	60
2	40
4	20
6	0
8	15
10	28
12	40
14	52
16	68

   (a) Plot a graph of conductivity against the volume of acid added, and then calculate the **concentration** of the sulphuric acid.
   (b) Use the solubility table in a data book to explain why the conductivity at the endpoint is zero.

7. The conductivity graph below was obtained when a 0.4 mol l^{-1} solution of sulphuric acid was used to titrate 20 cm³ of a sodium carbonate (Na$_2$CO$_3$) solution. Calculate the concentration of the sodium carbonate solution.

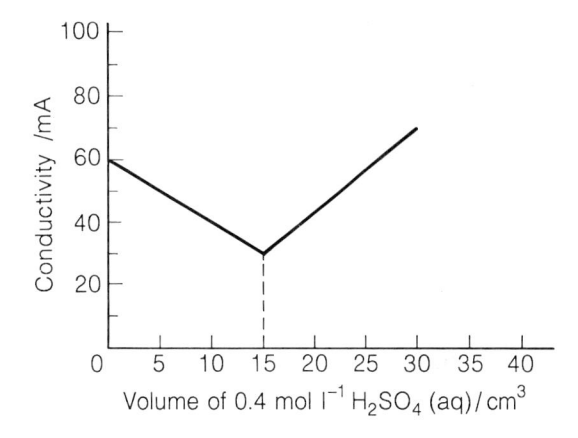

Acid and Alkalis – Study Questions

A	B	C
sodium sulphate	sulphur dioxide	calcium oxide
D	E	F
potassium hydroxide	hydrogen chloride	potassium chloride

○ **1** (a) Which box (or boxes) shows a substance which:
   (i) will neutralise an acidic solution?
   (ii) dissolves in water to give an acidic solution?
   (iii) is made up of more than two elements?
(b) Two of the substances in the grid can react together to produce a third substance which is also shown in the grid.
Which **two** boxes show the substances which can react in this way? **KU**

○ **2** As a homework exercise, pupils were asked to find the pH values of a number of substances found in the home. One pupil wrote down her results as follows:

bicarbonate of soda–9; vinegar–4; drain cleaner–14; cola drink–3; indigestion pill–10; window cleaner–12; washing-up liquid–7; lemon juice–3; milk–8.

Information can be presented in different ways: tables, diagrams, flowcharts, keys, pie charts, bar graphs, line graphs, etc.
Present the results of the home exercise in a suitable way. **PS**

○ **3** A pupil is given the task of separating copper metal from a mixture containing copper(II) oxide and copper metal.

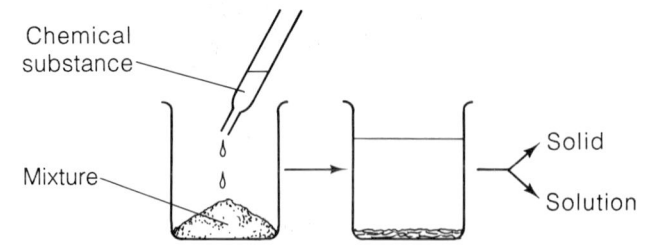

(a) Name a chemical substance that reacts with only **one** of the solids, forming a solution.
(b) Describe how the copper can be separated from a mixture of copper metal and copper(II) oxide. **PS**

● **4** Two white powders that are found in most houses are sodium carbonate (bath salts) and sodium hydrogencarbonate (bicarbonate of soda).

Both react with dilute hydrochloric acid to give sodium chloride, carbon dioxide and water. This is shown in the equations for the reactions:

$$Na_2CO_3 + 2HCl \rightarrow 2NaCl + CO_2 + H_2O$$
$$NaHCO_3 + HCl \rightarrow NaCl + CO_2 + H_2O$$

You are given a 1 mol l^{-1} solution of each powder.
(a) Describe briefly an experiment to decide which solution was sodium carbonate.
(b) Explain how the results would be used to reach a decision. **PS**

● **5** When a solution of metal nitrate is added to potassium chloride solution a white solid is formed.
Using only the table of solubilities in a data book, name metal nitrates which could cause this effect. **PS**

● **6** The reaction between sodium hydroxide solution and sulphuric acid can be represented by the following equation:

$$2NaOH(aq) + H_2SO_4(aq) \rightarrow Na_2SO_4(aq) + 2H_2O(l)$$

(a) Name the spectator ions in the reaction.
(b) Car batteries contain sulphuric acid. The concentration of acid is to be checked by carrying out a titration. For safety reasons, the battery acid has been diluted to exactly one hundredth of its original concentration.
   (i) The grid below contains a number of steps which could be used in the titration.
   Write down in the correct order the letters for the steps which should be used. **PS**

A	B	C
add Universal Indicator to solution in flask	evaporate to dryness	measure 10 cm³ of acid into a flask
D	E	F
fill burette or syringe with acid	repeat, using smaller additions near the end-point to get a more accurate result	note volume required for neutralisation
G	H	I
measure 20 cm³ of alkali into flask	run in acid, 1 cm³ at a time, shaking flask after each addition	repeat, using same volumes of acid and alkali, but with no indicator

(ii) It is found that 20.0 cm³ of sodium hydroxide solution (0.1 mol l⁻¹) is neutralised by 12.2 cm³ of the diluted acid solution. Calculate the concentration of the acid in the battery. (Show your working.) **KU**

- 7 Which box (or boxes) shows a statement that applies to 100 cm³ of:
  (a) calcium hydroxide solution (lime water)?
  (b) potassium sulphate solution? **KU**

A	more H⁺(aq) ions than 100 cm³ of pure water
B	the same number of H⁺(aq) ions as 100 cm³ of pure water
C	more OH⁻(aq) ions than 100 cm³ of pure water
D	the same number of OH⁻(aq) ions as 100 cm³ of pure water
E	equal numbers of H⁺(aq) and OH⁻(aq) ions
F	more OH⁻(aq) ions than H⁺(aq) ions
G	more H⁺(aq) ions than OH⁻(aq) ions

- 8 A pupil carried out an experiment with some acids which form ions in solution. The current flow is a measure of the extent to which the acid forms ions.

The results are shown in the table below.

Acid/0.1 mol l⁻¹	Current flow (mA)
CH_3COOH	24
$CH_2ClCOOH$	40
$CHCl_2COOH$	54
CCl_3COOH	71

(a) Explain how the current flow is related to the structure of the acid. **PS**
(b) Name the ion common to each of the solutions. **KU**

Metals and Corrosion

1 All About Metals

Key Ideas

Metals are important materials in everyday life.

Over three-quarters of the chemical elements are *metals*. Metals are found in the earth's crust. The *less reactive metals* can be found as free, *uncombined* elements and the *more reactive metals* are always found *combined* with other elements, in compounds called *ores*.

There is only a finite supply of metal elements in the earth's crust. We can *conserve* metals by *recycling* "used" metal objects. Recycling also saves energy.

The *properties* of metals can be *altered* by forming *alloys* with other metals.

Common household metal objects

Pouring steel in a foundry

Metals All Around

We come into contact with metals every day. As you climb out of bed in the morning, the *steel* springs in the matress relax. You fill the kettle with water from a *brass* tap, plated with *chromium*, and switch on the power so that electricity can flow through *copper* wires to the heating element.

As you stand waiting at the bus stop you think about how you are going to spend the ten pound note you were given for your birthday, with its *aluminium* strip down the middle.

You step onto the bus, made from a variety of *metals*, and pay the driver with coins made from *alloys* (metal mixtures) of *copper*, *nickel*, *zinc*, and *tin*. The bus passes under a *steel* railway bridge, just as a train, also made of many *metals*, thunders overhead on its *steel* railway lines and awakens you from your day-dreams.

Your first class is chemistry and you

METALS AND CORROSION

check that you have remembered your pencil. It is blunt, so you look for your *magnesium* alloy sharpener – you are not going to be caught out today. A friend admires your *gold* and *silver* rings.

Back home, after school, you feel hungry and so you open a *tin* plated *steel* can of beans and heat them in an *aluminium* pot. The television is turned on and you settle down with an *aluminium* can of juice and relax. Your *zinc-silver* battery powered watch tells you it's homework time, so you go to your room, and put on your personal stereo, powered by *nickel-cadmium* batteries. Soon it is bed time. Once again it has been a "metal" day.

Nearly all methods of transport are dependent on metals

Out of the Earth

Eighty-three of the 105 elements found in the periodic table are metals. Metals, however, are not common. Three-quarters of the earth's crust consists of two non-metals, oxygen and silicon.

Most metals can be found in the upper 20 kilometres of the earth's crust, and are easily mined. The unreactive metal elements are often found as free elements and are called **native** elements.

Elements in the earth's crust

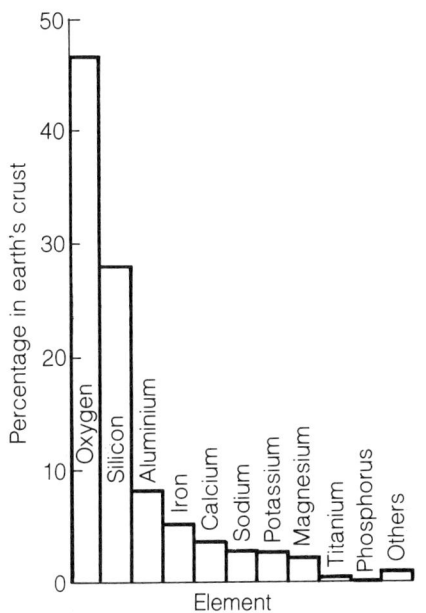

Other metal elements are found combined with non-metal elements, forming oxides, sulphides, carbonates and silicates, all examples of metal **ores**. There is a **finite** supply of metal ores. Presently we are rapidly using up metals such as copper, lead, tin, nickel and chromium. Copper is so scarce now, that ores containing only 1 per cent of copper are considered worth mining. You would have to dig up 100 tonnes of rock to obtain 1 tonne of copper! Mining is an expensive business, and as a result, copper is costly.

The demand for metals is so great, it has been predicted that if we continue to mine ores at the present rate, metals such as copper, zinc, tin and lead will run out by the end of the next century.

Fortunately it is possible to recycle a number of metals and save both energy, and consumption of metal ore. You may already collect aluminium "ring pulls" for associations such as "Guide Dogs for the Blind". The ring pulls are sold back to aluminium companies, who melt them down to make useful metal again.

Some Third World countries depend on metal ores as their most

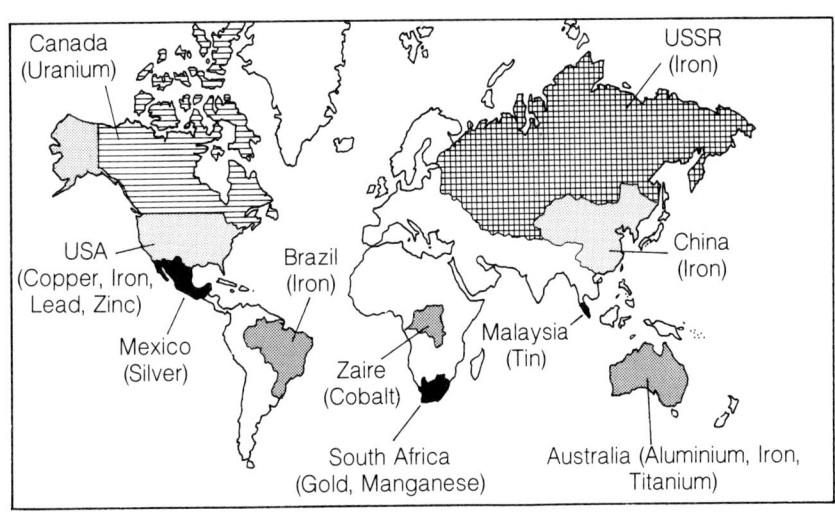

World producers of ore

METALS AND CORROSION

important natural resource. Their economies can go up and down with changes in the value of metals on the world market.

Certain metal ores are extracted from under the ground, but most are dug from near the surface by "open pit" or "open cast" mining. When the ore has been mined, the waste material (mainly rocks and soil) is separated from the ore.

The metal is then extracted from the ore. Although some metal extraction takes place in the country where the ore is mined, many millions of tonnes of ore are transported across the sea, in bulk ore carriers, to richer countries for **refining**.

The extraction process can be very expensive, since a lot of heat (or electrical) energy is required.

Physical Properties of Metals

Conduction of Electricity

All metals conduct electricity, both in solid and liquid form. We can use the property of **electrical conductivity**. The wires inside electrical cables are often made of copper. Gold connectors are used in computer circuits because the metal is a good electrical conductor.

Conduction of Heat

Metals are good at conducting heat. Metals feel cold to touch, because they quickly conduct the heat away from your hand. Most cooking pots and pans are made of metal, since they transfer the heat quickly from the heat source to the food.

How Heavy?

Have you ever noticed that some pots feel very heavy while others are very light? This property is related to the **density** of the metal. Density is measured in grams per cubic centimetre ($g\,cm^{-3}$). One cubic centimetre of aluminium feels light (density $2.7\,g\,cm^{-3}$) but one cubic centimetre of iron feels much heavier (density $7.9\,g\,cm^{-3}$). Lead is even more dense at $11.3\,g\,cm^{-3}$ and platinum has a density of $21.4\,g\,cm^{-3}$, almost eight times heavier than aluminium.

Bending and Shaping

Metals are useful to man because they can be shaped to suit our needs. The ease with which a metal can be shaped is called its **malleability**. If they are soft they can be beaten and bent into shape.

Gold can be beaten so thin that you can see through it. These thin sheets of gold are used in the visors of space helmets to act as "sunglasses" for astronauts.

If metals are harder, and more brittle (break easily), they need to be melted down and poured into moulds to form the desired shape.

Bar graph of some metal densities

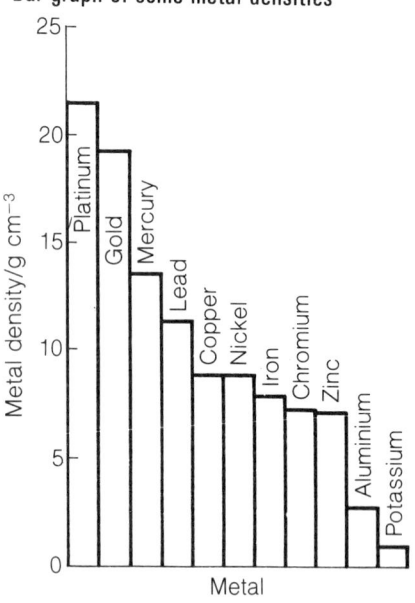

Bulk ore carrier discharging

Some metals are **ductile**. Ductile metals can be drawn into wires by forcing the metal through the tiny holes of a die.

How Strong?

Some metals are very strong and can be shaped in such a way as to withstand enormous pressures. A submarine must use strong metals to withstand the mass of the sea, squashing it from above, as it submerges into the ocean.

For obvious safety reasons, containers for transporting nuclear fuels must be able to withstand great forces. You may have seen a demonstration in which a train pulling one of these containers is made to crash at high speed. The nuclear flask is not damaged.

We can change the **strength** of some metals by treating them with

Nuclear flask experiment

heat. The half-shaft, which connects the wheel of a car to the engine, is sometimes weakened in a small area. In the event of the wheel locking, the weakened part snaps and prevents more serious damage to the engine.

The **physical properties** of many metals can be altered by simple processes like heating, cooling and hammering.

Alloys

Another way to change the physical properties of a metal, is to form an alloy with another metal (or non-metal). When two different metals are melted, mixed together, and allowed to cool, an **alloy** is formed. The alloy has physical properties different to those of the elements from which it was made. Pencil sharpeners, many coins, gold jewellery and bunsen burners are all made from metal alloys.

Why Make Alloys?

Iron is a very brittle metal, but if some **carbon** is added to molten iron it forms **mild steel**. Steel is less brittle than iron. If **chromium** and **nickel** are added to steel, **stainless steel** is formed.

Stainless steel is more resistant to chemical attack than mild steel, and it can be used in more corrosive environments. Knives, forks and spoons are often made of stainless steel, as is much of the machinery used in the food industry.

In the electronics industry, the components are joined to the circuit board with **solder**, an alloy of **tin** and **lead**. Solder melts at low temperatures and is a good conductor of electricity.

Alloy coins and jewellery

Silver coins, like a 50p piece, have no silver in them! They are actually made from an alloy of **copper** and **nickel** called **cupro-nickel**. The alloy is silver in colour and has the advantage of being cheaper, harder and more wear resistant than silver metal. When **zinc** is alloyed with **copper**, **brass** is formed. Brass is easily melted and cast into intricate shapes. It is also soft enough to be pressed, or stamped, into a new shape. Brass is used to make small statues, door handles and letter boxes.

Pure **gold** is very soft, and if it was used to make jewellery, it would soon wear away. Most jewellery is made from an alloy of **gold**, **silver** and **copper**. The amount of gold in jewellery varies. Pure gold is called 24 carat gold. Nine carat gold contains 37.50 per cent gold, 31.25 per cent copper and 31.25 per cent silver.

Aluminium is a very light metal. Its low density makes it suitable for building aircraft. However, because it is such a soft metal, long structures such as wings would bend under their own weight! The aluminium must be alloyed with **copper**, **manganese** and **magnesium** to strengthen it for use in the aerospace industry.

Activities

1. (a) Draw a table to show the composition of the following alloys, and their uses: solder; brass; cupro-nickel; 9 carat gold.
   (b) Why are alloys often preferred to the pure metal?

2. Using a periodic table, write down the name and symbol of the eighteen metals which have an atomic number between one and thirty.

3. The bar graph on page 141 shows the percentage of the ten most common elements found in the earth's crust.
   Name the elements from the graph which are not metals.

4. Explain what is meant by the **physical properties** of a substance. Illustrate your answer by describing four physical properties associated with metals.

2 Chemical Properties of Metals

Key Ideas

The reaction of metals with *oxygen, water* and *acid* can be used to indicate the *activity* of metals.

The *position* of a metal in the *activity* series can be used to explain why the metal is found either *combined* or *uncombined* in the earth's crust. The *history* of the use of metals is explained, in part, by the *activity series*. The least active metals were discovered and used first. The most active metals have been extracted on a large scale only in the last 100 years.

Reaction of Metals with Oxygen

Metals react with **oxygen** to form **metal oxides**. When magnesium reacts with oxygen, it burns with an intense white flame.

You should never look directly at burning magnesium, because the reaction gives out ultraviolet light, which can damage your eyes. When the reaction is over, a white ash of magnesium oxide remains:

magnesium + oxygen → magnesium oxide

$$Mg(s) + O_2(g) \rightarrow MgO(s)$$
● $2Mg(s) + O_2(g) \rightarrow 2MgO(s)$

The intensity of the flame shows that a lot of energy is being given out – an **exothermic reaction**. Magnesium is a reactive metal. A ball of fine magnesium wire is used inside some flash bulbs to produce light when taking indoor photographs.

Iron burning during welding

Iron powder will burn in oxygen, but it must be heated until it is quite hot. Hot iron powder only glows when it is put into a jar of oxygen. This suggests that iron is less reactive than magnesium:

iron + oxygen → iron oxide

$$Fe(s) + O_2(g) \rightarrow FeO(s)$$
● $2Fe(s) + O_2(g) \rightarrow 2FeO(s)$

By carrying out the same reactions with other metals we find that sodium, potassium, lithium and calcium produce intensely bright flames when burned in oxygen. Lead, copper and mercury react only slowly with oxygen and a change in colour of the final product is the only indication that a reaction has taken place. Silver and gold do not react easily with oxygen.

The amount of energy given out during these reactions can be used to compare how reactive different metals are.

It is interesting to note that when we heat iron filings in an iron spoon, the spoon itself does not appear to react with the oxygen. If we sprinkle iron filings onto a bunsen flame the iron will burn, rather like the fireworks called "sparklers". This is because reducing the **particle size** of a substance **increases** the **rate** of a reaction.

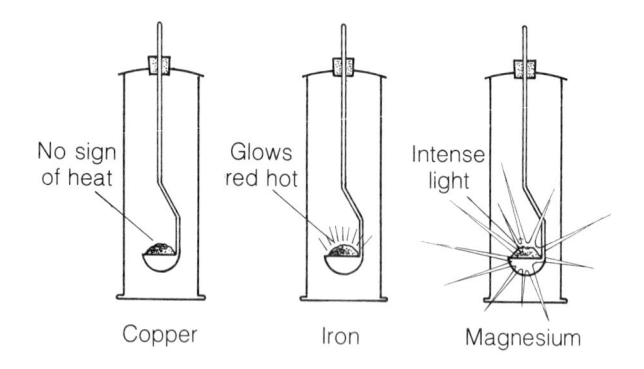

Different metals burning in oxygen

Reaction of Metals with Water

Some **metals** react with **water** to give off **hydrogen gas**, and form the **metal hydroxide**. Potassium reacts extremely vigorously with water. The potassium melts, catches fire, and then fizzes over the surface of the water as the reaction takes place:

potassium + water → potassium hydroxide + hydrogen

$$K(s) + H_2O(l) \rightarrow KOH(aq) + H_2(g)$$
● $2K(s) + 2H_2O(l) \rightarrow 2KOH(aq) + H_2(g)$

METALS AND CORROSION

Sodium reacts similarly. Lithium and calcium also react vigorously with water, but do not usually catch fire. Magnesium reacts only slowly with water. It may take a few days for a strip of magnesium to produce a small amount of hydrogen gas:

magnesium + water → magnesium hydroxide + hydrogen

$Mg(s) + H_2O(l) \rightarrow Mg(OH)_2(aq) + H_2(g)$
● $Mg(s) + 2H_2O(l) \rightarrow Mg(OH)_2(aq) + H_2(g)$

The magnesium reacts faster with boiling water and quicker still when steam is used. This is because **reaction** rate increases with **increase** in **temperature**.

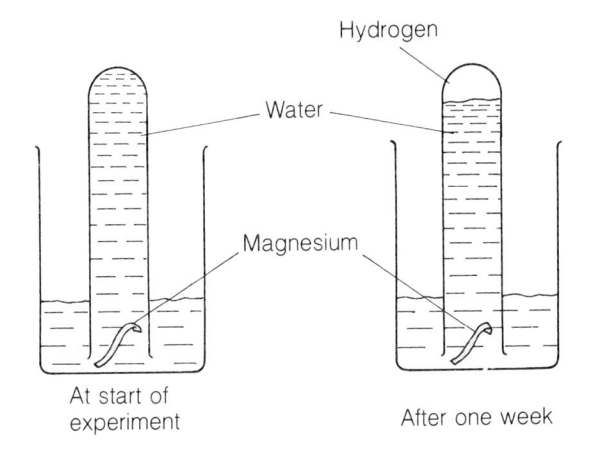

Reacting magnesium with water

Reaction of Metals with Dilute Acids

Some **metals** react with dilute **acids**, giving off **hydrogen** gas and forming **salts**. Magnesium reacts with sulphuric acid to form magnesium sulphate and hydrogen gas.

magnesium + sulphuric acid → magnesium sulphate + hydrogen

$Mg(s) + H_2SO_4(aq) \rightarrow MgSO_4(aq) + H_2(g)$

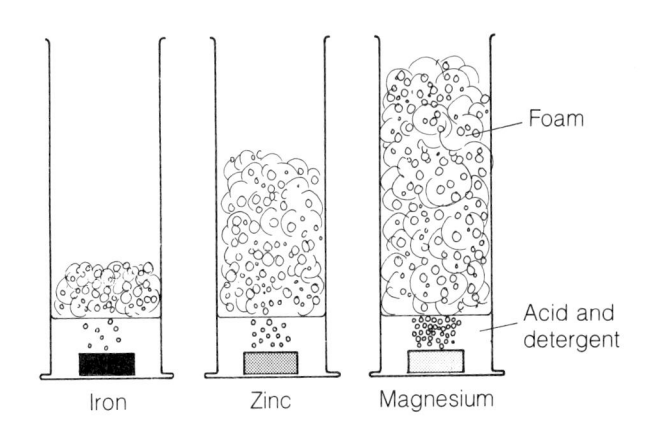

Reaction of iron, magnesium and zinc with acid, using detergent to measure the volume of hydrogen produced

We often use the reaction of zinc with sulphuric acid to prepare hydrogen gas. The salt zinc sulphate is formed.

zinc + sulphuric acid → zinc sulphate + hydrogen

$Zn(s) + H_2SO_4(aq) \rightarrow ZnSO_4(aq) + H_2(g)$

These reactions may also be used to place metals in a reactivity order. If we add some detergent to the acid, the hydrogen gas bubbles produce a foam. The amount of foam produced is related to the activity of the metal.

The Activity Series

As a result of reactions with oxygen, water and dilute acid, metals can be put in an order of reactivity. This is known as the **activity series** and is shown in table 5.1.

Table 5.1

Metal	
Potassium	Most reactive
Sodium	
Lithium	
Calcium	
Magnesium	
Aluminium	
Zinc	increasing activity
Iron	
Tin	
Lead	
Copper	Do not react with dilute acids
Mercury	
Silver	
Gold	Least reactive

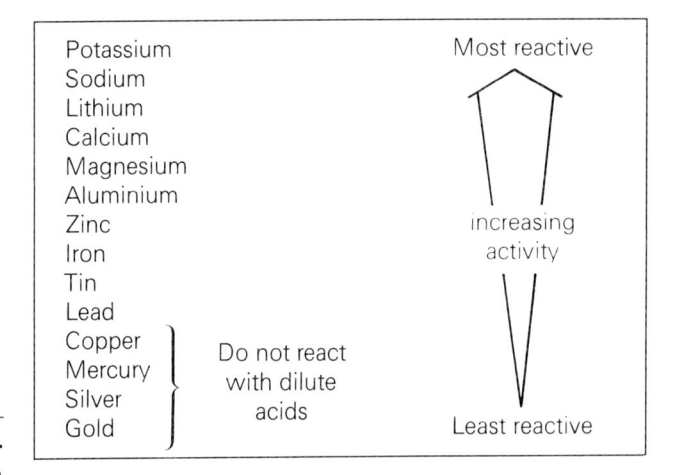

Table 5.2

Metal	Date Discovered	
Gold, Silver, Mercury	prehistoric (Stone Age)	
Copper	about 5000 BC (Bronze Age)	
Tin, Lead, Iron	about 4000 BC to 1500 BC (Iron Age)	increasing activity
Zinc	16th century	
Aluminium	1827	
Magnesium	1775	
Calcium	1808	
Lithium	1817	
Sodium	1807	
Potassium	1807	

146 METALS AND CORROSION

The Activity Series and the Discovery of Metals

Gold, silver and even copper can be found in the earth's crust as lumps of pure metal. We might deduce this from their position (at the bottom) in the activity series.

Man has made jewellery from these metals for thousands of years. When archaeologists discover ancient burial sites they often find such jewellery in perfect condition. This is because the metals are so unreactive. Even gold and silver coins, sunk with a ship thousands of years ago, remain in near-perfect condition despite years in salt water.

Bronze alloy sword

Gold recovered from the *Mary Rose*

During the **Stone Age**, people found gold and silver at the surface of the earth. Jewellery was easy to make from these metals because they are soft and could be easily beaten into new shapes. These metals also have low melting points and can be easily melted and poured into moulds.

The **Bronze Age** began when copper and tin were discovered. Bronze is an alloy of copper and tin. If rocks containing these metals are heated in a wood fire, lumps of the metal are left behind in the embers, after the fire has gone out.

The metals were probably discovered by accident, possibly by using metal-containing rocks to enclose a fire. They would have needed to be good scientists to observe what had happened and then to deduce (work out) where the metal had come from!

Copper is thought to have been discovered in Cyprus. Cyprus was famous in ancient times for its copper mines, and so the Greeks called the island "Kuprus". The Romans also mined copper ore in Cyprus, and called the metal "cuprum". This is how Cyprus got its name.

Bronze is harder than gold or silver, and so could be made into cutting implements and weapons. The nations who first made these discoveries soon conquered surrounding nations, on account of their superior weapons.

The Bronze Age was followed by the **Iron Age**. It requires higher temperatures to extract iron from its ore, and so hotter fires were needed before it was discovered. Iron gave a sharp cutting edge which did not blunt easily. Iron weapons were even better than bronze ones.

The element zinc was not discovered in its own right until the eighteenth century, although it had been accidentally made in Roman times. The Romans roasted a mixture of copper ore and calmine (an ore of zinc) with carbon. The resulting molten metal was not a form of copper as they thought, but the alloy of zinc and copper we call **brass**.

It was not until the **Industrial Revolution** in the eighteenth century, that technology progressed far enough to extract other metals from their ores. A great many metals were discovered in the hundred years between 1750 and 1850.

As the demand for metals, particularly iron, increased, the technology for making cheaper and purer metals was improved. Wars also increased the demand for metals, to make weapons. In response to this demand, the metal industries developed larger, continuous processing plants.

Very reactive metals form very stable compounds that require large amounts of energy to separate the metal from the ore. The discovery of the **most** reactive metals waited until electricity was invented. Aluminium requires the output of an electric power station to commercially separate it from aluminium oxide.

If we compare the date of discovery of metals with the activity series, we see that the two match quite well (table 5.2).

Finding the Ore

Many metal ores were discovered by chance rather than design. Today, the skill of the **geologist** ensures that when the miners start to dig a mine, there is likely to be a particular ore there.

The geologist uses sophisticated apparatus to help him locate ores. Satellites are even used to take special photographs from space, which help the geologist to pinpoint the location of ores.

It can take years of surveying, sampling and testing before mining begins. In some locations the ore is close to the surface, but in other places the ore is deep underground and expensive shafts have to be dug before mining can begin.

Concentrating the Ore

The mined ore is usually mixed up with a large amount of unwanted stone, clay and earth, and this needs to be removed.

The first step is usually to crush everything down to small pieces. The crushed ore is then treated in one of a number of ways.

1 Density Separation

The difference in density between the ore and the unwanted material can be used to separate them. Gold **panning** uses this method. The gold is swirled in a pan with water. The more dense gold sinks to the bottom of the pan and the lighter waste is swirled away.

2 Froth Flotation

Another method is called **froth flotation**. The crushed ore is mixed with water, a special chemical and some detergent. When air is bubbled through the mixture, the ore clings to the bubbles and floats to the top where it can be skimmed off. The unwanted material sinks to the bottom and is removed. Zinc ores are concentrated this way.

Panning for gold

3 Screening

Sometimes, simply washing the crude ore with water, and passing the solution through **screens** (sieves), can separate out the ore.

4 Leaching

Some ores are **leached** out. The ore is reacted with a chemical solution, which dissolves the metal and leaves unwanted material unaffected. The metal is then recovered from the solution. Copper is sometimes leached from its ore.

Activities

1. Examine the results of the following experiments, carried out on four metals labelled P, Q, R and S.
   (a) Metals Q and S react with hydrochloric acid to give off hydrogen gas. Metal P does not react with hydrochloric acid.
   (b) Metals Q and R burn in oxygen with intense flames. Metal S only glows when heated in oxygen.
   (c) Metal R reacts vigorously with water, but metal Q reacts only slowly with water.
   Place the metals in order of their reactivity. Give possible names for the four metals.

2. Explain why sodium and potassium are stored under oil, but aluminium and zinc can be stored in air.

3. Calcium reacts with water to form calcium hydroxide solution and hydrogen:
   (a) Write a balanced equation for this reaction.
   (b) What is the test for hydrogen?

3 Extracting the Metal from its Ore

Key Ideas

Before the extraction process begins, some metal ores have to be converted to the *metal oxide*. Some metal oxides *decompose* into the metal and oxygen by the action of heat alone.

Other metal oxides need to be reacted with a *reducing agent* such as *carbon* or *carbon monoxide* to produce the metal.

Iron is an important metal. It is extracted from its ore (iron oxide) in a *blast furnace*.

The *empirical formula* of a compound is the simplest ratio of all the atoms present. It can be deduced from the percentage composition of the compound, or by experiment.

The Activity Series and Metal Oxides

When we constructed the activity series from the reaction of metals with oxygen, we placed the metals which reacted most energetically at the top of the table. The result of these **oxidation** reactions (the metals lost electrons) was a **loss** of **energy**. The reactions are **exothermic**.

If we now wish to **reduce** the metal oxide (to get the metal ions to gain electrons), we must replace all the energy lost in the formation of the oxide:

metal + oxygen → metal oxide + **energy**
(oxidation)
metal oxide + **energy** → metal + oxygen
(reduction)

Oxides of metals low in the activity series will only require a small amount of energy to reduce their oxides to the metal. Oxides of metals from copper upwards are not affected by just heat. For these more reactive metals, heating with carbon, hydrogen or carbon monoxide reduces the oxide.

A chemical which causes reduction is called a **reducing agent**. Carbon, hydrogen and carbon monoxide are examples of reducing agents.

Heating Metal Oxides

1 Heat Alone

When we heat metal oxides, a few **decompose** to form the **metal** and **oxygen**. When silver oxide is heated, it forms silver metal and oxygen:

silver oxide → silver + oxygen
$Ag_2O(s) → Ag(s) + O_2(g)$
● $2Ag_2O(s) → 4Ag(s) + O_2(g)$

Silver is an unreactive metal, found near the bottom of the activity series. Oxides above mercury in the activity series are unaffected by heat alone.

You may have noticed that when zinc oxide is heated, it turns from white to yellow, but becomes white again on cooling. No overall chemical change has taken place.

2 Heating with Carbon

Some metal oxides react with carbon to form the metal and carbon dioxide. For example, if you mix powdered carbon with copper oxide and heat the mixture with a bunsen burner, small beads of molten copper form.

copper oxide + carbon → copper + carbon dioxide
$CuO(s) + C(s) → Cu(l) + CO_2(g)$
● $2CuO(s) + C(s) → 2Cu(l) + CO_2(g)$

The oxides of metals above zinc in the activity series do not react when heated with carbon.

3 Heating with Carbon Monoxide or Hydrogen

Both carbon monoxide and hydrogen can also be used to extract metals from their oxides. Great care must be taken when doing experiments with these gases, as they can form an explosive mixture with the oxygen in the air.

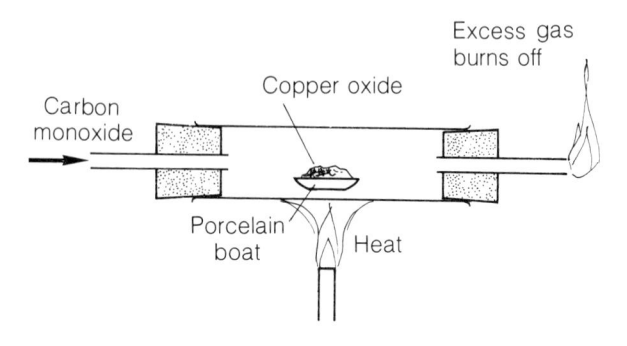

Reacting a metal oxide with carbon monoxide

Carbon monoxide reacts with metal oxide to form the metal and carbon dioxide:

$$\text{iron oxide} + \text{carbon monoxide} \rightarrow \text{iron} + \text{carbon dioxide}$$
$$FeO(s) + CO(g) \rightarrow Fe(s) + CO_2(g)$$

Hydrogen reacts with metal oxide to produce the metal and water:

$$\text{lead oxide} + \text{hydrogen} \rightarrow \text{lead} + \text{water}$$
$$PbO(s) + H_2(g) \rightarrow Pb(s) + H_2O(g)$$

Like carbon, hydrogen and carbon monoxide will react only with metal oxides up to zinc in the activity series. The oxides of metals higher than zinc in the activity series can only be converted to the metal by passing an electric current through their molten compounds. All these reactions are summarised in table 5.3.

Table 5.3

Metal Oxide	Heat Alone	Heat and Carbon	Heat and Carbon Monoxide	Heat and Hydrogen
Sodium Magnesium Aluminium	No reaction	No reaction	No reaction	No reaction
Zinc Iron Tin Lead Copper		Metal and carbon dioxide formed	Metal and carbon dioxide formed	Metal and water formed
Mercury Silver Gold	Metal and oxygen formed			

Converting Metal Ores to their Oxides

A number of metal ores are **metal sulphides**. When they are heated in a furnace, they react with oxygen in the air to form the metal oxide. Sulphur dioxide gas is also produced and this can be used to make sulphuric acid. For example, copper sulphide produces copper oxide when heated in air:

$$\text{copper sulphide} + \text{oxygen} \rightarrow \text{copper oxide} + \text{sulphur dioxide}$$
$$CuS(s) + O_2(g) \rightarrow CuO(s) + SO_2(g)$$
● $2CuS(s) + 3O_2(g) \rightarrow 2CuO(s) + 2SO_2(g)$

An ore of zinc, called zinc blende, contains mostly zinc sulphide. The ore forms zinc oxide when roasted in air:

$$\text{zinc sulphide} + \text{oxygen} \rightarrow \text{zinc oxide} + \text{sulphur dioxide}$$
$$ZnS(s) + O_2(g) \rightarrow ZnO(s) + SO_2(g)$$
● $2ZnS(s) + 3O_2(g) \rightarrow 2ZnO(s) + 2SO_2(g)$

The metal oxide can then be reduced to the metal by heating with carbon, carbon monoxide or hydrogen.

Industrial Extraction of Metal by Heat Alone

As we have seen, only the oxides of metals below copper in the activity series can be extracted from their oxides by heat alone. An ore called cinnabar contains mercury, which is present as mercury sulphide. Roasting cinnabar in air converts it to mercury oxide. Further heating reduces the oxide to liquid mercury:

$$\text{mercury sulphide} + \text{oxygen} \rightarrow \text{mercury oxide} + \text{sulphur dioxide}$$
$$HgS(s) + O_2(g) \rightarrow HgO(s) + SO_2(g)$$
● $2HgS(s) + 3O_2(g) \rightarrow 2HgO(s) + 2SO_2(g)$

then
$$\text{mercury oxide} \rightarrow \text{mercury} + \text{oxygen}$$
$$HgO(s) \rightarrow Hg(l) + O_2(g)$$
● $2HgO(s) \rightarrow 2Hg(l) + O_2(g)$

Usually these two reactions occur together and the mercury sulphide decomposes to form liquid mercury, sulphur dioxide and oxygen.

Heating with Coke

Both zinc oxide and lead oxide can be converted to the metal by heating them with **coke**, a form of carbon. Coke is made by heating coal in the absence of air. The coke lumps are a dark, silvery grey colour and are full of tiny holes – a bit like a sponge.

A plant process called the Imperial Smelting Process converts lead and zinc ores to both the metals at the same time. Lead ore, zinc ore and coke are mixed together and put in a furnace. The zinc oxide is reduced, and, at the temperature of the furnace, forms zinc vapour. This zinc "gas" is passed to another part of the plant where it is cooled and condensed into liquid zinc, to be poured into moulds. The lead oxide is also reduced and liquid lead is run off from the furnace.

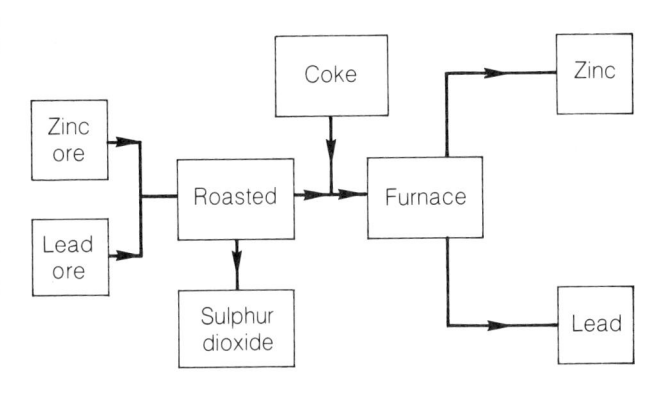

Flow diagram of the Imperial Smelting Process

150 METALS AND CORROSION

Making Iron in the Blast Furnace

Iron is a very important metal. Most of it is converted into steel, and used to make nuts, bolts nails and construction materials for vehicles and buildings.

Iron is found in most continents as **iron ore**. There are two common iron ores: **magnetite** (Fe_3O_4), which is found mostly in North America and Sweden, and **haematite** (Fe_2O_3), which is found in Australia and Brazil. The ore is found near the earth's surface and can be open pit mined. It is usually crushed and concentrated at the mine site. In Brazil, the concentrated ore is loaded onto trains to transport it to the shipping ports. The trains can be 1.5 km long and carry up to 17 500 tonnes of ore. Bulk ore carriers then transport the ore to the steel making countries. The ore is reduced to iron metal in a **blast furnace**.

The blast furnace is about 50 metres high and lined with heat resisting bricks. Each furnace can cost up to one million pounds to construct.

A large, deep water dock was recently completed at Hunterston in Ayrshire, which is capable of receiving bulk ore carriers. The crushed ore is carried by conveyor belt to the iron works. The iron ore is mixed with coke and limestone ($CaCO_3$), and the mixture is used to **charge** the furnaces.

The furnace is filled with coke and set alight. When the temperature is high enough, the charge of ore, coke and limestone is put into the top of the blast furnace. The charge falls onto the hot coke, through which a blast of hot air is forced. The hot air both increases the temperature of the furnace, and reacts with the coke to form carbon monoxide gas. The carbon monoxide converts the ore to iron.

The limestone breaks up at the high temperature to form calcium oxide and carbon dioxide. The calcium oxide then reacts with the impurities in the ore to form a material called **slag**. The slag floats on top of the molten iron and can be skimmed off. It is sold as material for building roads.

The molten iron is run off from the bottom of the furnace, and a fresh charge of ore, coke and limestone is put in at the top.

The furnace runs continuously, night and day, throughout the year. A typical blast furnace can produce more than 2000 tonnes of iron every 24 hours. If the furnace was stopped, or broke down, you can imagine the problems that would arise if it got so cold that the iron inside solidified!

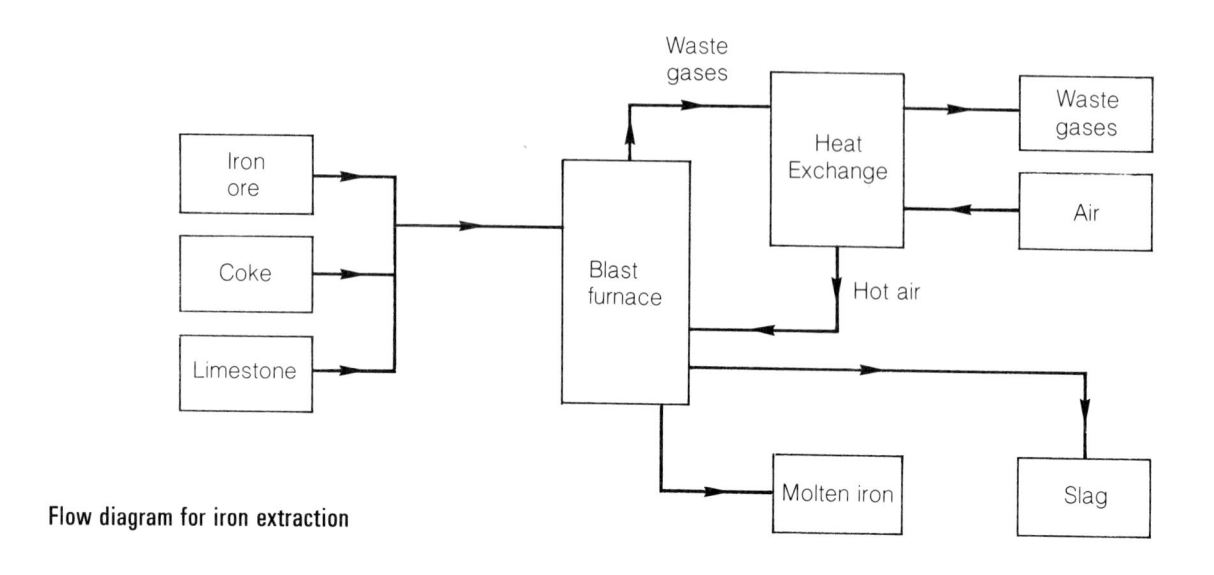

A blast furnace

Flow diagram for iron extraction

Inside the Blast Furnace

The following reactions take place inside the blast furnace:

Coke burns in the hot air to form carbon dioxide:

$$C(s) + O_2(g) \rightarrow CO_2(g)$$

Carbon dioxide reacts with coke to form carbon monoxide:

$$CO_2(g) + C(s) \rightarrow CO(g)$$
● $CO_2(g) + C(s) \rightarrow 2CO(g)$

Iron forms and flows to the bottom of the furnace:

$$Fe_2O_3(s) + CO(g) \rightarrow Fe(l) + CO_2(g)$$
● $Fe_2O_3(s) + 3CO(g) \rightarrow 2Fe(l) + 3CO_2(g)$

The molten iron is poured into moulds and allowed to cool. The iron at this stage is called **"pig iron"**, because of the shape of the moulds. Pig iron can be melted down later and made into cast iron gratings, manhole covers, vehicle engine blocks and gas stoves. It is also used to make **steel**.

The pig iron used to make steel is melted in a **converter**, sometimes with scrap or recycled iron and steel. Oxygen gas is blasted through the molten metal to burn out any impurities. The correct amount of carbon, along with any other additives are then added to the converter to form the alloy we call steel.

There are many different types of steel, made to suit the purchaser's requirements. Metals such as vanadium, manganese, chromium, tungsten, nickel and molybdenum can be added to alter the properties of the steel.

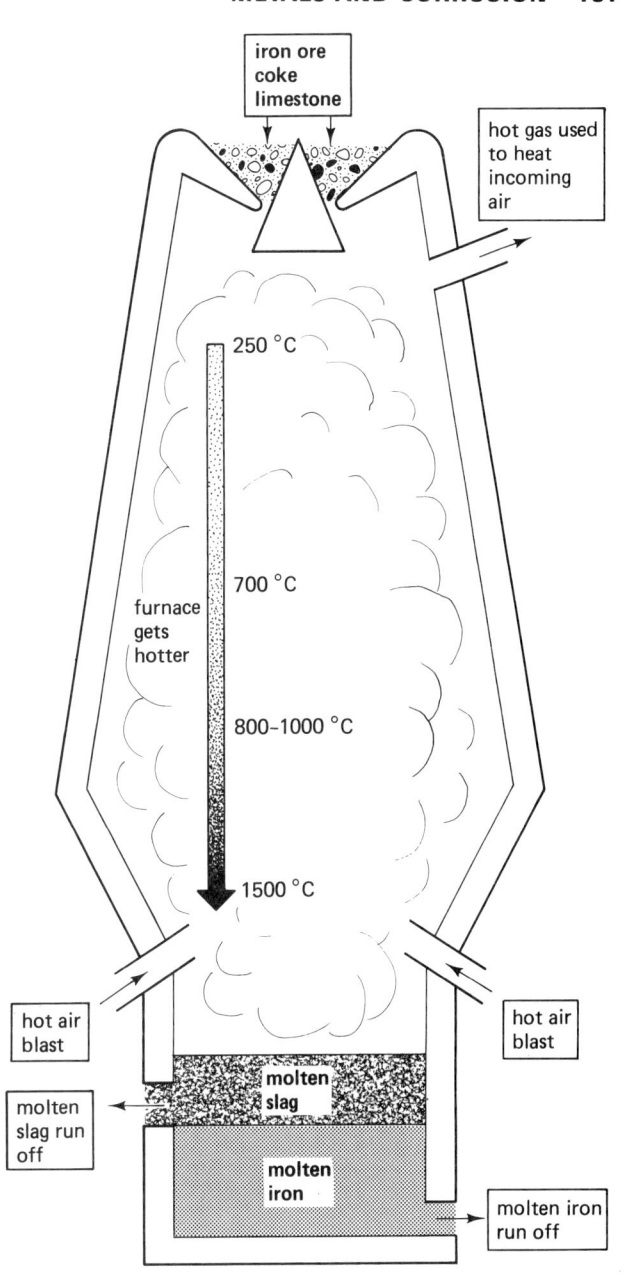

Empirical Formula

The **empirical** formula of a substance gives the simplest ratio of the atoms present in the compound. The empirical formula may have to be multiplied by a whole number to obtain the **molecular** formula.

Hydrogen peroxide, for example, which can be used for bleaching hair, has an empirical formula of HO, but its actual molecular formula is is H_2O_2.

The empirical formula can be obtained from the results of an experiment. For example, if copper oxide is heated in a stream of carbon monoxide, it is reduced to copper. If we weigh the copper oxide at the start of the experiment, and the mass of copper left at the end, we can calculate the amount of oxygen present in the oxide, by subtraction. The empirical formula can then be calculated.

Example

After 3.6 g of an oxide of copper had been heated in a stream of hydrogen, 3.2 g of copper remained. Find the empirical formula of the oxide.

Step 1 Find the mass of each element in the compound.

Copper oxide 3.6 g
Copper   −3.2 g
Oxygen   0.4 g

Step 2 Draw a table with a column for each element.

Step 3 Put in the mass of each element then the Relative Atomic Mass

Step 4 Convert the mass to moles by dividing by the Relative Atomic Mass

Step 5 Convert to a whole number ratio by dividing throughout by the smallest number of moles

	Copper	Oxygen	Step
	3.2	0.4	3
	64	16	
	$\frac{3.2}{64}$	$\frac{0.40}{16}$	4
=	0.05	0.025	
	$\frac{0.05}{0.025}$	$\frac{0.025}{0.025}$	5
=	2	1	

The ratio of copper to oxygen is therefore 2:1. So the empirical formula is Cu_2O.

Empirical formulae can also be calculated from percentage composition. The calculation is carried out in exactly the same way, substituting percentage for mass.

METALS AND CORROSION

Activities

○ 1 Copy and complete the flow diagram for the production of iron from iron ore.

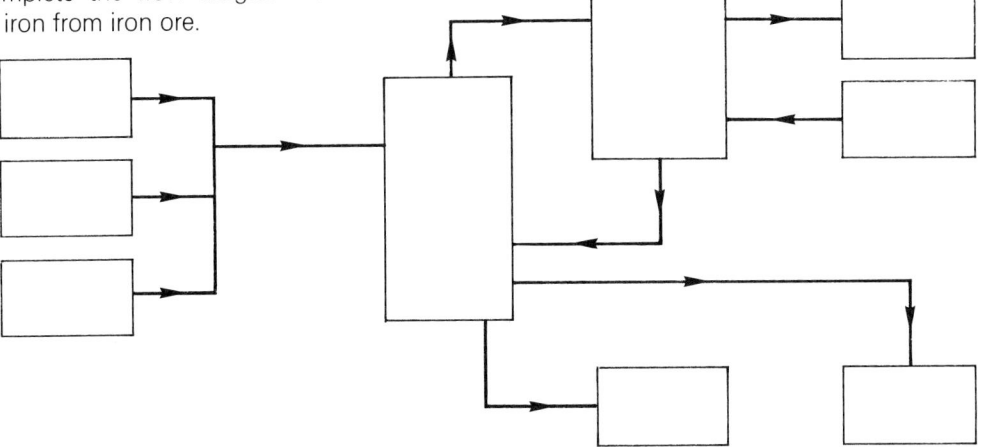

○ 2 Give the names of two metals which can be obtained from their metal oxides by:
   (a) heat alone;
   (b) heating with carbon;
   (c) by passing an electric current through the molten metal oxide.

◐ 3 The following data shows the iron ore production of various countries in 1981 (all figures are in millions of tonnes): USSR 243; Brazil 102; Australia 86; USA 75; China 70; Canada 50.5; India 40.5; South Africa 27.8; Sweden 23.2.
   ○ (a) Put the data into a table.
   ○ (b) Draw a bar graph to show the data.
   ● (c) If the total world production in 1981 was 864 million tonnes, what is the percentage of the world's iron ore produced by each country?

● 4 Some properties of the compounds calcium oxide, aluminium oxide, copper(II) oxide and silver(I) oxide are given below:

Test	A	B	C	D
Solubility in water	insoluble	insoluble	insoluble	soluble
Effect of heat	no reaction	forms metal	no reaction	no reaction
Heat with carbon	no reaction	forms metal	forms metal	no reaction

   (a) Use the table to identify the compounds A, B, C and D.
   (b) The metals in the three oxides, A, B and C can be placed in order of their reactivity from the information in the table. Put the three metals in order of **increasing** reactivity, and explain how you worked this out.

● 5 (a) If 0.2 g of hydrogen gas combines with 3.2 g of oxygen gas to form a compound, calculate the empirical formula.
   (b) If one mole of the compound has a mass of 34 g, what is the molecular formula of the compound?

● 6 A hydrocarbon contains 80 per cent carbon.
   (a) Calculate the empirical formula of the hydrocarbon.
   (b) What is the molecular formula of the hydrocarbon if one mole has a mass of 30 g?

● 7 Calculate the empirical formulae of the compounds, which have the following percentage composition by mass:
   (a) 40% calcium, 12% carbon, 48% oxygen;
   (b) 23.8% carbon, 5.9% hydrogen, 70.3% chlorine;
   (c) 42.5% potassium, 15.2% iron, 19.5% carbon, 22.8% nitrogen.

4 Extracting Ores by Electrolysis

Key Ideas

The more *reactive* metals can only be extracted from ores by the *electrolysis* of their *molten salts*.

During electrolysis, the metal ions move to the *negative electrode*, where they gain electrons to form the metal. The metal ions have been *reduced*.

Using Electricity to Extract Metals from their Ores

In Electricity in Chemistry we saw that the passage of electricity through a molten ionic substance causes a chemical change. The metal is formed at the negative electrode. This process is called **electrolysis**.

Many of the **reactive metals** can only be recovered from their ores by electrolysis. The concentrated metal ore is first purified and then melted. Electrodes are lowered into the molten ore and electricity is passed through the melt. Metal ions are attracted to the negative electrode, where they gain electrons to form liquid metal.

It is also possible to obtain some less reactive metals by electrolysis. The metal ion can be **leached** out of the ore by reacting it with a suitable chemical (e.g., an acid). Electrolysis of the solution formed, produces layers of pure metal on the negative electrode.

What Happens at the Electrodes

During the electrolysis of a molten ionic compound, the **positive** metal **ions** are attracted to the **negative** electrode. These ions **gain** electrons

$$M^+(l) + e \rightarrow M(s) \quad \text{reduction}$$

and form metal ions. They are **reduced**.

Negative ions are attracted to the **positive** electrode, where they **lose** electrons. The negative ions are **oxidised**.

Aluminium

Aluminium is the third most common element in the earth's crust, and the most common metal. However, it was not extracted from its ores until 1827. Most of the aluminium we use is in the form of **alloys**, in which the aluminium is mixed with other metals to change its properties.

Articles made from aluminium

Aluminium is a very light metal, and is very reactive. However, it quickly forms a coating of aluminium oxide on its surface which prevents further reaction (see Corrosion). It is used in the manufacture of window frames, soft drink cans, bottle-tops, cooking foil, step ladders, ships and aeroplanes.

It is also used to make overhead power cables because of its lightness and good electrical conductivity.

Occurrence and Extraction

Aluminium is extracted from the ore **bauxite** ($Al_2O_3 \cdot 3H_2O$). Aluminium is also found in many other rocks and clays, but it is very difficult to extract it from these sources. Bauxite is mined in Australia, Brazil, Jamaica and Yugoslavia. After mining, most of the ore is exported to other countries for processing. Canada and the USA process 40 per cent of the bauxite mined each year.

METALS AND CORROSION 155

Aluminium works at Holyhead

West Germany and Norway are the biggest European importers of bauxite. In the UK there are large plants at Holyhead in Wales, Lynemouth in England and Fort William in Scotland. Bauxite is generally about 45 per cent aluminium oxide, the main impurities being silicon dioxide (SiO_2), iron(III) oxide (Fe_2O_3) and titanium oxide (TiO_2).

The first stage in aluminium manufacture is to take out the impurities using the Bayer Process. The ore is crushed and mixed with hot sodium hydroxide solution, so that the aluminium oxide dissolves to form sodium aluminate:

bauxite + sodium hydroxide → sodium aluminate + water

$$Al_2O_3 \cdot 3H_2O(s) + 2NaOH(aq) \rightarrow 2NaAlO_2(aq) + 4H_2O(l)$$

The impurities sink to the bottom of the tank (sedimentation). The solution of sodium aluminate is then removed, diluted with water and cooled. A precipitate of aluminium hydroxide forms:

sodium aluminate + water → aluminium hydroxide + sodium hydroxide

$$NaAlO_2(aq) + 2H_2O(l) \rightarrow Al(OH)_3(s) + NaOH(aq)$$

When the aluminium hydroxide is heated to between 1200 and 1500 °C, pure aluminium oxide (called alumina) forms:

aluminium hydroxide → aluminium oxide + water

$$2Al(OH)_3(s) \rightarrow Al_2O_3(s) + 3H_2O(l)$$

The melting point of aluminium oxide is 2050°C and it is neither practical, nor economic, to electrolyse the molten salt to obtain the metal. Instead it is dissolved in another molten ore.

In 1876, Charles Hall (USA) and Paul Heroult (France) independently discovered that another aluminium ore called **cryolite** (Na_3AlF_6), which melts at 700–1000 °C, dissolved aluminium oxide. The Hall–Heroult electrolysis cell was developed and the commercial extraction of aluminium began.

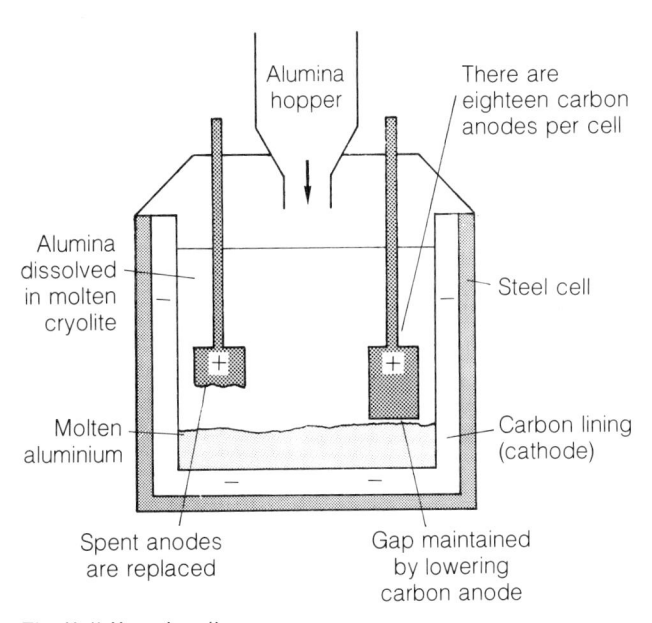

The Hall-Heroult cell

The positive carbon electrodes (anodes) for the cell are made on site from bitumen. The electrodes are used up during the electrolysis process and so a large part of the plant is devoted to their manufacture. The metal electrolysis tank is lined with carbon, and this forms the negative electrode (cathode). As the electricity flows, the aluminium oxide is decomposed into its elements.

Because so much electricity is required for the electrolysis of the melt, most aluminium smelters are built close to a power station.

156 METALS AND CORROSION

Reaction at the Anode

$$2O^{2-}(l) \rightarrow O_2(g) + 4e$$
$$\text{then } O_2(g) + C(s) \rightarrow CO_2(g)$$

The carbon anodes react with the oxygen and this is why they need to be replaced frequently.

Reaction at the Cathode

$$Al^{3+}(l) + 3e \rightarrow Al(l)$$

The molten aluminium sinks to the bottom of the tank and is sucked out into a large container. In a typical aluminium plant, each cell is capable of producing one tonne of aluminium, per day, on a continuous basis. The molten aluminium is poured into moulds to cool, and the solid "pigs" are then further processed into sheets, blocks or wire.

Environmental Problems

Bauxite is obtained by open cast mining and this leaves huge scars on the landscape.

The iron(III) oxide impurity in bauxite ore is a bright red colour. After purification of the bauxite this impurity is pumped into large lagoons to settle out. The iron(III) oxide cannot be discharged into rivers or the sea as it would kill marine life.

Exhaust gases from the smelters contain harmful substances which escape into the air. Gases are passed through **scrubbers**, which remove some of the harmful gases, but then the water used in the scrubbing process is contaminated, and can damage rivers.

Recycling aluminium helps to cut down pollution, and also reduces energy costs. Scrap aluminium needs only to be melted down and recast into pigs for further processing.

Aluminium metal is removed at the smelter

Purifying Metals

When a metal is first produced from its ore, it often contains some impurities. For many purposes these impurities do not matter, and the metal can be sold in an impure form. However, some customers require metal which is almost 100 per cent pure.

We saw that, in a blast furnace, pig iron could be purified by melting it and then blasting oxygen through it. The oxygen reacts with the impurities to form an easily removable slag.

Other metals are purified by a process involving electrolysis. It is called **electrolytic refining**.

The impure metal is made the positive electrode of an electrolysis cell.

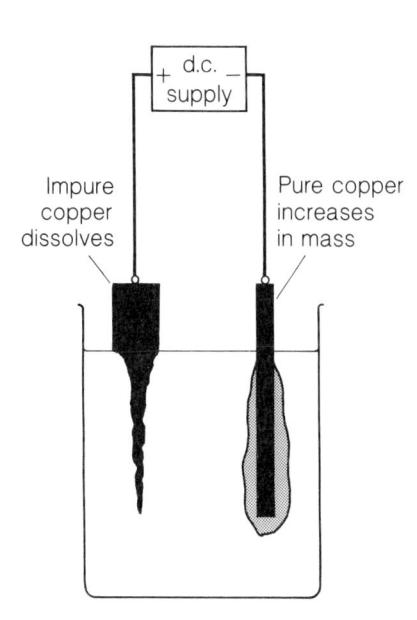

Electrolytic refining

A thin sheet of the pure metal forms the negative electrode. The electrolyte contains metal ions. When electricity is supplied, the impure electrode dissolves, forming metal ions. The ions are attracted to the negative electrode, where they gain electrons and deposit themselves as a layer of atoms on the electrode surface. The negative electrode "grows" until the positive electrode has completely dissolved.

Only one kind of metal ion at a time will deposit on the negative electrode during electrolysis, and so the layer on the electrode contains **only** the required metal.

The pure metal electrode is removed, melted down and cast into moulds for further processing.

Extracting Copper

The most important copper ore is chalcopyrites, which has the chemical formula $CuFeS_2$. Usually some arsenic, zinc, silver and gold is also found with this ore and they can be recovered during the processing.

The crushed ore is concentrated by the froth flotation process. The concentrated sulphide ore is then roasted in a furnace, where it melts to form two layers. The heavier layer is called **matte**, and sinks to the bottom of the container. The upper, lighter layer contains mainly waste material (the slag), which is skimmed off from the surface.

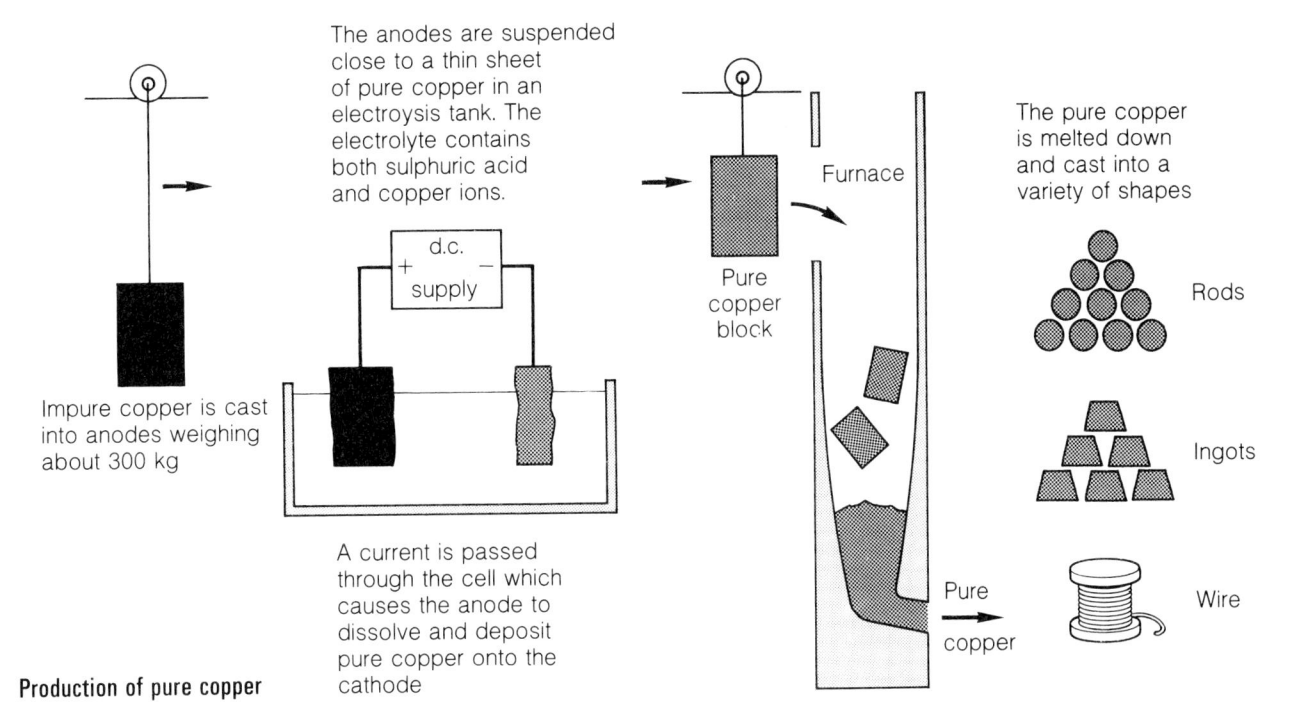

METALS AND CORROSION

Production of pure copper

Impure copper is cast into anodes weighing about 300 kg

The anodes are suspended close to a thin sheet of pure copper in an electroysis tank. The electrolyte contains both sulphuric acid and copper ions.

A current is passed through the cell which causes the anode to dissolve and deposit pure copper onto the cathode

The pure copper is melted down and cast into a variety of shapes: Rods, Ingots, Wire

The matte, which contains roughly 45 per cent copper, 30 per cent iron and 25 per cent sulphur, is poured into another container and air is blasted through it. The iron and sulphur both **react (oxidise)** to form their oxides.

The remaining copper is about 98.5 per cent pure and is called **blister copper**. The blister copper is poured into moulds, which are shaped to form the huge **anodes** (positive electrode) of an electrolysis cell. Each anode weighs about 300 kilogrammes.

A thin sheet of copper is made the **cathode** (negative electrode), and a copper sulphate solution is used as **electrolyte**.

When the electrolysis cell is switched on, the impure blister copper dissolves to form copper ions:

$$Cu(s) \rightarrow Cu^{2+}(aq) + 2e$$

The copper cathode begins to increase in size as copper metal is deposited onto it:

$$Cu^{2+}(aq) + 2e \rightarrow Cu(s)$$

When the anode has completely dissolved, the pure copper cathode is removed and melted down, before casting it into ingots, rods and wires.

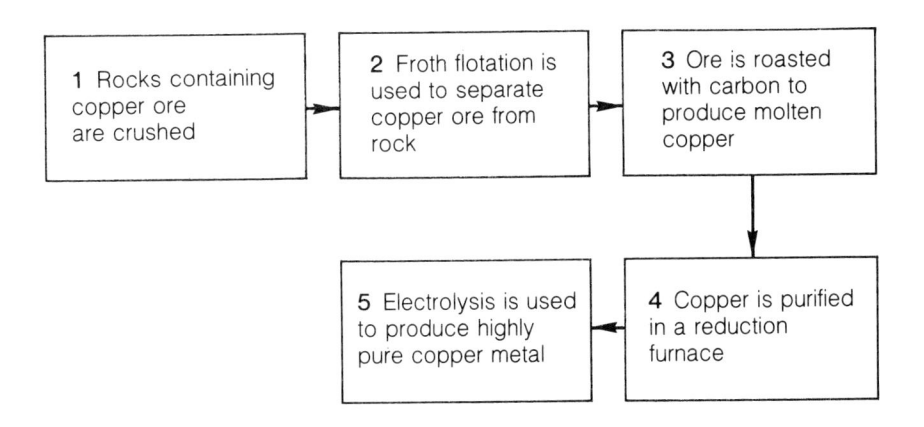

1. Rocks containing copper ore are crushed
2. Froth flotation is used to separate copper ore from rock
3. Ore is roasted with carbon to produce molten copper
4. Copper is purified in a reduction furnace
5. Electrolysis is used to produce highly pure copper metal

Flow diagram for copper manufacture

158 METALS AND CORROSION

Activities

1. The consumption of copper in 1981 was as follows:

Country	Copper Use (Thousand tonnes)
USA	1891
Japan	1254
Germany	727
France	440
Italy	366
UK	333
Belgium	258
Canada	243

   Present this information in a bar graph.

2. The growth in the production of copper ore over the last century is shown below:

Year	Copper Ore Production (Thousand tonnes)	Year	Copper Ore Production (Thousand tonnes)
1900	500	1940	2350
1910	850	1950	2500
1915	1050	1960	4400
1920	950	1970	6450
1930	1550	1980	7850

   (a) Draw a line graph showing these figures;
   (b) From your graph, predict what the output of copper ore will be in the year 2000;
   (c) Why do you think there was a drop in output between 1915 and 1920?

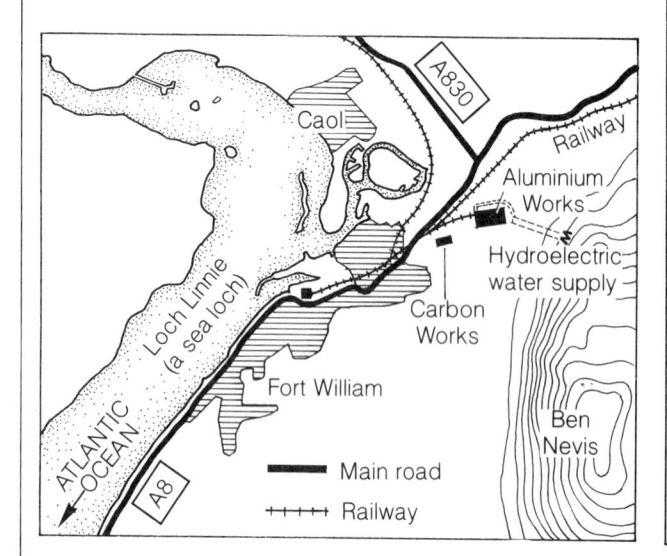

3. Copy and complete the flow diagram to show the industrial process for producing aluminium from bauxite.

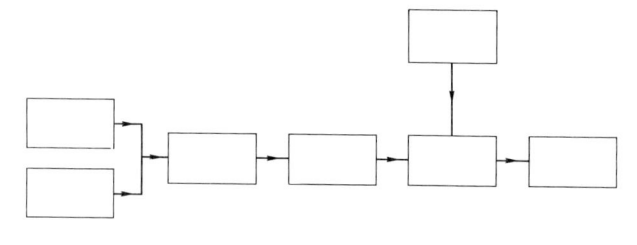

4. An aluminium plant needs:
   (i) A deep water port to discharge the bauxite;
   (ii) A cheap supply of electricity;
   (iii) Good road and rail links to transport the finished aluminium.

   Examine the maps of the Fort William and Holyhead areas and comment on their choice as sites for aluminium smelters.

Fort William

Holyhead

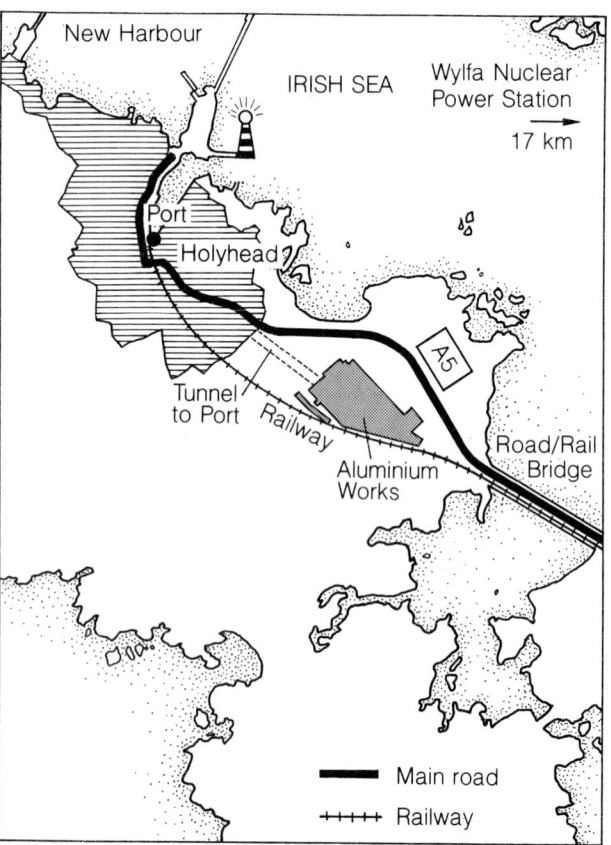

5. Explain why recycling aluminium can save energy and reduce pollution.

5 Corrosion

Key Ideas

Corrosion occurs when *metals* react with substances in their surroundings to produce *compounds*. The *atoms* at the surface of the metal change into *ions* by losing electrons. This is an *oxidation* process. *Rusting* is the special name given to the corrosion of *iron*. Both *water* and *oxygen* are required for *rusting* to occur. The presence of solutions of *ions*, speeds up the *rate* of *corrosion*. Iron ions and hydroxide ions can be detected using *ferroxyl indicator*.

Corrosion all Around

Corrosion is the name given to the chemical reaction in which the atoms at the surface of a metal change into **ions**. As a result of this, a metal compound forms, which may flake off or be washed away by rain, leaving the surface pitted with holes. The metal changes its appearance, weakens and becomes less fit for its intended use.

An example of rusting

You can see examples of iron or steel corroding all around you. Tin cans or bicycles left outside for a few weeks soon show the tell-tale brownish discoloration of corrosion. The corrosion of iron is given the special name **rusting**, and the brown marks are called **rust**.

If the body or chassis of a vehicle is allowed to rust it becomes unsafe to drive. Rust also lowers the resale value! Many cars are scrapped every year because of rust.

Corrosion costs the country many millions of pounds each year. Metal objects no longer fit for use have to be replaced. Vast amounts of money are also spent trying to prevent corrosion taking place. In many cases all we manage to do is slow the process down.

Corrosion and the Activity Series

Metals low in the activity series, such as gold, do not corrode at all. Silver does not corrode in pure air, but it forms a greyish surface film (tarnish) if certain other chemicals are present in air. The tarnish is removed by polishing.

Usher Hall

Lithium, sodium and potassium (group one metals) are very reactive and have to be stored in oil to protect them from reacting (corroding) with air and moisture.

You may have seen a piece of sodium being cut and noticed how quickly the shiny silver surface dulled and turned a blue/grey colour. The change in colour shows that a chemical reaction has taken place. The metal has reacted with oxygen in the air to form a compound – it has corroded.

Reactive metals also corrode rapidly in water. They melt with the heat produced in the reaction and displace hydrogen gas from the water. Magnesium and calcium (group two metals) do not need to be stored under oil. If you examine either of these metals, the surface is usually covered with a grey oxide coating. They too have corroded, but more slowly than the group one metals.

Even metals low in the activity series, such as copper, will corrode under the right conditions. The Usher Hall in Edinburgh has a copper dome. It was opened in 1914 and the copper dome had to be replaced in 1988. It had taken 74 years to corrode! The new dome will stay bright and shiny for a few years, but it will eventually dull and turn green again.

METALS AND CORROSION

The copper corrodes by reaction with chemicals in the air, forming green **verdigris**, a mixture of copper carbonate and copper sulphate.

Rusting of Iron

Iron and steel are used throughout the world. The rate at which they corrode and the prevention of corrosion is therefore of great importance to us all. We can set up a series of experiments to find out what causes iron and steel to rust.

In a normal environment, both air and water are present. Our experiments must test for each of these if we are to discover the cause of rusting.

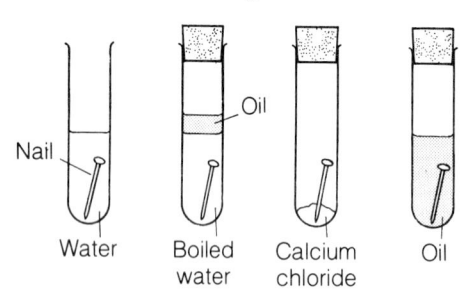

Tube	1	2	3	4
Chemical environment	Air + Water	Water only	Air only	Neither air nor water
Amount of rust	Lots	None	None	None

Test tube 2 contains boiled water. When water is boiled any gases dissolved in it are driven out. The oil prevents more air getting in. Test tube 3 contains calcium chloride, which removes water from the air. The results show that both **air** and **water** must be present for rusting to occur.

If wire wool is pushed to the bottom of a test tube, and the test tube is inverted in a beaker of water, the wire wool begins to rust.

As the wire wool rusts it uses up some of the air, and water is drawn up inside the test-tube. If we measure the volume of water sucked up we find that it is 20 per cent of the total volume of air originally present (air is about 20 per cent oxygen). A lighted splint placed in the tube, after the experiment, is immediately put out, suggesting that no oxygen is present.

We can conclude that both **oxygen** and **water** cause rusting.

In the first stage of rusting the iron atoms at the surface react with moist air to lose electrons and form iron ions:

$$Fe(s) \rightarrow Fe^{2+}(aq) + 2e$$

We can show that Fe^{2+} ions are present by using a **green** solution called **ferroxyl indicator**. The indicator turns a **navy blue colour** if Fe^{2+} ions are present.

The **iron ions** then combine with **hydroxide ions** (also formed during corrosion) to form **iron hydroxide**. The iron hydroxide eventually turns into **iron oxide**, the brown powdery material we call **rust**.

If a nail is left for a short time in water containing a little ferroxyl indicator, the solution begins to turn blue. Iron ions have formed. If we put some acid or salt into the water, the blue colour forms even quicker, suggesting that the presence of ions speeds up rusting. The presence of ions in the water causes it to act as an **electrolyte**, speeding up the rate at which the iron loses electrons.

Ions are present in rain water due to **carbon dioxide** dissolving in the water to form carbonic acid (H_2CO_3). Air pollution can lead to even more acidic rain. Both of these speed up rusting.

Motor vehicles near the sea will rust more quickly than vehicles kept inland. Salt spray from the sea is carried in the air and speeds up corrosion. In winter many roads are gritted with a mixture of salt and sand to melt the ice and snow. When vehicles drive along the road, salt spray covers the underside of the car, and accelerates rusting.

The exhaust pipe on a car rusts very quickly, because it gets very hot, and heat speeds up chemical reactions. New, mild steel exhausts are often "holed" with rust within two years. Stainless steel exhausts are available, which are guaranteed for the life of the car. However, they are more expensive than the mild steel exhausts.

The Chemistry of Rusting

Corrosion occurs when metal atoms **lose electrons** to form **ions**. This is an **oxidation** process.

An oxidation only occurs if a corresponding **reduction** also takes place. The electrons of the metal atom are **accepted** by both the **water** and **oxygen** to form hydroxide ions:

$$2H_2O(l) + O_2(g) + 4e \rightarrow 4OH^-(aq)$$

Rusting involves a number of complex reactions, but they are summarised by the equation:

iron + oxygen + water → iron(II) hydroxide
$$2Fe(s) + O_2(g) + 2H_2O(l) \rightarrow 2Fe(OH)_2(s)$$

The iron(II) hydroxide **further oxidises** in the presence of water and air to form iron(III) hydroxide. This in turn forms iron(III) oxide:

$$Fe(OH)_2(s) + air + water \rightarrow Fe_2O_3$$
$$Fe^{2+} \rightarrow Fe^{3+} + e$$

Water often contains **dissolved ions**, making it an **electrolyte**. These ions allow the electrons to move more easily from the iron to the water and oxygen. The rate of corrosion is speeded up.

When the electrolyte contains **acid**, the iron will displace **hydrogen ions** from the acidic solution, because it is above hydrogen in the electrochemical series.

$$Fe(s) \rightarrow Fe^{2+}(aq) + 2e \quad \text{oxidation}$$
$$2H^+(aq) + 2e \rightarrow H_2(g) \quad \text{reduction}$$
$$\overline{Fe(s) + 2H^+(aq) \rightarrow Fe^{2+}(aq) + H_2(g) \quad \text{redox}}$$

Rusting as an Electrochemical Cell

We can show that rusting involves both oxidation and reduction (redox), by setting up an electrochemical cell with ferroxyl indicator in the electrolyte. Ferroxyl indicator actually contains **two** indicators, one which turns from green to blue in the presence of Fe^{2+} ions and another, called phenolphthalein, which changes from colourless to pink in the presence of OH^- ions.

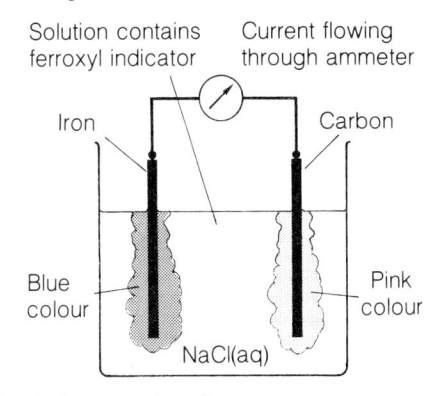

Electrochemical nature of rusting

The cell is set up, using an iron electrode, and a carbon electrode. A meter connected in the circuit shows that the electrons are flowing **from the iron** electrode to the carbon electrode. A blue colour forms at the iron electrode, showing that Fe^{2+} ions are being formed there. A pink colour at the carbon electrode shows the formation of hydroxide ions.

Steel is an alloy of iron and carbon, and the presence of water and oxygen on the surface of the steel provides the correct conditions for electrons to pass from the iron to the carbon and form rust.

Rusting can therefore be thought of as an electrochemical cell in which iron forms one electrode and carbon impurities the other electrode. Electrons move from the iron to the carbon, and hydroxide ions form around the carbon. The iron forms iron ions.

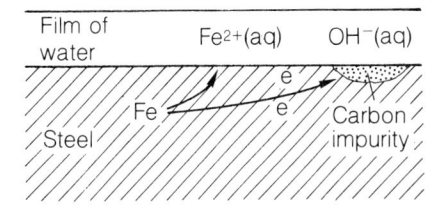

An iron cell at the surface of a sheet of steel

Activities

1. (a) What is the chemical name for rust?
   (b) What substances, other than iron, are needed to make iron rust?
   (c) Give three ways to speed up rusting?
   (d) Why will a car exhaust rust more quickly than other parts of the car?

2. Give examples of a metal which (a) corrodes very quickly, (b) takes some time to corrode and (c) does not corrode at all.

3. Explain why metal objects left by American astronauts on the Moon will not corrode.

4. Corrosion of copper roofs involves the formation of verdigris. What chemicals must be present in air for this to happen?

● 5. A pupil polished three samples of iron with sandpaper and placed one piece in each of three test-tubes marked A, B and C.
   Different solutions and a few drops of ferroxyl indicator were added to each tube. After a few hours it was found that corrosion had occurred in tube B. Tubes A and C showed only slight corrosion.

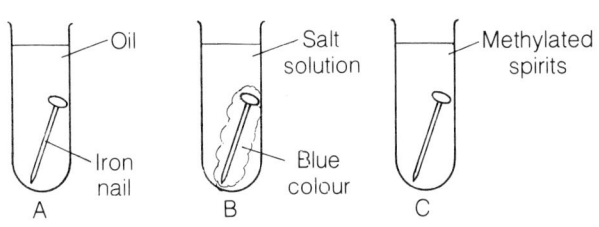

   (a) What was the purpose of the ferroxyl indicator?
   (b) Why were the pieces of iron polished before the experiment?
   (c) Why does salt speed up corrosion, whereas sugar does not?

● 6. Explain why rusting can be described as a redox reaction.

● 7. Ships which sail in fresh water rust more slowly than ships which sail in the sea. Explain this statement.

6 Protecting Metals from Corrosion

Key Ideas

Metals can be protected from corrosion by *sealing* the surface so that water and oxygen cannot get in.

Electrochemical methods can also be used to prevent corrosion. These include *sacrificial protection* and *cathodic protection*.

Metals can also be *electroplated* with another metal.

Coating steel with *zinc* is called *galvanising*.

Aluminium is protected from corrosion by a layer of *aluminium oxide*. *Anodising* is the process used to increase the thickness of the *aluminium oxide* layer on aluminium metal.

Using the Electrochemical Series

1 Sacrificial Protection

Rusting occurs when iron atoms lose electrons. One way of preventing rusting would be to ensure that iron atoms do not lose electrons. The electrochemical series is related to the ease with which atoms lose electrons. The higher the metal in the series, the easier it loses electrons.

The following experiment shows how we can use the position of metals in the electrochemical series to help prevent rusting.

Experiment

Some iron nails are cleaned with wire wool to remove any surface rust. A different metal is wrapped around each nail. The nails are then put into separate dishes and a warm gelatine/salt solution, containing ferroxyl indicator, is added. The gelatine sets. After a few hours the plates are examined.

The presence of a dark blue colour around the untreated nail shows that corrosion of the iron has occurred. A pink colouration also indicates that hydroxide ions have been formed.

The nail wrapped in copper has a very intense blue area around it, showing that corrosion is **more rapid** than for the untreated nail.

The nail wrapped in magnesium shows some pink colouration but no blue at all. The magnesium seems to have **prevented** corrosion of the iron.

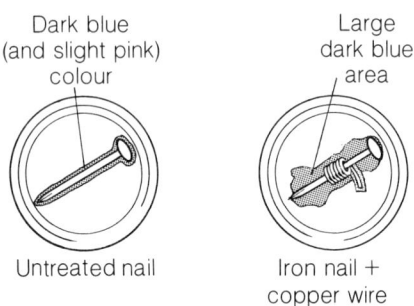

Each plate contains gelatine/salt solution and ferroxyl indicator

Effect of other metals on the rate of rusting

Conclusion

The experiment shows that metals **higher** in the electrochemical series will corrode, **pass electrons to the iron** and **prevent** rusting. A metal **lower** in the electrochemical series will **take electrons away from the iron** and so **speed up** the rusting process.

We can use this knowledge to slow rusting down.

If magnesium or zinc blocks are bolted onto oil rigs, which operate in the North Sea, the blocks will corrode and therefore protect the steel structure of the rig by passing electrons continuously to it. The metal blocks gradually disappear and require replacing at regular intervals.

Ships often have zinc or magnesium blocks bolted onto the hull, below the water line, to slow up the rusting process.

Underground oil and gas pipe lines rust in the damp soil. To prevent this, bags of scrap magnesium are connected at regular intervals along the pipeline.

In each case the more active metal "sacrifices" itself to protect the less active metal, and so this is called **sacrificial protection**.

What's Happening to the Metals

In each case an electrochemical **cell** has been set up. Electrons are flowing from one metal to the other. We can examine the ion electron equations for each cell.

Untreated Nail

$$Fe(s) \rightarrow Fe^{2+}(aq) + 2e \quad \text{oxidation}$$
$$2H_2O(l) + O_2(g) + 4e \rightarrow 4OH^-(aq) \quad \text{reduction}$$

Nail with Copper

Iron is higher than copper in the electrochemical series. The iron ions form more readily than copper, so electrons flow from iron to copper, and the hydroxide ions form at the copper.

At the iron nail $\quad Fe(s) \rightarrow Fe^{2+}(aq) + 2e \quad \text{oxidation}$
At the copper wire $\quad 2H_2O(l) + O_2(g) + 4e \rightarrow 4OH^-(aq) \quad \text{reduction}$

Nail with Magnesium

Magnesium is higher than iron in the electrochemical series. Magnesium ions form more readily than iron ions, so magnesium dissolves and pushes electrons to the iron. Hydroxide ions therefore form at the iron.

At the magnesium wire
$$Mg(s) \rightarrow Mg^{2+}(aq) + 2e \quad \text{oxidation}$$
At the iron nail
$$2H_2O(l) + O_2(g) + 4e \rightarrow 4OH^-(aq) \quad \text{reduction}$$

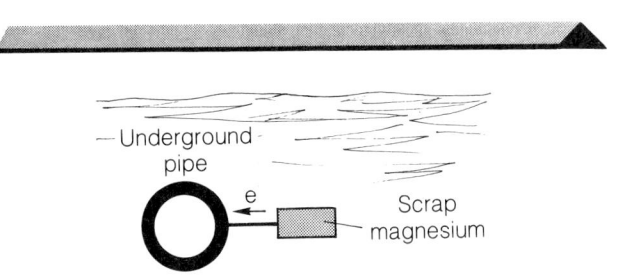

Sacrificial protection of a pipe (left) and a ship hull (right)

2 Cathodic Protection

Another way of protecting iron or steel is to supply electrons to the metal from a battery or electricity generator. The process is called **cathodic protection**. The object to be protected is connected to the **negative** terminal (**cathode**) of a **d.c.** electricity supply. The constant supply of electrons to the iron prevents rusting. Cars and lorries are protected in this way. The body of the vehicle is "negatively earthed" by connecting the negative terminal of the battery directly onto the bodywork.

At some ports, when a ship docks in harbour, it is connected to the negative terminal of a d.c. generator. The positive terminal is connected to some scrap iron, which is dumped on the sea bed. The sea acts as an electrolyte and so the circuit is complete. The scrap iron rusts in preference to the ship.

Physical Protection of Metals

You have seen that water and oxygen need to be present before corrosion can occur. We should be able to prevent corrosion by **sealing the surface** of a metal so that a **barrier** is set up, preventing water and oxygen getting in.

1 Painting

If a piece of metal is thoroughly cleaned and dried, and then coated in paint, the paint will prevent water and oxygen getting to the metal.

Many large metal structures (cars, ships, bridges) are coated in layers of paint to protect the metal from the corrosive atmosphere. Cars are often treated first with special undercoats to **inhibit** (slow up) rust, before the final, glossy coats of paint are sprayed on.

It takes almost a year to paint the Forth Rail Bridge. The surface of the paint is easily damaged, and any exposure of the bare metal to the atmosphere would soon start the rusting process. Consequently the bridge has been continuously

Cars coming out of treatment bath

METALS AND CORROSION

Forth Rail Bridge

painted for the last one hundred years! It has, however, been successful in preventing rust from weaking its structure.

2 Coating with Grease

Many engineering workshops ensure that steel tools and machinery are wiped down with grease or oil. This too provides a surface coating which repels water. However, the coating is very easily damaged and has to be repeated on an almost daily basis.

3 Coating with Plastic

It is also possible to coat a piece of metal with plastic to prevent corrosion. In some cases the metal is simply heated and dipped into plastic granules which melt and stick to the metal. Some lamp posts are coated this way. Plastic coatings can be very tough and withstand fairly extreme conditions. Wire plate racks and the wire netting seen around schools, are often coated in plastic.

4 Coating with another Metal

It is possible to **electroplate** one metal with another metal. The object to be coated is made the negative electrode of an electrolysis cell. The coating metal is made the positive electrode, and the electrolyte a solution of its ions. Some electroplating solutions are complicated mixtures of chemicals which are needed to ensure that the plating is firmly bonded onto the surface of the metal.

Electroplating totally covers the metal surface with atoms of the plating metal, and so it is very effective in preventing corrosion. However, it is expensive to apply, and uses up large amounts of electricity.

Chromium or zinc are often electroplated onto steel to prevent corrosion. Both these metals are more reactive than iron, and we might expect them to corrode even more quickly than iron. They do, but once a metal oxide layer forms at the surface, it prevents oxygen or water reaching the metal atoms underneath. Further corrosion cannot take place.

Iron also reacts with oxygen in the air to form a surface oxide coating, but this layer flakes off easily and exposes fresh iron to further reaction.

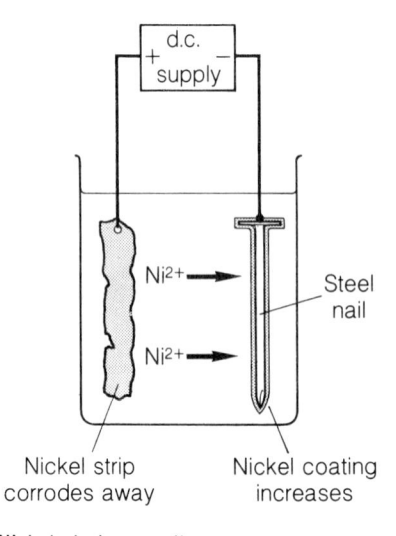

Nickel plating a nail

Car bumpers were often made of steel. They were chromium plated both to prevent corrosion and to enhance appearance. However, chromium does not plate easily onto steel. The steel must first be plated with copper, then with nickel and finally with chromium. This makes chromium plating expensive, both in terms of energy used and metal consumption. Most cars today have plastic bumpers which are easier and cheaper to produce, do not corrode, and more effective at reducing damage in an accident.

Water taps and cutlery are often chromium plated. You may have noticed on the back of cutlery or metal ornaments the letters EPNS. This stands for **E**lectro**P**lated **N**ickel **S**ilver. The article is often made from an alloy such as brass, which is plated first with nickel, and then with silver. The finished article looks like solid silver.

Galvanising

Coating steel with zinc is called **galvanising**. The zinc can be applied by two different methods.

1 Hot-dip Galvanising

The object to be coated is dipped under the surface of a bath of molten zinc. The zinc sticks to the steel forming an uneven surface coating. Steel buckets, gates, fences, watering cans, metal cages and wire netting are often galvanised by hot-dipping.

You can often tell if this method has been used by looking for runs of metal (like paint runs) on the surface, or for sharp drips of solid zinc sticking out from the edges.

2 Galvanising by Electroplating

Zinc can be electroplated onto steel. This method gives a more even coating of zinc, and a better finish.

Food cans cannot be galvanised because zinc is poisonous. The zinc may also react with acids in the canned food to produce hydrogen gas. The hydrogen pressure could eventually cause the can to explode!

Tin Plating

The position of tin in the electrochemical series suggests that it will corrode easily. However, like zinc and chromium, tin also forms an oxide coating which prevents water and oxygen getting to the metal. Once the oxide layer forms further corrosion of the tin stops.

Steel can be coated with tin both by electroplating and the hot-dip process.

Most food cans are made of steel coated with tin. Unlike zinc, the tin is not poisonous, and doesn't react with the food. If the can contains **very** acidic foods, the inside is often coated with lacquer or plastic, which prevents the acids from reacting with the tin.

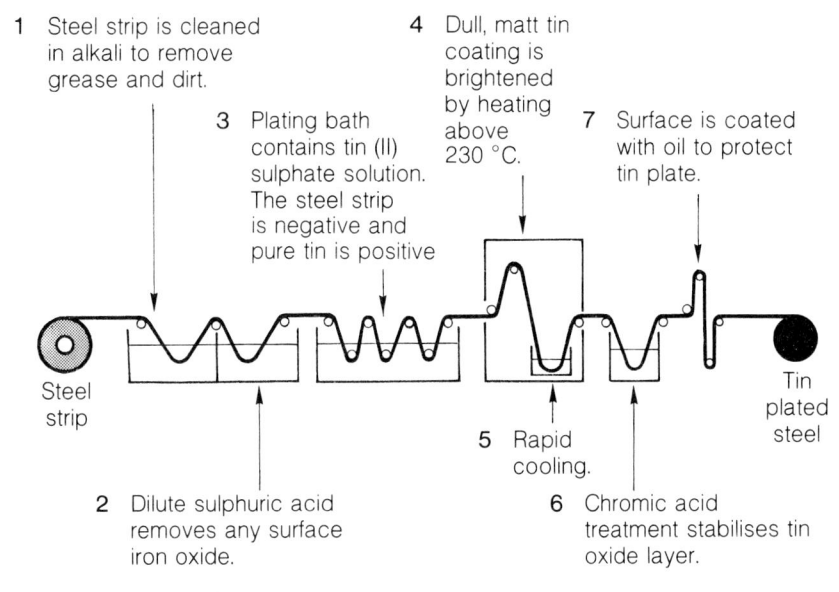

1. Steel strip is cleaned in alkali to remove grease and dirt.
2. Dilute sulphuric acid removes any surface iron oxide.
3. Plating bath contains tin (II) sulphate solution. The steel strip is negative and pure tin is positive.
4. Dull, matt tin coating is brightened by heating above 230 °C.
5. Rapid cooling.
6. Chromic acid treatment stabilises tin oxide layer.
7. Surface is coated with oil to protect tin plate.

Tin plating sheet steel

Comparing Zinc and Tin Plating

When steel is plated with **zinc**, a hard layer is formed which protects the steel. Zinc is above iron in the electrochemical series. If the zinc coating is deeply scratched to expose the steel to the atmosphere, the zinc continues to protect the steel by sacrificial protection. The zinc corrodes, passing electrons to the iron, and thus protecting it.

$$Zn(s) \rightarrow Zn^{2+}(aq) + 2e$$

Electrons flow towards iron (steel) as zinc corrodes

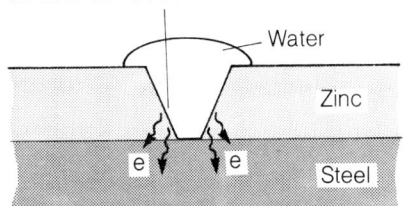

Scratched zinc plating

When steel plated with **tin** is scratched in the same way, the electrochemical process passes electrons from iron to tin, as tin is lower in the series. This time the iron is sacrificed to protect the tin, and the rate of rusting **increases**.

$$Fe(s) \rightarrow Fe^{2+}(aq) + 2e$$

Electrons flow towards tin as iron (steel) corrodes

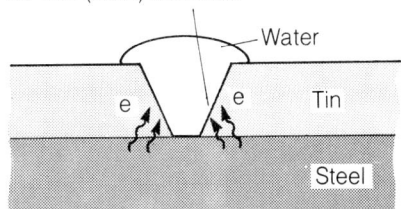

Scratched tin plating

During the Second World War, many air-raid shelters were built in people's gardens. They were made of corrugated steel which had been galvanised. Fifty years later, some are still being used as garden huts. Despite being partly or totally below the ground they show little signs of corrosion. The zinc has protected the steel very effectively.

The Country Code says we should not leave litter in the countryside when we go on picnics or hikes, yet the hillsides are littered with old cans, carelessly thrown away. The tin coated cans will eventually corrode and crumble into the ground. However, aluminium soft drink cans do not corrode and will litter the hills for many years to come.

166 METALS AND CORROSION

Protecting Aluminium

Aluminium is more reactive than zinc, yet it does not seem to corrode as quick. This is because as soon as aluminium is exposed to oxygen in the air, it rapidly reacts to form a layer of protective aluminium oxide. The oxide layer prevents more oxygen from reaching the aluminium and corrosion stops.

The thickness of the aluminium oxide layer varies along the piece of aluminium. A thicker, more even coat of aluminium oxide can be obtained using a process called **anodising**. In this process, the aluminium is cleaned and made the positive electrode (anode) of an electrolysis cell. Another piece of aluminium is made the cathode, and dilute sulphuric acid is used as electrolyte. During the electrolysis, oxygen is given off at the anode, and reacts with the aluminium to produce aluminium oxide.

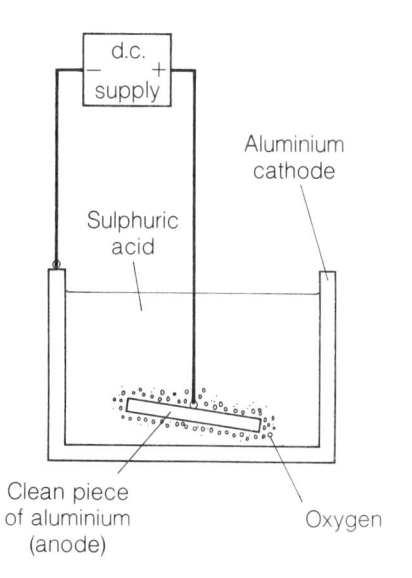

Anodising aluminium

The thick layer of aluminium oxide formed is harder and more difficult to scratch. It offers long term protection to the aluminium underneath, which can be given a high polish to obtain a mirror-like finish. You may well have seen aluminium mirrors in your local swimming baths.

The oxide layer can also be **dyed** to give it an attractive colour finish. Many aluminium pot lids are coloured this way.

Anodising a compact disc.

Activities

○ 1 Attaching another metal to steel can affect the rate of corrosion. Give an example of a metal which could
  (a) speed up rusting
  (b) slow rusting down.

○ 2 Describe, with examples, how surface coating, sacrificial protection and cathodic protection can help prevent rust.
  Electroplating and galvanising are common ways of protecting iron.
  (i) Describe how you would carry out both processes on a piece of iron.
  (ii) Explain how each method protects the iron.

● 3 (a) Explain why galvanised steel is preferred for waste buckets and tin plated steel for food cans?
  (b) What would happen if the bucket and food can were each badly scratched?

● 4 Wooden boats often have a brass or copper strip attached to their keel to prevent damage when the boat is dragged ashore.
  (a) What would happen if the metal strip was attached to the boat with steel (iron) nails?
  (b) What type of nails would you recommend?

● 5 The Germans sank their fleet at Scapa Flow at the end of the First World War. Many of these ships have been raised in recent years and sold as scrap. The ships are almost rust free on the sea bed, but rust rapidly when they are raised to the surface. Explain these observations.

Metals and Corrosion – Study Questions

1 Read the following passage:

Magnesium reacts readily with acids and oxygen. Aluminium might be expected to behave in a similar way. However, if you test aluminium, you will often find that this is not the case. This is mainly due to a layer of aluminium oxide forming very rapidly when the metal is first exposed to air. This oxide layer does not flake off or allow air and water to pass through it. It is this layer which prevents further corrosion of the aluminium.

(a) Which is the most suitable title for this passage?
A Corrosion of metals; B Reacting with air; C The oxidation of metals; or D The reactivity of aluminium. **PS**

(b) Write down the formula for aluminium oxide. (Show your working.) **KU**

(c) Use symbols and formulae to write the equation for the reaction of magnesium with oxygen to form magnesium oxide. (It is not necessary to balance the equation.) **PS**

2 The main constituent of steel is iron. Car bodies are made from steel. Rusting of car bodies is a major problem.

(a) Name the two substances which cause the rusting of iron.

(b) Salt is spread on roads in icy weather.
   (i) State the effect this has on the rate of rusting.
   (ii) Explain why salt has this effect.

(c) The body of a car is used as part of the circuit that operates the electrical equipment. The electrical circuit can be arranged to slow down rusting.
   (i) State which terminal of the battery should be attached to the car body to produce this effect.
   (ii) Explain why this terminal should be used. **KU**

3 Extraction means getting a pure metal from one of its compounds.

A	$Zn(s) + H_2O(g)$ → $ZnO(s) + H_2(g)$
B	$SnO_2(s) + C(s)$ → $Sn(l) + CO_2(g)$
C	$CaCl_2(l)$ → $Ca(s) + Cl_2(g)$
D	$Ni(s) + 2HCl(aq)$ → $NiCl_2(aq) + H_2(g)$
E	$2Ba(s) + O_2(g)$ → $2BaO(s)$
F	$CuCO_3(s)$ → $CuO(s) + CO_2(g)$

Which box (or boxes) shows an equation which describes extraction of a metal? **PS**

4 Consider the following statements about the reactions between selected metals and air:

Nickel is relatively inert to corrosion at ordinary temperature. It burns, producing its oxide (NiO), when it is roasted in air.

Cobalt is not affected by air at room temperature. However, when the temperature is raised, it forms a surface layer of oxide.

Strong heating of manganese brings about the following reaction, which does **not** occur under normal conditions:

$$3Mn(s) + 2O_2(g) \rightarrow Mn_3O_4(s)$$

Chromium burns well only at temperatures above 1727°C. Below this temperature, it is unreactive.

Use the information given to write out **two** general statements which could be applied to **all** of the four metals. **PS**

5 Corrosion of metals is a major problem. It can be prevented by putting a barrier between the metal and the atmosphere. The grid shows some ways of preventing corrosion.

Anodising	Silver plating
Galvanising	Tinplating

(a) Which method is suitable **only** for the protection of aluminium?

(b) Which method will involve sacrificial protection if the barrier is broken? **KU**

6 Our modern world depends on metals. Some metals such as gold are found uncombined. Others such as aluminium have to be extracted from their ores.

(a) Explain why gold is found uncombined.

(b) Some metals are extracted from their ores by heating with carbon. Name such a metal.

(c) The extraction of some metals involves passing electricity through the molten ore. Name this process. **KU**

7 Uranium metal is obtained from ores containing uranium(IV) oxide and uranium(VI) oxide. The extraction of the metal involves three steps:

1 The oxide is converted to uranium(VI) fluoride.
2 The uranium(VI) fluoride is reduced by hydrogen.

$$UF_6(g) + H_2(g) \xrightarrow{100°C} UF_4(s) + 2HF(g)$$

3 The uranium(IV) fluoride is reduced by magnesium metal.

$$UF_4(g) + 2Mg(s) \xrightarrow{1600°C} U(l) + 2MgF_2(l)$$

(a) Write the formula for uranium(IV) oxide. **KU**

(b) Using the information shown above,
   (i) State **two** facts that can be concluded about the melting point of uranium(IV) fluoride;
   (ii) State whether uranium is a more or less active metal than magnesium. **PS**

168 METALS AND CORROSION

8 Common salt is used to melt ice and snow on the roads. It also speeds up the corrosion of steel in car bodies.

When the salt **dissolves** in water its **ions** make the water a better conductor of electricity. This causes more ions to be formed from the metal.

The compounds in the grid could also melt ice and snow.

A	B	C
sucrose $C_{12}H_{22}O_{11}$	ammonium nitrate NH_4NO_3	ethanol C_2H_5OH
D	E	F
copper(II) sulphate $CuSO_4$	slaked lime $Ca(OH)_2$	barium sulphate $BaSO_4$

Which box (or boxes) shows a compound that would also speed up the corrosion of the steel in car bodies? **PS**

9 Magnesium metal is extracted from sea water as outlined below.

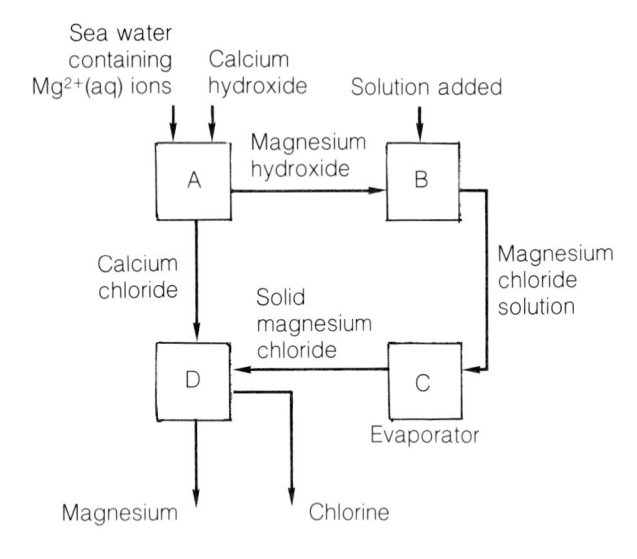

The reaction occurring in A is:

$$Mg^{2+}(aq) + 2Cl^-(aq) + Ca^{2+}(aq) + 2OH^-(aq)$$
$$\downarrow$$
$$Mg^{2+}(OH^-)_2(s) + Ca^{2+}(aq) + 2Cl^-(aq)$$

(a) What method could be used to separate magnesium hydroxide from the calcium chloride in A? **PS**
(b) Name a solution that would react with the magnesium hydroxide to form magnesium chloride solution in B. **KU**
(c) Describe a method that could be used to obtain magnesium metal from solid magnesium chloride in D. **KU**

10 We can work out the formulae for simple compounds through our knowledge of electron arrangements. The formulae for many compounds, however, were known long before electrons were discovered. They were found by experiment.

A pupil decided he would try to work out the formula for magnesium oxide by an experimental method.

He made magnesium oxide by burning magnesium and measured the change in mass. This allowed him to work out the masses of magnesium and oxygen in the sample of the compound. He used the following apparatus:

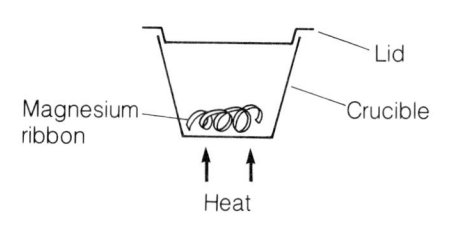

The grid below shows **all** the steps used in the experiment.

A	Weigh the crucible, lid and magnesium ribbon.
B	Clean the magnesium ribbon with emery paper.
C	Stop heating and allow crucible and contents to cool.
D	Weigh the crucible, lid and magnesium oxide.
E	Weigh the empty crucible and lid.
F	Heat the magnesium ribbon in the crucible.

Write down the letters for **all** the steps **in the correct order**. **PS**

11 Iron and aluminium are two metals which are widely used in our modern world. In blast furnaces, iron is extracted from haematite (iron(III) oxide) by a reduction process:
(a) Balance the following equation for this reaction:

$$Fe_2O_3 + CO \rightarrow Fe + CO_2$$

(b) Aluminium cannot be extracted from its oxide using carbon monoxide.
  (i) Explain why carbon monoxide can reduce iron(III) oxide but not aluminium oxide.
  (ii) Outline briefly how aluminium is extracted from aluminium oxide. **KU**

12 Over 60 different metals occur in the earth and we have found uses for almost all of them. Gold has been known since the earliest civilisation. It is too soft to make into tools but is used to make jewellery and coins. Copper was discovered around 4000 BC. It is one of the best conductors of electricity, which makes it useful for electrical wiring. Its lack of reactivity makes it a good choice for making hot or cold water pipes. About 1000 BC, iron was first extracted from its ores. Its hardness makes it very useful, and when converted to steel it is the raw material for cars, ships, railway lines and machinery. The first of the modern metals to be discovered was aluminium, in 1825. This light metal does not corrode to a large extent. Aircraft, window frames, milk bottle tops and wrapping foil are all made from aluminium.

(a) Present the above information in a table with four headings. **PS**
(b) Explain why aluminium was not discovered until 1825. **PS**
(c) Outline the method of industrial extraction of aluminium from its ore. **KU**

1 Our Hungry World

Key Ideas

The *world's population* is increasing fast. As a result the demand for food is increasing too. *Plants* are the source of all food. They require *nutrients* to make them grow properly. Plants take many nutrients from the *soil*. Nutrients can be replaced by *natural* and *synthetic fertilisers*. Some plants can *fix* nitrogen from the air.

Feeding People

Few of us can have failed to have seen on TV, or read in the newspapers, about people starving in Africa. Food is so short in some areas that people are starving to death. It is not just a problem in Africa. India and parts of Asia have similar problems. All this is made worse by the human population increasing so rapidly. By the year 2000 it is estimated that the world's population may be twice as high as it was in 1970!

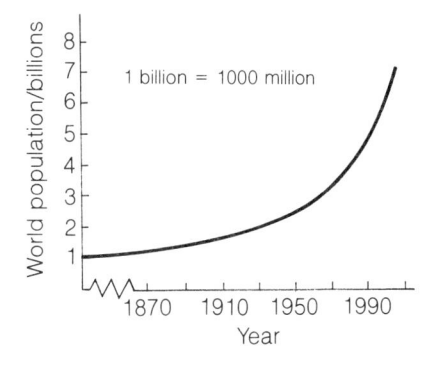

The increasing world population

Although the global birth rate is falling, people are living longer than they used to, partly due to better medical treatment – and more people need more food. Compare the situation in the Third World to that in Europe and North America. In Europe and America food is plentiful, and the population is not increasing very much. It is not difficult to see people who are overweight. Surveys of people's eating habits (and their weight) in the USA, suggest that about 40 per cent of the population is overweight!

To feed the world (both the overfed West and the underfed Third World) more and more **plants** need to be grown. Plants are the source of **all** our food. We often think of plants as only flowers, trees and grass, but **vegetables, fruits** and **cereals** (like corn, wheat and rice) are also plants. A typical daily menu is shown in table 6.1 on page 170.

Millions of people in the world are starving

Many people in the Western World are overweight

Fertilisers

170 FERTILISERS

Table 6.1

Meal	Food	Food Source
Breakfast	orange juice	orange tree
	corn flakes	corn
	milk	cow
	sugar	sugar cane
	bread	wheat (flour)
	butter	cow
Lunch	bread	wheat (flour)
	cheese	cow
	apple	apple tree
Evening Meal	potatoes	plant
	lamb	sheep
	peas	plant
	rice	
	pudding	rice

From table 6.1 it is easy to pick out the plants which we eat, but we also eat animals. Think about what the animals eat. Cows and sheep eat grass, and grass is a plant. The importance of plants to animals is shown in the **food chain**.

Feeding Our Animals

Cereals are the main "energy foods" for both rich and poor countries.

Table 6.2 (in kg per person)

	1965–66	1973–74
USA	730	840
USSR	500	650
EEC	410	450
Japan	240	280
Third World	170	180

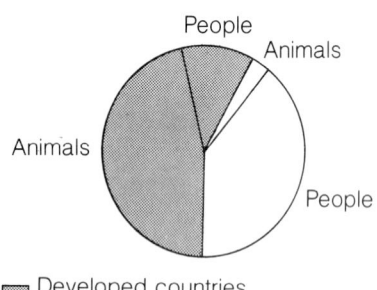

How the world cereal crop is used as food

A typical food chain

Table 6.2 shows how much the developed world eats compared to the Third World countries.

Much of the cereal crop in rich countries is used to feed animals, as shown in the pie chart. The animals are then eaten by us. However, animals are very poor at converting the cereals into meat. It has been estimated that 90 per cent of the food cattle eat is not turned into meat. If we all ate less meat, more cereals would be available to provide energy and protein directly to humans.

Feeding Pets

Feeding pets uses up valuable food. In the past, most of Peru's anchovies (a type of fish) ended up as pet food in North America. Today, because of overfishing in the waters around Peru, the catching of anchovies has been drastically cut. In Britain alone, it has been estimated that cats and dogs eat enough protein to satisfy over half a million people!

No matter where food is grown, or who (or what) eats it, the amount required is increasing all the time. This means that farming methods must be constantly improved to produce food more efficiently.

What Makes Plants Grow?

All food comes from plants. Before plants can be harvested, and the food they produce used, they themselves need **food** and **water** to grow. The materials that all plants need to grow are called **nutrients**. Plants get nutrients from the soil. There are **three** important **elements** that must

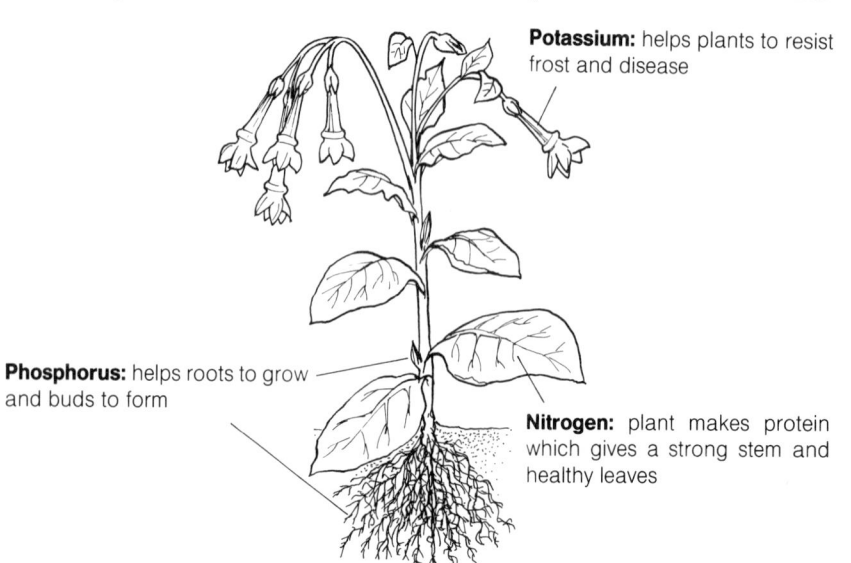

Potassium: helps plants to resist frost and disease

Phosphorus: helps roots to grow and buds to form

Nitrogen: plant makes protein which gives a strong stem and healthy leaves

FERTILISERS

be present in the nutrients – **nitrogen**, **potassium** and **phosphorus**. These elements exist in the soil as **compounds**, such as soluble nitrates and phosphates. They dissolve in water and are taken into the plant through the roots.

Table 6.3 shows the main elements required by plants.

Table 6.3

Major Elements	Trace Elements
Carbon	Iron
Hydrogen	Manganese
Oxygen	Copper
Nitrogen	Zinc
Phosphorus	Molybdenum
Sulphur	Boron
Potassium	Chlorine
Calcium	
Magnesium	

Carbon comes from carbon dioxide in the air (see Carbohydrates). Hydrogen and oxygen come from water. All the other elements are in the soil. The quantity of each element present depends on the type of soil. Nitrogen, phosphorus and potassium are all quickly removed from the soil by plants no matter how much is present. They may also be easily washed out of the soil by rainwater.

Plants need **trace** elements too. Trace elements are present in very small amounts and are important to both plants and animals. They are listed in table 6.3.

Replacing Nitrogen

Nitrogen, phosphorus and potassium are quickly removed from soil by plants, so they need to be replaced. For nitrogen, this happens **naturally**.

Leguminous Plants

A **legume** is a plant, like clover, beans or peas, which can use nitrogen in the air to make **nitrates**. Taking nitrogen from the air and changing its form, so that plants can absorb it, is known as **fixing** nitrogen. The plants absorb the soluble nitrates and use the nitrogen in them to make protein. Legumes can fix nitrogen because they have small **nodules** on their roots which contain **nitrifying bacteria**. These are living microbes which fix the nitrogen from the air. Plant scientists are trying to grow the nodules on plants which do not normally have them. Why do you think they are doing this?

Bacteria containing nodules on the roots of a legume

Compost

Once plants die, they eventually rot and **ammonium** salts containing nitrogen are released. Bacteria in the soil converts these into nitrates again. The nitrates are soluble and readily absorbed through plant roots.

Animals and Manure

Animal **waste** is also rich in ammonium salts. When animals **die** they too release ammonium salts into the soil. These are then converted to nitrates. The decomposition of plants and animals is part of the "nitrogen cycle".

Fertilisers

Substances which replace the essential elements in the soil are called **fertilisers**. Natural fertilisers, like compost and manure, were once able to replace all the nutrients taken from the soil by crop plants.

Farmers used to **rotate** crops, so that the crop grown on a particular field was changed every year. The farmer might grow wheat on a field one year, followed the next year by a legume which could fix nitrogen and increase the fertility of the soil. Sometimes a field was left **fallow**. This meant not planting a crop at all, and letting grass, clover and weeds grow. These plants were then ploughed into the ground where they would rot and fertilise the soil.

You may use natural fertilisers like compost in your garden. Some people like to eat vegetables and cereals produced **organically**, meaning that only natural fertilisers have been used.

Compost (seen in the wheelbarrow) is a natural fertiliser

172 FERTILISERS

However, modern farming also uses **synthetic** (manufactured) fertilisers. These are used for several reasons: the demand for food is now so great that few fields can be left without a crop; there is not enough compost or animal manure to spread on the fields; some parts of the world have no source of natural fertiliser. Synthetic fertilisers replace elements which have been removed from the soil by plants, and also supply essential elements that may already be missing. You can find out about synthetic fertilisers in the next section.

Organically grown foods are becoming more popular

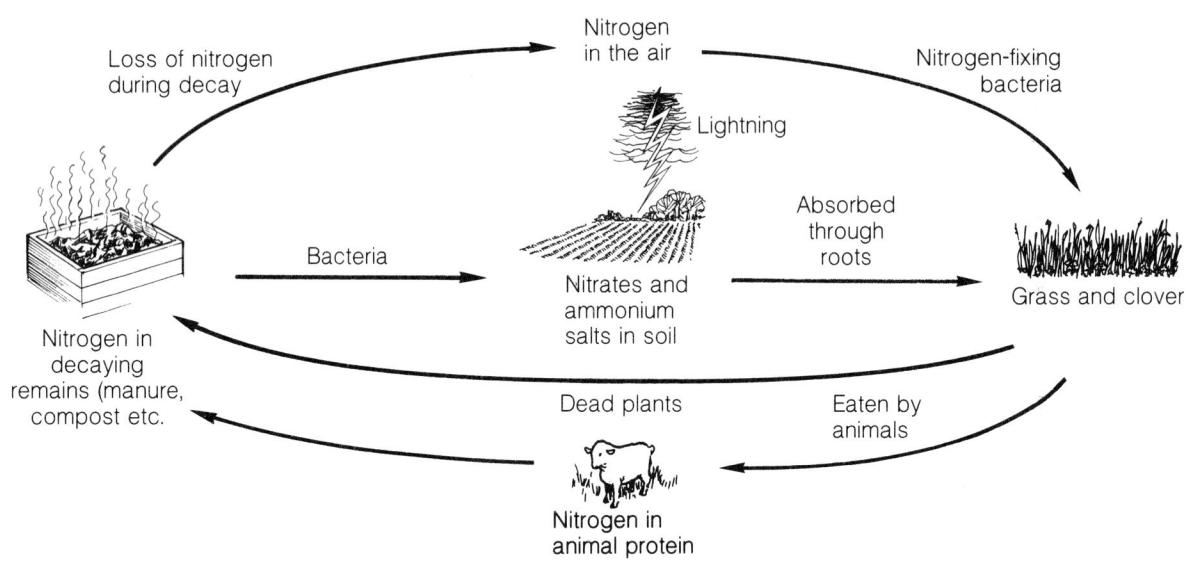

The nitrogen cycle without human interference

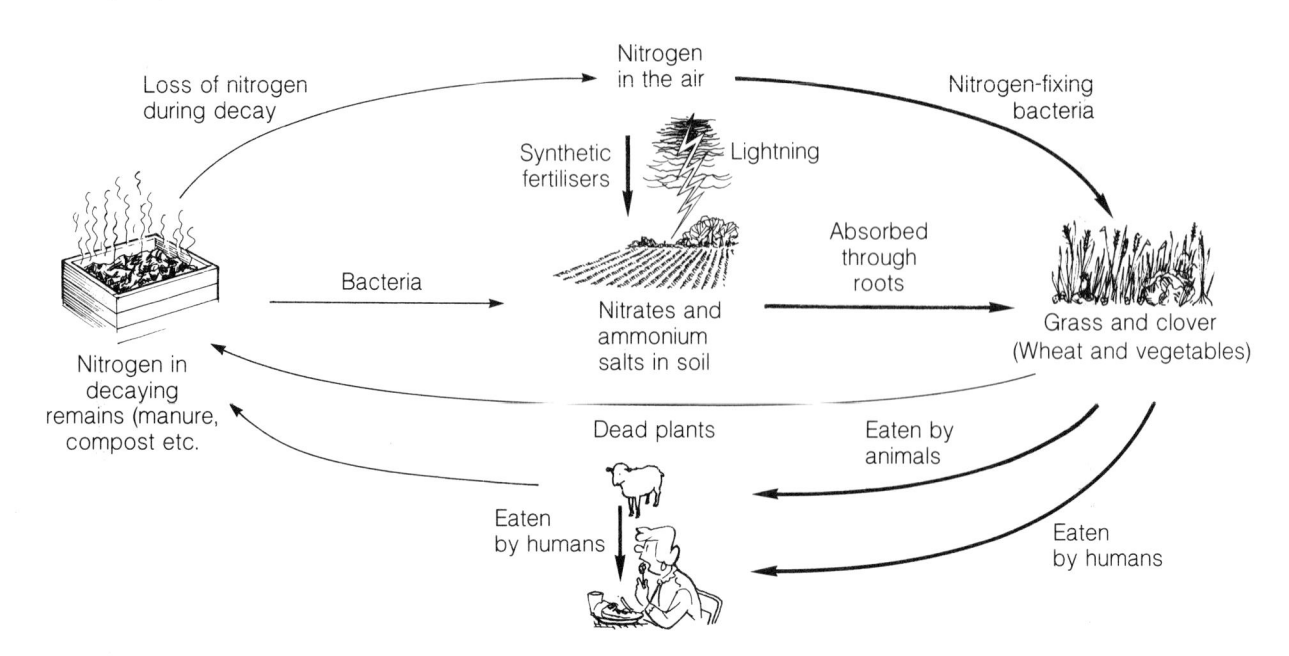

The nitrogen cycle showing how humans have effected it

FERTILISERS

Activities

1. Look at the graph of world population estimates on page 169.
   (a) Write down the approximate world population in 1890 and 1990.
   (b) From the graph, predict the likely world population in 2010.
   (c) What sort of problems will an increase in world population be likely to cause?

2. All food chains start with plants. Make up a food chain with at least two animals in it.

3. (a) What are the essential elements that plants need to ensure healthy growth?
   (b) Explain how plants like beans and peas are able to "fix" nitrogen.
   (c) How do plants which cannot fix their own nitrogen, obtain an adequate supply?

4. The following table shows the trace elements we require in our diet. Use the information in the table to construct a bar chart showing our daily needs (in mg) of these elements. Label the bar graph with the symbols of the elements.

Element	Recommended Daily Intake (RDI, in mg)
Zinc	9.4
Manganese	5.1
Fluorine	1.8
Copper	1.5
Iodine	0.3
Selenium	0.1

5. Look at the diagrams showing the nitrogen cycle on the page opposite.
   (a) Describe the natural (first) cycle diagram in words.
   (b) Describe humanity's effect on this nitrogen cycle.

2 Synthetic Fertilisers

What's New?

The fact that plant growth needs nitrogen, phosphorus and potassium is not new. In 1842, John Lawes set up a long-running experiment to study the growth of winter wheat. It was soon shown that the wheat produced more grain when it was fed with nitrogen fertiliser. By the end of the nineteenth century, nitrogen compounds like "chile saltpetre" (sodium nitrate, $NaNO_3$) and ammonium sulphate (($NH_4)_2SO_4$) were being used as **nitrogen fertilisers** in Britain. Phosphorus containing compounds called "superphosphates" were also being used. These were mixtures of **water soluble** phosphate compounds. By the 1930s superphosphates were replaced by "triple superphosphates" which had a much higher phosphorus content.

In Germany, during the 1860s, potassium chloride (KCl) was being extracted from huge underground deposits. A method known as the Cyanamide process was used to produce **ammonia (NH_3)**. This could either be used on its own as a nitrogen fertiliser or reacted with acids to form a variety of **soluble** compounds (e.g., ammonium sulphate). The Cyanamide process was both complicated and expensive. By 1906, Fritz Haber had developed a method for combining **nitrogen** with **hydrogen** to produce ammonia, using a catalyst. The **Haber process** is still used today, and produces millions of tonnes of ammonia every year (see page 183).

Fertilisers Today

The manufacture of synthetic fertilisers is now a massive industry throughout the world. At the beginning of the century only one million tonnes of fertiliser per year were used worldwide. Today this figure is over 100 million tonnes. North America, Europe and the USSR use approximately 70 per cent of this total. Table 6.4 shows fertiliser production in the UK over the past 100 years or so.

Compare the figures for 1874 and 1980. They show that the production of nitrogen containing fertilisers has risen most dramatically. Nitrogen is required by plants in large amounts. Also, many nitrogen compounds are easily washed out of the soil and lost to the atmosphere (see page 178). Nitrogen fertilisers must therefore be applied to fields regularly.

The figures also show that the production of phosphorous fertilisers has fallen since 1950. However, this does not mean that phosphorus is no longer important. Unlike many nitrogen compounds, phosphorus compounds are not so easily washed out of the soil. Once the soil has enough phosphorus to make it fertile, less fertiliser needs to be added.

What Makes a Good Fertiliser?

Compounds used as fertilisers must contain at least one of the **essential elements**, nitrogen, phosphorus and potassium. They must also be **soluble** in water, so that they can be absorbed through the roots of the plants. Table 6.5 shows compounds which would make good fertilisers.

Check with a data book and you will find that all of these, except **urea**, are very soluble in water. Although

> ## Key Ideas
>
> **Synthetic fertilisers** are chemicals made by industrial chemists. They contain the **essential elements** nitrogen, phosphorus and potassium. These chemicals must be **soluble** so that they are easily dissolved and absorbed by plant roots. This high solubility can cause **problems**. Different crops need different amounts of essential elements. **Compound fertilisers** contain a mixture of synthetic fertilisers. The **percentage mass** of a particular element in a compound can be calculated from its formula.

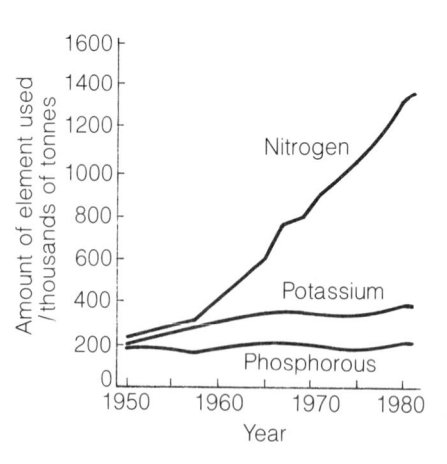

The graph shows the amount of each fertiliser *used* in the UK

Table 6.4

Year	Fertiliser		
	Nitrogen	Phosphorus	Potassium
1874	35 000	40 000	2 500
1939	61 000	76 000	63 000
1950	229 000	204 000	198 000
1980	1 268 000	192 000	320 000

(Figures give tonnes of each **element** contained in fertiliser.)

FERTILISERS

Table 6.5

Compound	Formula
Ammonium nitrate	NH_4NO_3
Calcium nitrate	$Ca(NO_3)_2$
Sodium nitrate	$NaNO_3$
Ammonium sulphate	$(NH_4)_2SO_4$
Potassium sulphate	K_2SO_4
Potassium chloride	KCl
Ammonium phosphate	$(NH_4)_3PO_4$
Ammonia solution	$NH_3(aq)$
Urea	$CO(NH_2)_2$

urea is not very soluble, it does contain a lot of nitrogen. It is useful in areas where there is a lot of heavy rainfall. In India and South East Asia, the monsoon rains wash soluble fertilisers away, but urea stays in the soil.

Fertilisers need to be easy to spread. Large lumps are difficult to spread evenly, and do not dissolve very well either. Small pellets or concentrated solutions are much better. Ammonia solution, for example, is sprayed onto fields. Sometimes it is pumped into the ground to cut down evaporation of ammonia gas. Solid fertilisers such as ammonium nitrate are made so that they do not "cake" into lumps.

▪ Nitrates

Ammonium nitrate (NH_4NO_3) has all the properties of a good fertiliser. It is very soluble and contains a lot of nitrogen. It is made by reacting **ammonia gas** (NH_3) and **nitric acid** (HNO_3):

$NH_3(g) + HNO_3(aq) \rightarrow NH_4NO_3(aq)$

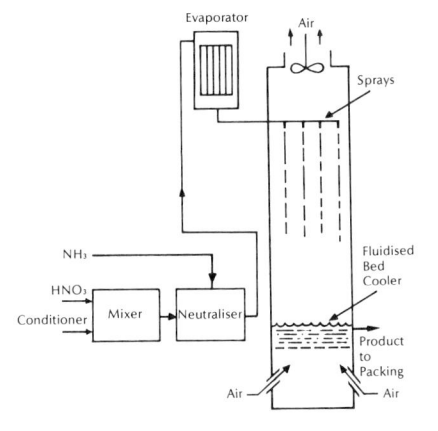

Manufacture of ammonium nitrate prills

You can find out more about these two important chemicals in sections 3 and 4.

Solid ammonium nitrate will cake to form lumps. To avoid caking, a conditioner is added to a hot, concentrated solution of ammonium nitrate. The mixture is sprayed from the top of a large tower. As the droplets fall, the water evaporates and leaves small, smooth, round grains of solid, called "prills". These are easy to handle, and the conditioner prevents the prills from caking. Ammonium nitrate made by ICI has the trade name "**Nitram**".

▪ Phosphates

Natural phosphates found in rocks are usually very insoluble. To make a soluble phosphate, **phosphoric acid** must be made first. The acid is then **neutralised**, with say **ammonia**, to make soluble **ammonium phosphate**.

▪ Potassium Compounds

Potassium chloride (KCl) is the most widely used source of potassium. It exists underground in certain parts of the country. At Boulby in the north-east of England, potassium chloride is found in the rock "sylvinite", over 1000 metres below the ground. Sylvinite contains sodium chloride and clay impurities, which have to be removed.

▪ Ammonium Compounds

Ammonium nitrate and ammonium phosphate are not only used because of the nitrate and phosphate content. The ammonium ion (NH_4^+) itself is a source of nitrogen. It is converted into the nitrate ion (NO_3^-) by bacteria in the soil. Nitrates are easily absorbed by plants.

▪ NPK Compound Fertilisers

Nitrogen fertilisers such as ammonium nitrate are often spread alone on fields to replace lost nitrogen. Phosphate and potassium compounds are seldom spread on their own. Instead, a mixture of compounds containing all three essential elements (nitrogen, phosphorus and potassium) are used. Such a mixture is called a **compound** fertiliser. They are also called **NPK** fertilisers. Can you think why? (The periodic table may help!)

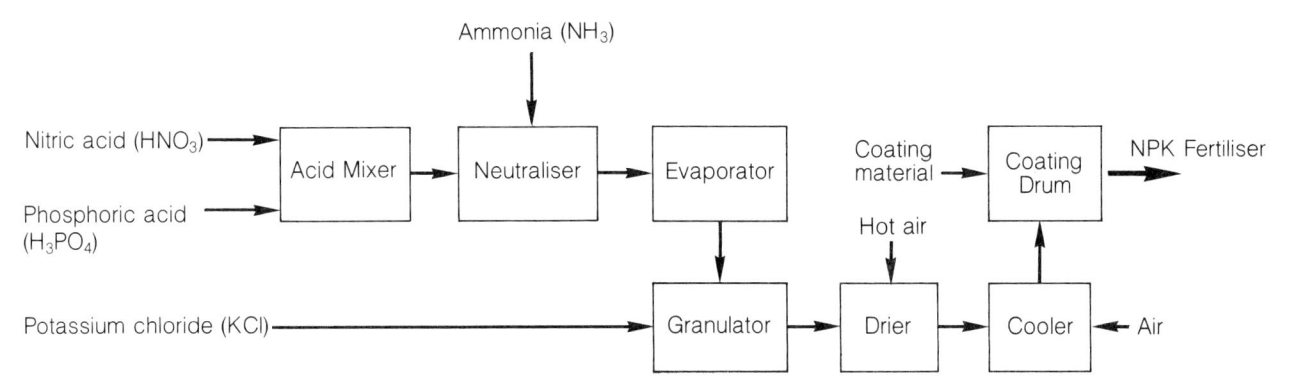

Simplified flow diagram showing NPK production

176 FERTILISERS

The Importance of Ions

Compounds used in the most common fertilisers in Britain, are all ionic:

e.g.,
ammonium nitrate $NH_4^+NO_3^-$
ammonium phosphate $(NH_4^+)_3PO_4^{3-}$
potassium chloride K^+Cl^-

This is important for several reasons. Generally, ionic compounds are **soluble** in water. However, ions do get washed out of the soil by rainwater, some more easily than others. This is partly due to the nature of the soil.

Most soils contain **humus** (mainly rotting vegetation) and **clay** particles, which are very large and have **negative** charge. **Positive ions** are attracted to these particles, stick to the surface, and so are not easily washed away. Potassium ions (K^+) are held particularly well, as are ammonium ions (NH_4^+).

Bacteria in the soil converts the ammonium ions into nitrate ions (NO_3^-), which is the form of nitrogen most easily taken up by plants.

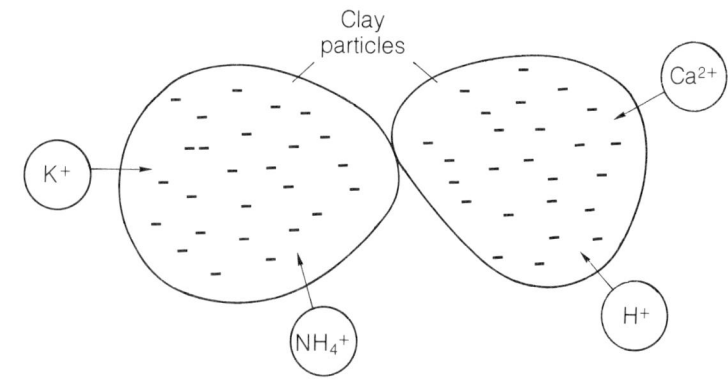

Positive ions are attracted to the surface of the negative clay particles

However, nitrate is a negative ion and it is not held by the negative clay and humus particles (like charges repel). It is therefore easily washed out of the soil in a process called **leaching**. Nitrate ions may also be broken down into nitrogen by **denitrifying** bacteria in the soil.

Testing for Ions

Compound fertilisers are made up of a mixture of ions: potassium (K^+), ammonium (NH_4^+), nitrate (NO_3^-) and phosphate (PO_4^{3-}). Each of these ions can be tested for.

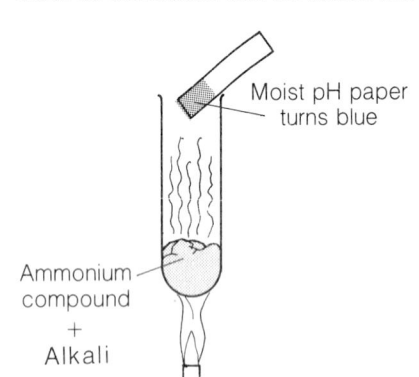

Ammonium compounds give off *ammonia* gas when heated with alkali. Ammonia gas turns pH paper *blue*. This can be used as a test for *ammonium ions* (NH_4^+)

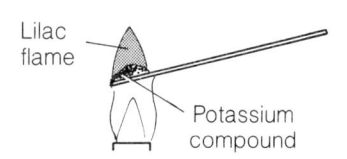

Potassium compounds burn with a *lilac* flame. This can be used as a test for *potassium ions* (K^+)

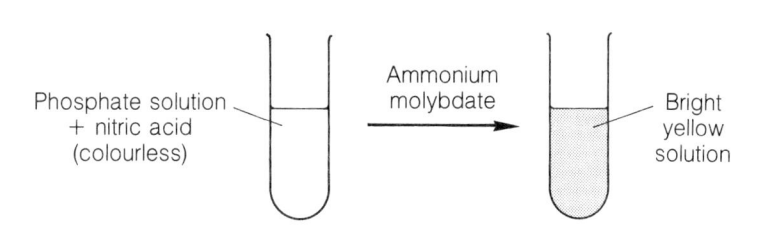

- The formation of the bright *yellow* solution shows that *phosphate ions* are present. This can be used as a test for *phosphate* ions (PO_4^{3-})

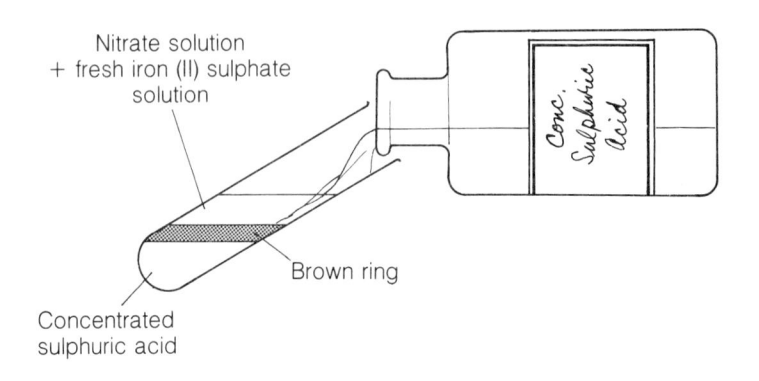

- The *brown ring* forms where the acid and the two solutions meet. This can be used as a test for the *nitrate ion* (NO_3^-)

Which Fertiliser?

Not all crops require the same amount of nitrogen, phosphorus and potassium. Table 6.6 shows the estimated amounts of these elements removed from the soil by certain crops.

Grass, which farmers grow for animal feed, needs a lot of **nitrogen**. The farmer may use only a nitrogen fertiliser like ammonium nitrate (NH_4NO_3) for grass. **Wheat** requires all three essential elements and so an **NPK** compound fertiliser is used. NPK fertilisers are usually a **mixture** of ammonium nitrate, ammonium phosphate and potassium chloride. The proportions of each compound in the mixture varies. When deciding which NPK fertiliser to use, the farmer has to think about which crop he is going to grow. Adding the wrong mixture will reduce the crop yield and be very wasteful.

In India, the use of an NPK fertiliser high in nitrogen and phosphorus has lead to a 50 per cent increase in rice yields. In southern England, NPK fertilisers high in potassium have led to a 400 per cent increase in barley yields.

Table 6.6

Crop	Mass of element removed (in kilogrammes per hectare, kg/ha)		
	N	P	K
Wheat	115	22	26
Barley	72	14	13
Oats	72	13	18
Potatoes	109	14	133
Beetroot	86	14	302

(One hectare is about the size of two large football pitches. All measurements are taken from planting to harvesting.)

Different NPK mixtures

How Much Nitrogen?

Many soluble compounds containing essential elements could in theory be used as fertilisers. So which one do you choose? If you require a nitrogen fertiliser, the **percentage by mass** of nitrogen for each compound can be calculated and the values compared. We can calculate the percentage by mass of nitrogen in ammonium nitrate and ammonium sulphate, using the following equation:

Percentage mass of element =
$$\frac{\text{total mass of element in compound}}{\text{relative formula mass of compound}} \times 100$$

Calculating M_r:

Element	A_r	No. of atoms in formula	Mass
N	14	2	28
H	1	4	4
O	16	3	48
		Total (M_r) =	**80**

Percentage nitrogen = $\frac{28}{80} \times 100$

= **35%**

For ammonium nitrate (NH_4NO_3):

Percentage nitrogen =
$$\frac{\text{mass of nitrogen in compound}}{M_r} \times 100$$

178 FERTILISERS

For ammonium sulphate ((NH$_4$)$_2$SO$_4$):

Percentage nitrogen = $\dfrac{\text{mass of nitrogen in compound}}{M_r} \times 100$

Calculating M_r:

Element	A_r	No. of atoms in formula	Mass
N	14	2	28
H	1	8	8
S	32	1	32
O	16	4	64
		Total (M_r) =	**132**

Percentage nitrogen = $\dfrac{28}{132} \times 100$
= **21%**

We can see that ammonium nitrate contains more nitrogen. This type of calculation can be done for any element in any compound. Table 6.7 compares the percentage by mass of nitrogen, phosphorus and potassium in some fertilisers and manures.

Table 6.7

		Percentage by Mass		
		N	P	K
Fertiliser	Ammonium nitrate	35.0	0.0	0.0
	Ammonium phosphate	28.0	21.0	0.0
	Potassium Chloride	0.0	0.0	52.0
Manure	Farmyard	0.6	0.1	0.6
	Digested sewage	1.4	0.4	0.1
	Bone meal	3.6	10.3	0.0

Counting the Cost

The industrial manufacture of fertilisers uses up a lot of energy. It has been argued that valuable fuel is wasted because it takes more energy to produce the fertiliser than is gained from an increase in food crop. It has been estimated, however, that almost **six times** as much extra energy can be produced. The increase in crop yield is immense.

In 1976, workers at the Massachusetts Institute of Technology showed that over a 15 year period, fertilisers accounted for 40 per cent of the increase in world crop production. In India, between 1951 and 1973, it was estimated that fertiliser use increased yields by as much as 80 per cent. Fertilisers do cost money though, and this cost is passed on to the farmer. In Britain in 1988, an NPK fertiliser cost around **70 pounds per tonne**. About 7 million tonnes of fertiliser are used in Britain every year, so farmers must spend a lot of money on it.

Using bacteria to fix nitrogen is a much cheaper way of fertilising the soil. If more plants could fix nitrogen, there would be less need for chemical fertilisers and a great saving in energy. Scientists at Sussex University have had some success in making a **catalyst** which helps to fix nitrogen from the air. Imagine being able to spread a catalyst in a field only once, and then watching it produce nitrogen for plants for ever!

New microbes may possibly be designed to fix nitrogen in all types of plants. There has been some success in using bacteria to make protein, but it is only fit for animal feed. Bacteria could well be a cheap source of food.

Waste and pollution

Nitrates

Nitrogen fertilisers are widely used by British farmers. In 1988, 1.6 million tonnes of nitrogen fertiliser were spread at a cost of around 600 million pounds. It has been calculated that only 70–80 per cent of this is taken up by crops. The rest is either lost to the atmosphere or drains off the fields into our water supply (leaching).

Some scientists and doctors are concerned about the high levels of nitrate ions (NO$_3^-$) in our drinking water. They think this could be bad for our health, possibly causing stomach cancer and "blue baby syndrome", which is a very rare disease in babies, last recorded in Britain in 1972. At the moment there is only some evidence to support each of these claims. However, the EEC have now set a safety limit of 50 milligrams of nitrate per litre of drinking water (50 mg l^{-1}).

Pollution of water by nitrates is not thought to be a problem in Scotland, because of different agricultural methods. However, heavily farmed areas like south Staffordshire and East Anglia do have this problem. In 1989 it was estimated that around 800 thousand people in these areas were drinking water with a nitrate level higher than the EEC safety limit.

Pie chart showing what happens to nitrogen fertilisers after they are added to soil

FERTILISERS

What is Being Done About It?

Water authorities often mix water of a high nitrate content with water of a low nitrate content. However, nitrate pollution is getting so bad that new (and expensive) chemical and biological ways of removing nitrate ions are being tried. Farmers working in the **"nitrate zones"** of East Anglia are being told to use less nitrate fertiliser.

Nitrates in the Nineties

Nitrate levels in Britain's water are going to have to be reduced during the 1990's. Many doctors and scientists are concerned that our health is being affected by high levels of nitrate in our water.

Such is the concern in Europe, that the EEC have made a safety limit of 50 mg of nitrate per litre of water. Excessive use of nitrate fertilisers is being blamed for the high nitrate levels in the south east of England. However, the Fertiliser Manufacturers Association (FMA) claim that most people consume more nitrate in their food, particularly if they eat a lot of vegetables, than they do when they drink water. The Association also argues that there is little or no evidence to support the idea that excess nitrate causes cancer.

Phosphates

Unlike nitrogen, little or no phosphorus is ever returned to the soil naturally.

About 17 million tonnes of phosphorus is carried out to sea by our rivers every year.

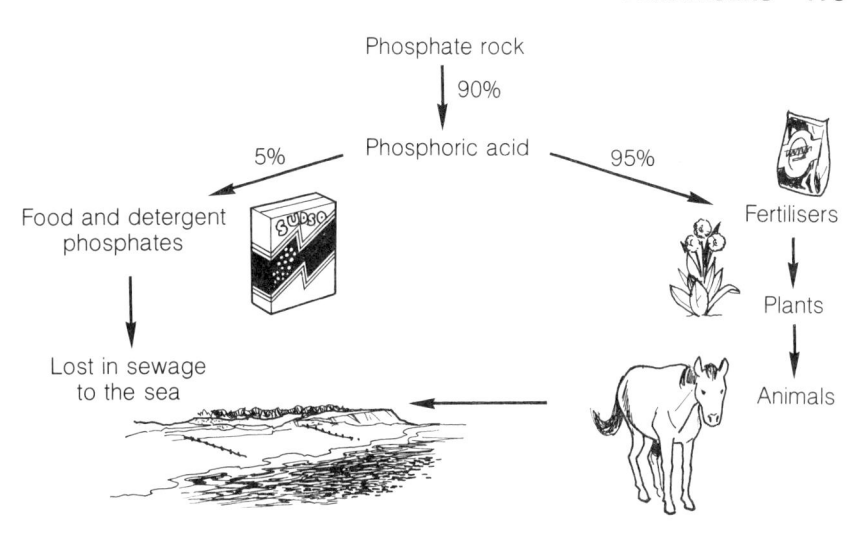

Very little phosphorus is returned to the soil

Very little of this waste is due to the leaching of phosphate fertilisers. Most comes from the manufacture of detergents. However, the loss is still enormous. Large deposits of phosphate rock still remain in the world, but few are in Europe. It therefore costs a lot of money to make soluble phosphates. It would be very worth while to gather, process and recycle some of the "lost" phosphorus.

Some countries, like Holland, already remove phosphates from sewage because they are also **pollutants**. Phosphates are thought to help the formation of **algae** in water. Algae are plant cells and grow very quickly. The green "slime" on stagnant water is algae, as are some seaweeds.

Algae growth eventually stops sunlight reaching the plants deeper in the water which need the light to produce oxygen. There is then less dissolved oxygen in the water and fish are unable to breathe.

Many algae are rich in protein, minerals and vitamins. In some hot countries like Israel, algae is grown in artificial ponds and used as a food. Table 6.8 compares the amount of protein in the algae "spirulina" with cattle and wheat.

Table 6.8

Type of Food	Amount of Protein (kg/ha)
Beef cattle	100
Wheat	4 000
Spirulina	50 000

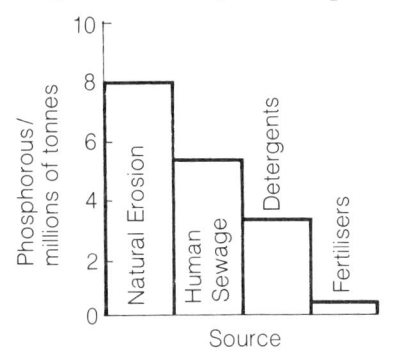

Source of phosphorus carried to the sea by our rivers every year

Recycling Human Waste

Industrial waste and waste products from our bodies (urine and faeces) are carried away by water to form a liquid called **sewage**. Sewage must be treated before it is discharged into a river or the sea, otherwise it will cause **pollution**.

At a sewage works, naturally occurring bacteria break down the pollutants in the sewage. Gases like carbon dioxide and methane are formed. The water is purified and solids (**sludge**) are left.

The methane can be used as fuel, and the purified water may be discharged into the sea or a river. The sludge can be used as a **natural fertiliser** or soil conditioner.

One of the main problems with using sludge is that it is often contaminated by "heavy" metals. They include the metals lead and mercury, which come from industry. Heavy metals are toxic to animals and must be removed.

180 FERTILISERS

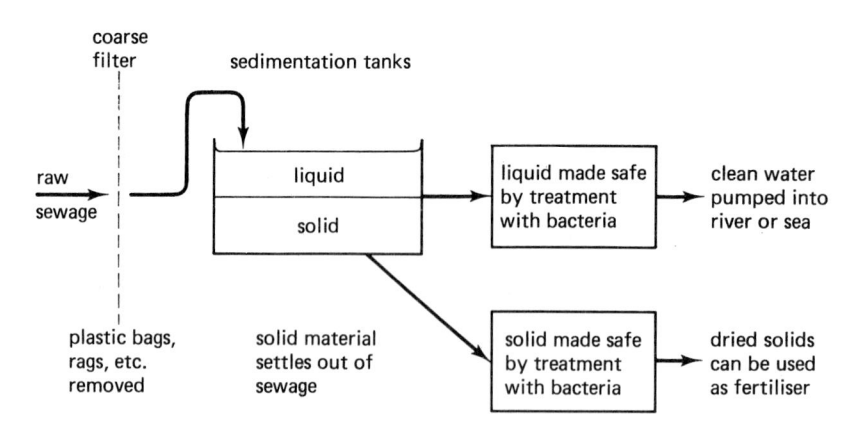

Sewage is purified in a sewage treatment plant

```
raw sewage → [coarse filter: plastic bags, rags, etc. removed] → [sedimentation tanks: liquid / solid; solid material settles out of sewage]
   liquid → [liquid made safe by treatment with bacteria] → clean water pumped into river or sea
   solid → [solid made safe by treatment with bacteria] → dried solids can be used as fertiliser
```

Britain dumps millions of tonnes of sewage sludge in the North Sea every year. In March 1990 the Government announced that this would have to stop by the end of 1998. The environmentalist group Greenpeace say that this is too late. They claim that the UK will dump another 50 million tonnes of contaminated sludge into the sea by that date.

In 1990, the estimated cost of using alternative methods to dispose of our sewage was put at 3.5 billion pounds. Most of this will have to be paid by us. Mr Chris Patten, the Environment Secretary at the time, said "I think people will be prepared to pay a bit more for a much cleaner environment." What do you think?

Pesticides

We have seen how fertilisers improve crop yields. However, there is little point in growing a diseased crop or one contaminated by weeds. Insects can also damage large amounts of crop, and in a very short time. In Africa, a large swarm of locusts will eat over 3 thousand tonnes of crop in a day! Chemicals called **pesticides** are therefore used to control weeds, insects and fungi which would otherwise destroy millions of tonnes of plants every year. Table 6.9 summarises the action of various types of pesticide.

Insecticides are the most widely used pesticide. Over half of the pesticides used in the world are insecticides. Herbicides are of great importance too. The type of pesticide chosen depends on the climate and the crop. In tropical areas, insecticides are most needed, but in temperate areas like Britain, herbicides are more widely used.

It is essential that we know what kind of organism a pesticide will kill.

Spraying weed killer

We must also know what effects a pesticide has on the environment. Living things which do not harm crops might also be killed off unnecessarily. However, it is unlikely that the perfect pesticide will ever be made, because it is very difficult to find a chemical which will kill the pests but not harm crops, humans or other animals.

Some pesticides have had disastrous effects. During the Vietnam war in the late 1960s, a herbicide called **Agent Orange** was sprayed onto jungle areas by the USA to kill off all vegetation. This was done to expose possible hiding places of the Vietcong fighters. However, the herbicide contained small amounts of an impurity called **dioxin**. Dioxin has terrible effects on unborn babies, and Vietnamese women later gave birth to badly deformed children. US servicemen, who returned home after the war, started families only to find their babies were affected too.

Another example is **DDT**. This insecticide was used to wipe out insects carrying diseases like malaria

Table 6.9

Pesticide	Action
Insecticide	Kills insects which attack crops, animals and ourselves
Herbicide	Kills weeds
Fungicide	Controls fungus forming on both growing and stored crops
Nomaticide	Kills microscopic eel worms which attack the roots of crops
Molluscucide	Kills slugs and snails

and typhus. DDT also killed insects like locusts which could cause famine in some countries. The World Health Organisation (WHO) estimates that the use of DDT has saved over 5 million lives. However, DDT is banned in Europe and the USA. This might seem incredible when it does such a good job, but DDT also has a damaging effect on humans. It is a very stable compound, and will build up in the body. It is neither broken down nor excreted. The main concern is that levels of DDT could eventually be high enough in the body to kill.

Lindane is another insecticide which kills malaria mosquitoes. It is used today to fumigate aircraft travelling from tropical countries. Small amounts of lindane are sprayed in the passenger cabins to kill mosquitoes. In March 1989, 5 tonnes of lindane were washed overboard from the Indonesian ship *Perentis*, into the English Channel. French mine sweeping ships and a remote controlled submarine searched unsuccessfully for the containers of insecticide. Lindane is very toxic and also builds up in animals to fatal levels. Environmentalists fear that if the lindane leaks into the sea it will have a disastrous effect on marine life.

For or Against Fertilisers?

In this section you have read about the use of fertilisers. You have also read about some of the problems with using them. Look at the points listed below. Some of the arguments both for and against the use of fertilisers are summarised. They may help you make up your own mind about using fertilisers today.

For
- Increase crop yields dramatically
- Reduce cost of food
- Don't harm the soil
- Nitrates have not yet been proven harmful to animals
- Manufacturing fertilisers uses only about 1 per cent of all fossil fuels used in Britain

Against
- Natural fertilisers being wasted
- Some plants fertilised by chemicals have a higher nitrate content than those fertilised naturally
- Nitrates may damage your health
- Nitrates take years to get into our water supply (they will still be a problem in 20 years time, even if the spreading of fertilisers is reduced now)
- Expensive to make and use

Activities

1. Millions of tonnes of **synthetic** fertiliser are used in Britain every year.
   (a) What does the word "synthetic" mean?
   (b) Why are synthetic fertilisers used?
   (c) Table 6.4 on page 174 shows the amounts of fertilisers produced in Britain over the past 100 years.
      (i) Draw a **line** graph to show the amount of **nitrogen** fertiliser produced each year.
      (ii) Extend your graph and **predict** the amount which might be produced by the year 2000.

2. One property that a good fertiliser must have is high solubility in water.
   (a) Why is this so?
   (b) Urea and ammonium phosphate are two good fertilisers.
      (i) Describe an experiment to find out which is the most soluble.
      (ii) List the things you would do to make sure your comparison was a fair one.
      (iii) If you did the experiment you would find that urea was not very soluble. However, it is still widely used as a fertiliser in India. Explain why this is so.
   (c) Explain why the high solubility of nitrate fertilisers is causing problems in some parts of the country.
   (d) Write an equation for ammonia reacting with nitric acid to produce ammonium nitrate.

3. Potassium chloride and ammonium nitrate are both white solids. When ground up they look very similar. You are given a sample of each, but not told which is which. Describe the chemical tests you would do on **each**, to tell them apart.

4. Ammonium phosphate $((NH_4)_3PO_4)$ is a widely used fertiliser. Calculate the percentage by mass of phosphorus in the compound.

5. NPK fertilisers contain different proportions of nitrogen (N), phosphorus (P) and potassium (K). Some are high in nitrogen, others high in potassium. Explain, giving examples, why this variety is necessary.

6. Scientists are working hard to produce a bacteria that will fix nitrogen in all plants. Explain how this would benefit farmers.

7. The table shows the sources of nitrate in our diet.

Source	Amount (%)
Green Vegetables	45
Water	20
Milk	15
Potatoes	10
Cheese and Processed Meat	10

The information in the table can be presented in a number of different ways. Present this data in another way of your own choosing.

3 Making Ammonia

Key Ideas

Ammonia gas *(NH₃)* is one of the most important chemicals used in the manufacture of synthetic fertilisers. It is made industrially by reacting *nitrogen* with *hydrogen*. The process requires a *catalyst, high pressure* and a *reasonably high temperature*. Ammonia can also be prepared in the laboratory and its *properties* investigated. It is *very soluble,* forming an *alkaline* solution.

The Haber Process

The Haber process is the name given to the **industrial** production of **ammonia gas (NH₃)**. It is named after the German chemist Fritz Haber (1868–1934). At the beginning of the twentieth century many scientists were trying to "fix" nitrogen from the air, in the form of ammonia. At that time, it was not just because ammonia was a useful fertiliser. It could be used to make **explosives** and Germany was preparing for war.

Early Experiments

Haber began work on preparing ammonia around 1904. He was interested in reacting **nitrogen** with **hydrogen** to make ammonia. This involved some major problems.

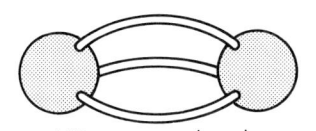

Nitrogen molecule

Nitrogen has a strong triple bond

At room temperature and pressure, **hardly any** nitrogen and hydrogen reacted. The atoms in a nitrogen molecule (N₂) are very difficult to break apart. It is a **very** unreactive molecule. This is because there is a **strong triple covalent bond** holding the atoms together.

Haber calculated that by increasing the temperature and pressure he would increase the amounts reacting. However, this meant building very **complicated apparatus** to withstand high temperature and pressure. Temperatures around 500–600 °C and a pressure of about 175 times normal atmospheric pressure were used. The nitrogen and hydrogen mixture was passed over a very expensive osmium catalyst. The process increased the amount of ammonia produced.

Scaling up the Process

In 1909 BASF, a large dye manufacturer, built a reactor based on Haber's laboratory arrangement. A chemical engineer called Carl Bosch was given the job of building it. There were a few problems to overcome.

■ Designing the Reactor

The reactor had to withstand high temperatures and very high pressures. A double-walled reactor, made of special steel, which would not react with hydrogen, had to be built.

■ Finding a Catalyst

Haber's catalyst worked, but it was very expensive. Eventually another catalyst, made mainly of iron, was found.

■ Cheap Hydrogen and Nitrogen

At first the hydrogen came from breaking up water (H₂O) by passing electricity through it. Nitrogen came from liquefying air and then letting it warm up. The liquid nitrogen in the air changes into a gas at −196 °C. All this was very expensive. Bosch developed less expensive methods, based on burning coke (from coal) in air. By the end of 1913, a complete ammonia works was operating on the River Rhine.

Making Ammonia Today

In Britain, the Haber process is still the most important way of making ammonia. The design of modern industrial plants, however, makes the production of ammonia **more efficient** and **cheaper** than in the past.

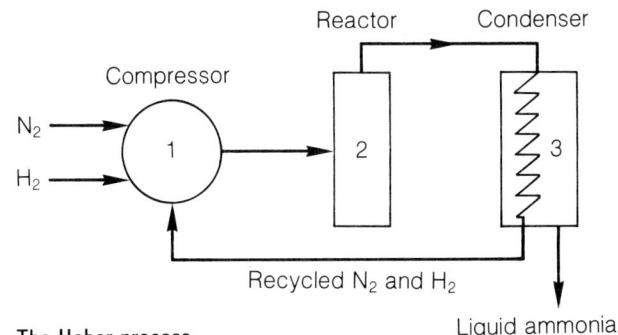

The Haber process

At (1), a mixture of pure nitrogen and hydrogen is passed into a compressor. This raises the gas pressure to around **250 atmospheres**. (250 times the pressure of the air around you just now!)

At (2), the compressed gases are passed over an **iron catalyst**, which has a "promotor" added. A promotor is added to the catalyst to make it more efficient. The temperature is raised to between **380 and 450 °C**.

At (3), the ammonia produced is either **condensed** (cooled until it forms a liquid) or **dissolved** in water, to make a **solution**. Only about 15 per cent of the gas mixture is converted to ammonia. The unreacted gases are not wasted, but are **recycled**, and passed back over the catalyst.

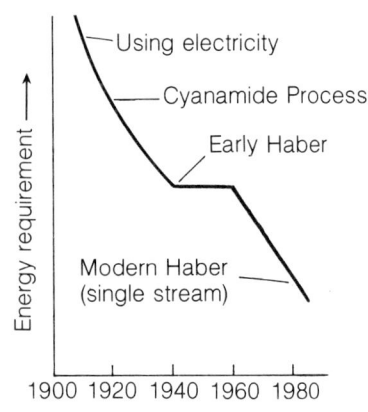

FERTILISERS

The graph shows how ammonia production has become more energy efficient

Nitrogen and Hydrogen

It is essential to have a cheap and plentiful supply of raw materials (**feedstocks**). Today, **hydrogen** comes from either **methane** (in natural gas) or **naphtha**, a petrol-like fraction of crude oil. **Nitrogen** comes from the **air**. Pure hydrogen and nitrogen are eventually obtained by a series of complicated reactions.

The flow diagram (page 183) is a simplified description of the single stream process used in plants like ICI's at Billingham in the north-east of England.

Why not 100 per cent Ammonia?

The reaction between nitrogen and hydrogen to produce ammonia is **reversible**. This means that any ammonia produced can also break up to form nitrogen and hydrogen again. The symbol for a reversible reaction is $\rightleftharpoons$.

For the Haber process, the equation is:

$$N_2(g) + 3H_2(g) \rightleftharpoons 2NH_3(g)$$

Eventually the rate (speed) at which ammonia is made is the **same** as the rate at which it is breaking up. This is called **equilibrium**. Raising the pressure helps nitrogen and hydrogen to combine, and more ammonia is formed. Increasing the temperature has a similar effect, but raising it **too** high causes ammonia to break up. At lower temperatures nitrogen and hydrogen combine too slowly. A **compromise** temperature must therefore be used to produce ammonia at an economical rate. Many important industrial reactions are reversible, and similar decisions have to be made about pressure, temperature and other operating conditions.

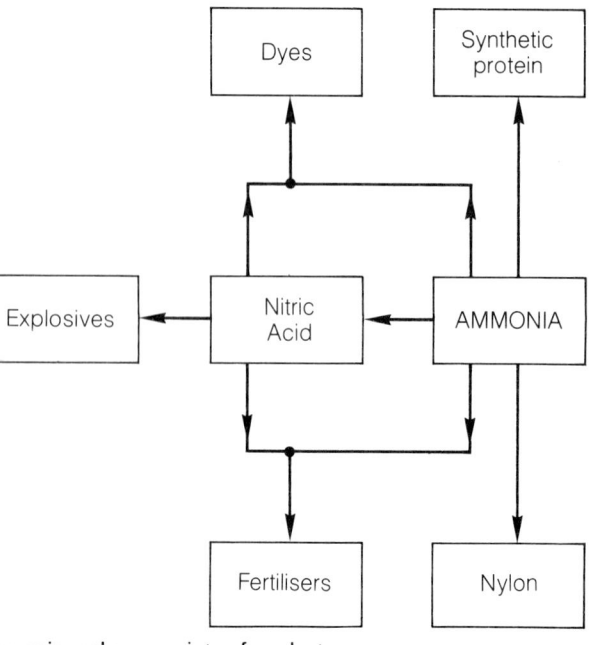

Siting an Ammonia Plant

Ammonia plants have always been built close to sources of:

(1) **energy**, whether coal, oil or natural gas, to cut down on transport costs.
(2) **water**, needed in fairly large amounts for dissolving chemicals and cooling processes.
(3) **transport**, either by road, rail, river or sea.

In Britain, the main production site for ammonia is at Billingham, on the River Tees, in the north-east of England. There are four large ammonia plants. It was originally chosen by the Government because it was close to the Durham coalfields. There are also large power stations in the area, and today it is convenient for North Sea oil and gas.

Building and Running the Plant

The larger a chemical plant is, the more economic it is to run. Even so, a 1 200 tonne per day plant, like the Number Four plant at Billingham, cost 50 million pounds to build in 1976.

Large chemical plants take a long time to start up and shut down, so it is more economical to run a plant continuously, 365 days a year. Every so often, however, it must be shut down for safety checks. The catalyst, which can last for between two and eight years, must also be changed. Control of the plant is now highly computerised, and operated from a central control room.

The Future

The world's population is still growing fast. People have to be fed. This means that more food has to be grown, and more fertilisers have to be made. It has been estimated that another 500 ammonia plants will be needed worldwide in the next 25 years. To keep costs down, these plants will have to be built close to where the ammonia is needed.

Each plant will have to use as little energy as possible. Once natural gas and oil are used up, coal could become the major source of hydrogen. Coal is already used in countries like South Africa, which has no gas or oil. Table 6.10 shows possible alternative sources of fuel and feed (raw materials) for ammonia production.

Ammonia makes a variety of products

FERTILISERS

Making Ammonia in the Lab

Ammonia gas can be made in the laboratory by heating an **ammonium salt** with an **alkali**.

e.g.,

calcium + ammonium → calcium + ammonia + water
hydroxide   chloride (a salt)   chloride

$Ca(OH)_2(s) + 2NH_4Cl(s) \rightarrow CaCl_2(s) + 2NH_3(g) + 2H_2O(g)$

The ammonia can be dried by passing it through a column containing lumps of calcium oxide. Ammonia is **less dense** (lighter) than air so it can be collected in an upturned test tube.

Making ammonia in the lab

Properties of Ammonia

Physical

Ammonia is a **colourless gas** which is lighter than air. It has a **very powerful "fishy" smell**.

Wet nappies give off ammonia gas!

Chemical

(1) Reaction with water

Ammonia is **very soluble** in water. Over one litre of ammonia gas will dissolve in one millilitre (ml) of water. Ammonia solution ($NH_3(aq)$) is formed:

$NH_3(g) \xrightarrow{H_2O(l)} NH_3(aq)$

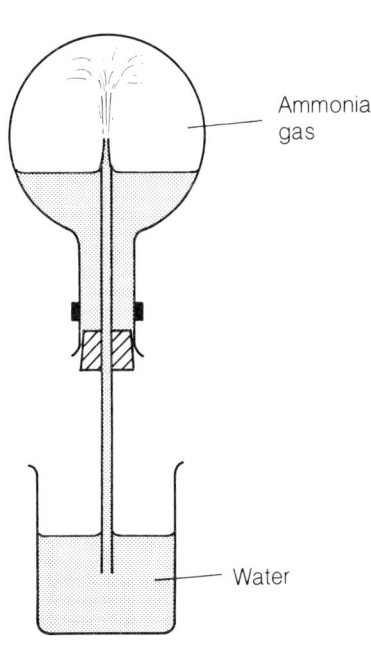

The Fountain experiment shows just how soluble ammonia is

If the ammonia solution is tested with damp pH paper or universal indicator, the pH is around nine or ten. This tells us ammonia solution is **alkaline**, and suggests that some hydroxide ions (**OH⁻**), which make solutions alkaline, are present.

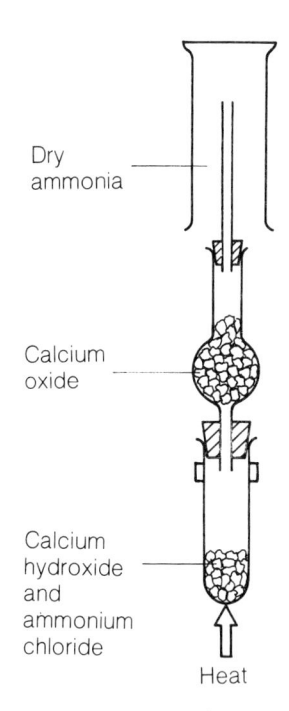

Some of the ammonia molecules react with water to form hydroxide ions and ammonium ions (NH_4^+).

(2) Neutralisation

Since ammonia solution is alkaline it can **neutralise** acids. **Ammonium salts** are formed in this way:

e.g.,

ammonia + hydrochloric → ammonium
solution   acid   chloride solution

$NH_3(aq) + HCl(aq) \rightarrow NH_4Cl(aq)$

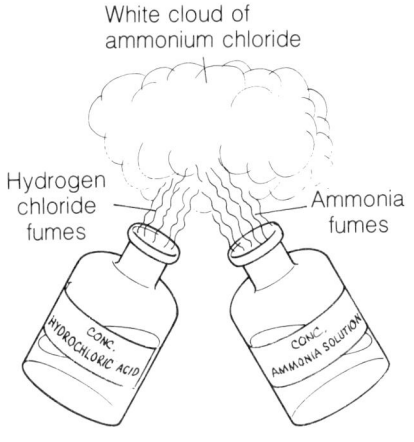

The white ammonium chloride fumes show ammonia gas is present

Table 6.10

Source	Fuel/Feed
Coal	Coke, obtained from coal, is reacted with steam to produce hydrogen (feed)
Nuclear Power	To make electricity which can be used to break up water and produce hydrogen (feed)
Vegetation	A renewable energy source (fuel)

FERTILISERS

Ammonia gas is given off from ammonia solution at room temperature. Hydrogen chloride gas is given off from hydrochloric acid. **Thick white** fumes of ammonium chloride gas are formed when the two gases react.

This can be used as a chemical **test** for ammonia gas.

Making Ammonium Salts

An ammonium salt can be made in the laboratory by **titrating** ammonia solution with the required acid.

Ammonium Nitrate

Dilute **nitric** acid is added from a burette into a flask containing ammonia solution and an **indicator**. When the indicator **just** changes colour the ammonia solution has reacted completely. To obtain a **pure** salt, the titration is repeated using exactly the same volumes of nitric acid and ammonia solution, but with **no** indicator. The solution formed is left to dry. The water evaporates and crystals of ammonium nitrate are left behind.

Titrating ammonia solution with nitric acid

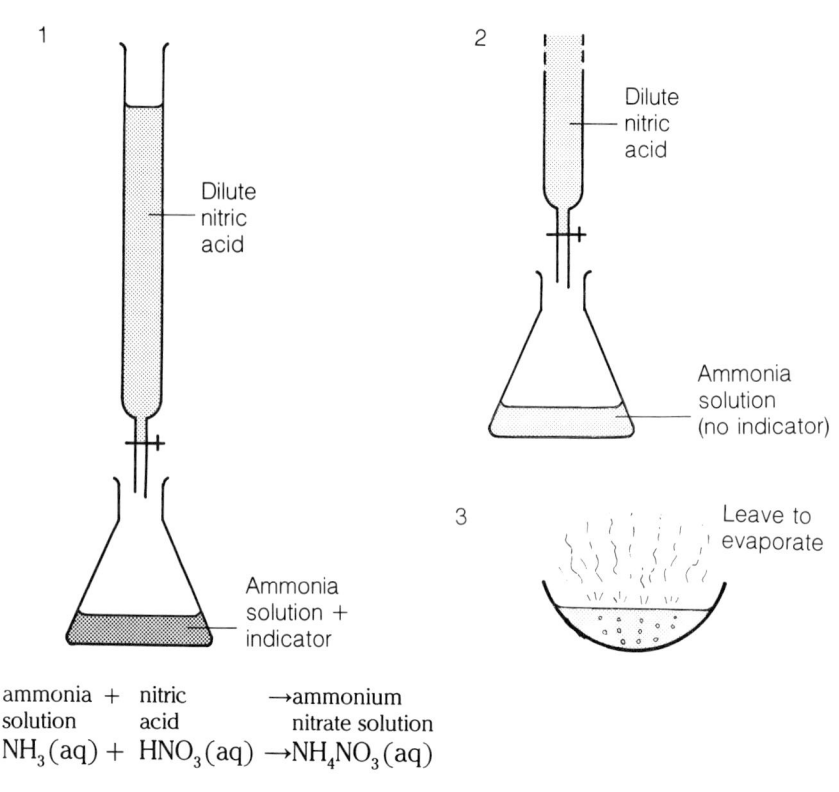

ammonia + nitric → ammonium
solution   acid   nitrate solution

$NH_3(aq) + HNO_3(aq) \rightarrow NH_4NO_3(aq)$

Ammonium sulphate can be made in a similar way, using **sulphuric acid**.

Activities

1. Early this century Fritz Haber developed a process for making ammonia (NH_3).
   (a) Which elements did he combine to make ammonia?
   (b) Write down the formulae of the elements in (a).
   (c) Write a formula equation for the production of ammonia.
   (d) What was the source of reactant elements at the beginning of the century?
   (e) Where do we get the elements from now?

2. (a) Outline the conditions needed to make ammonia in industry.
   (b) What sort of engineering problems do these conditions create?
   (c) Why is ammonia such an important compound?

3. Appearance, solubility, pH and types of reaction are all properties of substances which can be recorded. Look at the properties of ammonia and present the information in a table.

4. (a) Explain why the temperature at which the Haber process is carried out is a compromise.
   (b) An important part of the Haber process involves recycling unreacted gases. Explain why all the nitrogen and hydrogen are not converted into ammonia.
   (c) Ammonia plants operate continuously. Why do firms not like to stop the process?
   (d) Outline how you could make ammonia in the laboratory.
   (e) Look at the graph on page 184 which shows the changes in energy consumption in the manufacture of ammonia this century. Do you think the energy needed will ever drop to zero? Explain your answer.

4 Making Nitric Acid

Key Ideas

Nitric acid (HNO_3) is important for making nitrate fertilisers. It is made by dissolving a mixture of nitrogen dioxide (NO_2) and oxygen (from the air) in water. Nitrogen dioxide, however, is difficult to make. Nitrogen gas is not very reactive. In industry nitrogen dioxide is made from ammonia (NH_3). Nitrogen dioxide in the atmosphere is one cause of acid rain.

It's in the Air!

Nitric acid is essential for making **nitrate fertiliser**. It is easily made by dissolving a mixture of **nitrogen dioxide (NO_2)** and oxygen (from the air) in water:

nitrogen + oxygen + water → nitric
dioxide   acid
$NO_2(g) + O_2(g) + H_2O(l) → HNO_3(aq)$
• $4NO_2(g) + O_2(g) + 2H_2O(l) → 4HNO_3(aq)$

However, nitrogen dioxide is very difficult to make from its elements (nitrogen and oxygen). It's maybe just as well. The air around us is almost entirely made up of nitrogen and oxygen. If they reacted easily our atmosphere would be a mixture of nitrogen dioxide and nitric acid!

Why Don't They React?

Nitrogen and oxygen do not react easily because nitrogen molecules are difficult to break (see page 183). It takes a lot of **energy** to break the strong triple bond between the nitrogen atoms. In nature, the energy comes from **lightning**. A similar thing happens in the car **engine**. When the petrol/air mixture is sparked, the nitrogen molecules break up. Nitrogen and oxygen combine to form nitrogen oxide (NO) and nitrogen dioxide (NO_2) both in a car engine and during lightning storms.

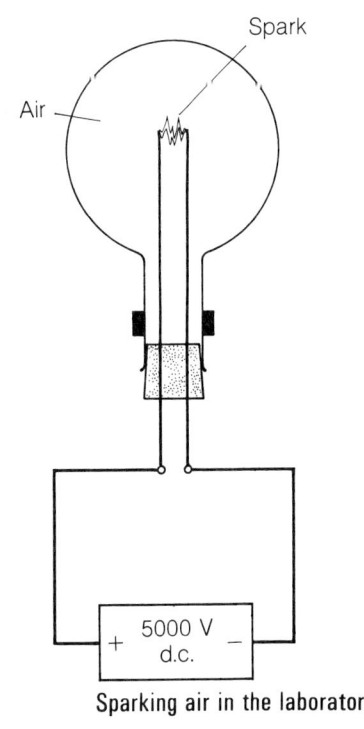

Sparking air in the laboratory

Nitrogen Oxides in the Air

Nitrogen oxide reacts with oxygen in the air to form nitrogen dioxide. This is very soluble and dissolves in moisture in the air to form part of the mixture called **acid rain**. Acid rain can have a pH between 2 and 5. "Normal" rain has a pH of between five and six, mainly due to dissolved carbon dioxide.

Acid rain pollutes rivers and lochs, and attacks buildings and unprotected metal structures (see Acids and Alkalis pages 122–125). Nitric acid (HNO_3) in the rain does help replace nitrogen in the soil, in the form of nitrate ions (NO_3^-), but it can also make the soil too acidic for many plants to grow properly.

Acid in the soil also lowers the solubility of compounds which contain the essential elements required by plants.

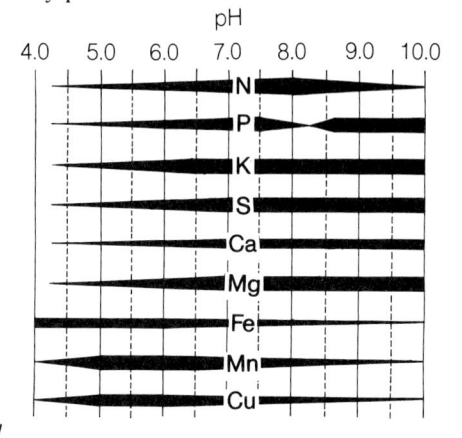

The pH of soil too acidic for a plant to grow can be raised by adding **lime**. Lime acts as a **neutraliser**.

Making Nitric Acid Industrially

We have seen how difficult it is to make atmospheric nitrogen and oxygen react. At the beginning of the century, in Scandinavia, nitrogen dioxide was made on a large scale using electricity. There was a lot of hydro-electricity available, which was relatively cheap. However, the process was so inefficient that overall

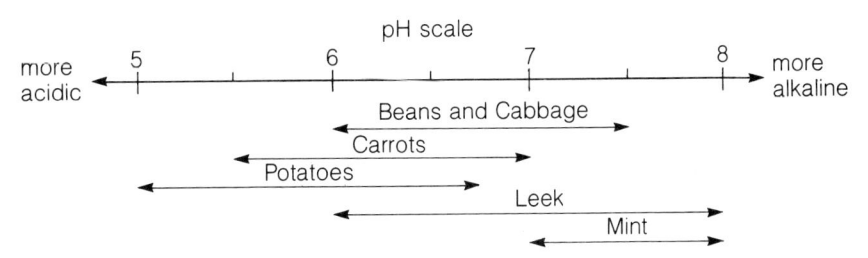

Preferred pH range of some plants

188 FERTILISERS

it was very expensive. The modern way of making nitric acid uses **ammonia**. It is often called the **Ostwald process**, after the chemist who developed it.

The Ostwald Process

Stage 1
Air is cleaned and **compressed** to twice atmospheric pressure. The air is used to react with ammonia and also in the final stage of the process.

Stage 2
The air/ammonia mixture is passed over a **platinum/rhodium gauze catalyst**, at 900 °C. Nitrogen oxide (NO) is formed. The gauze provides a large surface area on which the reaction can take place. It also lets the gases flow freely through it.

Stage 3
Nitrogen oxide and air are passed through a cooler. They react to form **nitrogen dioxide** (NO_2).

Stage 4
Nitrogen dioxide and air are passed up an absorption tower. The tower is packed with small glass beads over which water falls freely. The nitrogen dioxide, the oxygen from the air and the water meet at the surface of the beads and react to form **nitric acid**. The acid is collected at the bottom of the tower. At this stage the mixture is about 65 per cent nitric acid and 35 per cent water. The acid is concentrated by separating the water by distillation.

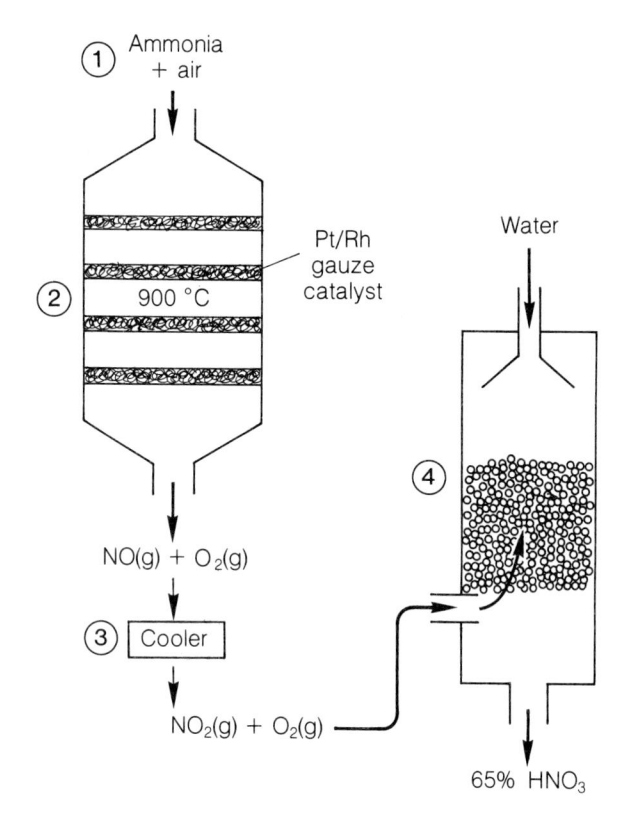

Simplified flow diagram of Ostwald process

Saving Energy and Money

Reasonably high temperatures are needed to start the catalytic conversion of ammonia. The catalyst is electrically heated to around 900 °C. This uses up a lot of energy and costs a lot of money. However, the reaction is very **exothermic**. This means that heat energy is produced during the reaction, and so the amount of electricity supplied can gradually be reduced. This saves both energy and money.

Due to the high temperatures, the thin catalyst gauzes used in the process wear out and have to be replaced. There are about eight layers of gauze, and they are not all replaced at the same time. Usually, the top layer is removed and replaced by a new one at the bottom.

In the Laboratory

We can show the catalytic conversion of ammonia to nitrogen dioxide in the laboratory.

The products are difficult to see. This is because only small amounts of nitrogen dioxide gas are produced, and some of this reacts with the ammonia gas. However, we can tell that the ammonia is reacting because the platinum catalyst continues to glow at the mouth of the flask.

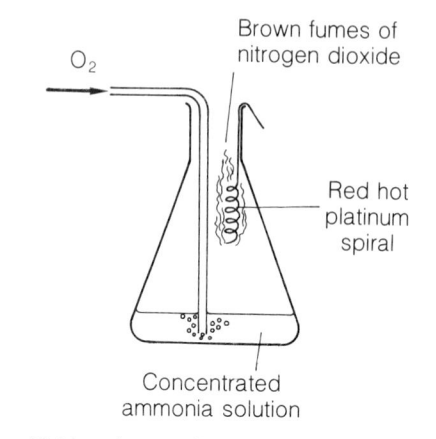

Making nitrogen dioxide in the laboratory

Using Nitric Acid

The most important use of nitric acid is in the manufacture of nitrate fertilisers. Another major use is in making explosives.

Nitroglycerine is an explosive made from nitric acid. It explodes if it is shaken fiercely or dropped. In the 1860s, the **Nobel** family developed a way of making nitroglycerine safer. They absorbed it in a type of clay, so that it could only be ignited with a fuse. This new explosive was called **dynamite**. Alfred Nobel made a fortune out of selling the explosive, and when he died left 2 million pounds to be awarded to people working for world peace or in medical research. The **Nobel Prizes** have been awarded every year since 1901 by the Nobel Foundation in Stockholm.

Activities

1. Nitric acid is made by dissolving a mixture of nitrogen dioxide and air in water.
   (a) Give **two** examples of how nitrogen dioxide is produced electrically, in everyday life.
   (b) Why is nitrogen dioxide not usually produced electrically in industry?
   (c) Why is it difficult to get nitrogen to react?
   (d) Oxides of nitrogen pollute the air. Explain how they do this.

2. Nitric acid is produced industrially by the Ostwald process.
   (a) Name the reactants in the process.
   (b) Outline the main stages of the process. State the conditions required.
   (c) Give two uses of nitric acid.

3. Look at the graph on page 187 of the range of soil pH preferred by some vegetables.
   (a) State the pH range in which cabbage grows best.
   (b) Name a vegetable that would grow well in fairly acidic soil.
   (c) Suggest one factor which might cause the pH of the soil to become more acidic.
   (d) What could be added to acidic soil to reduce its acidity?

4. The Ostwald process is a high energy consumer. However, it uses less energy as the reaction proceeds. Explain why this happens.

5. Look at the graph on page 187 which shows the availability of plant nutrients over a range of pH values. Use it to help you answer the following: Potatoes need nitrogen, phosphorus and potassium. What would happen to the uptake of nitrogen, phosphorus and potassium by the potato plant as the soil became more and more acidic? Explain your answer.

5 Spotlight on Industry

Key Ideas

Building a chemical plant of any kind is a complicated and costly business. When choosing a site and designing a plant, a number of factors have to be considered:
- Is the site close to the materials to be processed?
- Is there a workforce available?
- Are the communications good?
- Is there a good supply of energy close by?

The Billingham fertiliser works

Bringing it all Together

Often in industry a product is made from two or more different chemicals, which have to be made in separate plants and then brought together. It is sometimes cheaper if these chemicals are made by the same firm, with all the various plants close to each other. The Imperial Chemical Industries' fertiliser plant at **Billingham** (the biggest fertiliser producer in Britain), is a good example of this. The flow diagram of the processes carried out at Billingham, shows how nitric, sulphuric and phosphoric acid are made in separate plants and then transferred to another two plants to make fertiliser.

The carbon dioxide produced as a by-product at the ammonia plant is not wasted. Some is reacted with ammonia to form another fertiliser, **urea** $(CO(NH_2)_2)$. Carbon dioxide is also liquefied and sold to drinks manufacturers. Carbon dioxide is the "fizz" in fizzy drinks like lemonade and coke. Fizzy drinks can be made at home with a machine which uses a small cylinder of carbon dioxide.

Why Choose Billingham?

Billingham was developed as a fertiliser plant between the First and Second World Wars. It was chosen because:
- There was good access by road, rail and sea.
- There were plenty of workers.
- A new power station had been built in the area.
- There was plenty of coal, both for fuel and making hydrogen.
- Raw materials were ready available – salt, water, iron ore, limestone and anhydrite (a source of sulphur).

Even though many of the raw materials have changed, Billingham has been well sited to accommodate change. Natural gas from the North Sea is piped ashore, and potassium chloride is mined at nearby Boulby. Sulphur from France and phosphate rock from the USA can be imported directly, by ship.

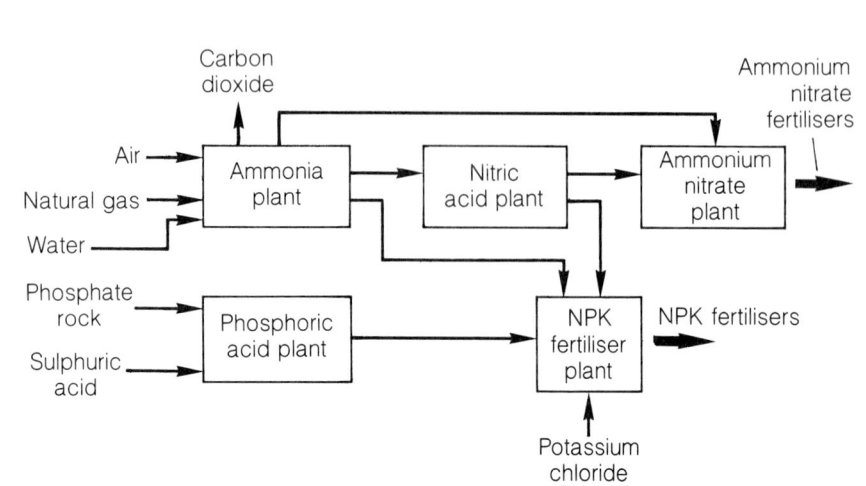

Bringing it all together at Billingham

FERTILISERS

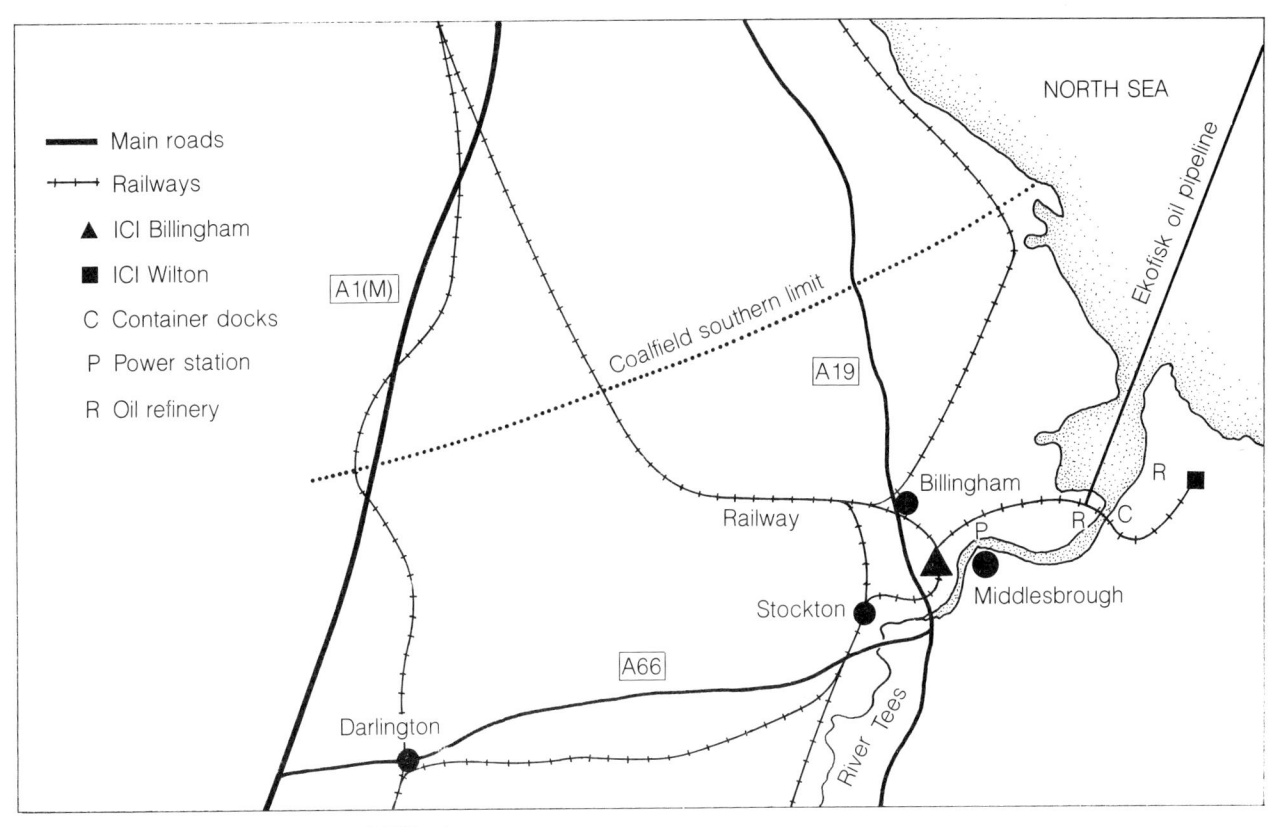

Communications and resources around Billingham

Activities

1. Look at the flow diagram showing the processes at Billingham. Use it to help you answer these questions.
   (a) Pick out the **main** chemicals made there.
   (b) Which chemicals go into making compound fertilisers?
   (c) Where does the natural gas and potassium chloride come from?

2. You have been asked by a large chemical firm to look for a site for a new fertiliser plant. What sort of things would you be looking for when choosing a site?

3. Suppose the nitric acid plant in a fertiliser complex has a major break-down. Describe the effect this would have on other parts of the complex.

Fertilisers – Study Questions

○ **1** Several potassium compounds are sold as fertilisers. "Phosphate of potash" and "sulphate of potash (K_2SO_4)" are two examples. The correct chemical names are potassium phosphate and potassium sulphate.
   (a) Write the formula of potassium *phosphate*.
   (b) Calculate the mass of 1 mole of potassium *sulphate*.
   (c) Describe a chemical test and result which would prove potassium to be present in a substance. (You may wish to refer to a data book.)
   (d) Potassium phosphate contains two elements which are essential for plant growth.
   Name an element *not* found in potassium phosphate which plants require in large amounts.
   (e) Compounds which are used as fertilisers contain elements that are essential for plant growth. They must also have a particular property.
   State this property. **KU**

○ **2** Heating a mixture of solid ammonium sulphate and sodium hydroxide pellets produces ammonia gas. Ammonia reacts with iron oxide.
Draw a diagram to show the apparatus you would set up to make ammonia gas and to pass it over hot iron oxide.
In your diagram, label the apparatus and chemicals used. **PS**

○ **3** The approximate composition of air is nitrogen (80 per cent) and oxygen (20 per cent).
   (a) Draw a pie chart to show the proportion of nitrogen to oxygen in the air. Label the gases.
   (b) Some bags of potato crisps are filled with pure nitrogen gas instead of air. Suggest why this is done. **PS**

○ **4** The chemical industry produces large quantities of nitric acid by the catalytic oxidation of ammonia.

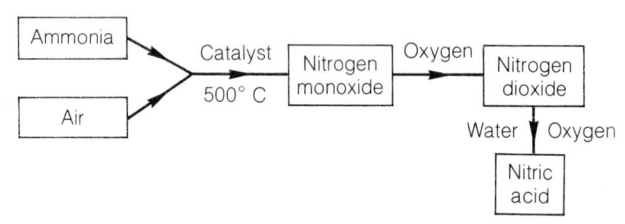

Ammonia + Air → (Catalyst 500°C) → Nitrogen monoxide → Oxygen → Nitrogen dioxide → Water, Oxygen → Nitric acid

   (a) State the name of this industrial process.
   (b) Name the catalyst used to speed up the reaction.
   (c) The nitric acid can be used to make potassium nitrate fertiliser.
   Write the formula for potassium nitrate. **KU**

● **5** As the world population increases, the demand for food grows. In order to meet this demand, farmers are using more and more synthetic fertilisers to improve crop yields. One of these synthetic fertilisers is NITRAM. The following flow diagram shows how NITRAM can be made industrially.

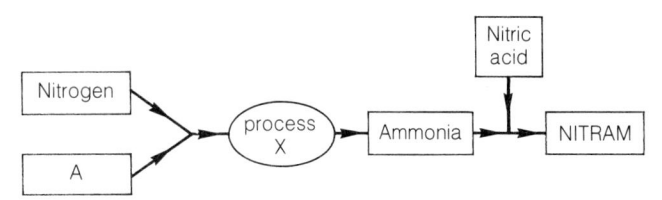

Nitrogen + A → process X → Ammonia + Nitric acid → NITRAM

   (a) (i) Name reactant A. **KU**
       (ii) Name industrial process X.
   (b) In process X, the percentage conversion of nitrogen to ammonia decreases as the temperature increases.
   Why then is process X carried out at the relatively high temperature of 450°C? **KU**
   (c) What is the chemical name for NITRAM? **KU**
   (d) NITRAM is very soluble in water and this allows essential elements to be taken in by the roots of crop plants very quickly.
   Suggest why NITRAM's high solubility can also be a disadvantage in its use as a fertilizer. **PS**
   (e) Ammonium phosphate is another important synthetic fertiliser.
       (i) Write the formula for ammonium phosphate.
       (ii) Name a substance which will react with ammonium phosphate to produce ammonia. **KU**

1 The Plastic Age

Key Ideas

Plastics and *synthetic fibres* are substances which are made from *oil*. *Plastics* are *light, durable* materials and are good *insulators* of heat and electricity. Because of their *durability*, many plastics can cause *environmental problems*. Some plastics also give off *toxic fumes* when they *burn. Biodegradable* plastics can now be manufactured. These slowly disintegrate if they are thrown away.

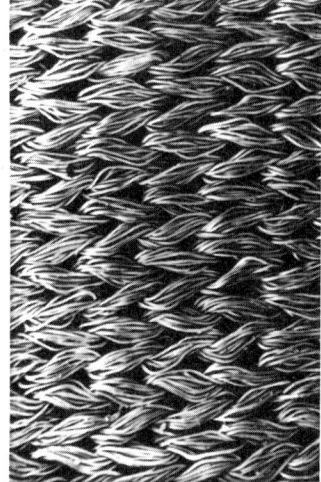

Different textures applied to synthetic fibres

Plastics All Around

If you look around your home, much of what you see is made from, or contains, **plastics** and **synthetic fibres.** These include kitchen work tops, knife handles, telephones, washable wallpaper, paint, clothes, shopping bags, radio and television cabinets, carpets, soft drink bottles, records, tapes and compact discs, electrical fittings and cables, shoes, toys and even the bath. The list goes on and on!

Plastics are **synthetic** – they are made by us. The plastics used to make articles such as lemonade bottles and washing-up basins, have all been melted and **moulded** into shape. However, the plastics used to make carpet backings and ropes have been melted and **drawn out** (**extruded**) into thin threads called **fibres**. The synthetic fibres are then woven or twisted together. They can also be texturised to make them feel soft and fluffy like wool.

Why Not Use Natural Materials?

As the world population has increased the demand for materials has also increased. The demand for substances like rubber, wool, cotton, leather, wood and metal cannot be

Plastics in the kitchen

Plastics

194 PLASTICS

met by natural sources alone. Plastics and synthetic fibres are now common alternatives to these materials. At the beginning of the century, about 4 million tonnes of natural fibres were being produced, consisting of around 80 per cent cotton and 20 per cent wool. By 1950, 10 per cent of cloth being made was from synthetic fibres. Today the figure is nearer 50 per cent and rising.

Paper packaging (made from wood) has largely been replaced by plastic packaging, and most wooden kitchen furniture is now plastic coated chipboard.

Shoes often have a large synthetic content and much of our clothing is made either partly, or entirely, from synthetic fibres. The same clothing made from natural fibres is a lot more expensive.

Electrical fittings using plastics as insulating material

Wasting Oil?

Although "synthetics" have helped to preserve some of our natural resources, some people say that they are only using up other valuable resources, such as **oil**. Oil is the main source of the chemicals used to make plastics. In fact, only 3 per cent of all crude oil produced today, is turned into plastics and synthetic fibres. Most of the crude oil is still used for fuel.

Some geologists estimate that oil will run out within the next fifty years, and we will have to find an alternative to plastics and synthetic fibres. Maybe we should find alternative energy sources and save oil for making plastics?

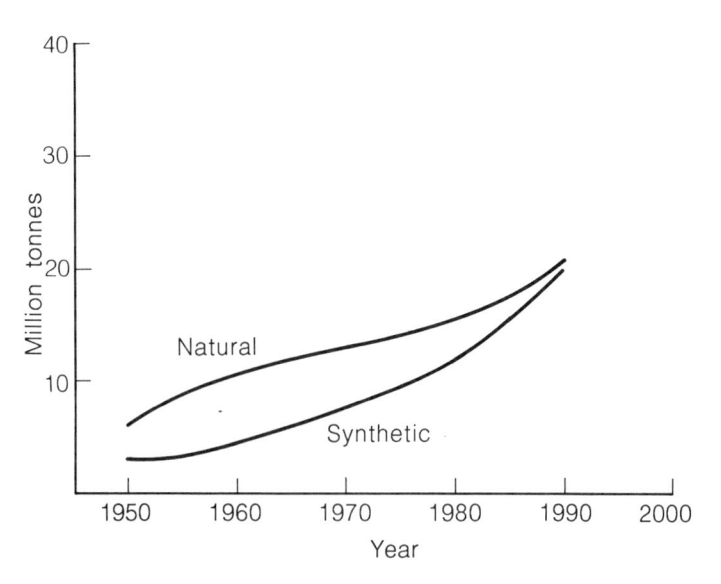

World fibre production

Properties of Plastics

Plastics have many uses. They can be made with almost any property to suit the customer's requirements. The plastic used to make carrier bags is **thin** and **flexible**, yet very **strong**. Plastics can also be made very **rigid** (inflexible) and able to **withstand high temperatures**. These are suitable for electric kettles, and some types of oven-ware.

Most plastics do not conduct electricity and and so they make good insulators. Plastic is used to insulate electrical cables, and to make light switches and plugs. A relatively modern plastic, **kynar** film, is unusual. It can sometimes be made to conduct electricity. You may have come across it in physics. It is used to produce a small electric current when it is heated or given a sharp knock.

Plastics are also very **light** materials and are used in the fittings of ships and aeroplanes to help reduce weight. Household plastics are often soft and easily damaged. There are other plastics like **kevlar** which can be as **strong** as steel – especially if it is reinforced with carbon fibres. The wings and bodies of some jet fighters use kevlar because it is both strong and light.

You may have the opportunity to do some canoeing at school. Competition-standard canoes use carbon reinforced kevlar so that they can withstand collisions with rocks, and yet be flexible enough to put up with

Kevlar/carbon canoe

the buffeting they receive in the wild-water.

Kevlar is also used to reinforce radial tyres and to make body armour for the police and army. Body armour will stop a pistol bullet fired at a distance of 3 metres.

Climbing ropes, and mooring ropes for ships, must be strong enough to support heavy weights. They must also be light for carrying about, and tough to withstand the wet, windy conditions, without rotting, shrinking or expanding. Many ropes today are made from synthetic fibres twisted together.

Plastics are good **insulators** of **heat**. Plastic fibres can be used to insulate your loft and plastic foam to fill the cavity between the walls of your home. The lining of your anorak may well be padded with wads of texturised plastic fibre to keep out the cold.

There are even strong **transparent** plastics, which can be used as bulletproof windows!

Pollution from Plastics

Plastics are so **durable** (long lasting) that if they are carelessly thrown away they will not rot for many years. You only have to look around you to see plastic litter all over the place and realise the scale of such pollution. Even in the remotest of hills you can often see plastic litter scattered about the pathway.

The sea has its share of plastic waste, as a walk along the beach will show you. Sometimes dead dolphins and sharks are washed ashore, having choked on plastic bags or bottles they ate.

To help prevent plastic pollution, a French scientist invented a **biodegradable** plastic made from maize **starch** and some other chemicals. If it is left on the ground it breaks down to form water and carbon dioxide. In water, it simply dissolves. Some carrier bags are made from biodegradable plastic. It is hoped that in future many more articles will be made from biodegradable plastic too.

Unfortunately, most plastics used today are not biodegradable and their disposal remains a problem. Part of the solution is to be more careful about how we dispose of such litter. If the plastics waste is buried along with other waste, it only hides the problem, rather than solving it. One advantage of using natural fibres like cotton, silk and wool is that they are biodegradable. They are broken down by bacteria in the soil and rot away. However, natural materials like wood have their disadvantages too. Although wood is strong and can be shaped for different uses, it is also attacked by pests such as woodworm, and infested by wet or dry rot. This destroys the strength of the wood and can be very dangerous if the wood is part of the structure of a building.

Plastic litter

A biodegradable plastic bag

Burning Plastics

Many plastics burn very easily, giving off a lot of smoke. Even if they don't burn, they often smoulder, producing yet more smoke. If the smoke is inhaled it can seriously damage your lungs. Too much smoke can cause death by suffocation.

Some plastics give off **toxic (poisonous)** fumes when they burn. This is one of the reasons why firemen wear breathing apparatus when they enter a burning house.

Many people who die in house fires have been overcome by toxic fumes and smoke produced from burning plastics.

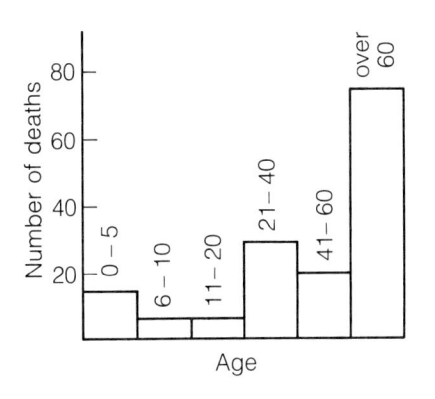

Deaths from house fires in Scotland in 1988

196 PLASTICS

Chairs and settees used to be filled with plastic foam which gave off toxic cyanide gas when it burned. The government brought in laws to ban this type of plastic in furniture.

Burning foam filled furniture

Why are Toxic Gases Produced?

Most plastics are made up of long chains of hydrocarbons, so when they burn carbon dioxide and water are the main products. In a limited supply of air, however, **poisonous carbon monoxide** is produced.

The more carbon a plastic contains the smokier the flame will be. If plastic is burning in a room, it soon fills with black, choking smoke. Some plastics give off other gases when they burn. PVC, which is used to make records and cover electrical wire, contains both hydrogen and chlorine in its structure. It burns to give off carbon dioxide, water and **hydrogen chloride** (HCl) gas. Hydrogen chloride gas irritates the lungs and eyes because it dissolves to form hydrochloric acid.

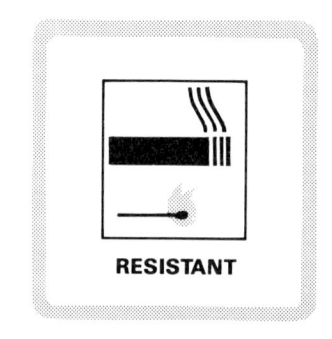

RESISTANT

Symbol for fire retardant material

Polyurethane foam, once common as padding in chairs, has a **cyanide** group (–CN) in its structure. When the foam burns, extremely toxic **hydrogen cyanide** (HCN) gas is given off, which can kill. If you are buying furniture it should be labelled with the sign shown.

This tells you that it has been manufactured with a fire retardant material, which has been treated to make burning difficult. Even if it still burns, it does not give off toxic fumes.

Plastics often melt before they burn. Some people used to line the ceilings of their kitchen with polystyrene tiles. If the tiles accidentally caught fire, the burning, molten plastic dripped on to the floor, spreading the fire further.

Activities

1. Give three properties of a plastic material and describe how some plastic products make use of these properties.

2. Look at the graph of "World Fibre Production" on page 194, and estimate what the synthetic fibre production will be in the year 2000.

3. Explain why the government had to bring in laws to control which materials were used to fill settees and armchairs.

4. (a) Either design a poster or make up a slogan to make people aware of the dangers of pollution from plastics.
   (b) Some biodegradable plastics are now available. Describe how this will help cut down plastic pollution.

5. Make a table to show the advantages and disadvantages of both natural and synthetic materials.

6. A–D are all parts of the structures of well known plastics:

$$\begin{array}{c}\text{H}\quad\text{CN}\;\text{H}\quad\text{CN}\;\text{H}\quad\text{CN}\\|\quad|\quad|\quad|\quad|\quad|\\-\text{C}-\text{C}-\text{C}-\text{C}-\text{C}-\text{C}-\\|\quad|\quad|\quad|\quad|\quad|\\\text{H}\quad\text{H}\quad\text{H}\quad\text{H}\quad\text{H}\quad\text{H}\end{array}$$

A

$$\begin{array}{c}\text{H}\quad\text{H}\quad\text{H}\quad\text{H}\quad\text{H}\quad\text{H}\\|\quad|\quad|\quad|\quad|\quad|\\-\text{C}-\text{C}-\text{C}-\text{C}-\text{C}-\text{C}-\\|\quad|\quad|\quad|\quad|\quad|\\\text{H}\quad\text{H}\quad\text{H}\quad\text{H}\quad\text{H}\quad\text{H}\end{array}$$

B

$$\begin{array}{c}\text{H}\quad\text{Cl}\;\text{H}\quad\text{Cl}\;\text{H}\quad\text{Cl}\\|\quad|\quad|\quad|\quad|\quad|\\-\text{C}-\text{C}-\text{C}-\text{C}-\text{C}-\text{C}-\\|\quad|\quad|\quad|\quad|\quad|\\\text{H}\quad\text{H}\quad\text{H}\quad\text{H}\quad\text{H}\quad\text{H}\end{array}$$

C

$$\begin{array}{c}\text{H}\quad\text{CH}_3\;\text{H}\quad\text{CH}_3\;\text{H}\quad\text{CH}_3\\|\quad|\quad|\quad|\quad|\quad|\\-\text{C}-\text{C}-\text{C}-\text{C}-\text{C}-\text{C}-\\|\quad|\quad|\quad|\quad|\quad|\\\text{H}\quad\text{H}\quad\text{H}\quad\text{H}\quad\text{H}\quad\text{H}\end{array}$$

D

(a) Which of the plastics A–D give off toxic fumes when they burn, even in a plentiful supply of oxygen?

(b) Name the gas produced, for each of your answers to (a).

2 Making Plastics (Polymers)

Key Ideas

All plastics are made up of *giant molecules*, which are built up from thousands of small molecules (*monomers*) joined together. Any substance made of long chains of repeating units is called a *polymer*. Many plastics are formed by the *addition polymerisation* of *small unsaturated* monomers obtained by *cracking* heavy crude oil fractions. *Condensation* polymers form when monomers link together, and simple molecules like *water* or *hydrogen chloride* are also produced.

Polymers

There are many different kinds of plastics in use today. One thing they all have in common is that they are made up of very **large molecules**, often called **polymers**. The large polymer molecules are formed when thousands of very small molecules called **monomers** join together. This is called **polymerisation**.

```
+M+M+M+M+M+M+M+
       monomers
       ↓ polymerisation
—M—M—M—M—M—M—M—
       a polymer
```

Natural Polymers

All plants and animals contain **natural polymers**. Plants produce glucose by photosynthesis (see Carbohydrates). Many small glucose molecules (**monomers**) then link up to form the long **polymer** chain we call **starch**.

Glucose is also the monomer for **cellulose**, a longer polymer than starch. Many more glucose molecules need to join up to form one molecule of cellulose. **Cotton** is made from cellulose, and about 40 per cent of the structure of **wood** is cellulose.

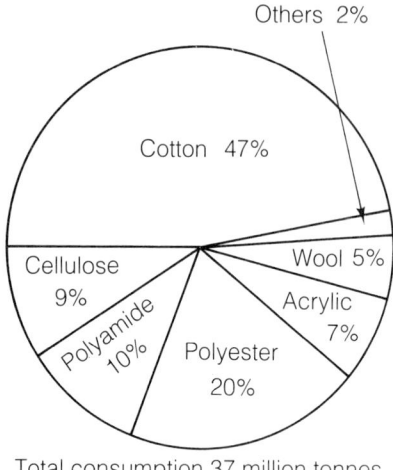

World consumption of fibres (1987)
- Cotton 47%
- Polyester 20%
- Polyamide 10%
- Cellulose 9%
- Acrylic 7%
- Wool 5%
- Others 2%

Total consumption 37 million tonnes

Tapping a rubber tree

Proteins are polymers made from monomers called amino acids. Wool and silk are examples of natural protein fibres. Wool and cotton still account for around 50 per cent of the total world fibres market. **Rubber** is another natural polymer. It is formed from latex, the sap from rubber trees.

From Natural to Synthetic Polymers

Rayon was the first **synthetic polymer** to be mass produced. It was first manufactured in the UK in 1905, by treating **cellulose**, in the form of wood pulp, with sodium hydroxide solution and carbon disulphide. This

Wet spinning rayon thread

broke the polymer fibre down into smaller units. The reaction produces a syrupy substance called **viscose**, which is forced through a series of small holes into a solution of sulphuric acid. The syrupy solution reforms into fine polymer fibres, which can be spun into **rayon** thread and then woven into fabric.

The manufacture of rayon converts a natural fibre into a synthetic fibre. Scientists had already discovered the complex structure of proteins like wool, and researchers aimed to produce a synthetic fibre which was similar to wool. In 1935, an American scientist, called Carothers, made a material which could be formed into fibres and woven into cloth. He called it **nylon**. It was the first mass produced, wholly synthetic fibre.

Commercial production of nylon in the UK started in 1941. In the same decade, **polyester** was also made in the UK, and **acrylic** in Germany. The age of synthetic materials had begun.

Addition Polymerisation

Addition polymers are formed when thousands of small **unsaturated** molecules add together. Most of these monomers come from crude oil. The larger, less useful molecules from crude oil are **cracked** to produce mixtures containing **alkenes** (see Fuels and Hydrocarbons).

Table 7.1 gives the names of some common addition polymers and their monomers. It clearly shows that given the name of the polymer, the monomer can easily be identified, and vice versa.

Poly(ethene)

Poly(ethene) is formed when thousands of **ethene** (C_2H_4) molecules add together. The ethene itself is obtained either by cracking fractions from crude oil, or cracking ethane from natural gas.

The carbon atoms in the ethene molecule are joined by a double bond:

During polymerisation the double bonds of the ethene molecules open up, and immediately join up with adjacent molecules to form new single bonds. This continues until a giant chain is formed. The process is called **addition polymerisation** because each monomer **adds on** to the next monomer. The reaction is similar to joining up a large number of "poppet beads" to form a long chain.

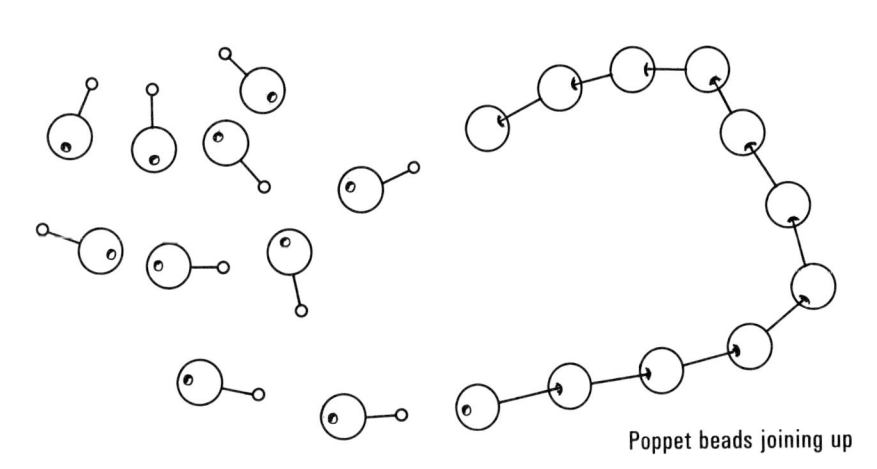

Table 7.1

Monomer	Polymer	Common Name	Uses
ethene	poly(ethene)	polythene	carrier bags, washing up bowls
propene	poly(propene)	polypropylene	ropes, carpet backing
chloroethene	poly(chloroethene)	PVC	records, hose pipes
tetrafluoroethene	poly(tetrafluoroethene)	PTFE	non-stick pans, coating on skis
phenylethene	poly(phenylethene)	polystyrene	packaging, disposable cups and cartons

section of a poly(ethene) molecule

Poppet beads joining up

PLASTICS

The polymer is often represented as the repeating unit enclosed by brackets with a subscript "n" outside. The **n** represents the number of repeating units in the molecule. This is usually a very large number. For poly(ethene) **n** is between 1 000 and 50 000.

e.g.,

$$n\ \underset{H\ H}{\overset{H\ H}{C=C}} \rightarrow \left[\underset{H\ H}{\overset{H\ H}{-C-C-}}\right]_n$$

$$50\,000\ \underset{H\ H}{\overset{H\ H}{C=C}} \rightarrow \left[\underset{H\ H}{\overset{H\ H}{-C-C-}}\right]_{50\,000}$$

You may know poly(ethene) by its commercial name **polythene**. It is the most widely used polymer in the world.

Low density poly(ethene) is made industrially by compressing ethene gas to about 2 000 times atmospheric pressure, and then heating it to 200°C. Low density poly(ethene) is floppy, and loses its shape in boiling water. It is used to make squeezy bottles, plastic food wrapping and carrier bags.

If ethene is reacted with a special **catalyst**, made of aluminium and titanium, at a pressure of only 30 atmospheres, **high density** poly(ethene) is formed. This is much more rigid than low density poly(ethene) and does not lose its shape in boiling water. It can be used to make washing-up bowls, buckets, milk crates and dustbins.

Poly(propene)

The next alkene in the homologous series after ethene is **propene** (C_3H_6). It too forms an addition polymer – **poly(propene)**:

$$n\ \underset{H\ H}{\overset{H\ CH_3}{C=C}} \rightarrow \left[\underset{H\ H}{\overset{H\ CH_3}{-C-C-}}\right]_n$$

Notice how the propene monomer is similar in structure to ethene. This allows polymerisation to take place in the same way as for poly(ethene). Poly(propene) is more rigid than poly(ethene) and keeps its shape at higher temperatures. It is used to make plastic chairs, ropes, carpet backings, and fishing nets.

Poly(chloroethene)

Poly(chloroethene) is better known by its commercial name **polyvinyl chloride (PVC)**. Another name for chloroethene (CH_2CHCl) is vinyl chloride, so its polymer is called **p**oly**v**inyl **c**hloride (or **PVC**).

$$n\ \underset{H\ H}{\overset{H\ Cl}{C=C}} \rightarrow \left[\underset{H\ H}{\overset{H\ Cl}{-C-C-}}\right]_n$$

Again the structure of the monomer clearly shows how addition polymerisation takes place.

PVC is used to make plastic bottles, records, floor tiles, wallpaper coatings, hose pipes, car window stickers, drain pipes and insulation for electric cables.

In France, PVC bottles are collected and recycled. The bottles are ground to a powder, treated to remove unwanted material (like paper and inks) and then melted down to be reformed into plastic piping and telephone cables.

Poly(tetrafluoroethene)

Poly(tetrafluoroethene) or PTFE is also known by one of its commercial names, **Teflon**. Its monomer is tetrafluoroethene (C_2F_4).

$$n\ \underset{F\ F}{\overset{F\ F}{C=C}} \rightarrow \left[\underset{F\ F}{\overset{F\ F}{-C-C-}}\right]_n$$

PTFE is used as non-stick coating for frying pans and oven ware, and, because it is so unreactive, it is also used to line tanks containing corrosive chemicals.

Poly(phenylethene)

Poly(phenylethene) is much better known as **polystyrene**.

$$n\ \underset{H\ H}{\overset{H\ C_6H_5}{C=C}} \rightarrow \left[\underset{H\ H}{\overset{H\ C_6H_5}{-C-C-}}\right]_n$$

The large –C_6H_5 group in phenylethene makes this polymer much more rigid, and therefore more brittle than poly(ethene). Toys, cotton reels, handles, switches and construction kits like "Airfix" models, are all made from polystyrene. Polystyrene can also be made into a foam. This is used to make ceiling tiles, packaging for delicate objects, and plastic cups. Polystyrene foam is formed by blowing a gas, such as carbon dioxide through the molten plastic. As the mixture cools, bubbles of the gas are trapped in the plastic, and the polystyrene expands. It is often called **expanded polystyrene**.

Sometimes **chlorofluorocarbon** (**CFC**) gases are used to create the foam. This also gives the final product good insulation properties, but CFCs are thought to be destroying the ozone layer in the earth's atmosphere. This causes more ultraviolet light to reach earth, which is thought could lead to dramatic changes in climate. CFCs are also used as propellant in spray cans such as deodorant and hair spray. Many manufacturers are now using more "environment friendly" gases in place of CFCs.

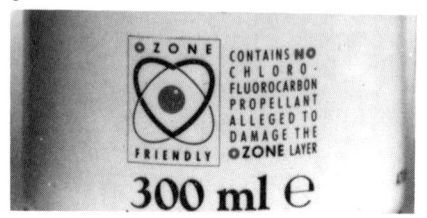

By polymerising two different monomers at the same time (**co-polymerisation**), polystyrene can be made much tougher. This is used to make motor cycle crash helmets.

Poly(methyl 2-methylpropenoate)

This polymer is better known by one of its commercial names, **perspex**. Although the monomer for this polymer is more complicated than ethene, it polymerises in the same way.

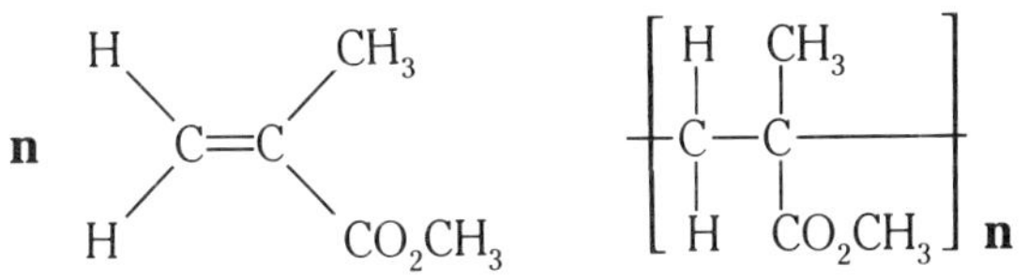

$$n \; \underset{H}{\overset{H}{\diagdown}}C=C\underset{CO_2CH_3}{\overset{CH_3}{\diagup}} \longrightarrow \left[\begin{array}{cc} H & CH_3 \\ | & | \\ -C-C- \\ | & | \\ H & CO_2CH_3 \end{array} \right]_n$$

Perspex is used to make aeroplane windows, dentures, light fittings and spectacle lenses. Perspex is an **acrylic** polymer.

Thermosetting Plastics and Thermoplastics

When plastics are heated, some melt and others retain their shape. If molten plastic is poured into a mould, it will solidify into the shape of the mould. If the new shape can be melted down and cast into another shape, the plastic is called a **thermoplastic polymer**. Most addition polymers are thermoplastic (see table 7.1).

Some other plastics do not have this property. Once they have been formed into a particular shape they cannot be melted down again. Instead, they swell and crack when heated. These are called **thermosetting** polymers.

In industry, monomers used for thermosetting polymers are put into moulds and heated under pressure. The monomers polymerise and take up the shape of the mould. Thermosetting polymers are used to make electric plugs, sockets, and light fittings, because they do not soften or melt when they are hot. Ash trays and table tops also have to withstand moderate heat and are often made from thermosetting polymers.

Polyester and **epoxy** resins are also thermosetting plastics. Polyester resins are used to make glass fibre reinforced products such as boats and car bodies. They are also used to repair dents or rust holes in metal car bodies. The polyester resin monomer is bought in a tub or tube, and must be mixed with a quantity of **catalyst** paste. The mixture is spread over the hole or dent and left to **cure** (harden). The curing process is actually polymerisation. When the polyester resin is set, it can be rubbed down and shaped. After spraying the repair is invisible.

Epoxy resins are used to make paints and glues. The paint (or glue) comes in two packs, again one containing the monomer resin and the other the catalyst. The two are mixed in the correct proportions and applied to the surfaces being treated. Polymerisation sets the resin hard. If you touch the resin while polymerisation is taking place you may feel that it is warm. It is a sign that a chemical reaction is occurring.

Repairing a car body

A Closer Look at Addition Polymerisation

Ethene has the structural formula:

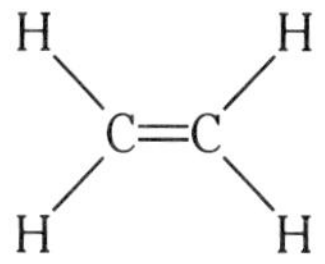

$$\underset{H}{\overset{H}{\diagdown}}C=C\underset{H}{\overset{H}{\diagup}}$$

Each carbon atom has four electrons in its outer energy level. Two of these electrons are involved in the carbon–hydrogen bonds and the other two in the carbon–carbon double bond.

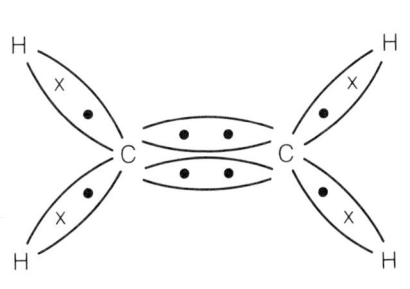

• = electron from carbon
x = electron from hydrogen

When polymerisation begins, the carbon–carbon double bonds in the ethene molecules break open:

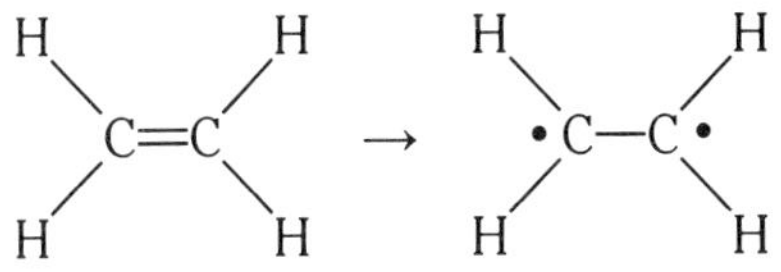

$$\underset{H}{\overset{H}{\diagdown}}C=C\underset{H}{\overset{H}{\diagup}} \longrightarrow \underset{H}{\overset{H}{\diagdown}}\bullet C-C\bullet \underset{H}{\overset{H}{\diagup}}$$

PLASTICS

New single bonds are formed with neighbouring ethene molecules. A long polymer chain grows from the initial ethene molecule until polymerisation stops:

$$\begin{array}{c}H\\ \\ H\end{array}\!\!>\!\!\overset{\bullet}{C}\!\!-\!\!\overset{\bullet}{C}\!\!<\!\!\begin{array}{c}H\\ \\ H\end{array} + \begin{array}{c}H\\ \\ H\end{array}\!\!>\!\!\overset{\bullet}{C}\!\!-\!\!\overset{\bullet}{C}\!\!<\!\!\begin{array}{c}H\\ \\ H\end{array} + \begin{array}{c}H\\ \\ H\end{array}\!\!>\!\!\overset{\bullet}{C}\!\!-\!\!\overset{\bullet}{C}\!\!<\!\!\begin{array}{c}H\\ \\ H\end{array}$$

↓ polymerisation

a polyethene chain with repeating $-CH_2-CH_2-$ units

Any compound containing a C=C bond is able to form an addition polymer in this way.

If you know the structure of an addition polymer, its monomer can be worked out by looking for the reactive unit and adding a double bond. For example, a section of the poly(propenonitrile) structure is shown below:

[structure of poly(propenonitrile) chain with alternating H and CN substituents]

The repeating unit is:

$$\left[\begin{array}{cc}H & CN\\ |&|\\ C-C\\ |&|\\ H & H\end{array}\right]$$

So the monomer is:

$$\begin{array}{cc}H & CN\\ |&|\\ C=C\\ |&|\\ H & H\end{array}$$

Poly(propenonitrile) withstands high temperatures. If propenonitrile and chloroethane are polymerised together (co-polymerisation) the polymer formed can be spun into fibre. These fibres are sold under the trade names of **Orlan** and **Acrilan**. You may have some clothes made from these fibres – check the care label and see!

Condensation Polymerisation

A **condensation** reaction is one in which a small molecule like **water** (H_2O) or **hydrogen chloride** (HCl) is one of the products. These reactions can be quite complicated. We can simplify things by representing the two reactants in a condensation reaction as:

$$H-[X]-OH \quad \text{and} \quad H-[Y]-OH$$

They react as follows:

$$H-[X]-\underline{OH+H}-[Y]-OH$$
↓ condensation
$$H-[X]-[Y]-OH + \underline{H_2O}$$

It does not really matter what X and Y are, so long as the molecules have an H and OH available to react. Similarly, for

$$H-[A]-Cl \quad \text{and} \quad H-[B]-Cl$$

$$H-[A]-\underline{Cl+H}-[B]-Cl$$
↓ condensation
$$H-[A]-[B]-Cl + \underline{HCl}$$

Condensation **polymerisation** involves thousands of monomers of this type reacting to form a polymer. Proteins and starches are natural condensation polymers (see Carbohydrates). Nylon and polyester are both synthetic condensation polymers.

Making Nylon

There are a number of different types of nylon polymer. They vary depending on the structure of the monomers. One nylon polymer is called nylon 6.6 because both repeating units contain six carbon atoms. The monomers are 1.6-diaminohexane ($NH_2(CH_2)_6NH_2$) and hexanedioyl dichloride ($ClOC(CH_2)_4COCl$).

$$\begin{array}{c}H\\ \\ H\end{array}\!\!>\!\!N\!\!-\!\!(CH_2)_6\!\!-\!\!N\!\!<\!\!\begin{array}{c}H\\ \\ H\end{array}$$

1.6-diaminohexane

$$\begin{array}{c}Cl\\ \\ O\end{array}\!\!>\!\!C\!\!-\!\!(CH_2)_4\!\!-\!\!C\!\!<\!\!\begin{array}{c}Cl\\ \\ O\end{array}$$

hexanedioyl dichloride

During polymerisation, hydrogen chloride is eliminated. We can show this with just three monomer units:

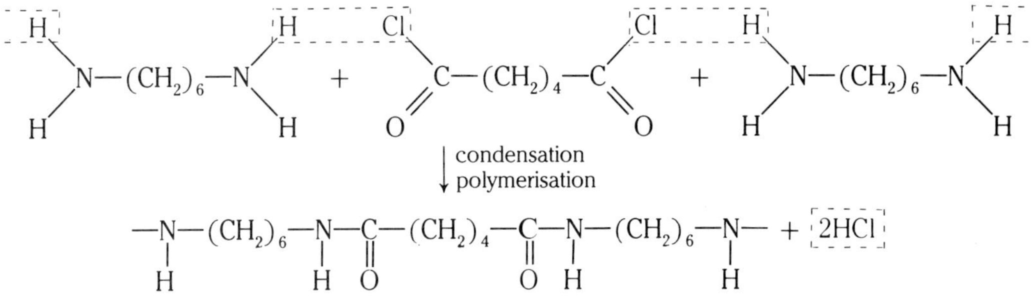

$$\underset{H}{\overset{H}{\diagdown}}N-(CH_2)_6-N\underset{H}{\overset{H}{\diagup}} \;+\; \underset{O}{\overset{Cl}{\diagdown}}C-(CH_2)_4-C\underset{O}{\overset{Cl}{\diagup}} \;+\; \underset{H}{\overset{H}{\diagdown}}N-(CH_2)_6-N\underset{H}{\overset{H}{\diagup}}$$

$$\downarrow \text{condensation polymerisation}$$

$$-\underset{H}{N}-(CH_2)_6-\underset{H}{N}-\underset{O}{\overset{\|}{C}}-(CH_2)_4-\underset{O}{\overset{\|}{C}}-\underset{H}{N}-(CH_2)_6-\underset{H}{N}- \;+\; 2HCl$$

part of nylon 6.6 chain

We can simplify the formation of nylon by using A and B to represent the hydrocarbon groups:

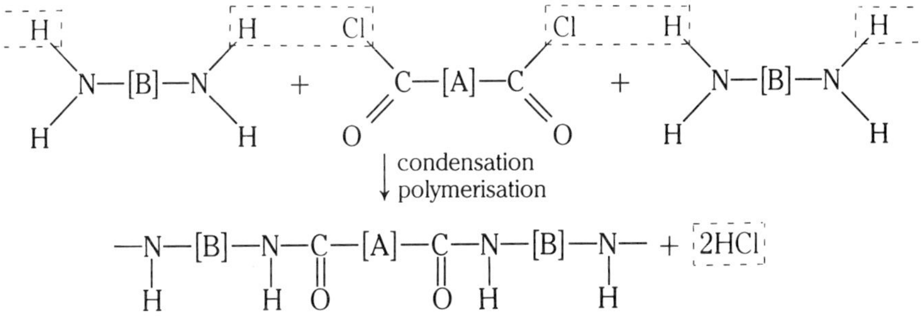

$$\underset{H}{\overset{H}{\diagdown}}N-[B]-N\underset{H}{\overset{H}{\diagup}} \;+\; \underset{O}{\overset{Cl}{\diagdown}}C-[A]-C\underset{O}{\overset{Cl}{\diagup}} \;+\; \underset{H}{\overset{H}{\diagdown}}N-[B]-N\underset{H}{\overset{H}{\diagup}}$$

$$\downarrow \text{condensation polymerisation}$$

$$-\underset{H}{N}-[B]-\underset{H}{N}-\underset{O}{\overset{\|}{C}}-[A]-\underset{O}{\overset{\|}{C}}-\underset{H}{N}-[B]-\underset{H}{N}- \;+\; 2HCl$$

Monomers with a –NH$_2$ and –COOH group can also be used to make a nylon polymer:

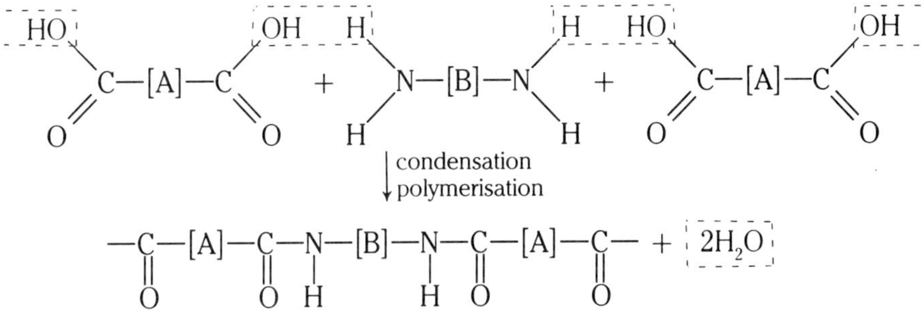

$$\underset{O}{\overset{HO}{\diagdown}}C-[A]-C\underset{O}{\overset{OH}{\diagup}} \;+\; \underset{H}{\overset{H}{\diagdown}}N-[B]-N\underset{H}{\overset{H}{\diagup}} \;+\; \underset{O}{\overset{HO}{\diagdown}}C-[A]-C\underset{O}{\overset{OH}{\diagup}}$$

$$\downarrow \text{condensation polymerisation}$$

$$-\underset{O}{\overset{\|}{C}}-[A]-\underset{O}{\overset{\|}{C}}-\underset{H}{N}-[B]-\underset{H}{N}-\underset{O}{\overset{\|}{C}}-[A]-\underset{O}{\overset{\|}{C}}- \;+\; 2H_2O$$

Notice that the same group appears between each group of hydrocarbons. This is called the **peptide link**. It is also found in all natural **proteins**.

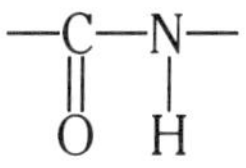

$$-\underset{O}{\overset{\|}{C}}-\underset{H}{N}-$$

the peptide link

204 PLASTICS

The peptide link joins the repeating carbon chains together. When Carothers was doing his research (which led to the discovery of nylon) he was looking for monomers which would link together by forming a peptide link.

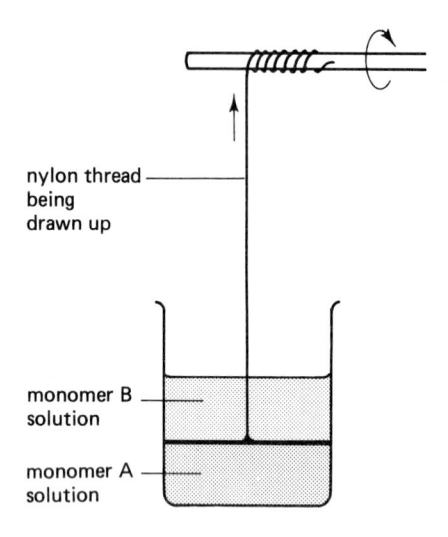

Making nylon in the laboratory

Polyesters

Terylene is an example of a polyester. Polyesters are formed from monomers such as:

$$HO-CH_2-CH_2-OH$$

$$HO-\underset{\parallel}{C}(=O)-(CH_2)_4-\underset{\parallel}{C}(=O)-OH$$

These monomers join as follows:

$$HO-CH_2-CH_2-OH \quad HOOC-(CH_2)_4-COOH \quad HO-CH_2-CH_2-OH$$

↓ condensation polymerisation

$$-O-CH_2-CH_2-O-\underset{\parallel}{C}(=O)-(CH_2)_4-\underset{\parallel}{C}(=O)-O-CH_2-CH_2-O- + 2H_2O$$

Simplifying the molecules:

$$\text{HO-[A]-OH} + \text{HO-}\underset{\text{O}}{\overset{\text{O}}{\text{C}}}\text{-[B]-}\underset{\text{O}}{\overset{\text{O}}{\text{C}}}\text{-OH} + \text{HO-[A]-OH}$$

$$\downarrow$$

$$\text{-O-[A]-O-}\underset{\text{O}}{\overset{\text{O}}{\text{C}}}\text{-[B]-}\underset{\text{O}}{\overset{\text{O}}{\text{C}}}\text{-O-[A]-} + 2H_2O$$

Identifying Monomers from Condensation Polymers

We can identify the monomers in a condensation polymer like nylon by looking for the peptide link. If we split the chain through each peptide link, the repeating units become apparent:

polymer

$$\text{-N-(CH}_2)_6\text{-N-C-(CH}_2)_8\text{-C-N-(CH}_2)_6\text{-N-C-(CH}_2)_8\text{-C-}$$
$$\text{H} \quad\quad \text{H} \;\; \text{O} \quad\quad \text{O} \;\; \text{H} \quad\quad \text{H} \;\; \text{O} \quad\quad\quad \text{O}$$

6.10 nylon

repeating units

$$\text{-N-(CH}_2)_6\text{-N-} \quad + \quad \text{-}\underset{\text{O}}{\overset{}{\text{C}}}\text{-(CH}_2)_8\text{-}\underset{\text{O}}{\overset{}{\text{C}}}\text{-}$$
$$\text{H} \quad\quad\quad \text{H}$$

The formulae for both monomers are still incomplete. We need to replace the simple molecule (HCl or H$_2$O) which was removed when the polymer formed. The monomers could be:

$$\underset{\text{H}}{\overset{\text{H}}{\text{N}}}\text{-(CH}_2)_6\text{-}\underset{\text{H}}{\overset{\text{H}}{\text{N}}} \quad \text{with either} \quad \underset{\text{O}}{\overset{\text{Cl}}{\text{C}}}\text{-(CH}_2)_8\text{-}\underset{\text{O}}{\overset{\text{Cl}}{\text{C}}} \quad \text{or} \quad \underset{\text{O}}{\overset{\text{HO}}{\text{C}}}\text{-(CH}_2)_8\text{-}\underset{\text{O}}{\overset{\text{OH}}{\text{C}}}$$

If the peptide link is not present, you need to study the polymer chain carefully and identify the repeating units:

$$\text{-O-}\underset{\text{O}}{\overset{\text{O}}{\text{C}}}\text{-(CH}_2)_6\text{-}\underset{\text{O}}{\overset{\text{O}}{\text{C}}}\text{-O-(CH}_2)_4\text{-O-}\underset{\text{O}}{\overset{\text{O}}{\text{C}}}\text{-(CH}_2)_6\text{-}\underset{\text{O}}{\overset{\text{O}}{\text{C}}}\text{-O-(CH}_2)_4\text{-O-}\underset{\text{O}}{\overset{\text{O}}{\text{C}}}\text{-(CH}_2)_6\text{-}\underset{\text{O}}{\overset{\text{O}}{\text{C}}}\text{-O-}$$

part of a polyester molecule

The monomers are:

$$\text{HO-(CH}_2)_4\text{-OH} \quad \text{and} \quad \underset{\text{HO}}{\overset{\text{O}}{\text{C}}}\text{-(CH}_2)_6\text{-}\underset{\text{OH}}{\overset{\text{O}}{\text{C}}}$$

Activities

1. (a) Draw the structure of the polymer formed if butene is polymerised.

    $$\begin{array}{cc} CH_3 & CH_3 \\ | & | \\ C\!\!=\!\!\!=\!\!C \\ | & | \\ H & H \end{array}$$

    (b) Name the polymer.

2. Examine the section of polymer chain shown below:

    $$-\underset{H}{\overset{H}{C}}-\underset{Br}{\overset{H}{C}}-\underset{H}{\overset{H}{C}}-\underset{Br}{\overset{H}{C}}-\underset{H}{\overset{H}{C}}-\underset{Br}{\overset{H}{C}}-\underset{H}{\overset{H}{C}}-\underset{Br}{\overset{H}{C}}-\underset{H}{\overset{H}{C}}-\underset{Br}{\overset{H}{C}}-\underset{H}{\overset{H}{C}}-\underset{Br}{\overset{H}{C}}-\underset{H}{\overset{H}{C}}-\underset{Br}{\overset{H}{C}}-$$

    (a) Name the monomer and draw out its structure.
    (b) Name the polymer.

3. (a) Explain the difference between thermosetting and thermoplastic polymers.
    (b) Give examples of how the properties of these polymers can be put to use.

4. Some glues and polymer resins, which come in two separate containers, can be purchased from DIY stores. One container is marked "catalyst".
    (a) What is a catalyst?
    (b) Why are the resin (or glue) and catalyst kept in separate containers?
    (c) What does the catalyst actually do when it is mixed with the substance in the other container?
    (d) Give two possible ways of telling when the catalyst has done its job.

5. (a) Identify the repeating units in the structure below, and draw the monomers involved.

    $$-\underset{O}{\overset{\|}{C}}-(CH_2)_3-\underset{O}{\overset{\|}{C}}-\underset{H}{\overset{|}{N}}-(CH_2)_5-\underset{H}{\overset{|}{N}}-\underset{O}{\overset{\|}{C}}-(CH_2)_3-\underset{O}{\overset{\|}{C}}-\underset{H}{\overset{|}{N}}-(CH_2)_5-\underset{H}{\overset{|}{N}}-\underset{O}{\overset{\|}{C}}-(CH_2)_3-\underset{O}{\overset{\|}{C}}-$$

    (b) Is it an addition or condensation polymer?

6. Chloroethene (C_2H_3Cl) is the monomer used to make the plastic PVC.
    (a) Draw the structural formula of chloroethene.
    (b) Draw a section of a PVC molecule, showing clearly how three of the monomers link together.
    (c) Is the polymer formed by addition or condensation?

7 Shown below is part of the polymer chain of the synthetic fibre sold under the trade name **Orlon**:

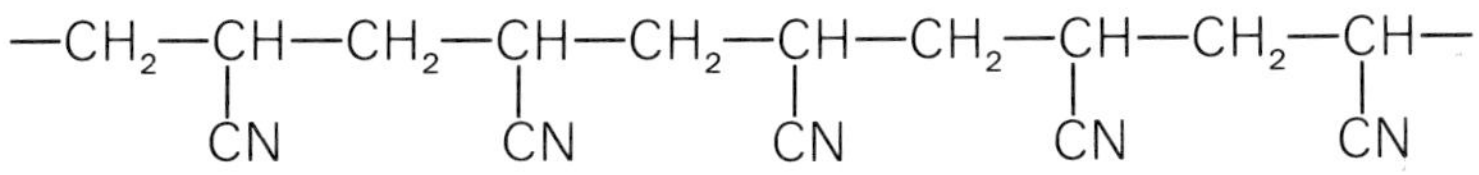

$$-CH_2-CH(CN)-CH_2-CH(CN)-CH_2-CH(CN)-CH_2-CH(CN)-CH_2-CH(CN)-$$

(a) Identify the monomer used to make Orlon.
(b) What type of polymer is Orlon?
(c) All polymers can be dangerous when they burn. What extra danger is there if Orlon burns?

3 Spotlight on Industry

> **Key Ideas**
>
> Chemists and engineers often work together. Once a chemist has made a new material, it is up to the engineer to find ways of using its properties to make useful products the customers will buy.

Processing Thermoplastics

Thermoplastic polymers are often manufactured in long rods, which are then chopped up to form small moulding **granules**. The granules can be melted and processed in a variety of ways to make the finished product.

Injection Moulding

The granules are forced under pressure through a heater to melt them. The molten plastic is **injected** into a mould, which is shaped like the finished article, such as a bowl, a bucket or the parts of an aeroplane construction kit.

The mould is quickly cooled and opened up to reveal the finished article. The mould is emptied, closed and the process begun again. If you look closely at plastic objects you will find a small pimple which has been left just at the point where the liquid plastic was injected into the mould.

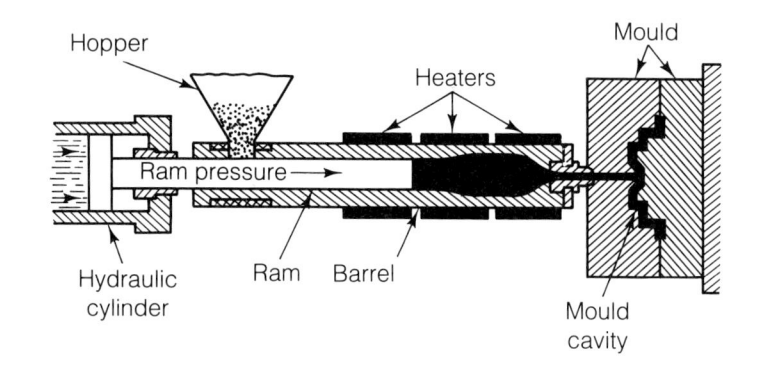

Injection moulding

Extrusion Moulding

In this process the moulding granules are poured into a heated screw which forces the plastic into an extruder. The extruder forces the molten plastic through a **shaped die**, rather like toothpaste coming out of a tube.

The die can be shaped to produce objects like drain pipes or curtain rails. The extruder produces the pipe (or rails) continuously, so it is cut into suitable lengths once the plastic has cooled.

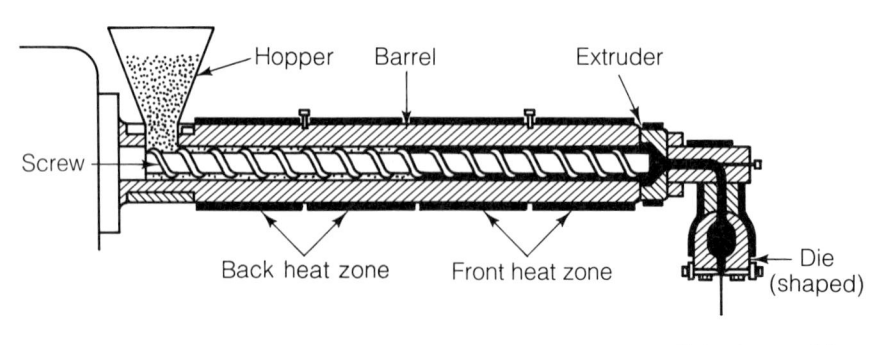

Extrusion moulding

Blow Moulding

Many plastic bottles are now made by **blow** moulding. A lump of warm, soft plastic from an extruder is put into a hollow mould. It is blown up by air pressure until the plastic fills the mould. The thickness of the bottle is determined by the amount of plastic put into the mould.

Blow moulding

Vacuum Forming

Plastic shop signs and many toys are formed by **vacuum** moulding. A sheet of thermoplastic is heated by an electric heater. When the plastic is soft (but not molten) the heater is removed and a mould is pushed up to the sheet. A vacuum is applied which sucks the soft plastic into every corner of the mould. The plastic cools rapidly and is removed when it is rigid.

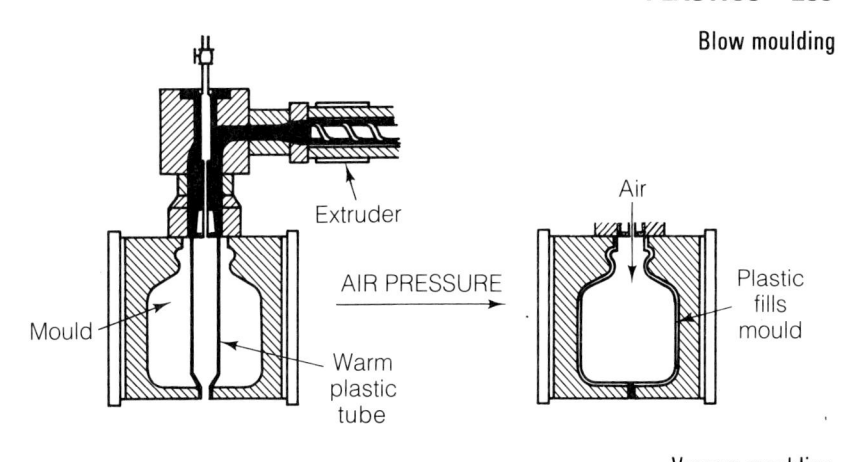

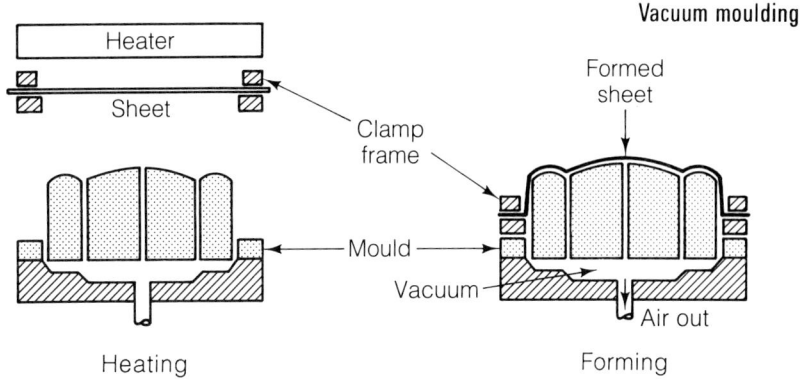

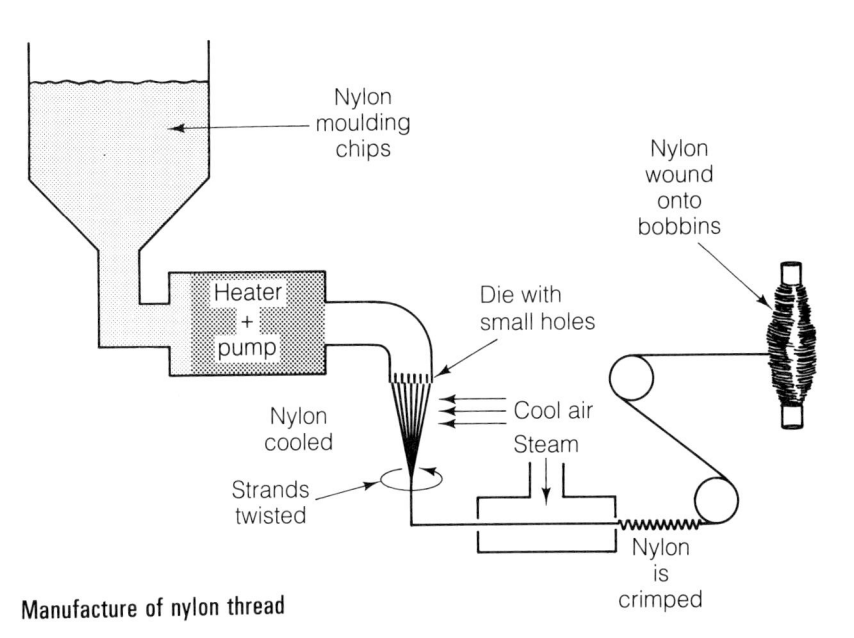

Vacuum moulding

Spinning Synthetic Fibres

Nylon **chips** are converted into nylon **fibres** for weaving into clothing material. The chips are melted and forced through a die made up of small holes, rather like a mincer. Thin strands of nylon are formed, which are cooled and twisted together. The fibres are passed through a steam chamber which crimps the nylon. The nylon is finally wound onto bobbins which feed the weaving machines.

Manufacture of nylon thread

Activities

1. For each of the everyday objects listed below, suggest which method was used to shape them:
   (a) a wellington boot
   (b) a plastic football
   (c) plastic guttering
   (d) a polypropylene rope
   (e) a child's plastic car.

2. Thermosetting polymers cannot be manufactured by any of the methods mentioned in this chapter.
   (a) Explain why.
   (b) How are thermosetting plastic objects manufactured?

Plastics – Study Questions

1 Synthetic materials are widely used in modern society. Name **two** synthetic materials, and state a use for each. **KU**

2 (a) Most polymers are insoluble in water. Some hospitals collect dirty clothing and bedding in bags made from a special polymer which dissolves in hot water. These bags can be sealed and put into washing machines. The risk of infection by touching the dirty material is lowered.

You have been given several samples of different water-soluble polymers, and have been asked to find out which of them dissolves quickest in warm water. You are given these instructions:

1. Pour water into beaker.
2. Add polymer being tested, and start stopclock.
3. Stir, once every 30 seconds.
4. When the polymer has completely dissolved, stop the clock.

It is necessary to make a fair comparison of the different polymers. State **two** factors which must be kept the same in all tests. **PS**

(b) (i) Draw the full structural formula for ethene.
(ii) Draw part of the structure of a poly(ethene) chain to show **three** ethene molecules joined together. **KU**

(c) Poly(ethene) is a thermoplastic. Explain what this means. **KU**

3 Terylene is a synthetic condensation polymer. It is made from the two monomers shown below. (The hexagonal symbol represents a particular group of atoms.)

```
    H  H
    |  |
H—O—C—C—O—H         H—O—C      C—O—H
    |  |                 ‖  ⌬   ‖
    H  H                 O      O
      A                        B
```

These monomer molecules join in the order
—A—B—A—B—

(a) Name the small molecule which is usually a product in a condensation reaction.
(b) Draw the structure of part of the polymer, showing **two** of each monomer unit.
(c) Name any other synthetic condensation polymer
KU

4 The following passage contains information about polymers.

> Most plastics can be made in a variety of processes. One common method is the solution method where the monomer is dissolved in a suitable solvent. This is used for high density poly(ethene), poly(propene), and poly(phenylethene).
>
> Poly(phenylethene), along with polyesters, polyamides and low density poly(ethene) can also be made by the bulk method where the monomer is the reaction fluid.
>
> Another method uses the monomer emulsified in water. This emulsion method is used for poly(chloroethene), poly(tetrafluoroethene), and poly(buta-1,3-diene).
>
> Finally, in the fluid catalysed bed method, used for poly(ethene) and poly(propene), the gaseous monomer flows through the solid catalyst.

Draw a table with columns to present this information. Each column should have a suitable heading. Fill in only **one line** of the table to show what data you would put in each column. **PS**

5 Perspex is as transparent as glass but does not break as easily. The polymer is therefore used to make safety screens, spectacle lenses and aeroplane windows. The following diagram shows part of a perspex molecule.

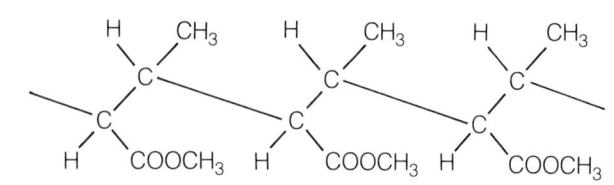

```
     H    CH₃      H    CH₃     H    CH₃
      \  /          \  /         \  /
       C             C            C
      / \           / \          / \
     /   C         /   C        /   C
    H   COOCH₃   H   COOCH₃   H   COOCH₃
```

(a) Draw the structural formula for the repeating unit in perspex.
(b) Draw the structural formula for the monomer used to make perspex.
(c) What type of polymerisation takes place when perspex is produced from its monomer? **KU**

1 The Energy Foods

Carbohydrates

Key Ideas

Glucose, a *carbohydrate*, is made by green *plants* during *photosynthesis*. Carbohydrates are broken down by plants and animals (including humans) during *respiration*. This produces *energy*. Photosynthesis and respiration maintain the balance of oxygen and carbon dioxide in the air. The destruction of *rainforests* and the production of carbon dioxide from *burning fossil fuels* may upset this balance.

Some well-known carbohydrate foods

We Need Energy

"A .... a day helps you work, rest and play." Can you fill in the missing word? This well-known slogan advertises Mars Bars as the chocolate bar which will supply us with energy. Chocolate and sweet tasting foods contain **sugars** such as **glucose** and **sucrose**. Sugars belong to a class of compounds called **carbohydrates**. **Starch** is another carbohydrate. Potatoes and rice contain a lot of starch.

Carbohydrates give us **energy** when they are broken down in our body. This energy keeps us warm and allows us to move about. In Britain, starch supplies around 25 per cent of our food energy needs. The starch comes mainly from vegetables like potatoes and from the wheat in bread. In some parts of the world, like the Far East, starch in the diet provides up to 80 per cent of energy needs. Rice, which has a high starch content, is one of the most common foods.

Take care with the amount of sweet foods you eat. Eating a lot of sweets and cakes can make you overweight. Foods like chocolate and chips also contain **fat**. Fat is high in energy too. If you take in more food than your body can burn up, it is stored inside you – as fat!

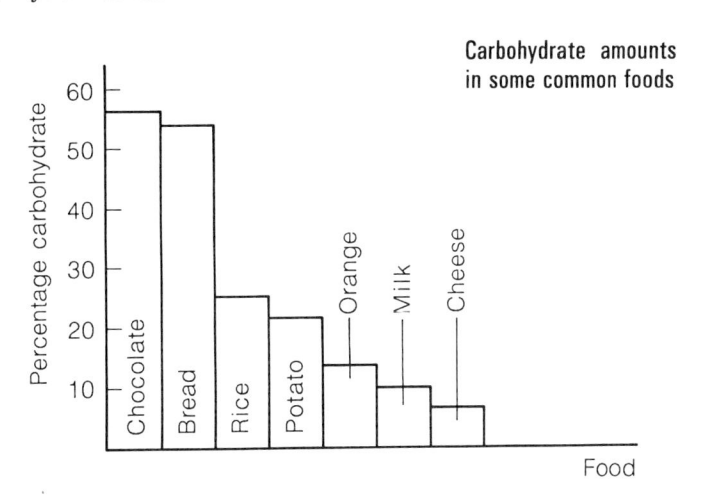

Carbohydrate amounts in some common foods

CARBOHYDRATES

Making Carbohydrates

Green plants make carbohydrates. They take in **carbon dioxide** (CO_2) and **water** (H_2O), which are small molecules, and change them into larger, more complicated carbohydrate molecules. This process usually needs **light**. Green leaves contain a chemical called **chlorophyll**, which absorbs the light energy needed for the reactions. Plants **produce oxygen** at the same time as the carbohydrate. The gas is released into the atmosphere. This whole process is known as **photosynthesis**.

Carbohydrates are made up of carbon, hydrogen and oxygen. These elements come from the carbon dioxide and water. Glucose is one of the smallest carbohydrate molecules and has the formula $C_6H_{12}O_6$. Starch molecules vary in size and can be up to **one million** times bigger than a glucose molecule.

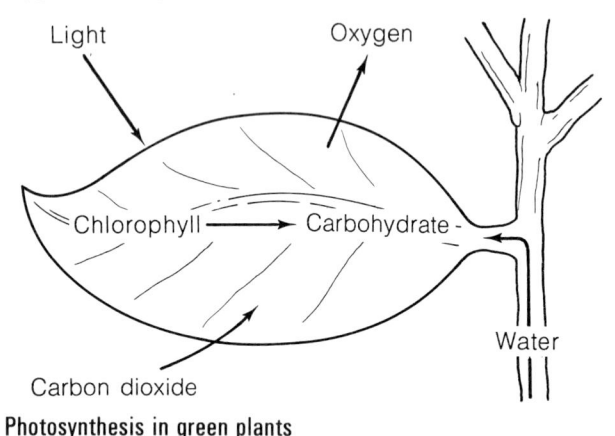

Photosynthesis in green plants

$$\text{carbon dioxide} + \text{water} \xrightarrow[\text{chlorophyll}]{\text{light}} \text{carbohydrate} + \text{oxygen}$$

Energy from Carbohydrates

The energy we get from carbohydrates is released only after a series of complicated reactions involving **oxygen**. These reactions take place in our body **cells**. Oxygen gets into the blood from our lungs. Large carbohydrate molecules like starch are broken down into smaller molecules like glucose in our digestive system. The smaller molecules pass from the small intestine into the blood. Carbohydrate and oxygen then pass into the body cells. Glucose and oxygen react producing carbon dioxide and water as chemical waste products, which are breathed out. This is known as **respiration**.

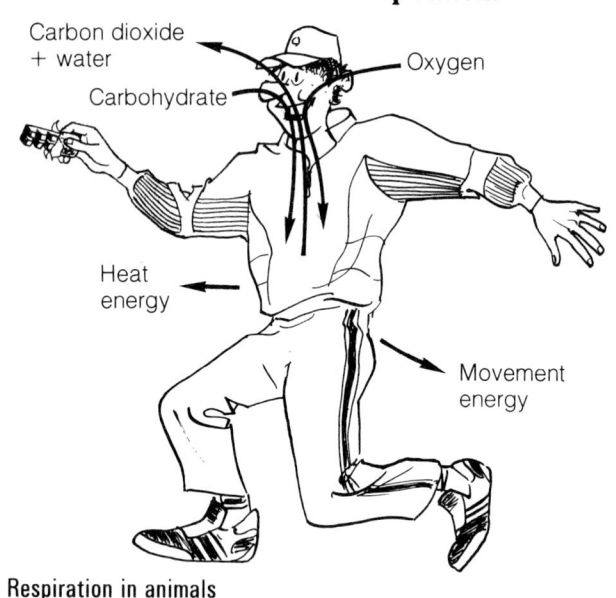

Respiration in animals

$$\text{carbohydrate} + \text{oxygen} \rightarrow \text{carbon dioxide} + \text{water}$$

Respiration in the Lab

We can carry out some simple experiments to show that energy is produced when a carbohydrate burns, and that carbon dioxide and water are the chemical waste products.

1 The Exploding Can

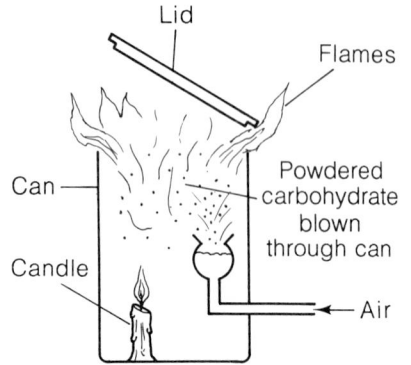

When air is blown through the carbohydrate, the mixture catches fire and explodes

2 Burning Carbohydrates

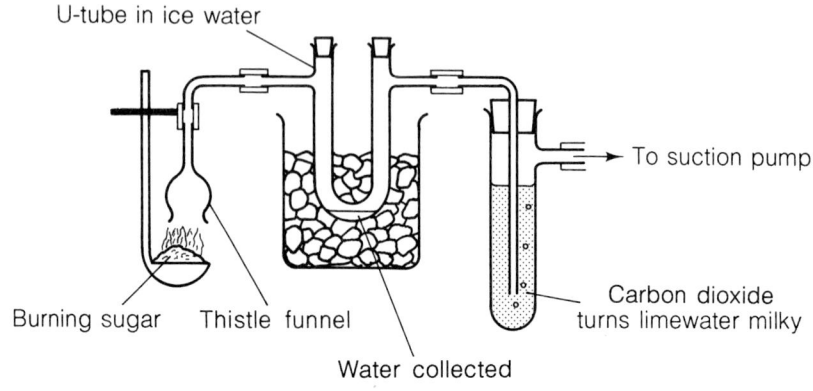

Burning carbohydrate produces carbon dioxide and water

CARBOHYDRATES

3 Breathed Air

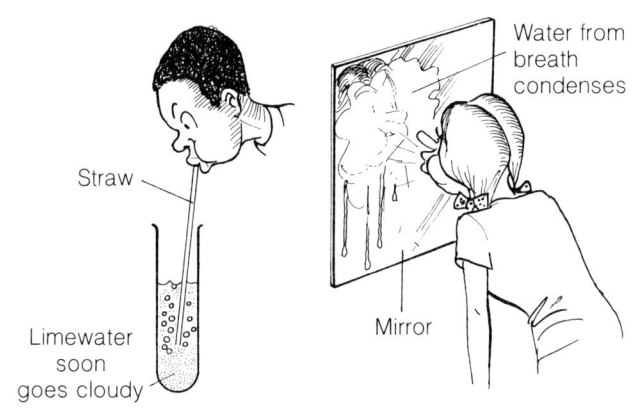

Breathed air contains both carbon dioxide and water vapour

Plants Need Energy

Plants use some of the carbohydrate made during photosynthesis to produce energy. They undergo respiration at night.

The energy is needed for important reactions which help the plant cells to develop and multiply.

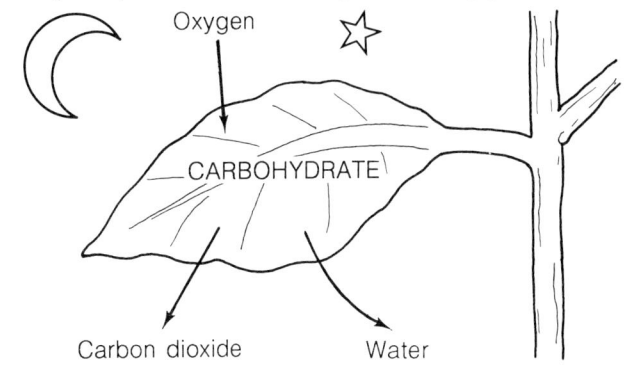

Plant respiration happens at night

Maintaining the Balance

A closer look at photosynthesis and respiration shows that the two are **chemically opposite** reactions:

Respiration: carbohydrate + oxygen → carbon dioxide + water
Photosynthesis: carbon dioxide + water → carbohydrate + oxygen

Plants give oxygen to us, and in return we give carbon dioxide to the plants.

Plants and animals are dependent on each other. Air consists of around 21 per cent oxygen and 0.035 per cent carbon dioxide. Plants and animals between them maintain this balance of gases. What happens if the balance is upset?

Scientists have found that the concentration of carbon dioxide in the atmosphere is increasing. Animals breathe out carbon dioxide but it is also produced by **burning fossil fuels** (mainly coal). Some scientists believe that the build up of carbon dioxide has created the **greenhouse effect** (see Fuels and Hydrocarbons, page 54).

In 1957, carbon dioxide made up about 0.0315 per cent of the atmosphere. In 1989 this had risen to 0.035 per cent. Although most of this increase is due to burning fossil fuels, some of the increase may have been caused by the destruction of **tropical rainforests**. These huge numbers of trees absorb a lot of the carbon dioxide we produce.

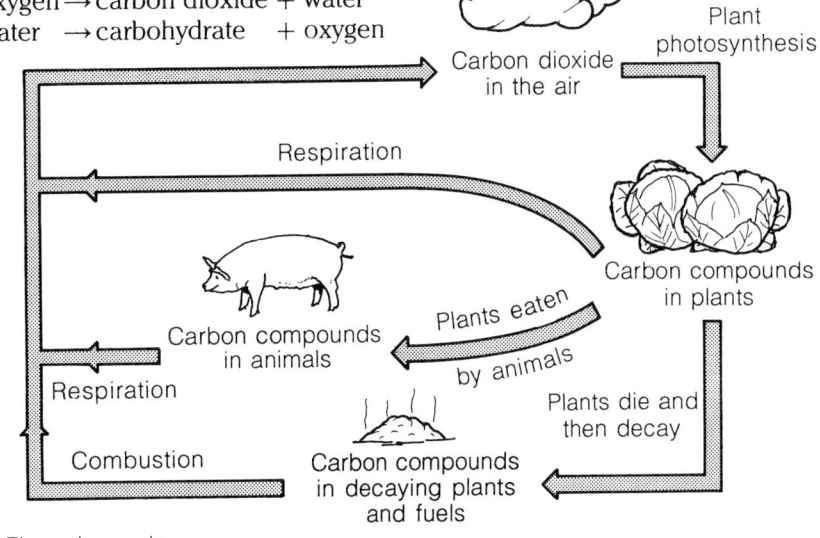

The carbon cycle

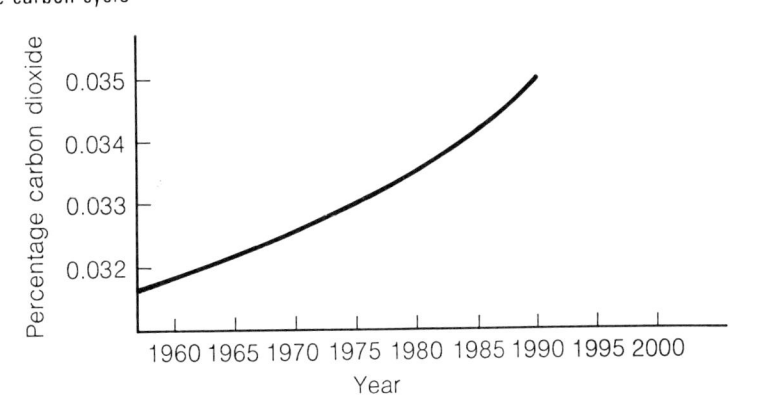

The build up of carbon dioxide in the atmosphere

The Rainforests

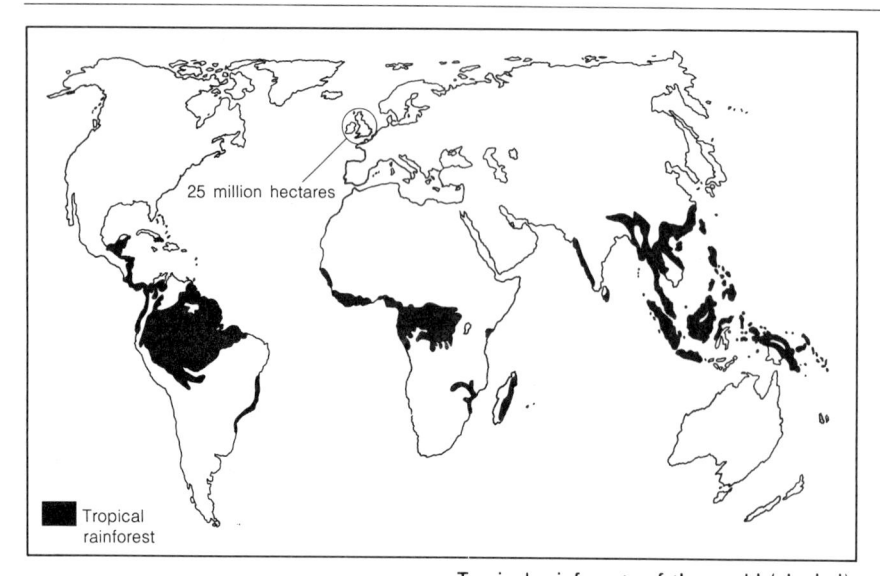

Tropical rainforests of the world (shaded)

The rainforests cover about 9 million square kilometres of the tropical zone – an area nearly the size of the USA. Almost half this area lies in Central and South America. At present, an area the size of England and Wales is being destroyed every year. At this rate, the rainforests will vanish within 40 years.

The trees are cut down for timber, which is used in the construction and furniture industries. Areas of forest are also cleared by people desperate for land on which to grow crops and make a living. Vast areas have also been flooded to build hydroelectric power schemes.

Nobody really thinks that all these activities can suddenly be stopped. However, groups like Friends of the Earth believe that if people in the construction industry (and even do-it-yourself enthusiasts) use **board materials** (made from wood grown in Europe) then far fewer rainforests would have to be cut down. At least it might slow the destruction down until the forest could be managed properly. You can help by refusing to buy tropical hardwoods, or furniture made from them. Alternatives are available!

Conservationists argue that it is not only the carbon dioxide/oxygen balance that is being affected. Rainforests behave like a gigantic "sponge", absorbing the heavy rain of the tropical regions and then gradually releasing it. Without the forests, heavy rain causes soil erosion and severe flooding. Soil erosion partly caused by deforestation has begun to fill the Panama Canal with silt.

Although tropical rainforests cover only 7 per cent of the Earth, they contain half of all known species of plants and animals. Indian tribes also live deep in the forests, as they have done for thousands of years. Destroying the rainforests will destroy all of these.

Don't Desert The Rainforest

TROPICAL RAINFORESTS are the greatest reservoirs of life on the planet. They cover just seven per cent of the Earth's surface, yet hold half of all known species – and many more which have still to be discovered. Every day we use products from the forests: timber, rubber, bananas, chewing gum and coffee, to name but a few. Many key drugs, from curare to contraceptives, derive from rainforest plants and more are found each year; yet only 1% of the species in the forests have been examined for economic usefulness.

Rainforests are a vital part of the web of life. They protect fragile soils from erosion, prevent rivers flooding and have a profound influence on rainfall. Cutting them down creates a sterile desert. Even in Scotland, far away from the tropical zone, we are still dependent on its forests. If they are destroyed, the world's climate will change, with catastrophic consequences for us all.

Despite all their riches and benefits, the rainforests are under threat as never before. Every minute 100 acres are destroyed, an area the size of England and Wales each year.

Groups like Friends of the Earth are fighting to save the rainforests

Activities

1. Carbohydrates and oxygen are made in green plants, when carbon dioxide and water react in the presence of light.
   (a) Name this process.
   (b) Write a word equation for the process.
   (c) What part does light and chlorophyll (green chemical) play in the process?
   (d) Name **two** sources of carbon dioxide in the air.
   (e) Explain why the process in (a) is so important to us.

2. The carbohydrates we eat react in the body to produce energy. Carbon dioxide and water are the chemical products.
   (a) Name this process.
   (b) Write a word equation for the process.
   (c) Explain why the chemical products from this process are important to plants.
   (d) Explain why the process you named in (a) also takes place in plants.

3. Look at the line graph on page 213, which shows how the amount of atmospheric carbon dioxide has changed this century.
   (a) From the graph, predict what the percentage of carbon dioxide in the atmosphere will be in 2000 assuming it continues to increase at the present rate.
   (b) Suggest what might cause carbon dioxide levels to rise to your predicted value.
   (c) Describe the effects of increasing the amount of carbon dioxide in the atmosphere upon the Earth.
   (d) Outline what can be done **now** to cut down on the amount of carbon dioxide going into the atmosphere.

4. You are asked to write an article for your school magazine giving a balanced view on the effects of destroying the rainforests. Write a report, giving reasons why some people say forest areas have to be cleared and why some argue that it is essential to control the destruction.

2 A Closer Look at Carbohydrates

Key Ideas

Carbohydrates are made up of **carbon, hydrogen** and **oxygen**. There are **twice** as many hydrogen atoms as oxygen in each carbohydrate molecule. Some carbohydrates are **sweet** tasting and dissolve in water; others are not sweet and do not form true solutions. Carbohydrates can be classified as *monosaccharides*, *disaccharides* and *polysaccharides*. We can identify different types of carbohydrates by carrying out chemical tests.

Formulae for Carbohydrates

The previous section gave examples of foods which contain carbohydrates. Table 8.1 gives the names and formulae of some carbohydrates found in food.

Table 8.1

Name	Formula
Fructose	$C_6H_{12}O_6$
Glucose	$C_6H_{12}O_6$
Maltose	$C_{12}H_{22}O_{11}$
Sucrose	$C_{12}H_{22}O_{11}$
Starch	$(C_6H_{10}O_5)_n$

where n is a very large number

Table 8.1 shows that all the carbohydrates contain the elements **carbon, hydrogen** and **oxygen**. Look carefully at the number of hydrogen and oxygen atoms in each compound. There are **twice** as many hydrogen atoms as oxygen in each case. This is the same for **all** carbohydrates.

Isomerism

Some carbohydrates in table 8.1 have the same formula but different names. They are different molecules because they have different structures. They are **isomers**. Hydrocarbon molecules can also have isomers (see Fuels and Hydrocarbons, page 65).

The structures of carbohydrates are very complicated. Count the atoms in the glucose and fructose structures shown here to check that they do have the same number of carbon, hydrogen and oxygen atoms in their molecules.

Glucose (left) and fructose (right) are isomers

Grouping Carbohydrates

Carbohydrates are classified according to the number of carbon atoms in the molecule. The simplest carbohydrates have the formula $C_6H_{12}O_6$. They are **monosaccharides** ("one-sugar"). When two monosaccharides join they form a **disaccharide** ("two-sugars"). When thousands of monosaccharides join together they form giant molecules (or polymers) called **polysaccharides** ("many-sugars"). Table 8.2 gives some examples of the different types of saccharide.

Table 8.2

Monosaccharides $C_6H_{12}O_6$	Disaccharides $C_{12}H_{22}O_{11}$	Polysaccharides $(C_6H_{10}O_5)_n$
fructose galactose glucose	lactose maltose sucrose	cellulose glycogen starch

Properties of Carbohydrates

Many foods and drinks are sweet tasting. Often this is because they contain carbohydrates like glucose and sucrose which are **sweet** tasting and **dissolve** in water to form a solution. Sweet carbohydrates are often called **sugars**. The sugar you may have in your tea or on breakfast cereal is actually **sucrose**.

Too many sugary drinks can make us fat. Many soft drinks now contain artificial sweeteners instead of sugars. Although they taste sweet they don't make us fat. Next time you

CARBOHYDRATES

A beam of light shows up in the starch "solution" – this is called the Tyndall effect

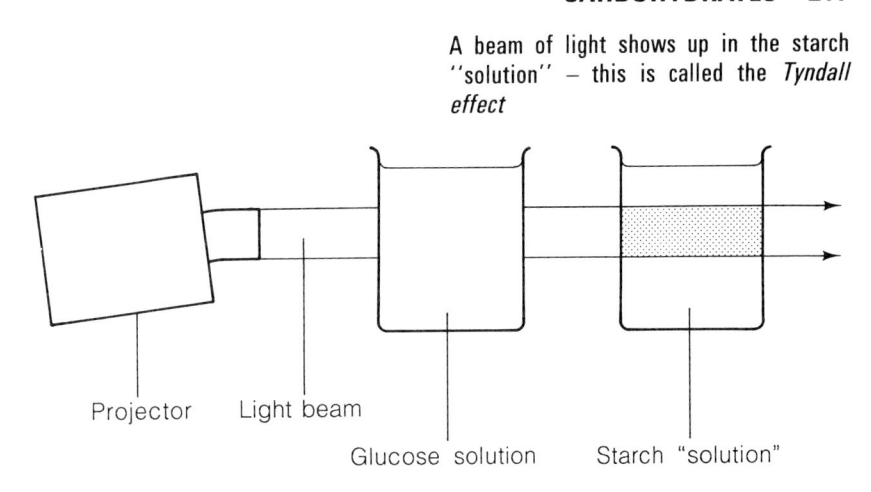

Lucozade contains glucose to give us energy

have a soft drink look out for artificial sweeteners like **saccharin** and **aspartame** in the ingredients.

INGREDIENTS:
CARBONATED WATER, COLOUR (CARAMEL), ARTIFICIAL SWEETENER (ASPARTAME), PHOSPHORIC ACID, FLAVOURINGS, CITRIC ACID, PRESERVATIVE (E211), CAFFEINE

Many diet drinks contain artificial sweeteners

Starch is **not sweet** tasting. Flour contains a lot of starch. Bread is not sweet tasting. If a small amount of starch is added to water and mixed thoroughly, it seems to dissolve. If a glucose solution (a true solution) is placed beside the starch "solution" you can't tell them apart. However, if you shine a beam of light through them both, you can see a difference. The light beam shows up in the starch, but not in the glucose solution.

Starch does not form a true solution when mixed with water. The starch molecules are too **big** to dissolve properly.

Testing Carbohydrates

Many carbohydrates look very similar as solids and in solution. We can identify them only by carrying out chemical tests.

Iodine Test

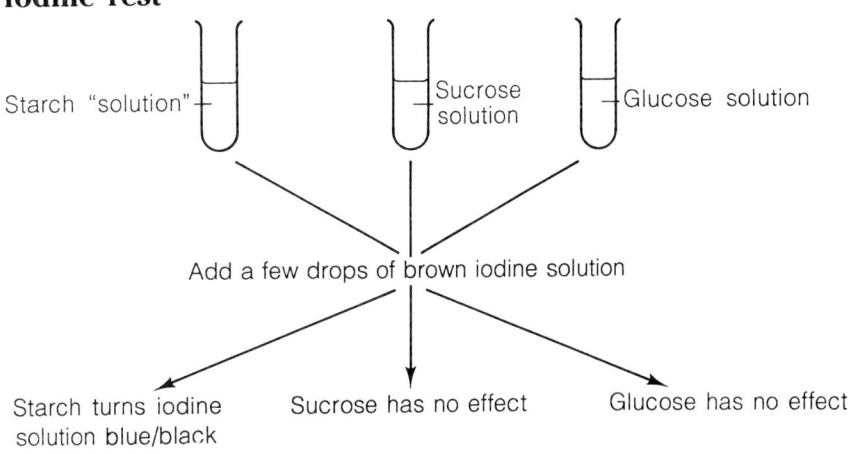

Starch "solution" / Sucrose solution / Glucose solution

Add a few drops of brown iodine solution

Starch turns iodine solution blue/black | Sucrose has no effect | Glucose has no effect

Iodine solution can be used to test for starch

Only starch turns **brown iodine** solution a **blue/black** colour. Iodine solution can be used to test for starch.

Benedict's Test

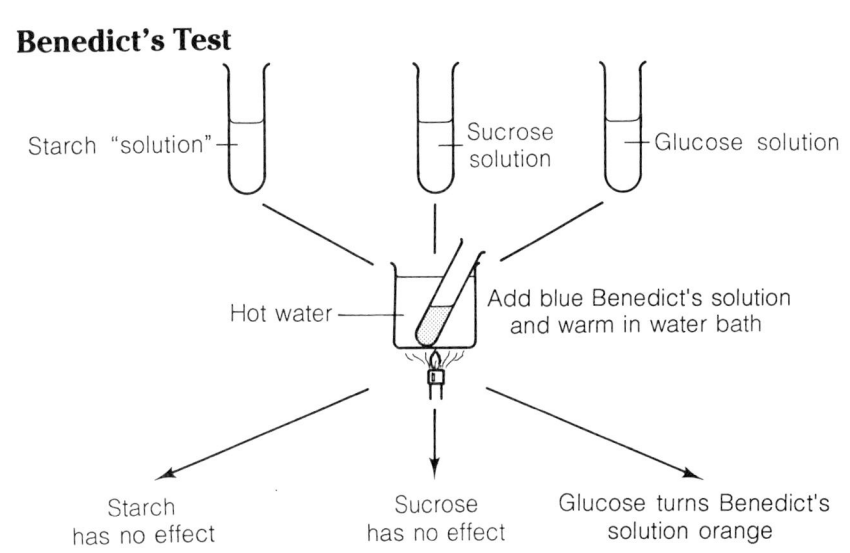

Starch "solution" / Sucrose solution / Glucose solution

Hot water — Add blue Benedict's solution and warm in water bath

Starch has no effect | Sucrose has no effect | Glucose turns Benedict's solution orange

Benedict's solution can be used to tell glucose from starch and sucrose

CARBOHYDRATES

Only **glucose** turns **blue Benedict's** solution **orange** (or brown). **Fehling's** solution, which is similar to Benedict's, gives the same result. The Benedict's test can be used to tell glucose from sucrose and starch. However, it is not just a test for glucose. Other sugars, like fructose, give the same result.

Reducing Sugars

Sugars which turn Benedict's solution orange are called **reducing** sugars. Fructose, glucose, lactose and maltose are all reducing sugars. However, sucrose is a **non-reducing** sugar.

Benedict's solution contains blue Cu^{2+} **(aq)** ions. When Benedict's solution reacts with a reducing sugar, the Cu^{2+} ion gains an electron and is **reduced** to the Cu^{+} ion.

$$Cu^{2+} + e \rightarrow Cu^{+}$$

Copper(I) oxide is formed. This is the orange (sometimes brown) colour seen.

Activities

○ 1

A C_6H_{12}	B Fructose	C Starch
D $C_{12}H_{22}O_{11}$	E C_2H_5OH	F Glucose

Which box (or boxes) in the grid contains the name or formula of:
(a) a carbohydrate?
(b) a disaccharide?
(c) a polysaccharide?
(d) a molecule which would give a positive test with Benedict's solution?

○ 2 You are given three white powders: one is starch, another glucose and the third sucrose. Outline tests you would do to identify each powder.

◐ 3 You are given a job as a "sweetness tester" in a chocolate factory. The job involves making solutions of different sugars and tasting them in order to compare sweetness. Describe exactly how you would prepare solutions of fructose and sucrose in order to do a **fair** sweetness test on each.

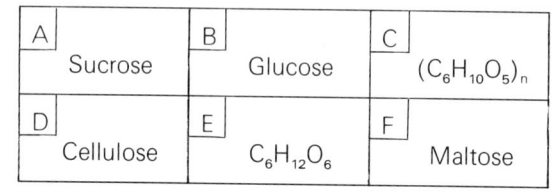

● 4

A Sucrose	B Glucose	C $(C_6H_{10}O_5)_n$
D Cellulose	E $C_6H_{12}O_6$	F Maltose

Which box (or boxes) in the grid contains the name or formula of:
(a) a molecule which does not give a positive test with Benedict's solution?
(b) an isomer of lactose ($C_{12}H_{22}O_{11}$)?
(c) a reducing sugar?

● 5 We can show that starch is made in the leaves of green plants as follows:
1 Boil a leaf in water for a few minutes.
2 Immerse the leaf in alcohol to take out the green colour.
3 Rinse the leaf and test for starch.

Given two identical plants and any chemicals you need, describe how you would prove that plants usually need **light**, in order to make starch.

3 Making and Breaking Carbohydrates

Key Ideas

Small carbohydrate molecules like glucose undergo *condensation polymerisation* to form giant carbohydrate molecules like starch. Starch itself can be *hydrolysed* (broken down) into smaller molecules in the laboratory using *acid*. *Enzymes* in the body *digest* the food we eat. Carbohydrates are hydrolysed by the enzymes. Mixtures of carbohydrates can be separated and identified using *paper chromatography*.

Making Large Molecules

In Plastics and Synthetic Fibres you read about **plastics** which are made up of large molecules (or polymers), formed when lots of small molecules (monomers) join together. Similar reactions happen in nature. Glucose ($C_6H_{12}O_6$) is made when small carbon dioxide (CO_2) and water (H_2O) molecules join during photosynthesis. Thousands of glucose molecules then join together to make **starch**, sometimes called "polyglucose". This process of joining small molecules together is called **polymerisation**.

small glucose molecules (monomers) —polymerisation→ large starch molecules (polymers)

A Closer Look at Polymerisation

When two glucose molecules join together, the disaccharide **maltose** is formed and one molecule of **water**.

$$\underset{C_6H_{12}O_6}{\text{glucose}} + \underset{C_6H_{12}O_6}{\text{glucose}} \rightarrow \underset{C_{12}H_{22}O_{11}}{\text{maltose}} + \underset{H_2O}{\text{water}}$$

Carbohydrates have very complicated structures. We can simplify the structure to let us see more easily how two small carbohydrate molecules join together. We can represent the glucose molecules by: HO—⬡—OH

We can then rewrite the equation above as:

HO—⬡—OH HO—⬡—OH
↓
HO—⬡—O—⬡—OH + H₂O

We can clearly see where the water molecules come from and how the two molecules join. We can extend the equation to starch molecules, which are made up of thousands of glucose molecules. However, it is difficult to show so many molecules joining. Three are shown below, but the rest of the glucose molecules join in exactly the same way.

HO—⬡—OH + HO—⬡—OH + HO—⬡—OH
↓
—O—⬡—O—⬡—O—⬡— + 2H₂O
part of a starch molecule

Polymers formed in this way are known as **condensation polymers.** The monomers join with the removal of a small molecule like water.

Chemical Detective!

We can prove that starch is a polymer of glucose by breaking down the starch molecules and then testing for glucose. This is done as follows:

Stage 1
Starch is broken down in the laboratory by boiling it with **dilute hydrochloric acid** for 15 minutes.

Stage 2
The broken down starch is tested with Benedict's solution.

Glucose, however, is not the only sugar that will give a positive test with Benedict's solution. Fructose and maltose also will. To show without doubt that only glucose has been formed we must use **paper chromatography**.

220 CARBOHYDRATES

Stage 3
Setting up a Chromatogram

1. A drop of broken down starch, and drops of known sugar solutions are spotted onto a piece of **chromatography paper**, and dried with a hair dryer.

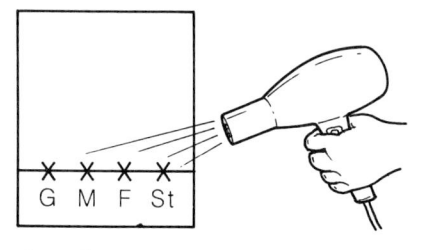

G = glucose
M = maltose
F = fructose
St = broken down starch

2. The paper is placed in a **tank of solvent**. The solvent moves slowly up the paper. The sugar spots travel up the paper with the solvent, but at **different rates**. The chromatogram is stopped when the solvent is almost at the top of the paper.

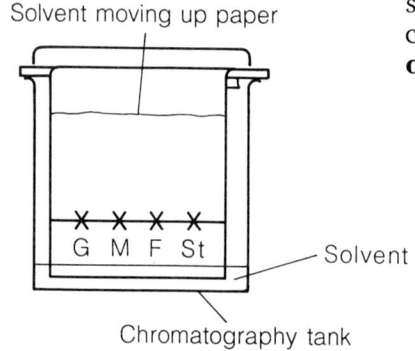

Solvent moving up paper
Solvent
Chromatography tank

3. The paper is removed and dried. At this stage the carbohydrate spots are invisible. The paper is dipped in a special solution, which colours the spots. The broken down starch spot and the glucose spot have travelled the **same** distance up the paper. This shows that broken down starch contains **glucose** molecules **only**.

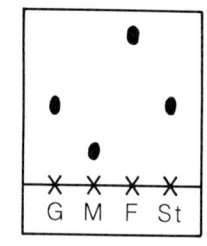

Digestion

The food molecules we eat are broken down in our body. This is called **digestion**. **Biological catalysts** called **enzymes** digest the food. Chemical digestion of carbohydrates starts in the mouth. Saliva contains the enzyme **amylase**. Amylase breaks down giant molecules into small molecules.

Digestion continues in the stomach and small intestine. Glucose molecules eventually pass through the small intestine and into the blood, where they are absorbed into the body cells. Any undigested food, and water, passes into the large intestine, where the water and salts are absorbed into the body. The undigested food is stored in the rectum and eventually passes out through the anus.

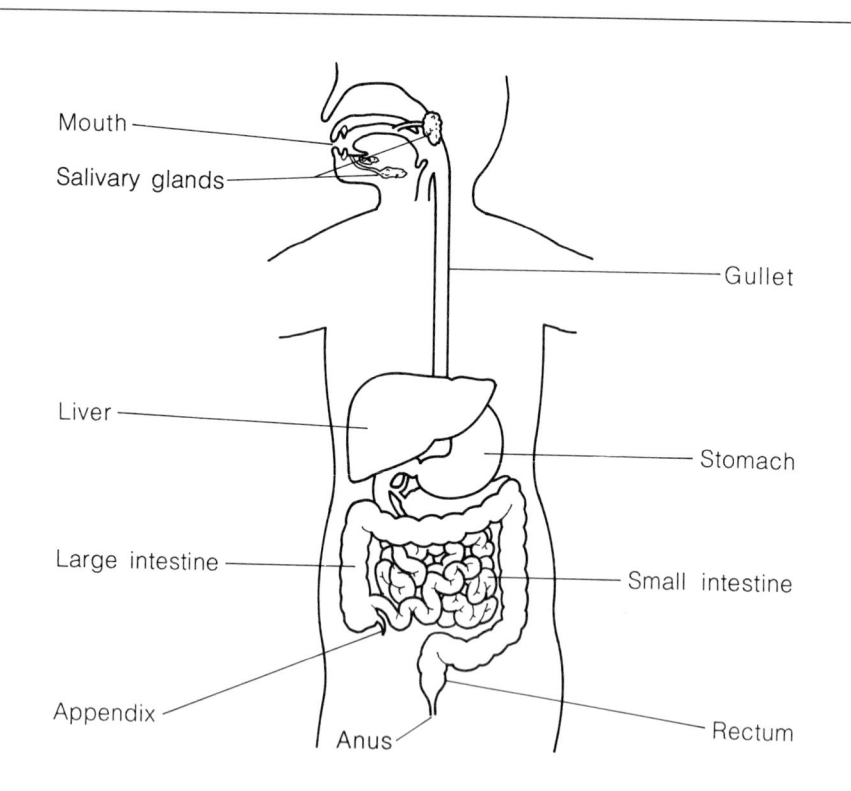

The human digestive system

Digestion in the Lab

We can show the action of amylase on starch in the laboratory.

The enzyme works best at around 37°C (body temperature), a much lower temperature than acid normally requires (see page 219). Enzymes are very efficient catalysts at this temperature.

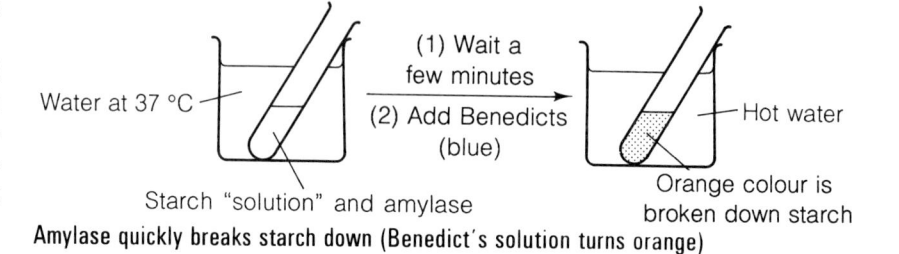

Water at 37 °C
(1) Wait a few minutes
(2) Add Benedicts (blue)
Hot water
Starch "solution" and amylase
Orange colour is broken down starch

Amylase quickly breaks starch down (Benedict's solution turns orange)

Absorption of Glucose

The glucose formed during digestion passes through the walls of the small intestine and into the blood. We can set up an experiment in the laboratory to model this. **Visking** tubing (plastic tubing with many tiny holes in it) represents the wall of the **small intestine**. The **water** in the large test tube represents our blood. The water in the test tube is tested with Benedict's solution and iodine at the start of the experiment and again after 30 minutes.

The starch molecules are too big to pass through the holes in the visking tubing. However, the glucose molecules are smaller and can pass through the visking tubing (small intestine) into the water (blood).

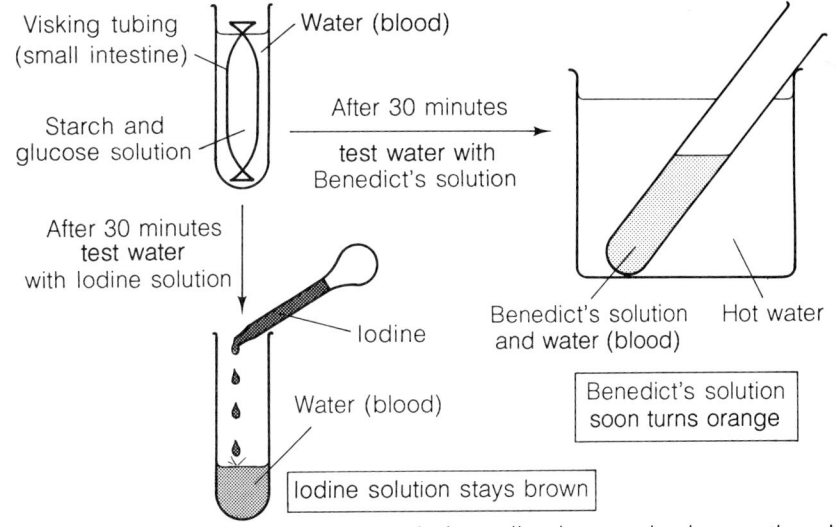

Absorption of glucose in the laboratory – only the smaller glucose molecules pass through the intestine

Hydrolysis

When a carbohydrate is broken down into smaller carbohydrate molecules, we say it has been **hydrolysed**. When starch is formed from glucose (by condensation polymerisation) water molecules are also produced. It is therefore reasonable to assume that when starch is broken down into glucose molecules, **water is added** back again (hydrolysis).

(The dashed lines show where hydrolysis occurs.) The water comes from the acid or enzyme **solution**.

Sucrose is a disaccharide formed when a **fructose** and a **glucose** molecule join together:

glucose + fructose → sucrose + water
$C_6H_{12}O_6 + C_6H_{12}O_6 \rightarrow C_{12}H_{22}O_{11} + H_2O$

This is a **condensation** reaction. When sucrose is **hydrolysed**, glucose and fructose are reformed:

sucrose $\xrightarrow[\text{or enzyme solution}]{\text{acid}}$ glucose + fructose

$C_{12}H_{22}O_{11} \rightarrow C_6H_{12}O_6 + C_6H_{12}O_6$

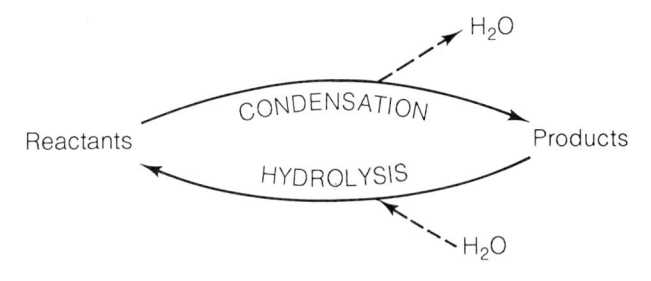

Condensation and hydrolysis are opposite reactions

Although they have the same chemical formula, glucose and fructose have different structures. They are **isomers**. A paper chromatogram of hydrolysed sucrose confirms that sucrose is made from fructose and glucose molecules.

HS = hydrolysed sucrose
G = glucose
F = fructose
M = maltose

A paper chromatogram of hydrolysed sucrose

222 CARBOHYDRATES

Making Jam

Making jam, both at home and in a factory, involves the breaking down of some sucrose into glucose and fructose. The jam mixture is about 60 per cent sugar (sucrose) and the rest is water and fruit. The mixture is heated to 105°C. At this temperature some of the sucrose reacts with water and breaks down into glucose and fructose. The acid in the fruit acts as a catalyst. The jam is therefore a mixture of sucrose, glucose and fructose. This is important because the mixture is much more soluble in water than just sucrose. This means that the sugar (sucrose) will not crystallize out when the jam is put into jars and allowed to set.

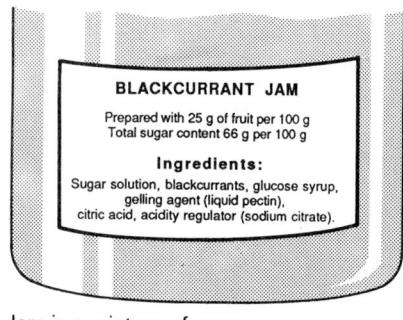

Bees make honey by breaking down sucrose. They use **enzymes** in their body to break down the sugar in the nectar collected from flowers.

BLACKCURRANT JAM
Prepared with 25 g of fruit per 100 g
Total sugar content 66 g per 100 g
Ingredients:
Sugar solution, blackcurrants, glucose syrup, gelling agent (liquid pectin), citric acid, acidity regulator (sodium citrate).

Jam is a mixture of sugars

Enzymes in Industry

Yeasts and their enzymes have been used for thousands of years to bake bread and brew beer. Today we find that there are many more ways in which we can use enzymes. Research into **biotechnology** aims at producing better and cheaper drugs, new types of food and alternative sources of energy. Table 8.3 shows some important industrial enzymes and their uses.

Table 8.3

Enzyme	Use
Invertase	Making soft centred chocolates
Lipase	Improving the flavour of ice-cream, cheese and chocolate
Proteases (bacterial)	Biological detergents
Rennin	Cheese production
Penicillin acylase	Semi-synthetic penicillin (a medical drug)

Using enzymes in large scale processes has improved production methods for some products. Some processes, such as brewing beer, are done in **batches**. Beer uses enzymes produced by yeast microbes to ferment sugar into alcohol (see page 230). This is usually done in a fermenting vessel. Only one lot of product is made at a time because the reaction vessel has to be cleaned out after each batch.

For some processes it is now possible to fix the microbes in one place and use them over and over again. This is a **continuous** process. For example, glucose can be obtained by breaking up sucrose using the enzyme **invertase** (found in yeast). The process is often called **inversion**. The glucose, which is much sweeter and more soluble than sucrose, is then used to make sweets. We can make a model of continuous inversion of sucrose in the laboratory.

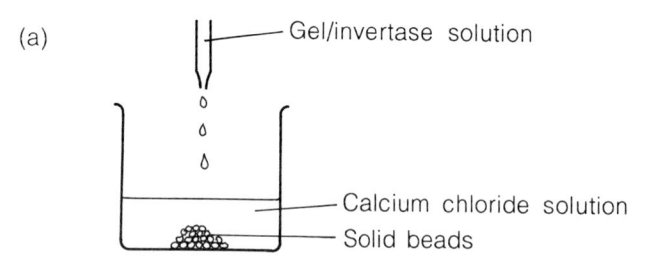

(a) Gel/invertase solution
Calcium chloride solution
Solid beads

Special solid beads of gel containing the enzyme are made by dropping a gel/invertase mixture into calcium chloride solution

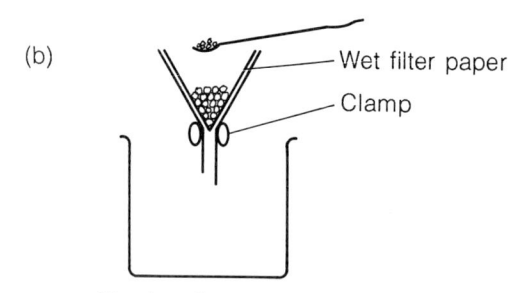

(b) Wet filter paper
Clamp

The beads are transferred into a filter funnel

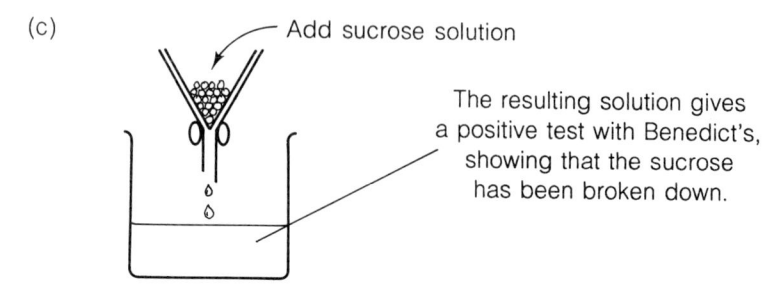

(c) Add sucrose solution

The resulting solution gives a positive test with Benedict's, showing that the sucrose has been broken down.

Sucrose solution is poured through the beads. This is repeated several times.

The continuous inversion of sucrose in the laboratory

Activities

1. Starch can be broken down into glucose molecules by acid or enzymes. Describe how you could prove that enzymes are much more efficient at lower temperatures. (Make it clear how you reached your conclusion.)

2. Glycogen is a carbohydrate which can be broken down by enzymes into smaller carbohydrate molecules. Describe how you could use paper chromatography to show that the small molecules formed are glucose molecules.

3. Describe what happens to the starch molecules in a piece of bread, from when it enters your mouth to when it finally reacts to give you energy.

4. (a) "Batch" and "continuous" are both methods of making an industrial product. Name one advantage the continuous process has over the batch.
   (b) Glucose is used to make a variety of sweets. It is more expensive to buy than sucrose. Describe how a sweet manufacturer can use enzymes to help reduce his costs.
   (c) Describe the problems you think there will be when scaling up the enzyme inversion of sucrose in the laboratory to large scale industrial manufacture.
   (d) Suggest **two** things you might try, to make the inversion of sucrose faster.

5. Glucose and fructose molecules can be represented as:

   HO—⬡—OH   HO—⬢—OH
   glucose   fructose

   (a) Use these representations to show what happens when a glucose and fructose molecule join together.
   (b) Name this kind of reaction.
   (c) Part of the glycogen molecule can be represented as:

   —O—⬡—O—⬡—O—⬡—O—

   Show, clearly, what happens to the molecule when glycogen is broken down in our body to form glucose.
   (d) Name this kind of reaction.
   (e) What is it that breaks down glycogen in the body?

4 Alcohol

Key Ideas

Alcohol can be made by adding yeast to any fruit or vegetable containing *starch* or *sugar*. Yeast is a living organism and its *enzymes* can change *carbohydrates* into alcohol. The process is known as *fermentation*. The efficiency of an enzyme depends on the *pH* of the solution. High *temperature* can also affect it. The alcohol/water mixture formed during fermentation can be *distilled* to concentrate the alcohol. Alcoholic *drinks* dull the body's senses. Alcohol can be used in cars, instead of petrol.

Both these newspaper articles are about the same thing – **alcohol**. There are different "families" of alcohols. However, the alcohol found in drinks such as beer and whisky is the same one which is used as fuel. It is called **ethanol**. It belongs to the **alkanol** family.

Alcohol as a Fuel

In the 1970s, the Brazilian Government decided to convert sugar cane (sucrose) to alcohol on a large scale, to use as fuel. The decision was made for several reasons:
1. To save money being spent on expensive foreign oil.
2. Many jobs would be created by growing huge amounts of sugar cane.
3. Any excess ethanol could be sold abroad.

The Good and the Bad

Young biker had too much alcohol

A seventeen year old boy, who was seriously injured after the motor bike he was riding was in a head-on collision with a lorry on Wednesday night, has died in hospital. The accident happened on a well-lit stretch of road not far from the youth's home. Friends say they had been with him at a party in a nearby sports club. Although he had drunk some beer, friends said "It wasn't very much." "He seemed fine when he left the party," said one girl.

A police spokesman has confirmed that the alcohol level in the victim's blood measured 120 milligrams per 100 millilitres of blood – above the legal limit of 80 milligrams. Police confirmed that the lorry driver, who was also seriously injured in the accident, had been breathalysed. The test established he had not been drinking on the night of the accident.

Ninety per cent of cars built in Brazil fuelled by alcohol

Brazil may have found the answer to the world oil shortage. Instead of using petrol to fuel their cars, they are using alcohol. Four million of Brazil's 12.5 million vehicles now run on alcohol produced from the fermentation of sugar cane. Massive reductions in oil imports have been achieved.

Sugar cane is a renewable energy source – it can be grown and harvested every year. In 1989, 13 billion litres of alcohol were produced in Brazil. However, they are not the only country to produce alcohol in this way. The USA are producing over 4.5 billion litres a year, using mainly maize as the source of carbohydrate.

Table 8.4

For	Against
Alcohol is a renewable energy source	Oil is cheaper to import and refine
In the USA, cars using ethanol have driven for more than 800 thousand million miles without any major problems	It is wrong to use food to make alcohol
	Too much energy is needed to make alcohol
A lot of sugar cane rots before it is eaten	
Burning alcohol cuts down on air pollution	The waste products of making alcohol pollutes rivers

Since that time, however, some people say that the Government have spent too much money keeping the industry going. Others say that the newly found oil reserves in Brazil, should be used to make petrol which would be cheaper to produce than the alcohol. Some more arguments for and against using alcohol as a fuel are given in table 8.4. They may help you to decide what you think of using alcohol as a fuel.

Alcoholic Drinks

The alcohol in **alcoholic drinks** is made from **carbohydrate**. Plants are a source of carbohydrate. Therefore, almost any fruit or vegetable can be used to make alcoholic drinks. The type of plant used determines the final flavour of the drink. Table 8.5 shows the plants used for various alcoholic drinks and the percentage of alcohol in them.

Table 8.5

Drink	Source of carbohydrate	% Alcohol
Beer	Barley	3–5
Cider	Apples	3–7
Wine	Grapes	9–13
Sherry	Grapes	18–20
Port	Grapes	
Whisky	Barley	40
Rum	Sugar Cane	

half pint (0.3 litres) of beer, cider or lager
1 glass of sherry
1 glass of wine
1 single spirit (brandy, gin, vodka, whisky)

All these drinks contain the same amount of alcohol – one unit

The Effects of Drinking Alcohol

Alcohol (ethanol) is very soluble in water. It doesn't have to be digested by the body. It is quickly absorbed into the bloodstream, where it can interfere with some of the chemical reactions of the body. Alcohol **slows** some of our reactions down. In small amounts it can relax a person, but in larger quantities alcohol slows down reactions so much that a person can have difficulty speaking, moving and thinking clearly. Judgement is badly affected and it is very dangerous to drive a car or operate machinery in this condition.

Regular heavy drinking can lead to alcohol addiction. Often people start drinking to help get over personal problems, but their **alcoholism** only makes them less able to cope. Heavy drinking can also damage your liver.

Over the Limit

In 1967 The Road Safety Act was passed by Parliament. It made some major changes to the law on drinking and driving. A limit was set to the amount of alcohol in the blood, above which it was illegal to drive. The limit was set at **80 milligrams of alcohol for every 100 millilitres of blood** (80 mg/100 ml blood).

Alcohol affects people in different ways. Some people can be above the legal limit after drinking just one pint of beer. This can depend on their size and whether or not they have just had something to eat. The only way to be sure you are not over the limit before you drive is not to drink anything alcoholic at all!

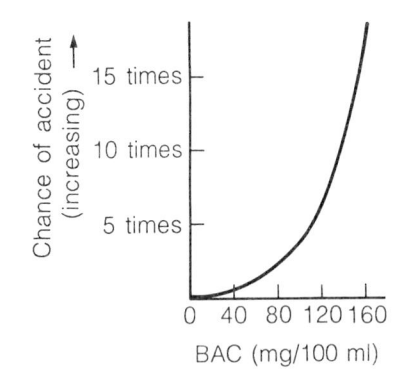

The chance of having an accident increases dramatically when you are above the legal limit

Measuring the Amount of Alcohol

The police can ask anybody committing a traffic offence, or involved in an accident, to take a roadside **breath test**. The driver is asked to blow into an alcotester (known as

Anyone committing a traffic offence can be asked to take a breath test

226 CARBOHYDRATES

the **breathalyser**) or an alcolmeter. Both give an indication of the **blood alcohol concentration (BAC)**. If either of these are positive, the driver is arrested and taken to a police station for a more accurate breath, urine or blood test.

A Weekend in the Life of...

People who drink regularly are constantly topping up their blood alcohol concentration. Take for example the drinking pattern of Frank Costello, age 21, over a typical weekend:

Friday: 6.00 pm (after work) — 2 pints of beer
9.00 pm–1.00 am (disco) — { 4 pints of beer
                             2 gins

Saturday: 1.00 pm (lunch) — 2 pints of beer
8.00 pm–12.00 pm (dinner) — { 1 gin
                              4 glasses of wine

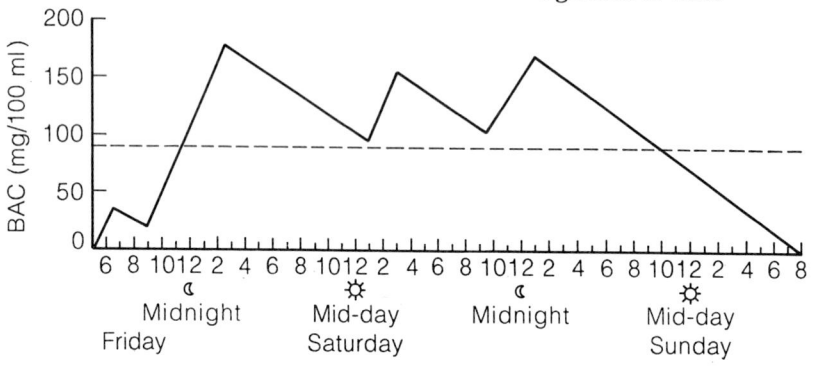

A weekend drink pattern

Making Alcoholic Drinks

The alcohol (ethanol) in drinks is produced by **fermentation**. During fermentation, **glucose** is broken down into **ethanol** and **carbon dioxide**. The process is speeded up by **enzymes**, which are biological catalysts. **Yeast** is a living organism containing enzymes.

Other sugars, like **sucrose** in cane sugar and **maltose** in barley can also be fermented. They must first be broken down into glucose. Enzymes in yeast can do this as well. The yeast gets its energy from the fermentation process.

$$\text{glucose} + \text{water} \xrightarrow{\text{yeast}} \text{ethanol} + \text{carbon dioxide}$$

Making Whisky

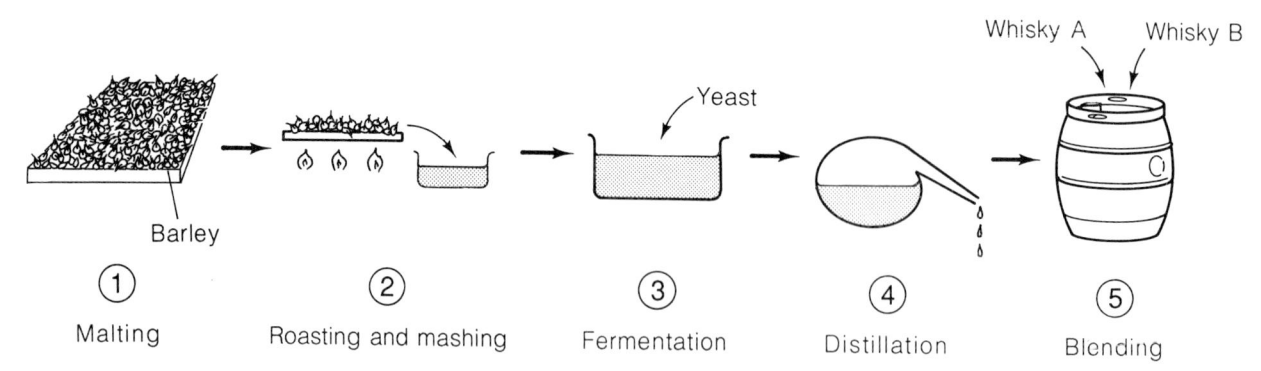

Stages in the whisky making process

1. Malting — Barley
2. Roasting and mashing
3. Fermentation — Yeast
4. Distillation
5. Blending — Whisky A, Whisky B

Whisky is made from barley. Barley contains a lot of starch but very little sugar. The starch is broken down into maltose. The maltose is converted to glucose and finally ethanol, during fermentation. The main steps are shown in the flow diagram.

Stage 1 Malting
The barley is soaked in water and spread on a warm floor, where it **germinates**. The starch changes to **maltose**. The barley is now called "green malt".

Stage 2 Mashing
The green malt is roasted above a peat fire which gives it a special flavour. It is then ground up and "mashed" with warm water. This dissolves the maltose and flavouring materials.

Stage 3 Fermenting
Yeast is added. The maltose is broken down into glucose, which is converted into **ethanol** and carbon dioxide.

Stage 4 Distilling
When the concentration of ethanol reaches about 8 per cent, the yeast is killed off and no

more ethanol is produced. The concentration of ethanol in whisky, however, is 40 per cent. To reach this, the ethanol and water needs to be partly **separated** by distillation. Ethanol has a boiling point of 79°C, whereas water boils at 100°C. When the mixture is heated the ethanol vapourises first. It is **condensed** as it passes through a water-cooled pipe. The whisky produced still has some water in it. Flavouring compounds are also distilled along with the ethanol.

Stage 5 Blending
Different distillations of whisky are often mixed together **(blended)** and then stored in wooden barrels and allowed to "mature" for several years. This improves the flavour. Water is added to reduce the ethanol content to around 40 per cent. Some whiskies are not blended. They are called **single malt** whiskies.

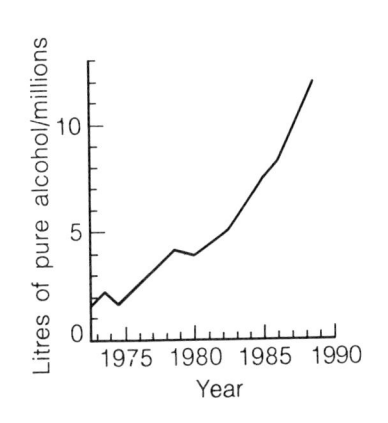

The making and selling of whisky has been going on in Scotland for centuries. Both blended and single malt whiskies are sold all over the world. Single malt is becoming more and more popular with the equivalent of 10 million litres of pure alcohol sold worldwide in 1988 alone.

Typical pot stills in a distillery

World sales of single malt whisky

A Closer Look at Enzymes

Enzymes generally work very fast. The speed of action of an enzyme is called its **turnover number**. This is the number of reactant molecules turned into product in one minute by one enzyme molecule. The turnover number for different enzymes ranges from a hundred to several million. The fastest known enzyme is **catalase**. It is found in the body. Catalase turns toxic hydrogen peroxide into harmless water and oxygen. It has a turnover number of six million.

Catalase is very **specific**. This means it only catalyses one reaction – the decomposition of hydrogen peroxide. Most enzymes are specific. Some digestive enzymes, however, catalyse several similar reactions. Pancreatic lipase, for example, breaks down a variety of different fats.

Enzymes do not work very well if the temperature is too high. They are proteins and become **denatured** at high temperatures. Denaturing changes the enzyme structure so that they can no longer act as a catalyst. For this reason, none of the enzymes in our bodies work above 45°C. They work best at around 37°C – **body temperature**.

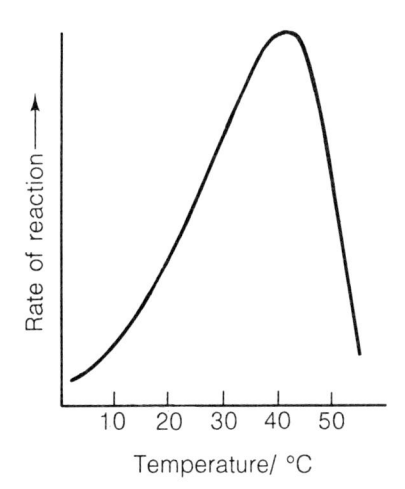

The effect of temperature on an enzyme-controlled reaction rate

A few living things have heat-resistant enzymes. Certain blue-green algae can live in hot springs. Their enzymes can operate at a temperature of 100°C.

Enzymes are also sensitive to changes in **pH**. Most enzymes work efficiently only within a narrow pH range. Enzymes in body cells work best at pH 7 (neutral). The digestive enzymes work at a number of pHs. Pepsin, found in the stomach, works best at pH 2 (acid), while trypsin, found in the small intestine, is most efficient at pH 8 (alkali). Table 8.6 shows the pH and temperature ranges over which some important brewing enzymes work best.

Table 8.6

Enzyme	pH	Temperature range/°C
amylase	5	62–75
pepsinase	2	37–40
phosphatase	6	50–65
polypeptidase	8	40–45

228 CARBOHYDRATES

Other Uses of Ethanol

Ethanol has a wide variety of uses. It is a very good **solvent** and dissolves many substances which are insoluble in water. It also **evaporates** quickly. These two properties make ethanol ideal for spreading certain solids evenly and thinly over surfaces. **Lacquer**, for example, when dissolved in ethanol can be sprayed on furniture. When the ethanol evaporates, it leaves behind a hard, smooth coating of lacquer, which protects the wood. The diagram shows products which can be made by dissolving substances in ethanol or solvents containing ethanol.

Synthetic Ethanol

Every year, hundreds of thousands of tonnes of ethanol are produced in Britain. To make these very large quantities, a process which is much faster and more efficient than fermentation must be used. A process is used in which **ethene** gas (C_2H_4) is combined with **water**:

$$C_2H_4(g) + H_2O(g) \rightarrow C_2H_5OH(g)$$
$$\text{ethene} \qquad\qquad\qquad \text{ethanol}$$

The simplified flow diagram shows how the process is carried out.

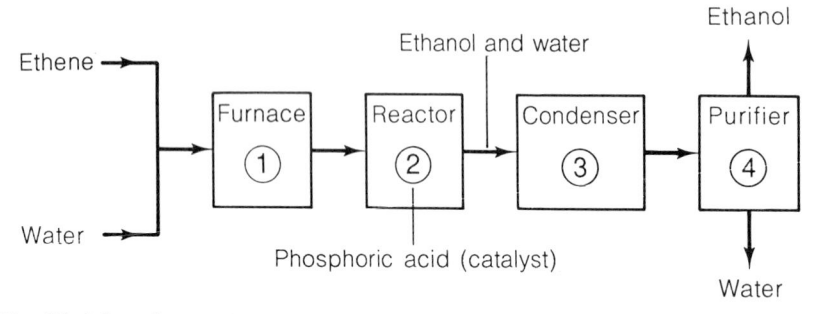

Simplified flow diagram for the industrial manufacture of ethanol from ethene

Stage 1 Ethene is made from oil and natural gas. It is mixed with water and passed through a furnace which is heated to about 300°C.
Stage 2 The hot mixture, under high pressure, is passed into a reactor containing a **catalyst**. A mixture of ethanol and water is produced.
Stage 3 The ethanol/water mixture is passed into a condenser where it is liquefied.
Stage 4 The ethanol solution is passed into a purifier, similar to a fractional distillation column used to separate oil fractions. The ethanol and water are separated.

Counting the Cost

Much of the ethene used to make ethanol comes from crude oil. Therefore, the cost of making ethanol from ethene is very dependent on **world oil prices**. In the mid 1970s oil was relatively cheap and so ethanol made from ethene was much cheaper than ethanol produced by fermentation (**bioethanol**). However, in the early 1980s the price of oil rose sharply and with it the cost of ethene. Ethanol from ethene cost four times as much in 1981 as it did in 1976. Bioethanol then became more competitive.

North Sea oil prices in the 1980s

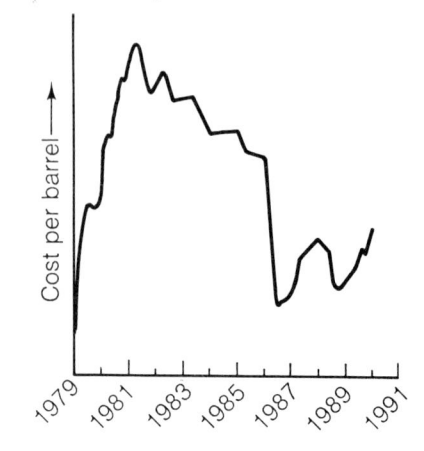

Activities

1. Table 8.5 on page 225 shows that beer and cider contain similar amounts of alcohol. Explain then why cider and beer have different tastes.

2. Alcohol can be made from the breakdown of glucose solution in the presence of yeast.
   (a) Show this process in a flow chart.
   (b) Name the alcohol formed.
   (c) To which family of alcohols does it belong?
   (d) Name the process described above.
   (e) What part does yeast play in the process?
   (f) A gas is also produced during the process.
      (i) Name the gas.
      (ii) Draw a labelled diagram showing how you would make alcohol from glucose and **collect** the gas produced.
      (iii) Describe how you would test the gas to confirm your answer to (i).

3. During whisky manufacture, the alcohol solution produced is distilled to separate the water and alcohol.
   (a) Why do manufacturers want to separate the alcohol from the water?
   (b) Explain why it is possible to separate alcohol and water in this way.

4. Read the newspaper article on page 224 about a young motor cyclist being killed in a road accident.
   (a) What does the article suggest was the cause of the accident?
   (b) Describe the effects of drinking too much alcohol can have on the body.

5. Dave and his girlfriend, Jenny, are at a party. Dave has 3 pints of beer and Jenny has 4 glasses of wine. Dave suggests that he drives home because he has had fewer drinks and so less alcohol.
   (a) What do you think of Dave's suggestion?
   (b) Use the information on page 225 to work out how many units Dave and Jenny each drank.
   (c) What advice would you give to them about drinking and driving?

6. Look at the graph on page 226, which shows the drinking pattern for Frank Costello over every weekend.
   (a) When is Frank's BAC at its highest?
   (b) Frank has to drive to work at eight o'clock on Saturday morning. Will he be above or below the legal limit?
   (c) How long does it take Frank to get rid of all the alcohol from his bloodstream?

7. Table 8.6 shows the temperatures and pHs some brewing enzymes work best at.
   (a) Describe what would happen to the reactions involved in the brewing process, if the temperature and pH of the solution was outside these ranges.
   (b) Even if the temperature and pH are kept within the ideal ranges, the conversion of sugar to alcohol eventually stops, even if there is sugar left. Explain why this is.

8. The graph on page 228 shows how the cost of North Sea oil changed during the 1980s.
   (i) In 1986, would you have advised an industrialist to use ethene as a feedstock for making ethanol?
   (ii) Would you have given the same advice today? Give a reason for your answer.

230 CARBOHYDRATES

5 Spotlight on Industry

Key Ideas

Manufacturers have to consider a number of factors when deciding what products they are going to make.
- Is there a demand for the product?
- Can it be made easily?
- Can the cost be kept down?

Making low-alcohol beer uses the scaled up laboratory techniques of *filtering* and *distillation*, to make a product for which there is a growing demand.

The Scottish and Newcastle brewery

Low Alcohol Beer – The Demand

Until around 1970, most of the beer drunk in Britain was dark beer, called Special or Bitter. Since then "blond" beers like lager have become more popular. By 1990 almost half the beer drunk in Britain was lager. In the late 1980s a new demand arose for **low** and **non-alcoholic** beers. The demand was from people who liked the taste of beer, but who wanted to:
- drink sensibly to comply with stricter drink-drive laws;
- drink beer without breaking religious rules;
- reduce health risks associated with drinking alcohol.

The alcoholic (ethanol) content of a typical British beer is about 4 per cent, though it can be higher. Reduced alcohol beers are usually sold as either:
1. **alcohol-free**: maximum alcohol content 0.05 per cent or
2. **low-alcohol**: alcohol content between 0.5 and 1.1 per cent.

Brewing Beer

Traditionally, beer is brewed from a mixture of **barley, malt, hops** and **sugar (sucrose)**.

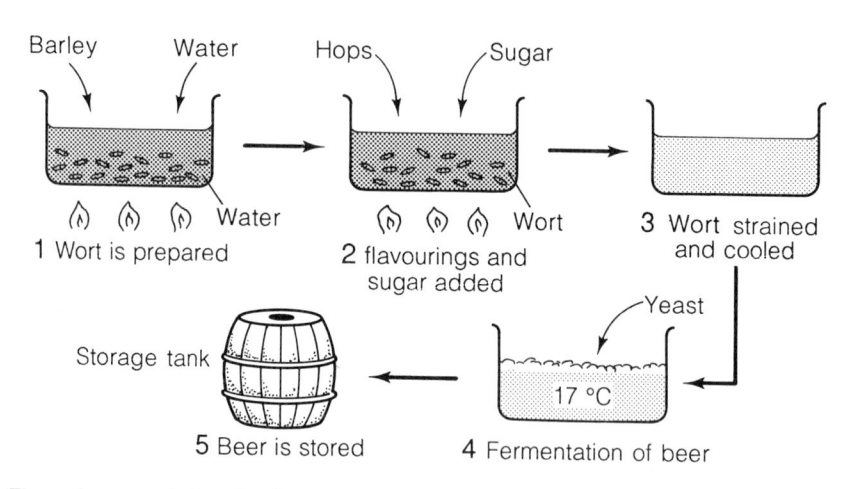

The main stages in brewing beer

Stage 1 The barley malt is boiled with water to produce **"wort"** (pronounced "wert").
Stage 2 The wort is strained into a boiling vessel to which hops and sugar are added. The hops give the beer a bitter **flavour**. The mixture is boiled for several hours.
Stage 3 After boiling, the wort mixture is strained before being cooled to around 17°C and passed into a fermentation tank.
Stage 4 Yeast is added and the mixture **ferments** for several days.
Stage 5 Once fermentation stops the beer is pumped into storage tanks before being canned or kegged.

Making Low-Alcohol Beer

There are various methods of making low-alcohol beer. Two of them are:
1. Fermenting only part of the wort (partial fermentation).
2. Fermenting the wort fully and then removing the alcohol.

Partial Fermentation

The fermentation is stopped when the required amount of alcohol is produced. This is done by rapidly cooling the mixture to 0°C. The yeast dies and is filtered off.

There are several problems with this method:
1. The beers tend to be sweet because of unreacted sugars.
2. Mould can form on the beer, because there is neither enough sugar nor alcohol to act as a preservative.

Simplified flow diagram of partial fermentation

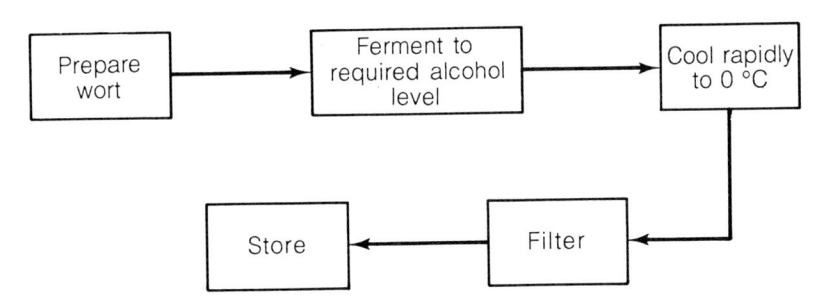

Prepare wort → Ferment to required alcohol level → Cool rapidly to 0 °C → Filter → Store

Removal of Alcohol after Fermentation

Distillation is used to separate the alcohol from the beer. A major problem, however, is that chemicals which give the beer **flavour** are also removed along with the alcohol. Chemists have devised several ways to solve this problem. One method is to remove the flavourings first, by distillation at low pressure. The alcohol is then removed by further distillation. This leaves a low-alcohol, low flavour beer. However, the flavourings removed earlier are added back into the low-alcohol beer, improving its taste.

A more complicated and costly process of separation, but one which keeps the flavour, involves using a **membrane**. The membrane is made from a material which has holes so small that only very small molecules, like alcohol and water, can pass through.

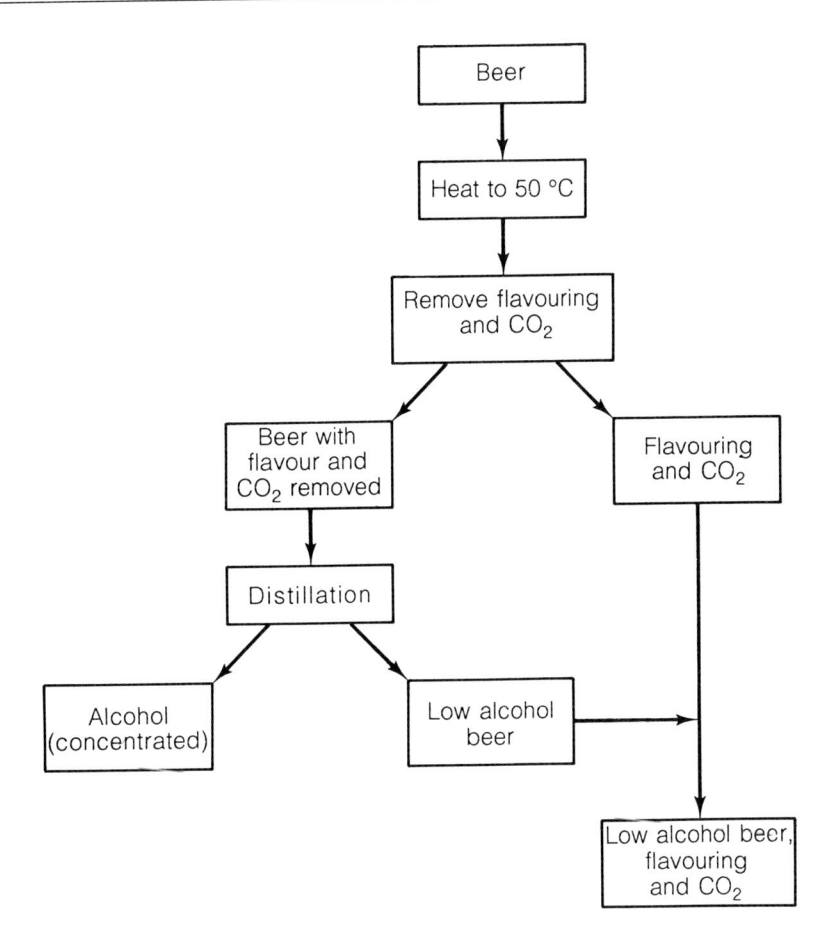

Beer → Heat to 50 °C → Remove flavouring and CO_2 → (Beer with flavour and CO_2 removed) + (Flavouring and CO_2)

Beer with flavour and CO_2 removed → Distillation → Alcohol (concentrated) + Low alcohol beer

Low alcohol beer + Flavouring and CO_2 → Low alcohol beer, flavouring and CO_2

Simplified flow diagram to show removal of alcohol after complete fermentation

Which Method to Use?

The exact methods of reducing the alcohol in beer are kept secret. Different brewers prefer different methods. Although the final taste of the beer is important, other factors must be considered:

- The ease of operating and maintaining the plant, especially those using a costly membrane.
- The rate at which the alcohol can be removed – if it is too slow, the method becomes uneconomical.
- Running costs, which are eventually passed on to the customer in the price of the beer.

One advantage to the brewer who makes low-alcohol beer is the amount of "**duty**" that needs to be paid. Duty is a tax on alcohol, which must be paid to the Government. It is only normally paid on drinks with an alcohol content above 1–2 per cent. Because low-alcohol beers are below this level, any duty paid can be claimed back by the brewer.

Activities

1. (a) Outline the reasons why brewers started producing low-alcohol beers.
   (b) Explain why low-alcohol beer costs around the same price as normal beer, even when less duty is paid by the brewers.

2. It is possible to make low-alcohol beer in the laboratory. Describe how you could separate the wort from the yeast and hops in the **laboratory**. How would you then remove the alcohol from the beer? (Use diagrams to show the arrangements you would use.)

3. Another way of making low-alcohol beer is as follows:
   "Two worts (A and B) are prepared. A is strong and high in flavour, and B is weak and low in flavour. Yeast is added to both A and B and they are fermented separately. Some of the flavouring is then removed from A and passed to B. The yeast is filtered from A and B and then they are blended (mixed) to get beer (C) of the required strength and flavour."
   Draw a simple flow diagram to show clearly what is happening in the process outlined in the passage.

Carbohydrates – Study Questions

1 The diagram below shows how some carbon compounds can be changed into others:

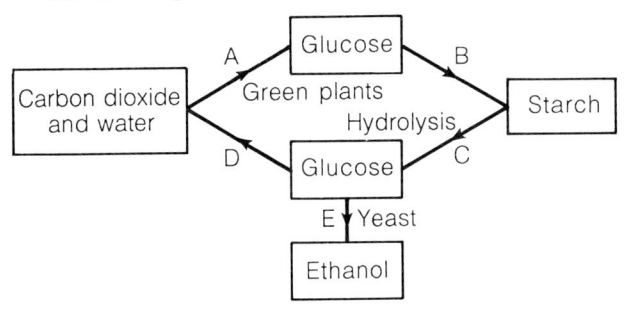

```
                    Glucose
              A  ↗          ↘  B
Carbon dioxide    Green plants      Starch
  and water       Hydrolysis
              D  ↘          ↙  C
                    Glucose
                      ↓ E  Yeast
                    Ethanol
```

(a) Which of the changes is an example of polymerisation?
(b) State one condition needed for change A to take place.
(c) Name one other substance produced during change E. **KU**

2 The flow chart shows part of the carbon dioxide cycle.

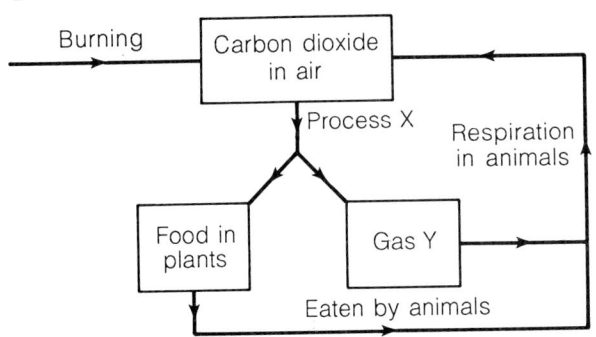

```
Burning  →  Carbon dioxide
              in air
                ↓ Process X         Respiration
                                    in animals
          ↙         ↘
    Food in        Gas Y
    plants
        ↓      Eaten by animals
```

(a) Name process X.
(b) Name gas Y.
(c) The amount of carbon dioxide entering the air has increased considerably in the last 50 years. Give a reason for this increase. **KU**

3 In Brazil, ethanol made from cane sugar has been used as a substitute for petrol. One advantage of using ethanol obtained in this way is that it is a "renewable source of energy".
 (a) Explain what is meant by a "renewable source of energy".
 (b) An important stage in the preparation of ethanol may be represented by the equation:

$$C_6H_{12}O_6(aq) \xrightarrow{enzymes} 2C_2H_5OH(aq) + 2CO_2(g)$$
$$\text{glucose} \quad \text{process X} \quad \text{ethanol}$$

  (i) Name process X.
  (ii) What part do the enzymes play in the process?
  (iii) Why is the reaction not speeded up by boiling?
  (iv) Use the equation to calculate the mass of ethanol which could be obtained from 18 g of glucose. **KU**

4 Large amounts of alcohol are made in industry. One way in which this is done is to treat ethene with steam in the presence of a catalyst.

$$\underset{\substack{H\ H \\ |\ \ | \\ H\ H}}{C=C} + H-OH \xrightarrow{catalyst} \underset{\substack{H\ H \\ |\ \ | \\ H\ H}}{H-C-C-OH}$$

(a) Give a suitable name for this kind of reaction. **PS**
(b) An industrial plant using this process has an input of 2500 kg of ethene per hour. Assuming only 70 per cent of the ethene is converted into alcohol, calculate the mass of alcohol produced each hour. **PS**
(c) Name another process used to make alcohol. **KU**

Relative Atomic Masses of Selected Elements (simplified for calculations)

Element	Symbol	Relative atomic mass (A_r)
aluminium	Al	27
argon	Ar	40
bromine	Br	80
calcium	Ca	40
carbon	C	12
chlorine	Cl	35·5
copper	Cu	64
fluorine	F	19
gold	Au	197
helium	He	4

Element	Symbol	Relative atomic mass (A_r)
hydrogen	H	1
iodine	I	127
iron	Fe	56
lead	Pb	207
lithium	Li	7
magnesium	Mg	24
mercury	Hg	201
neon	Ne	20
nickel	Ni	59
nitrogen	N	14

Element	Symbol	Relative atomic mass (A_r)
oxygen	O	16
phosphorus	P	31
platinum	Pt	195
potassium	K	39
silicon	Si	28
silver	Ag	108
sodium	Na	23
sulphur	S	32
tin	Sn	119
zinc	Zn	65

INDEX/GLOSSARY

acid an aqueous solution of a substance with a pH less than 7. There is an excess of H⁺(aq) ions in the solution 108–109
acid rain 52, **122–125**, 187
acrylic 199
activity series a list of elements arranged in order of how reactive they are 145–146
addition reaction 59
alcohol 224–232
alcoholism 225
alkali an aqueous solution of a substance with a pH greater than 7. There is an excess of OH⁻(aq) ions in the solution 111–112
alkali metals (group 1) 17–18
alkaline earth metals (group 2) 18–19
alkanes a family of hydrocarbons with the general formula C_nH_{2n+2}; where n = 1, 2, 3 etc. 55–57
alkanol 224
alkenes a family of hydrocarbons with the general formula C_nH_{2n}; where n = 1, 2, 3 etc. They all contain a C=C bond. They undergo addition reactions 58–60, 199
alloy a mixture of metals or metals and non-metals 143
aluminium
  manufacture 154–156
  sulphate 120–121
ammonia 183–186
ammonium chloride 91–92, **185–186**
ammonium ion 176
ammonium salts 175, **186**
anode a positively charged electrode **77**, 103–104, 155–157
anodising forming a coating of aluminium oxide on the surface of aluminium by electrolysis in a dilute sulphuric acid solution 166
(aq) – aqueous indicates that the substance has been dissolved in water 5
atom the smallest particle that can be obtained by chemical means 22–23
atomic number the number of protons in the nucleus of an atom. The elements in the periodic table are arranged in order of increasing atomic number 15, **24**
base a compound which neutralises an acid to form a salt and water. Bases can be soluble or insoluble. Metal oxides and metal hydroxides are bases. Soluble bases form alkaline solutions 117
batteries 91–95
beer 230–232
Benedict's Test 217

biodegradable a substance which will break down naturally 83, 195
blast furnace 150–151
bond
  covalent formed when two or more atoms share one or more pairs of outer electrons **28–30**, 78
  double 30, **58–59**, 201
  ionic strong attraction between oppositely charged ions 79
brass 143
breathalyser 225–226
brine **103**, 129
burning
  fuel **39–41**, 47
  plastic 195
calcium manufacture 77
carbohydrate compounds of carbon, hydrogen and oxygen. The ratio of hydrogen to oxygen is 2:1; made by green plants during photosynthesis 211–212, 216–222
carbon
  cycle 213
  dioxide **40**, 47, 54
  monoxide 49–50
catalyst a substance which changes the rate of a chemical reaction. The catalyst is unchanged chemically or in mass at the end of the reaction 13
catalytic converter may be fitted to car exhausts. They change harmful gases into harmless gases e.g., nitrogen dioxide into nitrogen and oxygen **51**, 125
cathode a negatively charged electrode 77, 103–104, 155–157, 163
cell a cell changes chemical energy into electrical energy during a reaction. A battery is one type of cell 91–93, **96**, 100–101, 161
cell
  rechargeable 93
cellulose 198
CFC's 19, **200**
chemical reaction a process that forms one or more new elements or compounds 1–2
chemical shorthand 26
chlor-alkali industry 103–105
chromatography **7**, 219–220
coal 40, **42**
combustion the chemical name for burning; a substance reacting rapidly with oxygen 39, **47**, 59
compost 171

INDEX/GLOSSARY

compound a substance formed when two or more elements are chemically joined together 3–4
concentrating ores 147
concentration the amount of substance dissolved in a solution. Usually measured in mol l^{-1} (mol/l) 112, 134–135
conductivity a measure of how well an electric current can pass through a metal, melt or solution at a particular voltage 72–76
conductivity titrations 136
conductor a substance which electricity is able to pass through. Metals and graphite are solid conductors. Ionic solutions and melts also conduct 72–76, 142
corrosion chemical reaction at the surface of a metal, changing the element into a compound 124, **159–161**
  prevention **162–166**
covalent network a large structure of covalently bonded atoms 78
cracking breaking down a large hydrocarbon molecule into smaller molecules. One of the products always contains a double bond 61–63
cracking
  ethene 67–69
  hydro 63
  catalytic 61–62
  thermal 62
current a flow of charged particles. Electrons flow through metals, and ions through ionic solutions or melts **73**, 75
cycloalkanes a family of hydrocarbons with the carbon atoms arranged in a ring. The general formula is C_nH_{2n} where n = 3, 4, 5 etc. 64–65

decomposition to break up or rot 171–172
density 142
diatomic molecules contain two atoms. They can be elements e.g., hydrogen (H_2) or compounds e.g., hydrogen chloride (HCl) 28
digestion the process by which food is broken down in the body into small molecules and then pass through the small intestine into the blood 220
dilution 113
direct current 76
disaccharides carbohydrates with the formula $C_{12}H_{22}O_{11}$ e.g., sucrose and maltose 216
displacement a chemical reaction in which a metal high in the electrochemical series takes the place of a metal lower in the series from a solution of its ions 97–98
dissolving 5, **81–82**
distillation
  fractional 7, **46**
  simple a method of separating a mixture of liquids by their difference in boiling point. It involves evaporation followed by condensation 7

electrochemical series metals and hydrogen arranged in order of how well they lose electrons and form ions 97–98
electrolysis the breaking down of an ionic compound into its elements by the use of an electric current **74–75,** 103, 154
electrolyte a solution or molten compound which conducts electricity **75,** 92, 96, 160–161
electrolytic refining 156
electrons the negatively charged particles which surround the nuclei of all atoms 22
  energy of 25
electron arrangement the arrangement of electrons in shells (or energy levels) around the nucleus of an atom 24–25
electroplating using electrolysis to coat one metal with another 164
element a substance containing only one kind of atom. It cannot be broken down further by chemical means **3,** 15–17
empirical formula the simplest ratio of atoms in a compound 152
emulsion 83
enzyme a biological catalyst 13–14, 84, 220, 222
epoxy resin 201
equation
  balancing 36, 88
  calculations from 37, 89–90
  chemical 36–37, 88
  word 2
  ethanol 224–228
  ethane **58–60,** 201
exothermic reaction a reaction in which heat energy is given out. There is a rise in temperature **41,** 188
extracting metals 148–151

fermentation the breakdown of glucose, using yeast, to form alcohol (ethanol) and carbon dioxide 226, 230
ferroxyl indicator a green coloured solution which turns deep blue in the presence of iron(II) ions (Fe^{2+}(aq)) and pink in the presence of hydroxide ions (OH^-(aq)) 160
fertilisers restore the essential elements of plant growth to the soil. They can be natural, e.g., rotten vegetation, or synthetic e.g., Nitram (ammonium nitrate) 171, 174–178
NPK **175,** 177
filtering 6
finite resources a limited amount of a resource e.g., fossil fuels and metals **44,** 141
flammable substances which burn easily 48
formulae
  elements 32
  ionic 85–86
  covalent **31–32**
fossil fuel formed from the remains of plants or animals that died millions of years ago. Coal, gas and oil are examples 42–43
  renewable 45
  shortage 44–45
fraction a mixture of similar sized compounds of boiling points within a narrow temperature range. Obtained by fractional distillation of crude oil 46
fuel any substance which reacts with oxygen to give out heat energy 39

galvanising coating a metal, usually steel, with zinc 164
glucose 211, **216,** 219, 221
graphite 72
Greenhouse Effect 54
group **17,** 85

Haber Process the name given to the industrial manufacture of ammonia from nitrogen and hydrogen 183–184
halogens (group 7) 19
homologous series a "family" of carbon containing compounds, with similar chemical properties, similar structures and a general formula. The series shows a regular change in physical properties 64
hydrocarbon a compound containing only hydrogen and carbon 46–47
  saturated contains single covalent bonds only 56–57
  unsaturated contains a C═C double bond **58,** 199
hydrogen ion 109
hydrogen test 109
hydrogenation 60
hydrolysis the breakdown of a compound by reaction with water, often in the presence of an acid or alkali 221
hydroxide ion 111

indicator a substance which changes colour at a particular pH 112
indigestion 119
insoluble
  bases 117
  carbonates 117
  salts 129–130
insulator 72–76
ion (or salt) bridge used in a chemical cell to connect two half cells together so that ions can flow between the two solutions 100
ion–electron equation an equation showing the gain and loss of electrons 76
ionic lattice a large structure of oppositely charged ions 79
ions atoms or groups of atoms with a positive or negative charge 23, 79–80
  coloured 80
  testing for 176
iron manufacture 150–151
isomer compounds with the same molecular formula but with a different structural formula **65–66,** 216
isotopes atoms of the same element but containing different numbers of neutrons. They have the same atomic number but different mass number, e.g., $^{35}_{17}Cl$ and $^{37}_{17}Cl$ 26

leaching 147, 176
legume 171
lemonade 110
lime 119

236 INDEX/GLOSSARY

magnesium oxide   130, **132–133**
manure   171
mass number the total number of protons and neutrons in the nucleus of an element   24
melts   73–74
metals
   physical properties   142–143
   reactions with acids   145
   oxygen   144
   water   144–145
methane   40, **55–56**
mixture two or more substances mixed together, but not chemically joined. They can be separated by physical means, e.g. filtering or distillation   5–7
molarity the concentration of a solution; the number of moles of substances dissolved in one litre of solution ($mol\,l^{-1}$ or mol/l)   134
mole one mole of an element is its atomic mass expressed in grams e.g., K = 39 so one mole is 39 g. One mole of a compound is its formula mass expressed in grams, e.g., NaCl = 23 + 35·5 = 58·5; so one mole is 58·5 g   34–35
molecule a group of atoms held together by covalent bonds   28–29
monomer the simple molecules from which polymers are made   **198,** 219
monosaccharide carbohydrates with the formula $C_6H_{12}O_6$ e.g., glucose and fructose   216

natural gas   43
negative electrode   76, 109
neutral a solution with a pH of 7. The concentration of H^+ (aq) ions is equal to the concentration of OH^- (aq) ions   112
neutralisation reaction when an acid and base (e.g., alkali) react to produce a salt and water   115
neutraliser   115, 119
neutron a particle found in the nucleus of an atom. It has mass (1 amu) but no charge   23
nitrates   **175.** 178–179
nitric acid   187–188
nitrifying bacteria convert atmospheric nitrogen into nitrogen compounds which can be absorbed by plants   171
nitrogen cycle shows how nitrogen is recycled between plants, animals and the atmosphere   172
nitrogen   183
   oxides   50, 187–188
noble gases (group 0)   20
non-conductor (or insulator) a substance which electricity cannot flow through. All non-metals, except graphite, are non-conductors 72–76
non-m,etal oxide   109
nucleus the central core of an atom made up of protons and neutrons   22–23
nutrients needed by plants to help them grow. The main (essential) nutrients are nitrogen, phosphorous and potassium   170–171
nylon   220–203

oil (crude)
   formation   43
   use of fractions   46–48
ore a naturally occurring metal compound   141
Ostwald Process the name given to the industrial manufacture of nitric acid from ammonia   188
oxidation occurs when a substance gains oxygen or loses electrons   101

percentage composition   177–178
periodic table the table of elements set out in order of their atomic number   15–17
pesticide   180–181
petrol
   leaded   51
   unleaded   51, 66
pH a number indicating the acidity or alkalinity of a solution, on a continuous scale. pH less than 7 is acidic, pH7 is neutral and pH greater than 7 is alkaline   112
phosphate   175, 179
photosynthesis the process by which plants make carbohydrates from carbon dioxide in the air and water, using light energy in the presence of chorophyll. Oxygen is given out in the process   212

pollution   40, 44, 49–53, 69, 83, 178–179
polymer a large molecule formed by reacting many small molecules (monomers) together. Poly(ethene) is a synthetic polymer. Starch and cellulose are natural polymers   198
   condensation a large molecule formed by reacting small molecules with the elimination of simple molecules like H_2O or HCl 202–205, 219
   addition a large molecule formed by reacting many small molecules containing the C=C group   199–202
polymerisation the reaction in which monomers join together to form a polymer   198
polysaccharide   216
population   44, **169**
positive electrode   76
precipitate the insoluble solid formed in a solution during a chemical reaction   129–130
processing plastics   208–209
properties
   chemical the way a substance reacts chemically with other substances   15
   physical things about a substance which can be observed and measured, such as colour, density and boiling point   15, 142
protons the positively charged particles found in the nucleus of an atom. Each has a mass of 1 amu. The number of protons in an element is its atomic number   22–23.

rainforests   214
recycled materials materials which are processed and used again e.g., aluminium cans, waste paper etc.   141
redox short for reduction and oxidation which both happen at the same time   101
reduction occurs when a substance loses oxygen or gains electrons   **101,** 218
relative atomic mass (A_r) a number which compares the masses of atoms from one element with the atoms of another   26
relative formula mass   87
relative molecular mass   34
respiration the process by which animals and plants obtain energy by breaking down carbohydrates (using oxygen) to give carbon dioxide and water   212–213
rusting the corrosion of iron to eventually form iron oxide   159–161

sacrificial protection process in which one metal corrodes and passes electrons to another metal to prevent it from corroding   162–163
salts (soluble) a substance formed when acids are neutralised. The positive ion comes from the neutraliser and the negative non-metal ion from the acid   5, 117, 126–129
saturated solution a solution which has the maxcimum possible amount of solute dissolved in it at a particular temperature   **5,** 81
sewage   179–180
soapless detergent   83
solder   143
solubility a measure of how well a solute dissolves in a solvent at a particular temperature. It is measured in grams of solute per 100 g of solvent (usually water)   **5,** 117, 126
solution formed when a solute dissolves in a solvent. Aqueous solutions are formed when a substance dissolves in water   5, 75, 81
solvent **5,** 81–82
speed (rate) of reaction   9–14
stainless steel   143
starch   211, **216–217**
   iodine test   217
states   5
sucrose   211, **216**
sulphur dioxide   **52–53,** 123
sulphurous acid   52, 123
symbols   3
synthetic a substance which is made by humans e.g., plastics   193

toxic   195–196
transition metals   20, 51, 88

valency   31–32
variables   10
volumetric titration   135–136

water treatment   121
whisky   226–227